Indian and Slave Royalists in the Age of Revolution

Royalist Indians and slaves in the northern Andes engaged with the ideas of the Age of Revolution (1780–1825), such as citizenship and freedom. Although generally ignored in recent revolution-centered versions of the Latin American independence processes, their story is an essential part of the history of the period.

In *Indian and Slave Royalists in the Age of Revolution*, Marcela Echeverri draws a picture of the royalist region of Popayán (modern-day Colombia) that reveals deep chronological layers and multiple social and spatial textures. She uses royalism as a lens to rethink the temporal, spatial, and conceptual boundaries that conventionally structure historical narratives about the Age of Revolution. Looking at royalism and liberal reform in the northern Andes, she suggests that profound changes took place within the royalist territories. These emerged as a result of the negotiation of the rights of local people, Indians, and slaves, with the changing monarchical regime.

Marcela Echeverri is Assistant Professor of Latin American History and MacMillan Research Fellow at Yale University.

Cambridge Latin American Studies

General Editor

Herbert S. Klein
Gouverneur Morris Emeritus Professor of History, Columbia University and
Hoover Research Fellow, Stanford University

Other Books in the Series

1. *Ideas and Politics of Chilean Independence, 1808–1833*, Simon Collier
2. *Church Wealth in Mexico: A Study of the 'Juzgado de Capellanias' in the Archbishopric of Mexico 1800–1856*, Michael P. Costeloe
3. *The Mexican Revolution, 1910–1914: The Diplomacy of Anglo-American Conflict*, P. A. R. Calvert
4. *Britain and the Onset of Modernization in Brazil, 1850–1914*, Richard Graham
5. *Parties and Political Change in Bolivia, 1880–1952*, Herbert S. Klein
6. *The Abolition of the Brazilian Slave Trade: Britain, Brazil and the Slave Trade Question, 1807–1869*, Leslie Bethell
7. *Regional Economic Development: The River Basin Approach in Mexico*, David Barkin and Timothy King
8. *Economic Development of Latin America: Historical Background and Contemporary Problems*, Celso Furtado and Suzette Macedo
9. *An Economic History of Colombia, 1845–1930*, W. P. McGreevey
10. *Miners and Merchants in Bourbon Mexico, 1763–1810*, D. A Brading
11. *Alienation of Church Wealth in Mexico: Social and Economic Aspects of the Liberal Revolution, 1856–1875*, Jan Bazant
12. *Politics and Trade in Southern Mexico, 1750–1821*, Brian R. Hamnett
13. *Bolivia: Land, Location and Politics Since 1825*, J. Valerie Fifer, Malcolm Deas, Clifford Smith, and John Street
14. *A Guide to the Historical Geography of New Spain*, Peter Gerhard
15. *Silver Mining and Society in Colonial Mexico: Zacatecas, 1546–1700*, P. J. Bakewell
16. *Conflicts and Conspiracies: Brazil and Portugal, 1750–1808*, Kenneth Maxwell
17. *Marriage, Class and Colour in Nineteenth-Century Cuba: A Study of Racial Attitudes and Sexual Values in a Slave Society*, Verena Stolcke
18. *Politics, Economics and Society in Argentina in the Revolutionary Period*, Tulio Halperín Donghi
19. *Politics in Argentina, 1890–1930: The Rise and Fall of Radicalism*, David Rock
20. *Studies in the Colonial History of Spanish America*, Mario Góngora
21. *Chilean Rural Society from the Spanish Conquest to 1930*, Arnold J. Bauer
22. *Letters and People of the Spanish Indies: Sixteenth Century*, James Lockhart and Enrique Otte, eds.
23. *The African Experience in Spanish America, 1502 to the Present Day*, Leslie B. Rout Jr.
24. *The Cristero Rebellion: The Mexican People Between Church and State, 1926–1929*, Jean A. Meyer
25. *Allende's Chile: The Political Economy of the Rise and Fall of the Unidad Popular*, Stefan de Vylder

26. *Land and Labour in Latin America: Essays on the Development of Agrarian Capitalism in the Nineteenth and Twentieth Centuries*, Kenneth Duncan and Ian Rutledge, eds.

27. *A History of the Bolivian Labour Movement, 1848–1971*, Guillermo Lora

28. *Coronelismo: The Municipality and Representative Government in Brazil*, Victor Nunes Leal

29. *Drought and Irrigation in North-east Brazil*, Anthony L. Hall

30. *The Merchants of Buenos Aires, 1778–1810: Family and Commerce*, Susan Migden Socolow

31. *Foreign Immigrants in Early Bourbon Mexico, 1700–1760*, Charles F. Nunn

32. *Haciendas and Ranchos in the Mexican Bajío, Léon, 1700–1860*, D. A. Brading

33. *Modernization in a Mexican ejido: A Study in Economic Adaptation*, Billie R. DeWalt

34. *From Dessalines to Duvalier: Race, Colour and National Independence in Haiti*, David Nicholls

35. *A Socioeconomic History of Argentina, 1776–1860*, Jonathan C. Brown

36. *Coffee in Colombia, 1850–1970: An Economic, Social and Political History*, Marco Palacios

37. *Odious Commerce: Britain, Spain and the Abolition of the Cuban Slave Trade*, David Murray

38. *Caudillo and Peasant in the Mexican Revolution*, D. A. Brading, ed.

39. *The Struggle for Land: A Political Economy of the Pioneer Frontier in Brazil from 1930 to the Present Day*, J. Foweraker

40. *Oil and Politics in Latin America: Nationalist Movements and State Companies*, George Philip

41. *Demographic Collapse: Indian Peru, 1520–1620*, Noble David Cook

42. *Revolution from Without: Yucatán, Mexico, and the United States, 1880–1924*, Gilbert M. Joseph

43. *Juan Vicente Gómez and the Oil Companies in Venezuela, 1908–1935*, B. S. McBeth

44. *Law and Politics in Aztec Texcoco*, Jerome A. Offner

45. *Brazil's State-Owned Enterprises: A Case Study of the State as Entrepreneur*, Thomas J. Trebat

46. *Early Latin America: A History of Colonial Spanish America and Brazil*, James Lockhart and Stuart B. Schwartz

47. *Capitalist Development and the Peasant Economy in Peru*, Adolfo Figueroa

48. *Miners, Peasants and Entrepreneurs: Regional Development in the Central Highlands of Peru*, Norman Long and Bryan Roberts

49. *Unions and Politics in Mexico: The Case of the Automobile Industry*, Ian Roxborough

50. *Housing, the State, and the Poor: Policy and Practice in Three Latin American Cities*, Alan Gilbert and Peter M. Ward

51. *Tobacco on the Periphery: A Case Study in Cuban Labour History, 1860–1958*, Jean Stubbs

52. *Sugar Plantations in the Formation of Brazilian Society: Bahia, 1550–1835*, Stuart B. Schwartz

53. *The Province of Buenos Aires and Argentine Politics, 1912–1943*, Richard J. Walter

54. *The Mexican Revolution, Volume 1: Porfirians, Liberals, and Peasants*, Alan Knight

55. *The Mexican Revolution, Volume 2: Counter-Revolution and Reconstruction*, Alan Knight
56. *Pre-Revolutionary Caracas: Politics, Economy, and Society 1777–1811*, P. Michael McKinley
57. *Catholic Colonialism: A Parish History of Guatemala, 1524–1821*, Adriaan C. van Oss
58. *The Agrarian Question and the Peasant Movement in Colombia: Struggles of the National Peasant Association, 1967–1981*, Leon Zamosc
59. *Roots of Insurgency: Mexican Regions, 1750–1824*, Brian R. Hamnett
60. *Latin America and the Comintern, 1919–1943*, Manuel Caballero
61. *Ambivalent Conquests: Maya and Spaniard in Yucatan, 1517–1570, Second Edition*, Inga Clendinnen
62. *A Tropical Belle Epoque: Elite Culture and Society in Turn-of-the-Century Rio de Janeiro*, Jeffrey D. Needell
63. *The Political Economy of Central America since 1920*, Victor Bulmer-Thomas
64. *Resistance and Integration: Peronism and the Argentine Working Class, 1946–1976*, Daniel James
65. *South America and the First World War: The Impact of the War on Brazil, Argentina, Peru and Chile*, Bill Albert
66. *The Politics of Coalition Rule in Colombia*, Jonathan Hartlyn
67. *The Demography of Inequality in Brazil*, Charles H. Wood and José Alberto Magno de Carvalho
68. *House and Street: The Domestic World of Servants and Masters in Nineteenth-Century Rio de Janeiro*, Sandra Lauderdale Graham
69. *Power and the Ruling Classes in Northeast Brazil, Juazeiro and Petrolina in Transition*, Ronald H. Chilcote
70. *The Politics of Memory: Native Historical Interpretation in the Colombian Andes*, Joanne Rappaport
71. *Native Society and Disease in Colonial Ecuador*, Suzanne Austin Alchon
72. *Negotiating Democracy: Politicians and Generals in Uruguay*, Charles Guy Gillespie
73. *The Central Republic in Mexico, 1835–1846, 'Hombres de Bien' in the Age of Santa Anna*, Michael P. Costeloe
74. *Politics and Urban Growth in Buenos Aires, 1910–1942*, Richard J. Walter
75. *Colombia before Independence: Economy, Society and Politics under Bourbon Rule*, Anthony McFarlane
76. *Power and Violence in the Colonial City: Oruro from the Mining Renaissance to the Rebellion of Tupac Amaru (1740–1782)*, Oscar Cornblit
77. *The Economic History of Latin America since Independence, Second Edition*, Victor Bulmer-Thomas
78. *Business Interest Groups in Nineteenth-Century Brazil*, Eugene Ridings
79. *The Cuban Slave Market, 1790–1880*, Laird W. Bergad, Fe Iglesias García, and María del Carmen Barcia
80. *The Kingdom of Quito, 1690–1830: The State and Regional Development*, Kenneth J. Andrien
81. *The Revolutionary Mission: American Enterprise in Latin America, 1900–1945*, Thomas F. O'Brien
82. *A History of Chile, 1808–2002, Second Edition*, Simon Collier and William F. Sater

83. *The Rise of Capitalism on the Pampas: The Estancias of Buenos Aires, 1785–1870*, Samuel Amaral
84. *The Independence of Spanish America*, Jaime E. Rodríguez
85. *Slavery and the Demographic and Economic History of Minas Gerais, Brazil, 1720–1888*, Laird W. Bergad
86. *Between Revolution and the Ballot Box: The Origins of the Argentine Radical Party in the 1890s*, Paula Alonso
87. *Andrés Bello: Scholarship and Nation-Building in Nineteenth-Century Latin America*, Ivan Jaksic
88. *Deference and Defiance in Monterrey: Workers, Paternalism, and Revolution in Mexico, 1890–1950*, Michael Snodgrass
89. *Chile: The Making of a Republic, 1830–1865: Politics and Ideas*, Simon Collier
90. *Shadows of Empire: The Indian Nobility of Cusco, 1750–1825*, David T. Garrett
91. *Bankruptcy of Empire: Mexican Silver and the Wars Between Spain, Britain, and France, 1760–1810*, Carlos Marichal
92. *The Political Economy of Argentina in the Twentieth Century*, Roberto Cortés Conde
93. *Politics, Markets, and Mexico's "London Debt," 1823–1887*, Richard J. Salvucci
94. *A History of the Khipu*, Galen Brokaw
95. *Rebellion on the Amazon: The Cabanagem, Race, and Popular Culture in the North of Brazil, 1798–1840*, Mark Harris
96. *Warfare and Shamanism in Amazonia*, Carlos Fausto
97. *The British Textile Trade in South American in the Nineteenth Century*, Manuel Llorca-Jaña
98. *The Economic History of Latin America since Independence, Third Edition*, Victor Bulmer-Thomas
99. *Black Saint of the Americas: The Life and Afterlife of Martín de Porres*, Celia Cussen
100. *Asian Slaves in Colonial Mexico: From Chinos to Indians*, Tatiana Seijas
101. *Indigenous Elites and Creole Identity in Colonial Mexico, 1500–1800*, Peter Villella
102. *Indian and Slave Royalists in the Age of Revolution: Reform, Revolution, and Royalism in the Northern Andes, 1780–1825*

Indian and Slave Royalists in the Age of Revolution

Reform, Revolution, and Royalism in the Northern Andes, 1780–1825

MARCELA ECHEVERRI

Yale University

CAMBRIDGE
UNIVERSITY PRESS

CAMBRIDGE
UNIVERSITY PRESS

University Printing House, Cambridge CB2 8BS, United Kingdom

One Liberty Plaza, 20th Floor, New York, NY 10006, USA

477 Williamstown Road, Port Melbourne, VIC 3207, Australia

4843/24, 2nd Floor, Ansari Road, Daryaganj, Delhi - 110002, India

79 Anson Road, #06-04/06, Singapore 079906

Cambridge University Press is part of the University of Cambridge.

It furthers the University's mission by disseminating knowledge in the pursuit of education, learning and research at the highest international levels of excellence.

www.cambridge.org
Information on this title: www.cambridge.org/9781107446007

First published 2016
First paperback edition 2017

A catalogue record for this publication is available from the British Library

Library of Congress Cataloging in Publication data
Names: Echeverri, Marcela, 1974–
Title: Indian and slave royalists in the Age of Revolution : reform, revolution, and royalism in the northern Andes, 1780–1825 / Marcela Echeverri (Yale University).
Description: New York, NY : Cambridge University Press, 2016. | Series: Cambridge Latin American studies ; 102 | Includes bibliographical references and index.
Identifiers: LCCN 2015045746 | ISBN 9781107084148 (Hardback)
Subjects: LCSH: Indians of South America–Colombia–Popayán Region–Politics and government–18th century. | Indians of South America–Colombia–Popayán Region–Politics and government–18th century. | Slaves–Political activity–Colombia–Popayán Region–History. | Royalists–Colombia–Popayán Region–History. | Social change–Colombia–Popayán Region–History. | Revolutions–Colombia–Popayán Region–History. | Popayán Region (Colombia)–Politics and government. | Pasto Region (Colombia)–Politics and government. | Andes Region–Politics and government. | Colombia–Politics and government–To 1810
Classification: LCC F2269.1.P66 E25 2016 | DDC 323.1198/0861–dc23 LC record available at http://lccn.loc.gov/2015045746

ISBN 978-1-107-08414-8 Hardback
ISBN 978-1-107-44600-7 Paperback

Contents

List of Figures   *page* xi
Acknowledgments   xiii

   Introduction: law, empire, and politics in the revolutionary age   1

1 Reform, revolution, and royalism in the northern Andes:
   New Granada and Popayán (1780–1825)   19

2 Indian politics and Spanish justice in eighteenth-century Pasto   62

3 The laws of slavery and the politics of freedom in late-colonial
   Popayán   92

4 Negotiating loyalty: royalism and liberalism among Pasto
   Indian communities (1809–1819)   123

5 Slaves in the defense of Popayán: war, royalism, and freedom
   (1809–1819)   157

6 "The yoke of the greatest of all tyrannical intruders, Bolívar":
   the royalist rebels in Colombia's southwest (1820–1825)   191

   Conclusion: the law and social transformation in the
   early republic   224

Bibliography   239
Index   265

Figures

I.1 Province of Popayán   *page* 4
1.1 District of Pasto and province of Los Pastos with selected
    Indian towns   24
1.2 Territorial aspirations of the Junta Suprema de Quito, 1809   42
1.3 New Granada and Peru   45
5.1 *Lista de negros de la mina de San Juan por quienes solicita la*
    libertad el síndico procurador general (List of *negros* from the
    San Juan mine for whom the state attorney requests freedom)   181
6.1 Pasto and Pacific lowlands, 1822–25   213

Table

1.1 Population of New Granada (1778) and Popayán, Pasto,
    and Pacific Lowlands (1797)   26

Acknowledgments

This book began as my dissertation project at New York University. From the days of research and dissertating until today I have enjoyed being part of a wonderful network of colleagues who contributed to making this a truly exciting project and a deeply formative experience.

For their inspiration and immeasurable support in every step of this project I am always thankful to Ada Ferrer, Margarita Garrido, Greg Grandin, Joanne Rappaport, Sinclair Thomson, and Barbara Weinstein.

For reading different versions of the entire manuscript and providing invaluable feedback, I thank Nicolas Ronderos, Sinclair Thomson, Peter Guardino, Ken Andrien, Joanne Rappaport, Herman Bennett, Sherwin Bryant, Rachel O'Toole, Tamara Walker, Cristina Soriano, Michelle Chase, Yuko Miki, Sarah Sarzynski, Gil Joseph, Stuart Schwartz, Laurent Dubois, Alejandro de la Fuente, and Alejandra Dubcovsky.

I also benefited greatly and learned from the advice and insights of the following scholars who read one or more chapters of the book: Lyman Johnson, Alejandro Cañeque, Chuck Walker, Brian Owensby, Jane Landers, Yanna Yannakakis, Kristen Block, Ernesto Bassi, Virginia Sánchez-Korrol, Renzo Honores, Anne Eller, Ed Rugemer, Kathryn Burns, Ben Vinson, Allan Kuethe, Matt Childs, Victor Uribe-Urán, Natalia Sobrevilla Perea, Alcira Dueñas, Chris Schmidt-Nowara, Alejandra Irigoin, Zara Anishanslin, Scarlett O'Phelan, Georges Lomné, Jaime Rodríguez, Amy Chazkel, Gabriel DiMeglio, Julie Gibbings, and Edgardo Pérez Morales.

I thank the participants at the workshops in which I presented my research, who engaged my work with interest: NYU's Atlantic World Workshop; Harvard's Atlantic History Seminar; CUNY's Center for the

Humanities "Freedom" Seminar; the Javeriana University History Department's faculty workshop; the Johns Hopkins History Department Seminar; the Omohundro Institute *WMQ-EMSI* Workshop "The Age of Revolutions"; U. Penn's McNeil Center for Early American Studies Atlantic Seminar; and the Newberry Library's 2014–15 Symposium on Comparative Early Modern Legal History, "Meanings of Justice in New World Empires: Settler and Indigenous Law as Counterpoints."

As I developed this project I received important guidance and encouragement, for which I am very grateful, from Lyman Johnson, Alejandro Cañeque, Kris Lane, Chris Schmidt-Nowara, Lauren Benton, Karen Kupperman, Fred Cooper and Jane Burbank, Jim Sidbury, Peter Blanchard, and James Sanders.

In New York, Providence, Colombia, Ecuador, Perú, and Spain, and all the places this project has taken me for research and conferences, I was lucky to meet and personally and intellectually learn from Andreas Kalyvas, Pablo Kalmanovitz, Valeria Coronel and José Antonio Figueroa, Natasha Lightfoot, Antonio Feros, Marta Irurozqui and Víctor Peralta, José Carlos de la Puente Luna, Emily Berquist, Joshua Rosenthal, Lina del Castillo, Ernesto Capello, Marta Herrera, Paula Ronderos, Daniel Gutiérrez, Cristóbal Gnecco, Santiago Muñoz, Mauricio Nieto, Claudia Leal, Carl Langebaek, Jairo Gutiérrez, Antonio Barrera, Geneviève Verdo, Clément Thibaud, Cecilia Méndez, Gabriela Ramos, Jordana Dym, Alex Borucki, Marixa Lasso, Reuben Zahler, Scott Eastman, Mark Thurner, Eric Van Young, Jorge Cañizares-Esguerra, T.J. Desch-Obi, Jessica Krug, Elena Schneider, Celso Castilho, Olga Gonzalez Silén, Guillermo Bustos, David Geggus, Manuel Barcia, Neil Safier and Iris Montero, Jeremy Mumford, Roque Ferreira, Sibylle Fischer, Bianca Premo, Erick Langer, Norah Andrews, Manuel Lucena Giraldo, Gabriel Paquette, Katherine Bonil, Yesenia Barragan, Camillia Cowling, David Wheat, Caitlin Fitz, Jason McGraw, David Sartorius, Oscar de la Torre, Zach Morgan, Gabriela Lupiáñez, Nuria Sala i Vila, José de la Puente Brunke, Karin Rosemblatt, Camilla Townsend, Renée Soulodre-La France, and Fabricio Prado.

At the College of Staten Island Zara Anishanslin, Ismael García Colón, Samira Haj, Marc Lewis, John Dixon, John Wing, Ben Mercer, Sarah Pollack, Oswaldo Zavala, Felipe Martínez, and Rafael de la Dehesa were wonderful colleagues. Special thanks to Francisco Soto, Jonathan Sassi, and Eric Ivison for their consistent support to my research. At CUNY I also enjoyed many conversations with Herman Bennett, Amy Chazkel, Virginia Sánchez-Korrol, and Namita Manohar.

At Yale and in New Haven I have had the mentorship and friendship of my colleagues Ned Blackhawk, Alejandra Dubcovsky, Rosie Bsheer, Rohit De, Ed Rugemer, Jen VanVleck, Alan Mikhail, Julie Stephens, Greta LaFleur, Vanessa Agard-Jones, Leslie Harkema, Dixa Ramirez, Albert Laguna, Laura Barraclough, Maria Jordan, David Blight, Carlos Eire, Paul Freedman, Glenda Gilmore, George Chauncey, Francesca Trivellato, Mary Lui, Naomi Lamoreaux, Anne Eller, Gil Joseph, and Stuart Schwartz. The students in my seminars at Yale in the past two years also deserve recognition for passionately engaging with this work and giving it a refreshing new life.

Yale's staff welcomed me warmly and it has been a pleasure to work with them. In the History Department I especially thank Denise Scott, Liza Joyner, and Dana Lee. Warm thanks to Jean Silk at the Council on Latin American and Iberian Studies and to David Spatz in the Gilder Lehrman Center.

The research and writing of this book was supported by New York University; the Instituto Colombiano de Antropología e Historia; Fundación Carolina; Harvard University; and the City University of New York. The book has been published with the assistance of the Frederick W. Hilles Publication Fund of Yale University.

I want to acknowledge the staff at the archival collections where I did research between 2001 and 2011, whose attention and generosity have made this book possible. In particular, Mauricio Tovar at the Archivo General de la Nación in Bogotá was always extremely supportive. Two wonderful archivists at the Archivo Central del Cauca, Yolanda Polo and Harold Puerto, deserve enormous recognition. At the Archivo Nacional del Ecuador I am grateful to Margarita Tufiño, Verónica Salazar, Piedad Mesías de Rubio, and Maria Teresa Carranco. At Biblioteca Luis Angel Arango I thank Margarita Garrido and Juan Ignacio Arboleda. Many thanks to the staff at the John Carter Brown Library, especially Michael Hammerly, Richard Ring, Valerie Andrews, and Ken Ward.

In the most recent phase of preparing the manuscript for publication, I am very grateful to Herb Klein and Debbie Gershenowitz from Cambridge University Press for their editorial advice and support in the process of writing this book. Thanks also to the three anonymous readers for their recommendations and encouragement.

Special thanks to Santiago Muñoz for his excellent and caring work on the maps in this book, to Marta Herrera and Daniel Gutiérrez for graciously allowing me to use maps from their books, and to Marsha Ostroff for patiently working through various versions of the manuscript and making adjustments to the language.

An earlier version of Chapter 3 was published in *Slavery and Abolition* 30:3 (2009), and parts of Chapters 4 and 5 appeared in an article with the *Hispanic American Historical Review* 91:2 (2011).

Last but not least, I want to acknowledge my friends and family who have nourished me with their love and affection, who have been and are there for me always. First, my closest kin: my parents Diego and Claudia, the sweetest people in the world; my little brothers Juan Pablo and Felipe; my sister-in-law Catalina Delgado and my niece and nephew Rebeca and Benjamín; *mi abuelita* Lolita (I love you); *mis tíos* Constanza Echeverri, Catalina Muñoz, and Sergio Camacho; Leonardo Ronderos, Maria Teresa Gaitan, and Nicolas Ronderos – to Nicolas I dedicate this book in appreciation for his inspiration, company, and support during the years when I developed the project, and in celebration of the time we lived together. My wonderful friends: Yuhayna Mahmud, Adriana Arjona, Camila and Maria Gamboa, Pedro and Miguel Salazar, Maria Fernanda Buriticá, Carolina Echeverri, Ana Paula Iglesias, Santiago Monge, Sandra Frieri, Diego Herrera, Renata Segura and Adam Lupel, Domingo Ledezma and Giovanna Roz, Eva Salcedo, Martha Lobo, Liliana Ujueta and Pablo Abitbol, Mariscal (Isho) Pérez, Michelle Standley, Carlos Granés, Camilo Martínez, Zara Anishanslin, Jack Lawson, Julieta Lemaitre, and Maria del Rosario Ferro.

Introduction

Law, empire, and politics in the revolutionary age

In the year 1810, in the midst of the Spanish monarchy's deepest crisis of sovereignty that took place during Napoleon's invasion of the Iberian Peninsula, the slave- and mine-owning elites across New Granada's southwestern Province of Popayán (in present-day Colombia) formed the first insurgent juntas, rejecting Spanish sovereignty. Their slaves who lived in gold-mining camps in the Pacific lowlands rebelled against their owners' rights to keep them in bondage and argued that they, on the contrary, were in favor of the monarchy. The slaves claimed that, up to that point, they had tolerated enslavement because their masters had been vassals of the king, who guaranteed the slaves protection. Unlike their masters who had ceased serving the Spanish Crown, the slaves preferred to remain vassals of the king and enjoy the freedom and rights that other vassals had. Over the next ten years, the slaves sustained a royalist rebellion and defended the Pacific lowlands from incursions by the forces seeking independence. In doing so, they acquired de facto freedom and lived autonomously throughout the decade.

Parallel events developed in the interior Andean highlands of Pasto where Indian communities united with Spanish forces to defend the king and the monarchy. As the monarchical crisis expanded into a long war that engulfed their homeland, the northern Andean Indians around the city of Pasto embraced the opportunity to manifest their loyalty to the Spanish king. Militia service became an avenue of social mobility for some. Collectively they received special concessions in exchange for their military service to the crown, providing a new means of protecting and expanding the Indians' rights in the imperial context.

In a remarkable moment in the history of slavery, the representatives of the Spanish king mobilized slaves against slave owners, and slaves allied with and defended the crown, which had historically promoted slavery. At the same time, the descendants of native people who three hundred years earlier had been conquered through force defended their status as tribute-paying vassals of the Spanish Crown. At this unprecedented juncture, people who had been the objects of imperial rule became its defenders.

When in 1822, after declaring independence in Venezuela and northern New Granada, Simón Bolívar arrived with his armies to the royalist bulwark of Popayán, the indigenous people in Pasto and the slaves in the Pacific lowlands rose to wage war against the republican invasion. Their rebellion lasted until 1825. These royalist militias not only threatened the stability of Bolívar's dream of an independent republic of Colombia, they also jeopardized his plans to defeat Spain in the heartland of its South American empire, Peru.

Given its strategic location, this royalist region and its peoples' fight against Bolívar made them legendary in popular and historiographic accounts of Colombian independence. The founding narrative of Colombian independence is José Manuel Restrepo's *Historia de la Revolución de Colombia*, published in Paris in 1827.[1] In Restrepo's tale of beginnings, the royalists were far from marginal characters. They enabled the literary creation of a constitutive antagonism between a morally superior Colombia and a decadent, tyrannical Spain. The *Historia de la Revolución* perfectly illustrates how nineteenth-century Creole nationalism cast the period of Spanish rule as a time of darkness, barbarism, and slavery. The royalists were not only military enemies of the Creole independentists, they also embodied the cultural dangers of centuries of Spanish domination and control. Restrepo portrayed the indigenous people and slaves who were core actors in the rebellion against Bolívar as victims of manipulation,

---

[1] José Manuel Restrepo, *Historia de la revolución de la República de Colombia en la América meridional* (1827; Besanzon: Imprenta de José Jacquin, 1958). Restrepo was Bolívar's Minister of the Interior and as a participant in and witness of the events in this period, he wrote a diary based on his insights into major turning points of history during the war and the first decades of republican life. Additionally, from his privileged position in the government, Restrepo gathered the most complete collection of documents in existence dealing with the independence wars in Gran Colombia. Known as the "Archivo Restrepo," the collection includes sources from Panama, Venezuela, Ecuador, and Colombia. In the historical writings that were informed by this archive, Restrepo laid the foundations of Colombia's nationalist "myth." See also José Manuel Restrepo, *Diario Político y Militar: Memorias sobre los sucesos importantes de la época para servir a la historia de la revolución de Colombia y de la Nueva Granada, desde 1819 para adelante*, 4 Vols. (Bogotá: Imprenta Nacional, 1854).

participating primarily as cannon fodder and always on disadvantageous terms. They were understood as symbols of backwardness and as obstacles to liberation, further obscuring the memory of the political goals, strategies, and achievements of these sectors of Popayán society.[2]

Thus, royalists and royalism have been integral to the Colombian nationalist story since the nineteenth century.[3] Indeed, the problem with the nationalist perspective inaugurated by Restrepo, which has framed all of the interpretations of the history of Popayán Province during the independence wars, is not a matter of erasure or silencing (see Figure I.1).[4]

Rather than simply including the Popayán royalists in the narrative of Colombian independence, this book corrects core assumptions about the region's isolation and about the royalists' backwardness and naïveté.[5] It carefully investigates who the royalists were by exploring the politics of indigenous people and slaves in Popayán Province before and during the independence wars. The book further uses royalism as a lens through

[2] Rebecca Earle, *The Return of the Native: Indians and Mythmaking in Spanish America, 1810–1930* (Durham, NC: Duke University Press, 2007), 26.

[3] Maya Jasanoff argues that patriotic portrayals of American independence excluded or "forgot" loyalists. Jasanoff, "The Other Side of Revolution: Loyalists in the British Empire," *The William and Mary Quarterly* 65, no. 2 (2008), 205–32.

[4] As Germán Colmenares, pioneer of social history in Colombia, rightly commented in the 1980s: "Since its publication, Restrepo's oeuvre has become a 'historiographic prison.'" Colmenares, "La Historia de la Revolución por José Manuel Restrepo: Una prisión historiográfica," in *La Independencia: Ensayos de Historia Social*, ed. Germán Colmenares, Zamira Díaz de Zuluaga, José Escorcia, and Francisco Zuluaga (Bogotá: Instituto Colombiano de Cultura, 1986), 9–23. For example, Jean Pierre Minaudier stated that during the independence wars in Pasto "*el pueblo* was not intentionally involved in them … but obeyed their masters (*a sus amos*)." Minaudier, "Pequeñas patrias en la tormenta: Pasto y Barbacoas a finales de la colonia y en la independencia," *Historia y Espacio* 3, nos. 11–12 (1987), 159, 163.

[5] Connecting popular riots and local politics in the Bourbon context with the independence crisis, some scholars have explained popular royalism in Popayán as the result of a regional tradition of resistance to the innovations of Bourbon reformism throughout the eighteenth century. See Sergio Elías Ortiz, *Agustín Agualongo y su Tiempo* (Bogotá: Editorial A.B.C., 1958); Edgar Bastidas Urresty, *Las guerras de Pasto* (Pasto: Ediciones Testimonio, 1979); Emiliano Díaz del Castillo, *El Caudillo: Semblanza de Agualongo* (Pasto: Tipografía y Fotograbado Javier, 1983); Brian Hamnett, "Popular Insurrection and Royalist Reaction: Colombian Regions, 1810–1823," in *Reform and Insurrection in Bourbon New Granada and Peru*, ed. John Fisher et al. (Baton Rouge: Louisiana University Press, 1990), 292–326; Rebecca Earle, "Indian Rebellion and Bourbon Reform in New Granada: Riots in Pasto, 1780–1800," *Hispanic American Historical Review* 73, no. 1 (1993), 99–124; and John Lynch, *The Spanish American Revolutions, 1808–1826* (1973; New York: W. W. Norton, 1986), 214, 241.

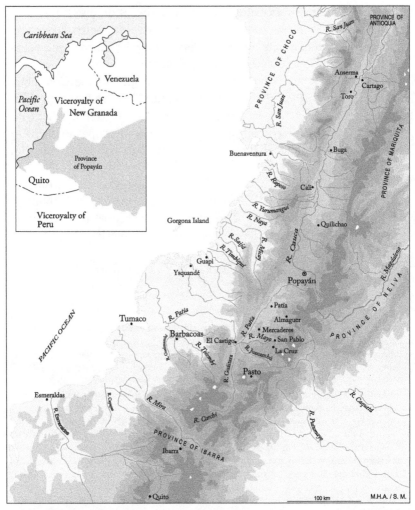

FIGURE I.1 Province of Popayán.
Map modified by Santiago Muñoz based on Marta Herrera, "Provincia de Popayán hacia 1797," and "Provincia de Popayán, siglo XVIII. Relieve e hidrografía," in *Popayán*, 13, 28.

which to rethink the temporal, spatial, and conceptual boundaries that conventionally structure historical narratives about the period generally known as Age of Revolution.

The royalist alliances found in Popayán had parallels elsewhere – for example, in modern-day Venezuela (Coro), Colombia (Santa Marta), Ecuador (Cuenca), and in northern and southern Peru (Piura and Cuzco) – proving that royalism was a powerful political force in the Latin American independence era. More broadly speaking, the structural opposition between the revolutionary faction and the royalist camp of course also characterized the earlier Atlantic Revolutions in the Americas – American and Haitian – where the defenders of empire were more commonly known as loyalists. Teleological assumptions about the implicit logic of political action as revolutionary in the eighteenth century have carved a deep conceptual antagonism in the historiographies of these revolutions. While scholarship about the Age of Revolution has expanded tremendously in the past decade, one of the themes from the revolutionary era that still needs to be understood is loyalty.[6] For example, historians continue to identify royalism as a theme exclusively linked to the colonial

---

[6] The recent literature on Latin America in the Age of Revolution includes: Heraclio Bonilla, ed., *Indios, negros y mestizos en la independencia* (Bogotá: Editorial Planeta/ Universidad Nacional de Colombia, 2010); Beatriz Bragoni, "Esclavos, libertos y solda- dos. La cultura política plebeya en tiempo de revolución," in *¿Y el pueblo dónde está? Contribuciones a la historia popular de la revolución de independencia rioplatense*, ed. Raúl Fradkin (Buenos Aires: Prometeo ediciones, 2008), 107–50; Gabriel Di Meglio, *¡Viva el bajo pueblo! La plebe urbana de Buenos Aires y la política entre la Revolución de Mayo y el Rosismo* (Buenos Aires: Prometeo Libros, 2007); Laurent Dubois, *Avengers of the New World: The Story of the Haitian Revolution* (Cambridge, MA: Belknap Press, 2004); Laurent Dubois, *A Colony of Citizens: Revolution and Slave Emancipation in the French Caribbean, 1787–1804* (Chapel Hill: Omohundro Institute of Early American History and Culture/University of North Carolina Press, 2004); Ada Ferrer, *Insurgent Cuba: Race, Nation, and Revolution, 1868–1898* (Chapel Hill: University of North Carolina Press, 1999); Ada Ferrer, *Freedom's Mirror: Cuba and Haiti in the Age of Revolution* (New York: Cambridge University Press, 2014); Peter F. Guardino, *The Time of Liberty: Popular Political Culture in Oaxaca, 1750–1850* (Durham, NC: Duke University Press, 2005); Peter F. Guardino, *Peasants, Politics, and the Formation of Mexico's National State: Guerrero, 1800–1857* (Stanford, CA: Stanford University Press, 1996); Aline Helg, *Liberty and Equality in Caribbean Colombia, 1770–1835* (Chapel Hill: University of North Carolina Press, 2004); Lyman Johnson, *Workshop of Revolution: Plebeian Buenos Aires and the Atlantic World, 1776–1810* (Durham, NC: Duke University Press, 2011); Marixa Lasso, *Myths of Harmony: Race and Republicanism during the Age of Revolu- tion, Colombia 1795–1831* (Pittsburgh, PA: University of Pittsburgh Press, 2007); Gabriel Paquette, *Imperial Portugal in the Age of Atlantic Revolutions: The Luso-Brazilian World, c. 1770–1850* (New York: Cambridge University Press, 2013); Rigoberto Rueda, "El 20 de Julio de 1810: una lectura en clave social," in *El Nuevo Reino de Granada y sus Provincias: Crisis de la Independencia y experiencias republicanas*, ed. Aristides Ramos et al. (Bogotá: Editorial Universidad del Rosario, 2009), 165–87; Kirsten Schultz, *Tropical Versailles: Empire, Monarchy, and the Portuguese Royal Court in Rio de Janeiro, 1808–1821* (New York and London: Routledge, 2001); Mimi Sheller, *Democracy after Slavery: Black Publics and Peasant Radicalism in Haiti and Jamaica* (Gainesville: Univer- sity of Florida Press, 2001); Camilla Townsend, "'Half My Body Free, the Other Half Enslaved': The Politics of the Slaves of Guayaquil at the End of the Colonial Era," *Colonial Latin American Review* 7, no. 1 (1998): 105–28.

elites.[7] Popayán's long-lasting multiethnic royalist alliances constitute a particularly fertile ground for analyzing the diversity, complexity, and impact of the politics of Indians and slaves during the Age of Revolution.

The book illustrates why we need to widen our geographic scope to areas beyond the North Atlantic/Caribbean region, where most of the work on the period has focused up to now. The North Andean/Pacific region of Popayán contrasts in important ways with the North Atlantic/ Caribbean cases most commonly studied by historians of the Age of Revolution.[8] This is particularly so because Popayán offers a single frame with which to analyze indigenous and Afro-diasporic politics and reveal

---

[7] See, for example, two recent books on the American Revolution: Eric Nelson, *The Royalist Revolution: Monarchy and the American Founding* (Cambridge, MA: Belknap Press, 2014); Andrew Jackson O'Shaughnessy, *The Men Who Lost America: British Leadership, the American Revolution, and the Fate of Empire* (New Haven, CT: Yale University Press, 2013). One analysis of slave resistance that dismisses loyalism can be found in Michael Craton, *Testing the Chains: Resistance to Slavery in the British West Indies* (Ithaca, NY, and London: Cornell University Press, 1982), 171.

[8] In their works, scholars such as Maya Jasanoff, Jane Landers, and David Sartorius have pointed to the key relevance of exploring how loyalty was expressed and experienced by people in the popular classes. Landers has highlighted the porous frontiers between revolution and counterrevolution in the Caribbean empires and proven that royalism was a strategy for mobility among people of African descent. Looking at the American and French Revolutions, Jasanoff noted that "the social extent and diversity of loyalism" are still rarely appreciated because of widespread stereotypes that loyalists were "socially elite, politically reactionary and essentially ... conservatives." Maya Jasanoff, "Revolutionary Exiles: The American Loyalist and French Émigré Diasporas," in *The Age of Revolutions in Global Context, c. 1760–1840*, ed. David Armitage and Sanjay Subrahamanyam (New York: Palgrave, 2010), 39; Jane Landers, *Atlantic Creoles in the Age of Revolutions* (Cambridge, MA: Harvard University Press, 2010); David Sartorius, *Ever Faithful: Race, Loyalty, and the Ends of Empire in Spanish Cuba* (Durham, NC: Duke University Press, 2013). For British North America, see also Maya Jasanoff, *Liberty's Exiles: American Loyalists in the Revolutionary World* (New York: Knopf/Harper Press, 2011); Ruma Chopra, *Unnatural Rebellion: Loyalists in New York City during the Revolution* (Charlottesville: University of Virginia Press, 2011), which deals with slave loyalists in New York City; and the classic study of Indian peoples who sided with the British in revolutionary North America, Colin Calloway, *The American Revolution in Indian Country: Crisis and Diversity in Native American Communities* (New York: Cambridge University Press, 1995). Among recent works on popular royalism in Latin America are Peter Blanchard, *Under the Flags of Freedom: Slave Soldiers and the Wars of Independence in Spanish South America* (Pittsburgh, PA: University of Pittsburgh Press, 2008); Jairo Gutiérrez, *Los indios de Pasto contra la República (1809–1824)* (Bogotá: Instituto Colombiano de Antropología e Historia, 2007); Armando Martínez and Daniel Gutiérrez, *La contrarrevolución de los pueblos de las Sabanas de Tolú y el Sinú (1812)* (Bucaramanga: Universidad Industrial de Santander, 2010); Cecilia Méndez, *The Plebeian Republic: The Huanta Rebellion and the Making of the Peruvian State, 1820–1850* (Durham, NC: Duke University Press, 2005); Gene E. Ogle, "The Trans-Atlantic King and Imperial Public Spheres: Everyday Politics in Pre-Revolutionary Saint-Domingue," in *The World of*

previously unexplored parallels and connections between the legal identities and political challenges of Indians and slaves in a territory under royalist control during a time of revolutionary change.

Indeed, Popayán is an ideal case study for bringing together the historiographies of indigenous people and people of African origin and descent, which are generally separated in historical studies. The indigenous society of Pasto, the second largest in New Granada, had not been part of the Inca Empire. Thus the northern Andean region provides a different perspective on the Andes than does Peru. Seen in the broader context of slavery in the Americas and the African diaspora, the two defining features of Popayán's slave society were the absence of plantations and the coexistence of enslaved Africans with indigenous people. At the same time that slavery was a legal identity that framed enslaved peoples' political options, these people also constructed their visions of freedom by drawing from the example that Indianness, as a legal status, represented.

While there were Indians and slaves all across the province, the indigenous population was concentrated in the highlands, around the city of Pasto, and the enslaved were especially important for gold extraction in the Pacific lowlands. Thus I study these two settings separately – the Andean highlands and the Pacific lowlands – while putting the indigenous people and the enslaved in the same analytical, political, and historical frame. I inquire into the ways in which legal definitions of Indianness and slavery were foundational to the individual and collective political identities of Indians and enslaved Afro-descendants. Most importantly, I explore what made each of these identities distinctive – in spite of the fact that we may be tempted to put them in a single category of subaltern or oppressed people – and show why a historical reconstruction of the

---

the Haitian Revolution, ed. David Geggus and Norman Fiering (Bloomington and Indianapolis: Indiana University Press, 2009), 79–96; Cassandra Pybus, *Epic Journeys of Freedom: Runaway Slaves of the American Revolution and their Global Quest for Liberty* (Boston: Beacon Press, 2006); Jaime Rodríguez, "Las primeras elecciones constitucionales en el Reino de Quito, 1809–1814 y 1821–1822," *Revista Procesos* 14 (1999): 13–52; Steinar Saether, *Identidades e independencia en Santa Marta y Riohacha, 1750–1850* (Bogotá: Instituto Colombiano de Antropología e Historia, 2005); Simon Schama, *Rough Crossings: Britain, the Slaves, and the American Revolution* (New York: Harper, 2006); James Sidbury, *Becoming African in America: Race and Nation in the Early Black Atlantic* (New York: Oxford University Press, 2007); Tomás Straka, *La voz de los vencidos: Ideas del partido realista de Caracas, 1810–1821* (Caracas: Facultad de Humanidades y Educación-Universidad Central de Venezuela, 2000); Eric Van Young, *The Other Rebellion: Popular Violence, Ideology, and Struggle for Independence* (Stanford, CA: Stanford University Press, 2001).

politics of indigenous people or slaves needs to pay close attention to the imperial shifts in legislation.

Although generally ignored in recent revolution-centered versions of the Latin American independence processes, the royalist Indians and slaves engaged with the ideas of the age, such as citizenship and freedom. Their story is an essential part of the history of the period, as this book will show. Placing the royalist Indians and slaves at the center of the narrative stresses the dynamism, creativity, and change intrinsic to monarchical political culture. It dismantles previous assumptions that the royalists were struggling to restore an old, static, conservative order. Royalist territories such as Popayán were theaters of deep political transformations, which were brought about by military dynamics and other liberal institutional innovations, such as the application of the 1812 Constitution conceived and promulgated in Cádiz.[9] In a time marked by antagonisms, uncertainty, disorder, and improvisation, political opportunities arose for all colonial subjects. Royalist Indians and slaves in Popayán championed imperial relations that would benefit them, and their military and political engagement with royalism had consequences for political relations in Popayán. That is to say, they were pivotal to the course of the war and shaped the range of changes brought about by independence. The negotiations that favored royalist Indians and slaves during the last twenty years of Spanish rule clearly set conditions and limits for the process of republican state formation after 1825, when Simón Bolívar and José de San Martín finally overcame the Pacific royalist forces.

The book draws a picture of the royalist region of Popayán that reveals deep chronological layers and multiple social and spatial textures. Tracing the historical meanings of royalism and understanding these multiethnic alliances outside their usual characterization as counterrevolutionary and antirepublican (or specifically anti-Bolivarian) requires reframing this story of the Indian and slave royalists in temporal and spatial contexts of broader proportions. Indeed, the royalist alliances involving Indians and slaves in Popayán cannot be understood at all from within the limited spatial and chronological boundaries of Colombian national history.

Empire is the framework for studying politics during the period, as it played a crucial role in shaping the strategies of Indians and slaves in the Province of Popayán leading up to the confrontation between the royalists and the Bolivarian Army in 1822. At the same time, it was in the cities and

---

[9] Which King Fernando VII overturned in favor of a repressive strand of absolutism when he returned to the throne in 1814.

rural areas, through the local events that were framed within the imperial crisis, that changes in the political structure and logic of the monarchy took place. In other words, it is important to acknowledge that the crisis in Spain, along with the diplomatic and constitutional efforts undertaken by the deputies in Cádiz to overcome it, had important consequences for the American territories. Yet it is equally fundamental to reconstruct the process whereby the people in the Americas produced and molded Spanish sovereignty at this moment of crisis. Thus, tracing the fluctuating rule of Spain in the Province of Popayán simultaneously produces a history of this region – encompassing the highlands and the mining frontier as well as the broader dynamics of the viceroyalties of Peru and New Granada – and a story of the imperial and interimperial dynamics involving Cádiz and France.

As in Restrepo's damning depiction, the term "royalism" was central to the political lexicon of the nineteenth century, signifying a primary pole of the ideological, military, and political spectrum in Spanish America after Napoleon invaded the Iberian Peninsula. In that critical context after 1808, the term "royalist" denoted the defenders and supporters of the King Fernando VII, who had been deposed by Napoleon. During his absence a widespread cult surrounded Fernando, known as "el deseado" (the beloved), which gave royalism the significant connotation of rejection of French rule and oppression. Over the course of the independence wars, however, royalism changed. It also began to imply the defense of the monarchy in opposition to the independence projects that were emerging across Spanish America. And because the source of Spanish sovereignty in the peninsula changed during the years 1808–14, when the king was absent, royalism became profoundly enmeshed with the Cádiz liberal experiment that instituted a constitutional monarchy to govern in the name of the absent king. These transformations, when seen from the perspective of the northern Andean royalist regions in the Pacific, reveal that the Age of Revolution cannot be understood on the basis of simplistic dichotomies such as revolutionary and reactionary, traditional and modern, or liberal and conservative. Rather, during the "revolutionary era," from the mid-eighteenth to the mid-nineteenth century, liberalism and monarchism were not necessarily antithetical and reform and revolution were deeply connected in the Spanish world.[10]

---

[10] This implies that the history of liberalism in Latin America starts earlier than it is traditionally thought to begin, in the early nineteenth century and within the Spanish Empire, and not later, with the creation of independent republics. There obviously were

Focusing on the micropolitics of the rural areas that the indigenous people and enslaved Afro-descendants inhabited, the book emphasizes long-term patterns (1780–1825) and broadens the geographic scope in order to reconstruct the ways in which the politics of Indians and slaves were articulated with the changes taking place in the Spanish Empire – from Bourbon reformism to the liberal revolution and then back to absolutism, though these transitions were never linear or complete given the upheavals brought by the war.

My first methodological strategy consists of looking at the political history of the region going back to 1780 and linking the reformist and revolutionary contexts in a single temporal frame. (In conventional historiographic terms these contexts would be called the late colonial period and the independence wars, respectively.) The Bourbon King Philip V came to the throne in 1700 aiming to restructure the Spanish Empire, and during the eighteenth century the Spanish monarchy went through deep reforms carried out by Philip's son Fernando VI (1746–59) and Charles III (1759–88). Following the 1808 Napoleonic invasion of the Iberian Peninsula, the crisis of the monarchy led to the rise of autonomist projects and to war in Spanish America, beginning in 1809. I look at these processes both together and from a broader Atlantic angle, seen as part of the revolutionary age.[11]

Between 1780 and 1825, at the same time that people in the northern Andean province of Popayán were experiencing the cycles of reform and revolution that characterized the entire period, they were also shaping the outcomes of reform and revolution. Here Popayán, Pasto, and the Pacific lowlands are not seen as backwaters that sought to remain outside broader processes of reform and change in the eighteenth century but instead

---

differences between these "liberalisms" through time. See, for example, Roberto Breña, *El primer liberalismo español y los procesos de emancipación de América, 1808–1824* (Mexico: Colegio de México, 2006).

[11] I agree with recent historical revisions of the period that have shown why we need to move away from an understanding of the Latin American *independence wars* that has stressed discontinuity with the late colonial years and has generally produced nationally bounded histories, which ignore the imperial dimension of such processes. See Jeremy Adelman, *Sovereignty and Revolution in the Iberian Atlantic* (Princeton, NJ, and Oxford: Princeton University Press, 2006); François-Xavier Guerra, *Modernidad e independencias: Ensayos sobre las revoluciones hispánicas* (México, D.F.: Editorial MAPFRE-Fondo de Cultura Económica, 1992); José María Portillo, *Crisis atlántica: Autonomía e independencia en la crisis de la monarquía hispana* (Madrid: Marcial Pons, 2006); Jaime Rodríguez, *La independencia de la América española* (1996; México, D.F.: Fondo de Cultura Económica, 2008).

are revealed as vigorous centers of political transformation, contestation, and innovation. In Popayán, as in much of Spanish America, the Bourbon reforms had mixed results. The antagonisms within indigenous communities and between them and colonial officials became more acute as authority and representation within the communities changed with the reforms. The tensions surrounding slavery between slaveholders and the enslaved, as well as with crown officials, were exacerbated by the crown's broader changes to legislation pertaining to slavery (which reflected Bourbon investment in expanding and modernizing slavery in the Caribbean). Thus, at the end of the eighteenth century, the reforms were sources of mobilization and contestation, and social conflicts proliferated.

Yet in spite of the increased tensions across Spanish America, the Spanish Empire's peculiarity at the dawn of the nineteenth century was its resilience. It was in 1808, as the peninsular crisis hit, that the unprecedented opportunities for involvement in the military defense of the crown opened new spaces for indigenous people from Pasto and its surrounding towns and for enslaved people who lived in the Pacific lowlands, all of whom played defining roles in maintaining the region under Spanish rule. In other words, in the context of the Spanish monarchical crisis and during the wars of independence, the region was a center of deep political experimentation. A look at royalism and liberal reform in the northern Andes suggests that profound changes took place within the royalist territories. The struggles and negotiations of local people, among them Indians and slaves, with the changing monarchical regime were at the heart of those transformations.

The second methodological strategy I use is spatial. The main shift here is telling the story of Popayán between 1780 and 1825 outside a preconceived Colombian national territorial frame and, instead, demonstrating how during the wars of independence this region was strategically articulated within what I call the "Pacific royalist block." Bordering the Pacific Ocean and comprising the gold-rich Pacific lowlands and a fertile Andean region, Popayán was a frontier area that lay between the Viceroyalty of New Granada's southern border, the Kingdom of Quito, and the Viceroyalty of Peru. During the crisis of the Spanish monarchy (1809–22), Popayán also lay at the strategic intersection of two divergent large-scale political processes, with most of New Granada embracing anticolonial ideals and experimenting with local rule while royalist Peru sustained a successful resistance against Creole-led insurgencies in New Granada and Río de la Plata (present-day Argentina). In this context, a royalist alliance took shape across the Pacific region of South America from Panama to

Chile, including Peru, Quito, and Popayán. The strategic location of the areas inhabited by Indians (Pasto) and slaves (the Pacific lowlands) in Popayán allowed them to negotiate local rule with the royalist authorities who had been seeking to defend the province from insurgent threats since 1809. This gold-mining region around which the provincial economy pivoted was especially coveted by all the regional powers north and south of Popayán (the cities of Cali and Quito), and during the war the Pacific lowlands were the gateway for information and military reinforcements arriving from Peru to Popayán.

A third conceptual and methodological strategy I employ here is to show that the politics of royalism was socially embedded and deeply tied to the legal identity of indigenous people and the enslaved. I build on scholarship produced in the United States and Latin America in the last twenty years about the relationship that indigenous people and people of African descent had to Spanish law. This body of scholarship has generated a sophisticated debate about the ways in which these people conceptualized the law and utilized legal institutions.[12] It has further offered definite evidence that the monarchical structure and its corporate organization of society provided all Spanish vassals with legal identities that ultimately granted them rights and protected their interests, particularly through the mediation of the crown.

My goal in this book is to take the political study of the law a step further by viewing it within the late-colonial context in conjunction with the transformative processes unleashed during the revolutionary age. I do

---

[12] In the twentieth century, discussions about the law in the Spanish Empire emerged within the contours of institutional history, privileging questions such as the role that metropolitan legislation had in shaping American societies. The work of Frank Tannenbaum, *Slave and Citizen: The Negro in the Americas* (1946; New York: Vintage Books, 1963), sparked a major debate focused on how variable legal regimes could account for the differences between slave societies. More recent approaches frame the study of the law according to the practical relevance it had for slaves in the particular contexts and circumstances in which they lived. See, for example, Alejandro de la Fuente, "Slaves and the Creation of Legal Rights in Cuba: *Coartación* and *Papel*," *Hispanic American Historical Review* 87, no. 4 (2007), 659–92; María Elena Díaz, *The Virgin, the King, and the Royal Slaves of El Cobre: Negotiating Freedom in Colonial Cuba, 1670–1780* (Stanford, CA: Stanford University Press, 2000). Steve Stern's *Peru's Indian Peoples* was foundational to the historiography on Indians' uses of the law. See also Brian P. Owensby, *Empire of Law and Indian Justice in Colonial Mexico* (Stanford, CA: Stanford University Press, 2008); Sergio Serulnikov, *Subverting Colonial Authority: Challenges to Spanish Rule in Eighteenth-Century Southern Andes* (Durham, NC: Duke University Press, 2003); Yanna Yannakakis, *The Art of Being In-between: Native Intermediaries, Indian Identity, and Local Rule in Colonial Oaxaca* (Durham, NC: Duke University Press, 2008).

so by exploring the significance of changes in legislation for the politics of Indians and the enslaved across Spanish America. Thus the book begins with a study of how Bourbon reformism framed politics among Indians and slaves in the late eighteenth century and then moves on to explore how local political dynamics changed in the nineteenth century, especially after the monarchical crisis that began in 1808. My analysis reveals that the Indians' and slaves' interpretation of the law, their recourse to violence in extreme circumstances, and their awareness of evolving legal and military opportunities had the potential to affect political relations at the local level and were, in turn, embedded within the longer history of imperial reform and crisis.[13]

I argue that notions of rights and freedom – which historians generally identify with republican thought and institutions – were part of Hispanic and monarchical political culture.[14] My analysis of eighteenth-century politics in the context of the Bourbon government and the monarchical crisis builds on the conception of a flexible legal practice that permitted people the sophisticated use of Spanish rhetoric to assert their interests.[15] In the history of the Hispanic imperial legal system, the political essence of the law can be best understood by looking at it in practice.[16] This practical approach to analyzing the law overturns the longstanding

---

[13] Yet even among scholars who acknowledge that enslaved people were acquainted with the law and used this knowledge to appeal to the crown's paternalism, some consider this as evidence of the slaves' mystical conception of the king's power. In other words, there is a sense among such historians that the slaves' pleas for justice reflected their naïveté. Renée Soulodre-La France, "'Los esclavos de su Magestad': Slave Protest and Politics in Late Colonial New Granada," in *Slaves, Subjects, and Subversives: Blacks in Colonial Latin America*, ed. Jane G. Landers and Barry M. Robinson (Albuquerque: University of New Mexico Press, 2006), 175–208.

[14] The concept of rights at the heart of Hispanic legal texts significantly affected the development of Western political theory. See Carlos Stoetzer, *El pensamiento político en la América española durante el período de la emancipación (1789–1825)* (Madrid: Instituto de Estudios Políticos, 1966); Anthony Pagden, *The Fall of Natural Man: The American Indian and the Origins of Comparative Ethnology* (New York: Cambridge University Press, 1987); Brian Tierney, *The Idea of Natural Rights: Studies on Natural Rights, Natural Law, and Church Law, 1150–1625* (Atlanta, GA: Emory University Press, 1997), 255.

[15] R. Jovita Baber, "The Construction of Empire: Politics, Law and Community in Tlaxcala, New Spain, 1521–1640" (PhD diss., University of Chicago, 2005), 258; John L. Phelan, "Authority and Flexibility in the Spanish Imperial Bureaucracy," *Administrative Science Quarterly* 5, no. 1 (1960), 47–65.

[16] See Owensby, *Empire of Law*, especially ch. 1. An interesting discussion of a "historical, processual, and social" approach to law that adds to our comparative perspective can be found in Jane Burbank, *Russian Peasants Go To Court: Legal Culture in the Countryside, 1905–1917* (Indianapolis: Indiana University Press, 2004), 10. Burbank's study of

assumption that the legal process turned Spanish vassals into objects, never allowing them to be their own agents.[17]

To understand the political logic and structure of imperial Spain, the concept of the political "pact" is particularly useful. Alliances, or pacts, between the king and his subjects had characterized Castilian governance and royal authority in the Middle Ages.[18] Such a contractualist understanding of monarchical power and society was crucial for defining the Spanish political community in the Americas, made up of autonomous corporate bodies that received protection and rights from the crown in exchange for their loyalty. The pact of reciprocity is also an important element of Andean historiography, which has given the colonial relationship a specific content by linking it to ethnohistorical interpretations of politics and government. Indian communities understood Spanish (and later republican) rule as based on the assumption that they shared a pact with the state at the economic as well as at the political level.[19]

The notion of a pact has been instrumental in challenging the more rigid definitions of colonial power that see it as stemming only from the top down, and of colonialism as a mere exercise of domination through force. It is also consistent with the Hispanic philosophy of government, which was based on scholastic principles that guaranteed a degree of flexibility to the monarchy's governmental structure. In other words, the "unwritten constitution" of the Habsburg Monarchy was indeed based on contractual principles that connected multiple social and ethnic groups

---

Russian peasants' uses of the courts proves that "through their choices of what to litigate and how to do so, [peasants] shaped the significance of the law."

[17] Yannakakis, *The Art of Being In-between*, 109–10; Baber "The Construction of Empire"; Rachel O'Toole, "'In a War Against the Spanish': Andean Protection and African Resistance on the Northern Peruvian Coast," *The Americas* 63, no. 1 (2006), 19–52; Bianca Premo, *Children of the Father King: Youth, Authority, and Legal Minority in Colonial Lima* (Chapel Hill: University of North Carolina Press, 2005); Renzo Honores, "Colonial Legal Polyphony: Caciques and the Construction of Legal Arguments in the Andes, 1550–1640" (paper presented at the 2010 Seminar on the History of the Atlantic World, *Justice: Europe in America, 1500–1830*); and José Carlos de la Puente, "Into the Heart of the Empire: Indian Journeys to the Habsburg Royal Court" (PhD diss., Texas Christian University, 2010) also contribute to the renewed methodological debate on legal history.

[18] Baber, "The Construction of Empire," 68; see also Pablo Fernández Albaladejo, *Fragmentos de Monarquía: Trabajos de historia política* (Madrid: Alianza Universidad, 1992).

[19] Tristan Platt, *Estado Boliviano y ayllu andino: tierra y tributo en el Norte de Potosí* (Lima: Instituto de Estudios Peruanos, 1982); Tristan Platt, "Liberalism and Ethnocide," *History Workshop Journal* 17 (1984), 6; Brooke Larson, "Explotación y economía moral en los Andes del sur: Hacia una reconsideración crítica," *Historia Crítica* 6 (1992), 75–97.

on both sides of the Atlantic.[20] Recent compelling Spanish historiography has recovered the importance of scholastic understanding of monarchical power and has shown its particular relevance to the study of the independence process in Spanish America. But few works have inquired into the implications that such a notion had among indigenous and Afro-descendant peoples because of their focus on elites and constitutional documents.[21]

As a consequence of the Bourbon state's attempts to claim control of the economy and to centralize governance, all popular legal action gained resonance.[22] Moreover, since Indian communities as well as the communities built by people of African origin and descent were internally differentiated, I have searched for traces of the unequal access they had to legal strategies before and after the start of the independence wars. For example, as native rulers, caciques had been crucial to the process of carving out a semiautonomous space for their communities in local politics, while at the same time guaranteeing their own permanence as a class that had accumulated economic and political prerogatives.[23] In a similar way, among the enslaved people in Popayán's Pacific lowlands,

[20] John L. Phelan, *The People and the King: The Comunero Revolution in Colombia* (Madison: University of Wisconsin Press, 1978) argues that in the early modern era the Spanish monarchy had an "unwritten constitution"; Manuel Lucena Giraldo, "La constitución atlántica de España y sus Indias," *Revista de Occidente* 281 (2004), 33; see also J.H. Elliott, *Empires of the Atlantic World: Britain and Spain in America, 1492–1830* (New Haven, CT, and London: Yale University Press, 2006), esp. part 2.

[21] Manuel Giménez, "Las doctrinas populistas en la Independencia de Hispanoamérica," *Anuario de Estudios Americanos* 3 (1946), 534–54; Mónica Quijada, "Las 'dos tradiciones': Soberanía popular e imaginarios compartidos en el mundo hispánico en la época de las grandes revoluciones atlánticas," in *Revolución, Independencia y las nuevas naciones de América*, ed. Jaime Rodríguez (Madrid: Fundación MAPFRE Tavera, 2005), 61–86; José María Portillo, *Revolución de Nación: Orígenes de la cultura constitucional en España, 1780–1812* (Madrid: Centro de Estudios Políticos y Constitucionales, 2001); Manuel Chust, *La cuestión nacional americana en las Cortes de Cádiz (1810–1814)* (Valencia: Instituto de Historia Social, 1999); Marie Laure Rieu-Millan, *Los diputados americanos en las Cortes de Cádiz* (Madrid: Consejo Superior de Investigaciones Científicas, 1990); Ángel Soto and León Gómez Rivas, "Los orígenes escolásticos de la independencia Iberoamericana (en el bicentenario de la emancipación 1810–2010)," *Bicentenario: Revista de Chile y América* 4, no. 2 (2005), 115–45; Carlos Stoetzer, *Las raíces escolásticas de la Emancipación en la América Española* (Madrid: Centro de Estudios Constitucionales, 1982).

[22] A process that also affected slaves in the mining district of Barbacoas, as shown in Chapter 3. See also Guardino, *The Time of Liberty*, 117.

[23] Yannakakis, *The Art of Being In-between*, 63, 190; Karen Graubart, "Learning from the Qadi: The Jurisdiction of Local Rule in the Early Colonial Andes," *Hispanic American Historical Review* 95, no. 2 (2015), 195–228.

the mining gang captains (who were also slaves) acquired a mastery of legal language of which they made effective use in the courts, thus guaranteeing their leading role within the enslaved communities. In both of these cases, the caciques and the gang captains employed their knowledge and use of the law to help assure the preservation of their internally sanctioned leadership roles. In external relations with colonial officials, the communication of Indian caciques and enslaved captains with the higher colonial authorities through their use of proper channels – the courts – to solve disputes and seek redress was regarded as a sign of their loyalty.[24] In all cases, the law helped shape collective political action and the political hierarchies within the communities of Indians and enslaved people.

During the monarchical crisis, Indians and slaves defined royalism through a dynamic process of the reinvention and negotiation of their rights and obligations that took place at the intersection of local and imperial contexts. Throughout the book I make a particular effort to avoid presupposing the interests of people in Popayán, given that in the turbulent years between 1780 and 1825 imperial policy shifted with dizzying speed, making it possible for all of the Spanish monarch's vassals to appropriate varying (and sometimes conflicting) strands of imperial discourse for their own purposes.

Based on extensive research in multiple archives in Colombia, Ecuador, Spain, and the United States, I use criminal documents dating from the late eighteenth century and on into the 1820s as well as speeches, sermons, pamphlets and numerous wartime memoranda, letters, and orders from the royalist armies in order to study the conflicts and strategies of Indians and slaves as they developed within the colonial context, in the independence period, and through the first years of the Republic. The Indians and slaves who form the core of my study did not leave a written trail of their own. For a long time, the major historians of independence have used the absence of such a trail to account for their sidelining of natives and people of African descent from their political narratives. Yet important traces of the strategic engagement of Indians and slaves with the law and royalist politics can be found both in the criminal records and in military and other official sources, which, when

---

[24] Garrett found that, for this reason, the Inca nobility in Cuzco believed the royal courts were the most effective means of challenging local authority. See David T. Garrett, *Shadows of Empire: The Indian Nobility of Cusco, 1750–1825* (New York: Cambridge University Press, 2005), 201.

read critically and creatively, are crucial to discerning the historical strategies of these groups during the period of this study.

Chapter 1 will provide a panoramic view of Popayán from 1780 to 1825, a narrative of the period covered in the book that frames the local political dynamics explored in the following chapters. This overview situates Popayán and its people within the spatial and temporal axes that linked New Granada to Peru and led up to the Bourbon reforms. Then it shows how politics in Popayán shifted as a result of the monarchical crisis in the Iberian Peninsula and its consequences.

Seeking to comprehend royalism beyond the negative definition of it as antirepublican or antirevolutionary, in Chapters 2 and 3 I explore the relations that Indians and slaves had with the Spanish monarchy before the independence crisis hit. This methodological starting point – identifying the historical background to royalist alliances in the ongoing engagement of both Indians and slaves in Popayán with the powerful rhetoric of monarchic justice – allows me to frame their political strategies within imperial history and not outside it (i.e., in a protonational context, following most narratives of the period). I highlight the issues that defined the political identity, priorities, and opportunities of Indians and slaves in late-eighteenth-century Popayán, and particularly stress the dynamism of colonial political culture: how it changed over time and how its interpretation varied according to the social position and political interests of its protagonists.

Building on the existing scholarship on the military participation of popular groups during the Atlantic Age of Revolution, Chapters 4 through 6 explain the practical dimension of the royalism of Indians and slaves in Popayán within the Atlantic context of imperial war, crisis, and reform. Similar to what happened earlier during the American and Haitian Revolutions, Indians and slaves in Popayán were central to the European powers' goal of guaranteeing the loyalty of their American subjects. This gave way to opportunities for alliances with colonial officials, based on the ability of the crown and its representatives to negotiate with Indians and slaves according to the most pressing interests of the latter. Ultimately, the collective participation of Indians and slaves in royalist alliances justifies interpreting monarchism as a political strategy that offered them opportunities and benefits, given that colonial elites were willing to accommodate the priorities of indigenous people and slaves to guarantee their loyalty.

The largely untold story of this royalist cause demonstrates that independence was hardly inevitable. Moreover, royalism's multiethnic appeal suggests that the conflict at the heart of the Age of Revolution in Latin America had complex social and ideological undertones. While the royalist alliances were explicitly based on the defense of the Spanish King's sovereignty at the turbulent juncture of the Napoleonic invasion, they were also deeply embedded in the political activities of Indians and slaves, who had had a long history of engagement with monarchic politics. In this work I will trace their struggles to define and defend specific rights in the colonial context and the transformations of and ruptures in those rights that were the result of the process of independence. With independence far from assured, or even necessarily desired, royalist Indians and slaves sought to position themselves favorably within the context of empire. This narrative focuses on the imperial identities that these subjects envisioned and shaped through legal and military strategies, showing the competing visions of empire, independence, freedom, and revolution that coexisted in Popayán from 1780 to 1825.

Reform, revolution, and royalism in the northern Andes

New Granada and Popayán (1780–1825)

In 1781, during the *Comunero* Rebellion in the Viceroyalty of New Granada, Spanish South America's northernmost jurisdiction, colonial officials in the Province of Antioquia recorded the news that a large community of mining slaves planned to revolt and ask to be granted freedom in exchange for a promise to remain as laborers in the gold mines, and to be responsible for paying tribute to the crown, "as if they were Indians."[1] The *Comunero* Rebellion was the largest popular mobilization against the Bourbon reforms in New Granada. Though its epicenter was in the provinces surrounding the capital, Santa Fe, it also had connections to unrest in other regions such as Antioquia, where the slave conspiracy raised concerns.

The slaves of Antioquia were keenly aware of the instability brought about by the Bourbon reforms and, under those circumstances, they were acting to negotiate their position within New Granada society. That they defined freedom as a condition regulated through the fiscal mechanism of paying tribute to the king suggests that, at the end of the eighteenth century, the political imagination of the enslaved in the mines of New Granada was shaped by their coexistence with indigenous peoples.[2] As the slaves themselves acknowledged, in the Spanish Empire paying tribute was first and foremost an obligation of the Indian population.

---

[1] Phelan, *The People and the King*, 110.

[2] Here I build on the idea that Frederick Cooper, Thomas Holt, and Rebecca Scott have posed, that "freedom is not a natural state." We need to inquire into the local histories of freedom, but not only in the postemancipation context. See Cooper, Holt, and Scott, *Beyond Slavery: Explorations of Race, Labor, and Citizenship in Postemancipation Societies* (Chapel Hill: University of North Carolina Press, 2000), 9.

Tribute was a head tax that indigenous people paid in exchange for the crown's protection of their communal rights.[3] The episode in Antioquia illustrates how, for slaves, freedom could be defined as the rights and bargaining power that vassals acquired through a fiscal relationship with the crown. Indeed, the enslaved seemed to recognize the legitimate mediating power of the king and were willing to enter into a relationship of vassalage, which they modeled on the Indians' position vis-à-vis the crown.

These types of connections between Afro-descendant and indigenous people were characteristic of the Spanish American mainland and specifically of the northern Andean region. The African Diasporic communities that emerged in places such as New Granada, Mexico, and Peru as a result of Spanish colonization and the expansion of African slavery were embedded in social settings marked by the transformations brought about in the native societies, which bore the brunt of the Spanish colonial project.[4] A case in point is the New Granadan province of Popayán, south of Antioquia, where free and enslaved people of African origin and descent, either living in the cities or working mostly as laborers in the mines and on haciendas, were in close contact with indigenous people across the province. Thus, it is particularly interesting, and necessary, to examine the political worlds of Indians and slaves

---

[3] Studying the case of seventeenth-century Mexico, Tatiana Seijas shows how Asian slaves also modeled their vision of freedom on the legal status and social category of the Indian population, seeking occupational rights and other protections or privileges that were granted to Indian vassals. Seijas writes that after manumission Asian (chino) slaves "changed their identity; they went from being chino slaves to being free Indians." See Seijas, *Asian Slaves in Colonial Mexico: From Chinos to Indians* (New York: Cambridge University Press, 2014), 159–63, 171. The crown also collected tribute from free blacks, as a means of counting the free population and acquiring revenue from their collective production as families and communities. See Norah Andrews, "Taxing Blackness: Tribute and Free Colored Community in Colonial Mexico" (PhD diss., Johns Hopkins University, 2014), 16, 21, 26, 30.

[4] In exploring an area of Latin America previously marginalized from broader discussions on slavery, this work contributes to what Sherwin Bryant et al. have called the "fourth-wave scholarship" on Afro-Latin American history. See Sherwin Bryant, Rachel O'Toole, and Ben Vinson III, eds., "Introduction" to *Africans to Spanish America*, 4–17. See also Lowell Gudmundson and Justin Wolfe, *Blacks and Blackness in Central America: Between Race and Place* (Durham, NC: Duke University Press, 2010), which illustrates the importance of exploring "historical trajectories that necessarily challenge both empirical and theoretical scholarship" on the African diaspora (p. 3); and Tiffany Ruby Patterson and Robin Kelley, "Unfinished Migrations: Reflections on the African diaspora and the Making of the Modern World," *African Studies Review* 43, no. 1 (2000), 11–45.

alongside one other. But it is also crucial to recognize that, legally, they inhabited different worlds.[5]

Intrinsic to Spanish colonial rule in the Americas was the legal differentiation of the two groups, Indians and enslaved people of African descent, and as colonial subjects this impacted them socially and politically. Moreover, from their different but interrelated positions, the individual and collective politics of indigenous people and of the enslaved were deeply grounded in and continuously adapting to the changing imperial legal context. That is to say, their legal identities as well as the institutions that defined them as Indians (tribute) and slaves (bondage) were in flux as the monarchy was constantly changing. In order to understand how the specific priorities and opportunities of indigenous people and the enslaved in Popayán evolved between 1780 and 1825 (which will be studied in detail in the following chapters), here we will examine the place of indigenous people and slaves in Popayán Province, the shifting terms of monarchic rule that shaped this region, and how, at the turn of the nineteenth century, war transformed politics in Popayán.

In the late eighteenth century, at the same time that the United States and Haiti were emerging from the first anticolonial wars in the hemisphere against, respectively, Britain and France, Spain was shaken by dissent and widespread reaction to the Bourbon reforms in America. Yet it was still able to counter rebellion and to hold on to its colonies. In the midst of a revolutionary age, when monarchies were being questioned and empires dismembered, the Spanish world seemed to be living up to the challenges of increasing threats to its security and the urgent need to revamp its economy and embrace free trade.

Then, in 1808, a major blow destabilized the Spanish monarchy from without: the Napoleonic invasion of Madrid and the removal of King Fernando VII from the throne. The invasion led to a war of independence from France in which the Spanish people fought against Napoleon's government. Furthermore, the years from 1808 to 1810 were also a time

---

[5] In her study of colonial Trujillo, Rachel O'Toole speaks of "legal locations." She outlines how the distinct legal locations and juridical positions of Africans and Andeans "informed strategies of resistance and adaptation to colonial rule." See O'Toole, *Bound Lives: Africans, Indians, and the Making of Race in Colonial Peru* (Pittsburgh, PA: University of Pittsburgh Press, 2012), 3, 21. Maria Elena Martínez argues that the relationship between the legal definitions of Indians and Africans was essentially antagonistic. See Martínez, "The Black Blood of New Spain: *Limpieza de Sangre*, Racial Violence, and Gendered Power in Early Colonial Mexico," *William and Mary Quarterly* 61, no. 3 (2004), 479–520.

of accelerated transformation within the Spanish monarchy. As a response to the monarchical crisis sparked by the French occupation, a liberal government sought to protect the king's sovereignty by writing a constitution. This reinvention of the monarchy in the early nineteenth century shaped the contours, limits, and meanings of institutional change, resulting in slow shifts in political subjectivities across the Hispanic world. But equally important were the reactions that people on the ground had to the new context and their interpretations of the exceptional circumstances. Loyalties were unstable, and this went hand in hand with jurisdictional disarticulations of multiple proportions: some had a deeper historical logic, while others were the product of transitional alliances at the local level.

It is well known that some American regions contested the authority of the government in the peninsula, and cities experimented with self-rule. Less known but equally significant is that other territories, such as Popayán, maintained a royalist stance and renewed their links to the imperial constitutional project underway in Spain. Everywhere, in the royalist territories as much as in those that sought to experiment with self-rule, the unprecedented combination of war and legal reform marked a turning point.

The royalist government in Popayán would not have been successful in defending the region from the insurgency encroaching on the province if it had not been for the mobilization of indigenous people and slaves in favor of the royalist cause. The royalist politics of Indians and slaves in Popayán, in turn, were framed in the circumstances that evolved in the Pacific-Andean region of Spanish America. The Viceroyalty of Peru became a crucial magnet that sustained the royalist government in the territory that spanned from Chile to Panama for more than a decade. This previously unappreciated Pacific alliance can be explained, in the long term, by looking at the southwestern region of New Granada in its broader geographic and jurisdictional context.

POPAYÁN AND THE NORTHERN ANDES

During the early colonization period in the sixteenth century, when the Viceroyalty of Peru encompassed all Spanish territory in South America, the Province (or *gobernación*) of Popayán was ruled from Lima. But as colonization at the northern end of the continent progressed and new centers of government were founded, the crown assigned the royal *Audiencias* or High Courts in Santa Fe (established in 1550 and located north of Popayán) and in Quito (established in 1563 and located south of Popayán) to oversee Popayán Province.[6] Thereafter, the *Audiencia* of Santa Fe governed the northern part of the province, and the *Audiencia* of Quito governed the territory south of Buenaventura – including Pasto, Popayán, Cali, and Barbacoas. This intermediate location between the New Kingdom of Granada and the Kingdom of Quito, along with its administration by overlapping jurisdictions, gave Popayán Province the character of a frontier area.[7]

Popayán Province (the present-day Colombian departments of Cauca, Nariño, and Valle del Cauca) was extremely large, encompassing an area that went from just below the southern border of the Chocó, then south to the Pacific coast, and east into the Andean highlands and the Amazonian territory, where the boundaries were undefined (see Figure I.1). While New Granada's most important port was Cartagena, on the Caribbean coast, the Pacific Ocean stretched along the entire western flank of Popayán Province, facilitating the entry of a significant legal and illegal trade in goods and slaves. Although its dynamics remain less studied than those of its Atlantic counterpart, the Pacific Ocean expedited contact between the inhabitants of Popayán and the maritime networks, which brought to the area people and news from Europe and the Caribbean as well as from other Spanish cities on the Pacific, such as Lima and Guayaquil, which were easier to reach by sea than by land. But in spite of the fact that it bordered the ocean and that the mining economy that flourished in the Pacific lowlands was pivotal to Popayán's regional economy, the province had an inward orientation. The majority of its trade with Spain took place along the Magdalena River (which traversed New Granada from north to south) because the Cauca River (which flowed between the western and central ranges) was only partially navigable. Thus, Popayán's three principal cities were in the interior, on the plateaus around the Cauca River or high in the cordilleras: Cali, the capital until 1628; Popayán, the seat of government thereafter; and Pasto, the southernmost city in the province (Figure I.1).

In Popayán, as in Mexico, Peru, and Santa Fe, the Spanish took advantage of existing native social hierarchies to establish their rule,

---

[6] Marta Herrera, *Popayán: La unidad de lo diverso: Territorio, población y poblamiento en la provincia de Popayán, siglo XVIII* (Bogotá: Ediciones Uniandes-CESO, 2009), 54–84.

[7] See the *Recopilación de las leyes de los reynos de las Indias* ([1681; Madrid: Viuda de Joaquín de Ibarra, 1791] Madrid: Facsimile reprint, 1941), Ley 2, título 15, libro 8 and libro 10; Herrera, *Popayán*, 71.

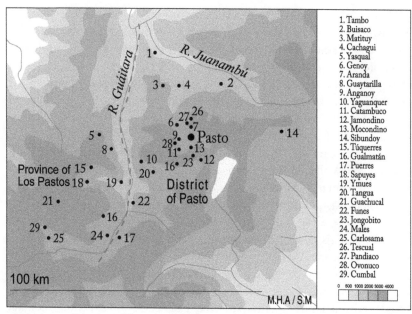

FIGURE I.I District of Pasto and province of Los Pastos with selected
Indian towns.
Map modified by Santiago Muñoz based on Marta Herrera, "Provincia de Popayán, 1797,"
in *Popayán*, 117–18.

perhaps disregarding the negative depictions of the Popayán natives by
Spanish chroniclers, who described the northern Andean chiefdoms (*cacicazgos*) as less advanced than the Inca state. In the sixteenth century,
Viceroy Toledo of Peru orchestrated a policy of *reducción*, which had the
intention of subjugating the South American Indians by resettling them
into more centralized communities. Natives living in settlements all across
Popayán were assigned to individual Spaniards (known as *encomenderos*)
for tribute and labor extraction. In many places in Popayán, such as
Chocó or Patía, native resistance to colonization hindered and delayed
Spanish settlement until the seventeenth century. That situation con-
trasted sharply with what took place in the highlands of Pasto, one of
the most populated areas in what later became New Granada, where the
natives acquiesced to *reducción*. Around the fertile soil at the foot of the
Galeras volcano (where the Spanish founded the city of Pasto in 1539), at
the time of conquest, three groups, Pasto, Quillacinga, and Abad, were
organized into chiefdoms. The population density of these chiefdoms
paralleled that of the Santa Fe and Tunja Muisca native societies, located

on the eastern range of the northern Andean cordillera, which also became epicenters of Spanish colonization.[8]

Pasto illustrates the impact of Spanish rule on native societies that had not been part of a pre-Hispanic empire or state. After the Spanish conquest of the northern Andes, their chiefdoms were reconstituted and their identities reinvented.[9] By the eighteenth century, the Indians living in the highlands surrounding the city of Pasto had not preserved their native languages. There also is no evidence that during the colonial period they used the pre-Hispanic names (Abad, Quillacinga, and Pasto) that the chroniclers had employed to classify them at the time of the conquest. But, identified as Indians, they actively preserved a communal territory and identity throughout the three hundred years of Spanish rule.[10] According to the census taken in 1797 (see Table 1.1), the highland native population was concentrated in two jurisdictions that comprised half of Popayán's native population. One was the area around the Andean city of Pasto, in the district governed by the city, and the other was the Province of Los Pastos, a sub-province of Popayán.[11] This division became official in the late eighteenth century, when the Province of Los Pastos was

---

[8] Chroniclers such as Pedro Cieza de León described people from the Andean highlands of Pasto as substantially less developed than the Inca. Although Inca forces successfully annexed the chiefdoms of the Ecuadorian Sierra to the Inca Empire, the chiefdom societies that existed around what would be called the city of Pasto had repelled the advances of the Inca forces only forty years before the arrival of Pizarro in Cajamarca. After the Inca expedition retreated, the Inca state's northern boundary was established at the Angasmayo River at Rumichaca. See Herrera, *Popayán*, ch. 1; *Luis Fernando Calero, Chiefdoms under Siege: Spain's Rule and Native Adaptation in the Southern Colombian Andes, 1535–1700* (Albuquerque: University of New Mexico Press, 1997).

[9] For the relevance of ecology to South American Andean peoples, see Larson, *Trials of Nation Making*, ch. 1; John V. Murra, *The Economic Organization of the Inca State* (Greenwich, CT: JAI Press, 1980). For the reinvention of Indian identities and ethnogenesis in the northern Andes, see Karen Powers, *Andean Journeys: Migration: Ethnogenesis, and the State in Colonial Quito* (Albuquerque: University of New Mexico, 1995); Tom Cummins and Joanne Rappaport, *Beyond the Lettered City: Indigenous Literacies in the Andes* (Durham, NC: Duke University Press, 2012).

[10] Derek Williams, *Acomodación, negociación y el actuar politico: Resistencia y revuelta indígena en el altiplano de los Pastos* (MA thesis, Universidad del Valle, 1994), speaks of the attacks from neighboring haciendas on Indians living on the Pasto *altiplano*. Gutiérrez, *Los indios de Pasto contra la República*, 132–34, highlights the success of the Pasto Indians' strategy to preserve their land throughout the nineteenth century. Joanne Rappaport, *Cumbe Reborn: An Andean Ethnography of History* (Chicago, IL: University of Chicago Press, 1994).

[11] Marta Herrera, *Popayán*, 99–158; Hermes Tovar, *Convocatoria al poder del número: Censos y estadísticas de la Nueva Granada, 1750–1850* (Bogotá: Archivo General de la Nación, 1994).

TABLE 1.1 *Population of New Granada (1778) and Popayán, Pasto, and Pacific Lowlands (1797)*

	New Granada 1778	Popayán Province 1797	District of Pasto 1797	Province of Los Pastos 1797	Barbacoas 1797	Iscuandé 1797	Micay 1797
Slaves	69,590	23,145	113	0	3,907	956	393
Indians	461,501	32,010	4,719	9,382	512	398	382
Free [people] of all colors	432,314	48,877	1,441	559	1,678	756	586
White	320,323	31,614	6,120	8,021	509	322	102
Total	1,283,728	135,646	12,393	17,962	6,606	2,432	1,463

Source: Hermes Tovar, *Convocatoria al poder del número. Censos y estadísticas de la Nueva Granada, 1750–1850* (Bogotá: Archivo General de la Nación, 1994), 69–73, 319.

recognized as an independent administrative unit with Túquerres as its center (see Figure 1.1). In spite of the decline of the native population in the Pasto and Los Pastos areas during the sixteenth and seventeenth centuries, taken as a whole this was the region in New Granada where the greatest number of natives survived into the eighteenth century.[12]

The founding elites of Popayán who received land grants were few in number, and they became privileged entrepreneurs who expanded their economic power through mining and commerce. The *encomendero* elite's dominion over the land translated into political power, which attracted peninsular Spaniards who were willing to establish family bonds with the traditional elites and provide the additional capital needed for investment in mining. Thus, Popayán had an elite that benefited from sugar production, gold mining, productive agricultural land, commerce, and control of the government. These colonists looked to the crown for approval to solidify their power and their social prominence in the region. They also tried to influence royal policy whenever possible, striving to obtain the government posts that were available to them in the *audiencia*, the *corregimientos* (political units administered by a *corregidor* or Spanish magistrate), and, most importantly, in the municipal council or *cabildo*. Modeled after urban political structures in Spain, the municipal council gave landowners the power to control the urban areas under its

[12] Calero, *Chiefdoms under Siege*, xiv.

jurisdiction. Thus, in Popayán, as elsewhere in Spanish America, the cities had a prominent role in the administration of adjacent rural areas, which, for the most part, were formally the property of the members of the *cabildo*.[13]

Slavery was more than an economic institution; it was foundational to the rise and expansion of the Spanish Empire. Africans had also arrived in significant numbers to the Pacific and the Andes during the period of exploration.[14] The Spanish elites combined the *encomienda*, which had constituted a mobile and flexible labor source since the sixteenth century, with African slavery.[15] As slaves of hacienda owners from Cali and Popayán, Africans colonized the Pacific lowland frontier in the late sixteenth century and were clearly essential to the rise of Popayán's gold-mining economy. Mine owners continued to supply the labor force for gold extraction with the importation of slaves, who came to the area from Africa passing through the hubs of Cartagena and Panama, thus profiting from a gold economy that was stable in the seventeenth century. The census data from 1797 counted 23,145 slaves in Popayán, which accounts for 17 percent of the provincial population (see Table 1.1). The enslaved worked on the haciendas around the cities of Popayán, Cali, and, to a lesser extent, Patía, as well as in gold mining in the Pacific lowlands.

---

[13] Germán Colmenares, *Historia económica y social de Colombia, vol. 2, Popayán: Una sociedad esclavista, 1680–1800* (1979; Bogotá: Tercer Mundo Editores, 1999); Peter Marzahl, *Town in the Empire: Government, Politics, and Society in Seventeenth-Century Popayán* (Austin: University of Texas, 1978).

[14] Although the roles of Africans during the conquest were largely ignored by Spanish chroniclers, we know that Nuflo de Olano, a *ladino* or Hispanized black slave, was part of Vasco Nuñez de Balboa's expedition that reached the Pacific Ocean in 1513. Like de Olano, many free and enslaved Africans participated in the conquest, from the Caribbean to Mexico and South America. Juan García, Miguel Ruiz, and Juan Valiente were all black conquistadors of Peru. See Jaime Arocha, "La inclusion de los afrocolombianos, ¿meta inalcanzable?," in *Geografía Humana de Colombia, Tomo VI, Los Afrocolombianos*, ed. Luz Adriana Maya (Bogotá: Instituto Colombiano de Antropología e Historia, 1998), 350; Matthew Restall, *Seven Myths of the Spanish Conquest* (Oxford: Oxford University Press, 2004), 52–63. On the movements of Afro-Iberians across the Atlantic World, see Leo Garofalo, "The Shape of a Diaspora: The Movement of Afro-Iberians to Colonial Spanish America," in *Africans to Spanish America*, ed. Bryant et al., 27–49. On slavery and the colonization of Quito and Popayán, see Sherwin Bryant, *Rivers of Gold, Lives of Bondage: Governing through Slavery in Colonial Quito* (Chapel Hill: University of North Carolina Press, 2014), esp. 41–45.

[15] The *encomienda* was a system of forced labor in which Spaniards received property rights over Indian labor from the crown. Kris Lane, "The Transition from *Encomienda* to Slavery in Seventeenth-Century Barbacoas (Colombia)," *Slavery & Abolition* 21, no. 1 (2000), 73–95.

The Pacific-Andean slave market was marked, first, by the Portuguese trade, which brought over captives mainly from Senegambia and West Central Africa, who were sold in Cartagena and Panama, and, later, by the rise of European traders from various countries, dominated by the British, who, throughout the eighteenth century, provisioned New Granada, legally and illegally, with captives from the Gold Coast and the Bights of Benin and Biafra.[16] These variations in the ethnic origins of these slaves and the low scale of imports compared with the numbers of slaves imported by the plantation economies in the Caribbean and Brazil explain in part why the enslaved population in Popayán was characterized by a deeply rooted heterogeneity. Thus, while the communities of people of African origin founded in the sixteenth century in Popayán had a high West African/Senegambian component, as the British began to dominate the slave trade in the eighteenth century, it was marked by the increased arrival of captives from the Gold Coast and the Bight of Benin.[17] However, particularly after 1750, Popayán's slave market increasingly traded locally born or creole slaves in greater numbers than

---

[16] On the Atlantic slave trade, see David Eltis, *The Rise of African Slavery in the Americas* (New York: Cambridge University Press, 2000), ch. 3; Herbert Klein, *The Atlantic Slave Trade* (1999; New York: Cambridge University Press, 2010), chs. 3–7; Christopher Schmidt-Nowara, *Slavery, Freedom, and Abolition in Latin America and the Atlantic World* (Albuquerque: University of New Mexico Press, 2011), chs. 1 and 2.

[17] In the early years of the trans-Atlantic slave trade and up to 1640, a period when the Portuguese dominated and supplied the main Spanish ports in the Caribbean (Santo Domingo, Veracruz, and Cartagena), Upper Guinea and Angola exported slaves in similar proportions, 41% and 43% respectively. A smaller percentage of slaves embarked from the Bight of Benin (only 8%). This was reflected in the slave populations on the ground in Popayán up to 1700, when the majority of enslaved Africans in the records used the name Angola while others that had probably been shipped from Senegambia used the names Yolof, Fulupo, Bran, and Mandinga. Nicolas del Castillo, *La llave de las Indias* (Bogotá: Ediciones El Tiempo, 1981); David Wheat, "The Afro-Portuguese Maritime World and the Foundations of Spanish-Caribbean Society, 1570–1640" (PhD diss., Vanderbilt University, 2009), 117; Sherwin Bryant, "Finding Gold, Forming Slavery: The Creation of a Classic Slave Society, Popayán, 1600–1700," *The Americas* 63, no. 1 (2006), 104. The literature on Senegambian ethnicities refers to Yolof as Wolof. See Michael Gomez, *Exchanging our Country Marks: The Transformation of African Identities in the Colonial and Antebellum South* (Chapel Hill: University of North Carolina Press, 1998), 43–47. While during the eighteenth century most slaves were taken to the British and French isles in the Caribbean, slaves from these shipments also arrived in Cartagena and on the Pacific coast. The ethnic profiles of African exports in this period are visible in the region of Barbacoas, where a majority of the slaves were classified as *arará* and *mina*, followed by people from Angola and Kongo. See Germán de Granda, "Onomástica y procedencia africana de esclavos negros en las minas del sur de la gobernación de Popayán, siglo XVIII," *Revista Española de Antropología Americana* VI (1971), 388–90.

bozales, or African-born slaves.[18] While millions of Africans were being exported to Brazil and the Caribbean to work on plantations in the late eighteenth century, the slave trade destined for Popayán actually slowed. This led to the rise of an Afro-Creole society that was proficient in Spanish, familiar with the territory, knowledgeable in the customary laws of slavery, and able to form and expand communities across Popayán.

In Popayán, African labor became fundamental to gold extraction, which, in turn, developed into the dynamo of the provincial economy and was the backbone of the overall economy of New Granada, from Quito to Cartagena, for much of the seventeenth and eighteenth centuries. Over time, New Granada's western regions became the largest gold-mining areas in Spanish America that used enslaved labor, as compared with the mining operations in Cuba, Veragua in Panama, and Venezuela, and stood in particular contrast to the mining centers in Peru and New Spain, where Indians were the majority of the workers and silver the metal they mined.[19]

Thus, Popayán had an important function in New Granada's economy, given the strategic weight that gold production had in the local and imperial contexts. In Popayán gold played the role that cocoa and sugar eventually would play in the economies of Venezuela and Brazil. In the immediate region, Popayán's gold flowed into Quito, contributing to the rise of the textile economy there. Other significant amounts of gold arrived in Santa Fe, the Viceroyalty's capital, where, until 1750, the only *casa de moneda* (mint) was located. Given that gold mining was dependent on the trade in slaves that was officially transacted through Cartagena, the two provinces, Cartagena and Popayán, were also strategically linked. In fact, Popayán's slave owners became intermediaries between Quito and Cartagena since they were the ones who generally brought slaves to the interior from the Caribbean and then sold them in the southwestern market to the Quiteños.[20]

---

[18] This was a distribution similar to the one found in Santa Fe in the mid-eighteenth century. Colmenares, *Historia económica y social, II*, 255. For Santa Fe, see Rafael Díaz Díaz, *Esclavitud, region y ciudad: El sistema esclavista urbano-regional en Santafé de Bogotá, 1700–1750* (Bogotá: Centro Editorial Javeriano, 2001), 80–81.

[19] Zamira Díaz, *Oro, sociedad y economía: El sistema colonial en la Gobernación de Popayán, 1533–1733* (Bogotá: Banco de la República, 1994); Bryant, *Rivers of Gold*, 18.

[20] Anthony McFarlane, *Colombia antes de la independencia. Economía, sociedad y política bajo el dominio borbón* (Bogotá: Banco de la República, 1997), 106, 134–137; Herrera, *Popayán*, 65; Marzahl, *Town in the Empire*; Robert West, *Colonial Placer Mining in Colombia* (Baton Rouge: Louisiana State University Press, 1952), 83.

By the eighteenth century, the Province of Popayán had three well-defined subregions, with the city of Popayán located on a plateau at its center. North of Popayán was the Cauca River Valley, with its center in the city of Cali. To the south lay the Pasto plateau, which was separated from Popayán by the Patía River Valley. To the west were the Pacific lowlands, where the mining centers of Barbacoas, Micay, and Iscuandé were located. The interrelationship of the Pacific lowlands to the Andean region was an important characteristic of Popayán's economy, as the mining centers were largely dependent on highland ranching and agricultural production. Mine- and slave-owning families generally also possessed large estates or haciendas in Popayán, Pasto, Patía, or Cali. Enslaved people also worked on the haciendas owned by Popayán mine owners, who kept their enslaved workforce rotating between the mines and the haciendas. Since the late seventeenth century, these families had used their capital to expand the mining frontiers northward into Chocó and to increase their commerce in slaves, tools, and basic goods to sustain the thriving economy. Landowners led expeditions into the western lowlands where, upon finding sources of gold, they established settlements along the rivers. These settlements were controlled by the cities located directly to their east, in the highlands and plateau regions, while landowners from Popayán, Pasto, and Cali competed to control the mining region, so jurisdiction over that area was contested. Thus, Pasto's area of influence roughly corresponded to the mining camps in Barbacoas, Popayán controlled the area between the Iscuandé and Micay rivers, and Cali ruled over the land between the Dagua and Naya rivers.[21]

Even though gold production in Popayán never reached the heights seen in Minas Gerais, it did contribute to making New Granada the largest exporter of gold to Spain during the eighteenth century.[22] As the Chocó frontier expanded and the gold economy there grew, the main beneficiaries were landowners and merchants from Cali, who had the easiest access to the northern Pacific region. In the eighteenth century, mine and slave owners from Popayán and Pasto allied with some elites from Quito to design a project for the creation of a road to the Pacific – *el camino de Malbucho* – in the Province of Esmeraldas. The project also involved the exploration for mines along the Santiago River. Most of the investment capital came from the elites in Popayán, and they took their

---

[21] Mario Diego Romero, *Poblamiento y sociedad en el Pacífico colombiano, siglos XVI al XVIII* (Cali: Universidad del Valle, Editorial Facultad de Humanidades, 1995).

[22] McFarlane, *Colombia*, 134.

slaves there to explore the area in the early 1800s. Thus, in the late eighteenth and early nineteenth centuries, the elites in Popayán and Quito were seeking to energize the Andean economy by opening up the Pacific maritime frontier with a view toward expanding exports to Spain through Panama.[23]

But this gold economy that was based on enslaved labor not only benefited whites or Creoles – it also provided opportunities for Indians and enslaved people to work and improve their financial situations. The Province of Los Pastos was located at the crossroads of the *camino real*, which went north to south, and the road that went east into the mining region of Barbacoas. In the seventeenth century, links between the growing hacienda economy and the developing mining economy made the Los Pastos region an especially strategic area for the production and transportation of agricultural goods to the mines. Indian men worked as porters (*cargueros*) carrying goods to Barbacoas and the mining region, which gave them access to the cash economy and provided funds for paying their tribute quota (or the Indian head tax).[24] Enslaved people who worked in mining were permitted to pan for gold for themselves on certain days, a practice that stimulated the growth of a substantial population of free people who had purchased their freedom with their savings.

In Popayán Province, the rise of "Indian" communities from among the native population around the city of Pasto reveals the interconnection between imperial judicial structures and the natives' collective interest in exercising their rights as vassals.[25] Their legal identity as Indians granted

---

[23] Rocío Rueda, "Rutas, caminos y la apertura de la frontera minera en la costa pacífica esmeraldeña (Ecuador, siglo XVIII)" (unpublished manuscript); Federica Morelli, "Quito en 1810: La búsqueda de un nuevo proyecto político," *Historia y Política* n. 24 (2010), 129.

[24] Archivo Nacional del Ecuador (hereinafter ANE) Popayán 344, doc. dated December 1, 1815.

[25] As Andrew Fisher and Matthew O'Hara have recently suggested, imperial subjecthood was the result of a process through which historical actors gained a sense of their relationship to the local and imperial community. Their identities were molded in the interaction with imperial categories of difference and with the representatives of the church and the crown. Fisher and O'Hara, "Introduction" to *Imperial Subjects: Race and Identity in Colonial Latin America*, ed. Fisher and O'Hara (Durham, NC: Duke University Press, 2009), 1–38. The literature on Indians as vassals is extensive. Two foundational texts of the historiography are Susan Kellogg, *Law and the Transformation of Aztec Culture, 1500–1700* (Norman: University of Oklahoma Press, 1995); and Stern, *Peru's Indian Peoples*. See also Sergio Serulnikov, "Disputed Images of Colonialism: Spanish Rule and Indian Subversion in Northern Potosí, 1777–1780," *Hispanic American Historical Review* 76, no. 2 (1996), 189–226, which deals with the Bourbon period and provides a sophisticated interpretation of how Indians defined colonial rule according to their ethnic interests.

them rights to protection on the part of the crown. The Indians' legal identity and their politics were linked by the legal provision that recognized them as vassals of the king.

The much more ambiguous position of enslaved Africans and their descendants stemmed from the fact that since they had been forcibly transplanted from Africa to America, slaves and their descendants were not considered to have a natural connection to the American territory and hence were not granted political rights in the same way as Indians were. But, as we will see in New Granada, further study of the lives of enslaved people of African origin and descent in the Spanish Empire suggests that they developed a keen sense of their potential for acquiring rights and, in many ways, acted as though they were indeed vassals. They familiarized themselves with Spanish law and used it to plead for better treatment, to legitimate their maroon communities, and to establish towns of free blacks, in addition to seeking autonomy to govern themselves. To that extent, in practice Africans and their descendants bridged the structural distance between their ambiguous legal position – stemming from their "depraved origin" – and the institutions and legal mechanisms afforded Indians, according to which indigenous people had a right to their own ethnic authorities and enjoyed relative autonomy or self-rule.[26] That provision gave Indians a direct entry into the imperial debates about governance as well as collective recognition as a corporate body within the state.[27] Although people of African descent initially lacked this privilege, the internal hierarchies that shaped their communities became instrumental in their attempts at political participation vis-à-vis the crown's officials. By claiming rights in the legal arena, enslaved people of African origin and descent sought their eventual entrance into the imperial polity and the crown's sanctioning of their communities.[28]

---

[26] As Alejandro de la Fuente has stated, "The colonial state was not necessarily beyond the reach of enterprising slaves." De la Fuente, "Slave Law and Claims-Making in Cuba: The Tannenbaum Debate Revisited," *Law and History Review* 22, no. 2 (2004), 350. See also Helg, *Liberty and Equality*, 91; O'Toole, "In a War Against the Spanish."

[27] See, for example, José Carlos de la Puente Luna, "The Many Tongues of the King: Indigenous Language Interpreters and the Making of the Spanish Empire," *Colonial Latin American Review* 23, no. 2 (2014), 143–70; Nancy Van Deusen, *Global Indios: The Indigenous Struggle for Justice in Sixteenth Century Spain* (Durham, NC: Duke University Press, 2015).

[28] This is illustrated clearly by the history of maroon communities that turned into towns. See Jane Landers, "*Cimarrón* and Citizen: African Ethnicity, Corporate Identity, and the Evolution of Free Black Towns in the Spanish Circum-Caribbean," in *Slaves, Subjects and Subversives*, 111–46; Charles Beatty-Medina, "Between the Cross and the Sword:

The highest political and judicial authority in Popayán province was a governor directly named by the king, whose domain included the sub-provinces of Los Pastos and Barbacoas as well as Iscuandé and Raposo, which were located in the Pacific lowlands. Within the institutional edifice of government that gave Indians, slaves, and *castas* (people of mixed parentage) access to royal justice, the *audiencias* played a crucial role. The internal composition of the *audiencias* was a reflection of political changes in Madrid that had to be adjusted to conditions in the local jurisdictions, which thus created shifts in local power arrangements among the elites. The *audiencia* was the dispenser of royal justice. It was the highest court of the land, the place where judicial disputes were ultimately resolved, and, especially in the American context, where the king's justice was represented.[29] The jurisdiction of the *audiencias* was subordinate to the Council of the Indies; they not only were judicial bodies but also wielded administrative and executive powers.[30] In New Spain, the creation of the Indian Court, a separate judicial arena for the protection of the Indian population, offered a "system of legal insurance" for Indian vassals of the crown. In places such as New Granada, where a special Indian court was not created to deal with Indian legal suits, the *audiencia* remained the essential embodiment of the king's justice for all Spanish vassals. Clearly, it was the government institution where all the subjects of the king could go to claim their rights and obtain justice.[31]

One functionary of the *audiencia* was the *fiscal protector general de los naturales*, who was in charge of overseeing that the laws protecting the

Religious Conquest and Maroon Legitimacy in Colonial Esmeraldas," in *Africans to Spanish America*, 95–113. See also Díaz, *The Virgin, the King, and the Royal Slaves of El Cobre.*

[29] As Alejandro Cañeque reminds us, "The king's chief mission was to administer justice, procuring the security and well-being of all his subjects." Calling the *audiencias* the "image of the king-judge," Cañeque adds that "the justice handed out by the *audiencias* [wa]s an extension of the justice that the king was supposed to administer directly." Cañeque, *The King's Living Image: The Culture and Politics of Viceregal Power in Colonial Mexico* (New York: Routledge, 2005), 55–57.

[30] Charles Cutter, "The Legal Culture of Spanish America on the Eve of Independence," in *Judicial Institutions in Nineteenth-Century Latin America*, ed. Eduardo Zimmerman (London: Institute of Latin American Studies, University of London, 1999), 50; Louis G. Kahle, "The Spanish Colonial Judiciary," *The Southwestern Social Science Quarterly* XXXII (1951), 31.

[31] As Woodrow Borah has put it, even with such local variations, the "basic outlines [of the judicial system] were present throughout the Spanish empire in America." Borah, *Justice by Insurance: The General Indian Court of Colonial Mexico and the Legal Aides of the Half Real* (Berkeley: University of California Press, 1983), 1. See also Serulnikov, *Subverting Colonial Authority*, 34.

Indian population were observed. This *protector general* had the right, and indeed the responsibility, to name the *protectores partidarios* for each district, whose duty it was to assist and defend Indians at every trial. An eighteenth-century protector's starting point was the legal stipulations or "privileges" that, according to Spanish law, specifically corresponded to Indians. The Indians' "privileges" essentially derived from their presumed "wretched" character (*miserables*), which was a category that applied to them as a class vulnerable to the abuse of powerful agents. These paternalistic laws favored native peoples in any cases in which they were involved, as defendants or plaintiffs.[32] Indigenous people, under the right circumstances, could mobilize a crucial ally in the person of the *protector partidario de naturales*, whose strategic position as a mediator accounts for his political significance in the years from 1780 to 1820.

For the enslaved there was not always a clear route to justice, but they also sought protection under the law. Some managed to get assistance from notaries, lawyers and informal scribes (*papelistas*) as well as from the judges who heard their cases in court.[33] In the cities the *defensor de pobres o de menores* represented them in court in cases where they had renounced their masters and sought to be sold to a different owner or were pleading for the right of self-purchase.[34]

IMPERIAL REFORM AND LOCAL POLITICS

In the eighteenth century, with the advent of the Bourbon dynasty to the throne, major reforms were designed and put into practice across the Spanish Empire. Undoubtedly, the most significant reform in New Granada was the creation of a viceroyalty in 1717. This implied reducing the jurisdiction of the Viceroyalty of Peru, which had previously included the Kingdom of New Granada, and increasing the power of the *audiencia* in Santa Fe. One of the main goals of this restructuring was to enhance the

---

[32] Charles Cutter, *The Protector de Indios in Colonial New Mexico, 1659–1821* (Albuquerque: University of New Mexico Press, 1986); Sonia Alda, *La participación indígena en la construcción de la república de Guatemala, S XIX* (Madrid: Universidad Autónoma de México, 2002); Baber, "The Construction of Empire." Owensby, *Empire of Law*, 56, notes that collectively marking natives as *miserables* (wretched people) was a juridical innovation because previously the category had only applied to individuals such as widows or orphans.

[33] Bianca Premo, "An Equity Against the Law: Slave Rights and Creole Jurisprudence in Spanish America," *Slavery and Abolition* 32, no. 4 (2011), 502.

[34] Premo, *Children of the Father King*, ch. 7.

crown's control over contraband trade, whose unrestrained growth needed to be curbed. Aside from improving the region's finances, it also aimed at increasing the protection of New Granada's Caribbean ports against attacks from Spain's enemies. This first attempt to modernize the government failed due to the lack of effectiveness of New Granada's first viceroy, Jorge de Villalonga, and in 1723 the Viceroyalty was suppressed. But the crown continued to view the reform of New Granada's government as a priority, and, in the pressing context of international war, in 1739 Sebastián de Eslava was named the second viceroy. After its restoration, the Viceroyalty lasted until 1810 when the Creoles in Santa Fe formed an autonomist junta and banished the viceroy.[35]

The impact of this administrative and fiscal reform was slow and modest, if judged by the absence of significant protests until the 1760s. This situation visibly changed in 1778 when Francisco Gutiérrez de Piñeres arrived from Spain to carry out a general tour of inspection, charged with the mission of transforming institutions and practices in order to strengthen the state. Gutiérrez de Piñeres was bold on two fronts: a reform of the Santa Fe *Audiencia* and the introduction of changes in fiscal policy to guarantee an effective and efficient collection of taxes for the benefit of the crown. The first reform, which followed José de Gálvez's vision of reform throughout the Americas, was a blow to Creole power. Its effect was somewhat mitigated by local politics in Santa Fe, but, ultimately, in the last quarter of the eighteenth century, the *audiencia* came to be dominated by peninsular *oidores* (judges). The fiscal reform had repercussions throughout the entire population and included the creation of tobacco and liquor monopolies, which brought about unrest, especially among the rural sectors of the population. Merchants, peasants, and consumers alike perceived such measures as hostile to their interests because the cost of buying and selling basic products increased.

Responding to the growing need for defense, the Bourbons planned to establish a system of disciplined militias that included free people of African descent in *pardo* or "all colors" militias. In New Granada the military reform was applied mainly on the coasts: in Santa Marta and Cartagena on the Caribbean and in Guayaquil on the Pacific. Although it was not unprecedented to have blacks or mulattos in the Spanish army,

[35] McFarlane, *Colombia*, 289–98. The most recent study of the Bourbon Reforms is Allan Kuethe and Kenneth Andrien, *The Spanish Atlantic World in the Eighteenth Century: War and the Bourbon Reforms, 1713–1796* (New York: Cambridge University Press, 2014).

the black men's leadership generated widespread fears and tensions.[36] It became an especially unpopular project among the Popayán Creoles, who rejected the crown's relaxation of racial divisions in the eighteenth century, for example, by making it easier for people of mixed racial ancestry to "purchase" whiteness (*gracias al sacar*), or allowing free blacks who entered the militias to earn special privileges. For this reason, following the first campaign to create the militias in the 1770s, they were reorganized during the regime of Viceroy Ezpeleta (1789–96). In 1794 he put into practice a new *reglamento* (regulation) promulgated in Spain that subsumed the military reform to the crown's fiscal interests, which emphasized maximizing remissions to Spain and allocating substantial revenue to cities with high strategic value (Cartagena, Havana). This was done to simultaneously minimize political conflicts in America, reduce military costs on land, and keep important cities and regions safe from foreign attack or encroachment. As a result, the number of men enrolled in the disciplined militias of New Granada shrank by almost half, from 15,000 to 8,060. Moreover, the authorities disbanded *pardo* units before white units with the result that the percentage of free blacks in the militias decreased considerably.[37]

Historiographic interpretations of Bourbon reformism as either total-izing or failed have been replaced by more nuanced notions of the com-plexity that permeated the imperial reformist thrust and its practical dimensions. Seeking the origins of independence in the absolutist turn the monarchy took and the destabilization this brought about throughout the eighteenth century, nationalist narratives generally depicted the reforms negatively.[38] Yet recently historians have begun to understand

[36] Margarita Garrido, "'Free Men of All Colors' in New Granada: Identity and Obedience before Independence," in *Political Cultures in the Andes, 1750–1950*, ed. Nils Jacobsen and Cristóbal Aljovín de Losada (Durham, NC: Duke University Press, 2005), 169–72. For Mexico, see Ben Vinson III, *Bearing Arms for his Majesty: The Free-Colored Militia in Colonial Mexico* (Stanford, CA: Stanford University Press, 2001).

[37] See Allan Kuethe, *Military Reform and Society in New Granada, 1773–1808* (Gainesville: University Presses of Florida, 1978), 77, 128, 162, 196–97, 199, 200; Allan Kuethe, "The Status of the Free Pardo in the Disciplined Militia in New Granada," *The Journal of Negro History* 56, no. 2 (1971), 115; Allan Kuethe, "More on 'The Culmination of the Bourbon Reforms': A Perspective from New Granada," *Hispanic American Historical Review* 58, no. 3 (1978), 478; Allan Kuethe, "The Early Reforms of Charles III in the Viceroyalty of New Granada, 1759–1776," in *Reform and Insurrection in Bourbon New Granada and Peru*, ed. John Fisher et al. (Baton Rouge: Louisiana University Press, 1990), 19–40.

[38] See, for example, David Brading, *The First America: The Spanish Monarchy, Creole Patriots, and the Liberal State, 1492–1867* (New York: Cambridge University Press,

the reforms as a process that was ultimately mediated by local relationships, which resulted in important levels of regional variation. Additionally, the reforms and the transformations they gave rise to in Spanish America have been recast in a positive light, allowing for an exploration of the ways in which some social groups adapted Bourbon reformism to their local interests. This approach enables a more sophisticated representation of the Spanish monarchy that does away with a dichotomist notion of power and emphasizes local negotiation of political relations and change.[39]

It is certainly true that the Bourbon reforms were unevenly introduced and received in New Granada. Historians have mostly noted the consequences they had in and around the viceregal capital, in particular, the results of the 1781 Comunero Rebellion that rocked the provinces of Socorro and Santa Fe.[40] Following that insurrection, among other things, reformers were forced to readjust aspects of their approach to indigenous land reform in the central highlands.[41] As in other regions of New Granada, Popayán's unique social landscape was a factor that mediated the priorities of reform at all levels. Indian communities in southwestern New Granada, including Quito, contested those aspects of fiscal reform that mainly targeted Indian lands and the expansion of revenues through demographic recalculations. As a result, either actual rebellion or the fear of widespread insurrection mitigated the effects of the fiscal changes.[42]

Yet there were other aspects of the absolutist project that were better received or, in other words, that created opportunities for certain sectors.

---

[39] 1993); Lynch, *The Spanish American Revolutions*; and Rodríguez, *La Independencia de la América Española*.

[39] See Serulnikov, *Subverting Colonial Authority*; Guardino, *The Time of Liberty*; and Yannakakis, *The Art of Being In-between*, 189.

[40] Studies of Bourbon reformism in New Granada include McFarlane, *Colombia*, and, more recently, Renée Soulodre-La France, *Región e Imperio: El Tolima Grande y las Reformas Borbónicas en el siglo XVIII* (Bogotá: Instituto Colombiano de Antropología e Historia, 2004); Helg, *Liberty and Equality*. The fundamental study of the Comunero Rebellion is Phelan, *The People and the King*.

[41] The dismantling of *resguardos* or community lands on the Bogotá plateau between 1750 and 1800 had structural impacts on Indians in that area, predating and resembling liberal reforms that the historiography would later equivocally interpret as an innovation of the Bolivarian republic. See Diana Bonnett, *Tierra y comunidad un problema irresuelto: El caso del altiplano cundiboyacense (Virreinato de la Nueva Granada) 1750–1800* (Bogotá: ICANH, Universidad de Los Andes, 2002).

[42] See Segundo Moreno Yáñez, *Sublevaciones indígenas en la Audiencia de Quito: Desde comienzos del siglo XVIII hasta finales de la Colonia* (Quito: Centro de Publicaciones Pontificia Universidad Católica del Ecuador, 1977).

As will be further discussed in Chapter 2, this was the case with the caciques of the Province of Los Pastos, whose role was pivotal to the fiscal reform at the level of the Indian communities. Although changes in the requirements for being appointed cacique created conflicts within the communities, the fiscal reform seemed to benefit those individuals who found it possible to become allies of the Spanish authorities, such as the *corregidor*. In this respect Pasto was part of the larger Andean eighteenth-century trend toward the alienation of the cacique authorities from the Indian commoners, but what happened in the Andes contrasts with the situation in Mexico, where the Bourbon reforms actually threatened cacique authority directly.[43]

For the enslaved population, the most significant aspect of the reforms was the change in the legal framework of slavery, a corollary of the Bourbon effort to increase revenue through greater control over the slave trade and economy in the Caribbean. In spite of the fact that the legislation was not put into effect because of slaveholder complaints, the enslaved were informed about the shifts in the crown's attempts to mediate between the slaves and their masters. As I will argue in Chapter 3, this crucial aspect of the transformations in the institution of Hispanic slavery during the Age of Revolution explains the increasing relevance of legal strategies to slave politics in the late eighteenth century. In a non-plantation context such as Popayán, where enslaved Africans were able to build communities, slaves invoked the crown's protection for their communities and the king's mediation to grant them rights to good treatment and self-purchase.

FROM REFORM TO REVOLUTION

Spain's War of Independence against Napoleonic France's invasion unleashed a perhaps inevitable and certainly irreversible process of political transformation in the peninsula as well as in Spanish America. The French intervention, which resulted in the replacement of Fernando VII with Napoleon's brother Joseph-Napoleon Bonaparte, fueled internal sociopolitical antagonisms that turned into a civil war that lasted from 1808 until 1843 and continued even after the Spanish monarch returned to power in 1814. The boldest legacy of these years was the transformation of an absolutist monarchy to a constitutional one.

[43] Yannakakis, *The Art of Being In-between.*

But there were other equally significant sides to the historical process inaugurated by the extraordinary events of 1808. The military aspect of the confrontations that ensued both in the peninsula and in Spanish America expanded the realm of politics in an unprecedented way. Thus, departing from the earlier logic in which the law was the political sphere par excellence and rebellion and violence were largely contained (with their outbursts expressing special interests), during the independence wars Spanish Americans formed new alliances around loyalties that transcended race and class but that were divided along deep lines – between royalists and insurgents – and that confronted each other with fury and passion through warfare. The dynamic of the wars brought to light new, sometimes competing, concepts of the structure and contours of the monarchy. Derived from warfare, novel rights were formulated, demanded, and put into practice.

1808–1810: Sovereignty and war

The slow mutation of political principles and institutions was the result of local dynamics unleashed by war as much as it was the evolution of a dialectic between American and peninsular interests. The ultimate configuration of a liberal monarchy owed much to the pressure that stemmed from the need to attract and sustain the allegiance of all social sectors in a context where loyalty was all but guaranteed. In Europe, Napoleon became one pole of a polarized magnetic field. Although he had allies (later to be called *afrancesados*), his regime was tinted with illegitimacy. At the other pole, the resistance aimed at preserving the sovereignty of the Spanish crown and keeping the empire unified. These might have seemed like quixotic goals, but the hardships wrought by the Napoleonic invasion heightened the collective spirit of the Hispanic community and enabled a productive negotiation to take place between the absolutist and liberalizing tendencies that coexisted in the peninsula.[44] The self-proclaimed representative body of the Spanish nation – in its three forms, the Junta Central (1808–09), the Regency (1809–10), and the Cortes (1810–12) – professed loyalty to an absent monarch whose power was nonetheless enduring. By the same measure, news of the king's abduction traveled across the Atlantic spreading fear

---

[44] See Scott Eastman, *Preaching Spanish Nationalism across the Hispanic Atlantic, 1759–1823* (Baton Rouge: Louisiana University Press, 2012), for a study of the rise of nationalism in Spain during the War of Independence against France.

and rejection of Napoleon's tyranny. Spanish Americans faced their tragic destiny, which called for unified heroism.

Between 1808 and 1810, the resilience of imperial structures and identities was evident when the Spanish American kingdoms claimed their right to juridical parity within the monarchy. Although American representation in Spanish constitutional debates was perceived as instrumental to keeping the monarchy united, Spanish liberals expressed a complicity with colonialism that undermined their attempts toward stability and unity. In contrast, the Spanish-American kingdoms struggled to achieve recognition as historically perfect communities with rights to representation equal to those of their Iberian counterparts.[45]

The Spanish-American municipal elites did not conceive of independence as their sole option because belonging to the monarchy had as much or more political purchase for them as they confronted an open-ended situation. The municipal councils that governed every urban center in Spanish America proclaimed juntas that did not necessarily envision breaking away from the monarchy. The juntas had complex ambitions, such as defending their sovereignty from the French attempt to gain control of the Empire while simultaneously exploring a degree of autonomy they had never had before. Until 1810, when achieving fair representation in the Spanish Cortes seemed a futile goal, every junta had proclaimed its loyalty to King Fernando VII.[46] But the dynamism of the moment offered multiple options that were imagined, weighed, and pursued. Breaking away from the Spanish resistance (while still embracing the king's sovereignty) enabled experimentation with autonomy, but it also generated risks. Some of the consequences that were unleashed threatened the maintenance of order, because once ties with Spain were severed, the colonial jurisdictional order came into question.

---

[45] Elliott, *Empires of the Atlantic World*, 377; Portillo, *Crisis atlántica*, 63; Jeremy Adelman, "Iberian Passages: Continuity and Change in the South Atlantic," in *The Age of Revolutions in Global Context, c.1760–1840*, ed. David Armitage and Sanjay Subrahmanyam (New York: Palgrave Macmillan, 2010), 70, 80. For the case of Santa Fe, see "Representación del Cabildo de Santa Fe, capital del Nuevo Reino de Granada, a la Suprema Junta Central de España" (1809), in *Constituciones de Colombia: recopiladas y precedidas de una breve reseña histórica*, Vol. 1, ed. Manuel Antonio Pombo and José Joaquín Guerra (Bogotá: Ministerio de Educación Nacional, 1951), 57–86.

[46] Manuel Chust, ed., *1808, la eclosión juntera en el mundo hispano* (México, D.F.: Fondo de Cultura Económica, 2007). Previous analyses of this moment argued that Creole declarations of loyalty were masking their anticolonial interests. See Marco A. Landavazo, *La máscara de Fernando VII: Discurso e imaginario monárquico en una época de crisis: Nueva España 1808–1822* (México, D.F.: Colegio de México, 2001).

During the Napoleonic invasion, the territories that were more vulnerable to defection were those that had suffered the most as result of the Bourbon reforms. The *audiencias* of Quito and Charcas had been separated from the Viceroyalty of Peru, when two new viceroyalties were established in South America during the eighteenth century. Quito became part of New Granada, and Charcas was separated from Lima to become part of the new Viceroyalty of Río de la Plata. Charcas and Quito were kingdoms in their own right, but they lost autonomy and importance with the Bourbon territorial reorganization. When the Junta Central called for the inclusion of American deputies but only recognized the viceroyalties as units of representation, Quito and Charcas rejected their exclusion and formed juntas of their own. La Paz formed a junta on July 16, 1809, and Quito's junta was proclaimed on August 10 of the same year; both of these juntas upheld the sovereignty of Fernando VII but did not recognize the authority of the Junta Central. With one bold move, Quito and La Paz took advantage of an unprecedented opportunity for maneuvering within the context of the Napoleonic invasion, seeking to regain the autonomy that had been lost during the Bourbon regime.[47]

Throughout the eighteenth century, Quito had been impacted negatively by the Bourbon reforms that had left the kingdom in a subordinate structural position vis-à-vis Peru and New Granada. Representatives of the Quiteño commercial elite struggled, without much success, to create alternative development strategies that would allow the Kingdom of Quito to compete within the context of the commercial reorganization taking place across the Atlantic world. Enlightened elites – such as Pérez Calama and the Baron of Carondelet – envisioned projects such as the *camino de Malbucho* to revitalize Quito's economy by opening a gateway to the Pacific Ocean. The Popayán mining region was an axis of that project, but the Quiteño elite also held ambitions to expand Quito's reach to the Pacific littoral – from Antioquia and Panama into Cartagena – to create a strong economic and political entity outside of the control of Lima and Santa Fe (see Figure 1.2). Thus, at the moment of creating a local junta, Quito was aiming to reconquer territories that had been lost to Popayán, namely Pasto and Barbacoas.[48] This was the background to

---

[47] Rodríguez, *La Independencia*, 122–31; Guerra, *Modernidad e Independencias*, 189.

[48] Carlos Landázuri Camacho, "La independencia del Ecuador (1808–1822)," in *Nueva Historia del Ecuador*, 6, ed. Enrique Ayala Mora (Quito: Grijalbo, 1994), 84–100; Kenneth Andrien, "Soberanía y Revolución en el Reino de Quito, 1809–1810," in *En el umbral de las revoluciones hispánicas, 1808–1810*, ed. Roberto Breña (México and

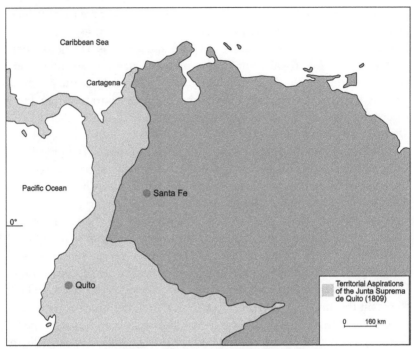

FIGURE 1.2 Territorial aspirations of the Junta Suprema de Quito, 1809.
Map modified by Santiago Muñoz based on Daniel Gutiérrez, *Un Nuevo Reino*, 161.

the 1809 Quito junta's aspirations to articulate its vision of a more beneficial order, once the monarchical crisis opened up real opportunities to attempt to put its plans into practice.[49]

In the Pacific-Andean region, repercussions from the creation of the junta in Quito were immediate. The junta sent emissaries to speak to the *cabildos* of Cuenca, Guayaquil, Popayán, and Ibarra, among others. The mission of these de facto diplomats was to convince the municipal authorities of the cities bordering Quito that at that critical juncture in time, that of the Napoleonic occupation of Spain, they should build alliances and commercial relations. The Quito junta's purpose was not only to create an expansionist power, as Popayán perceived it, or to rebel against the crown's sovereignty, as Santa Fe and Lima claimed, but to seek to preserve the king's rights during his absence and to maintain unity within

Madrid: El Colegio de México-Centro de Estudios Políticos y Constitucionales, 2010), 316–17.
[49] Morelli, "Quito en 1810," 129.

the monarchy.[50] The *cabildos* of Riobamba, Ibarra, Otavalo, Latacunga, Ambato, Guaranda, and Alausí initially recognized the new government. But the *cabildos* of Guayaquil, Pasto, Cuenca, and Popayán responded negatively to Quito's invitation to send delegates as representatives to the junta. Quito's response was aggressive, igniting a war, and as a result its goal to build a space independent of the two viceroyalties became untenable.[51] Instead of finding a positive echo and enabling horizontal relations to exist between provinces and cities, Quito's early junta produced repressive reactions in Santa Fe and Lima, as well as in Popayán, Cuenca, and Guayaquil – an economic blockade and a military campaign – which succeeded in causing the disbandment of the junta within two months.

After Fernando's abdication, established authority was in question and a crucial fear of anarchy was widespread. In spite of the Junta Central and the Regency's attempts to unify the resistance in Spain and maintain unity between the two hemispheres by calling for American representatives to the Cortes, in Spanish America the colonial jurisdictional hierarchy began to collapse.[52]

The Pacific royalist alliance

While the Creoles in the municipal councils were experimenting with autonomous rule and diplomacy, Spanish officials were deeply concerned about the situation. In 1809, the Peruvian Viceroy Fernando de Abascal y Sousa found himself at the center of two major crises, one in Quito and the other in La Paz. Abascal's fast response aimed at crushing any attempts at insurgency among the Creoles and keeping the Viceroyalty of Peru free of all danger, eradicating possible close-at-hand subversive influences, and demonstrating his power to repress insurgent behavior. In

---

[50] McFarlane, "The Rebellion of the *Barrios*," in *Reform and Insurrection in Bourbon New Granada and Peru*, 197–254; Phelan, *The People and the King*; Andrien, "Soberanía y revolución." After 1809 – following the declaration of the Quito junta – most of the juntas created in New Granada functioned as mini-states that communicated in diplomatic terms. Historian Daniel Gutiérrez has convincingly argued that the expansionist goal of the Quito junta was the singular most interesting aspect of its conception and dynamic of negotiation with neighboring provinces. Gutiérrez, *Un Nuevo Reino: Geografía política, pactismo y diplomacia durante el interregno en Nueva Granada (1808–1816)* (Bogotá: Universidad Externado de Colombia, 2010), 159–63, 167. See also María Teresa Calderón and Clément Thibaud, *La magestad de los pueblos en la Nueva Granada y Venezuela, 1780–1832* (Bogotá: Taurus, Instituto Francés de Estudios Andinos, Universidad Externado de Colombia, 2010).

[51] Morelli, "Quito en 1810," 129–30.   [52] Gutiérrez, *Un Nuevo Reino*, 153.

Lima the viceroy feared the risk that the revolt could spread to Guayaquil and Cuenca, so he swiftly moved to support both of these cities, as well as Popayán, in their resistance against Quito.[53]

By 1810, Abascal's counterrevolution found itself having to protect Spanish-Peruvian interests from dangers coming from Buenos Aires to the south, from Brazil to the east, and from New Granada to the north.[54] As Abascal's involvement in the military confrontations expanded and became more sustained, his ambitions grew and turned into a desire to extend the Peruvian frontier across South America. The flexibility with which Abascal expanded his forces obviously allowed him to amass power and add to the territories under his jurisdiction. To sum it up, the viceroy was trying to recover the territories lost during the Bourbon jurisdictional readjustment of the eighteenth century (see Figure 1.3).[55]

In Popayán, Governor Miguel Tacón was able to receive aid from authorities both north and south of Popayán (from Santa Fe and from Lima, respectively) partly because the province had a structural double-dependence on the *audiencias* in Quito and Santa Fe. However, in the unprecedented critical situation in which Quito had become a regional menace, Santa Fe was too far away and too inaccessible to be able to offer timely support, making Lima a preferable ally.

Governor Tacón lacked his own military forces to fight against Quito in 1809 and he centered his attention on the dangers posed by the large numbers of indigenous people and slaves who lived in the province of Popayán and were seen as vulnerable to "seduction" during the crisis. Tacón used this danger to persuade the viceroys in Santa Fe and Lima to send support. Moreover, since 1809 the governor had set out to gain the support of the indigenous and black population for the royalist project.[56]

---

[53] In his memoirs he described his reaction to the situation by saying that he sought to combat the slandering of the Spanish authorities, which aimed at planting distrust among the population. José Fernando de Abascal y Sousa, *Memoria de Gobierno*, Vol. 2 (Sevilla: Escuela de Estudios Hispano-Americanos de Sevilla, 1944), 82.

[54] Brian Hamnett, "El momento de decisión y de acción: El virreinato del Perú en el año de 1810," *Historia y Política* 24 (2010), 156. Juan Luis Ossa, *Armies, Politics and Revolution: Chile, 1808–1826* (Liverpool: Liverpool University Press, 2014), explains this process from the Chilean perspective.

[55] Hamnett, "El momento de decisión," 156–61; Scarlett O'Phelan Godoy, "Abascal y la reformulación del espacio del virreinato del Perú, 1806–1816," *Revista Política Internacional* 95–96 (2009), 30–46.

[56] See Chapters 4 and 5 in this volume. "Oficio de Tacón al Virrey del Perú, Barbacoas, September 18, 1811," in *Documentos Importantes de Nueva Granada, Venezuela y Colombia*, Vol. 5, ed. José Manuel Restrepo (Bogotá: Imprenta Nacional, 1969), 34; "Oficio del mismo [Tacón] al Presidente de Quito [Joaquín de Molina], Barbacoas, September 28, 1811," in *Documentos Importantes*, ed. Restrepo, 36; "Otro de Tacón

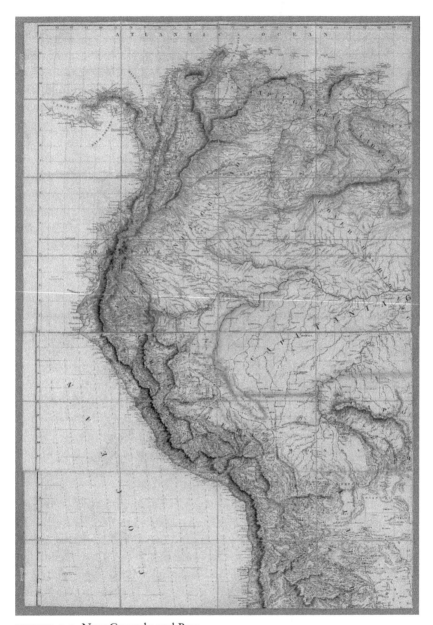

FIGURE 1.3 New Granada and Peru.
"Outlines of the Physical and Political Divisions of South America: Delineated by
A. Arrowsmith Partly from Scarce and Original Documents, Published before the Year
1806," London, 1811. Courtesy of the John Carter Brown Library at Brown University.

Under Abascal's protection, the royalist block that included the cities of Popayán, Pasto, and Barbacoas had as its immediate rivals first Quito and then Cali and Santa Fe. Thus Popayán was located in a strategic position that became the frontier between the two major insurgent territories that took shape in New Granada during the decade of 1810. The alliance between Tacón and Abascal was strengthened once a junta in Santa Fe deposed the viceroy in July 1810. Abascal's support for Tacón was very important both militarily and ideologically. Even though the insurgent offensive expanded and solidified to the north of Popayán, the ideological weight of the monarchy was kept alive in relation to Lima's vitality. Through the liaison with Peru, Popayán, Pasto, and Barbacoas found in Abascal a figure that offered the stability that had been lost in the New Granada viceroyalty. However, Tacón's shift to Abascal also increased the local elites' distrust of the governor. The elites of Cali rejected his willfulness and despotism, fueling the conflict.[57]

After mid-1810 and until 1814, autonomist projects emerged north of Popayán. Popayán Province was divided into a northern portion represented in the Confederation of the Cauca Valley and a southern part governed by Tacón from Popayán. The independence partisans were located north of Popayán in Cali, Buga, Anserma, Toro, Cartago, and Caloto, in alliance with Santa Fe. These cities struggled to construct confederations with Antioquia and Cartagena at different points in time. The city of Popayán was the focus of contention and military confrontation. It was attacked, sacked, and occupied intermittently by royalists and independence partisans. The royalists coalesced south of the city, in Pasto, Patía, Almaguer, and Barbacoas. They declared allegiance to and followed the policies of the liberal government in Spain until 1814, and after that they were ruled by Fernando VII.

The southwestern region of New Granada became a bastion of royalism, militarily tied to the forces of Viceroy Abascal in Peru as well as to the royalist poles of Guayaquil, Cuenca, and Panama. The Pacific region of Popayán became a strategic area because the ocean greatly facilitated communication between Popayán and Lima. In this context, the towns and people who lived along the rivers connecting Popayán to the Pacific

al Gobernador de Panamá [Juan Antonio de Mata], Barbacoas, October 4, 1811," in *Documentos Importantes*, ed. Restrepo, 40; "Otro del mismo [Tacón] al mismo [Gobernador de Panamá, Juan Antonio de Mata], Tumaco, December 4, 1811," in *Documentos Importantes*, ed. Restrepo, 41–42.

[57] Alfonso Zawadzky, *Las ciudades confederadas del Valle del Cauca en 1811: Historia, actas, documentos* (Cali: Imprenta Bolivariana, 1943), 111.

Ocean became strategic allies of the royalists. A bay and two rivers gave access inland from the coast: the Bay of San Buena Ventura, the Micay River, and the Patía River, which led first to Barbacoas and then into the Patía Valley, three days away from the city of Popayán. All along this territory, indigenous people, slaves, and free blacks joined the royalist forces and participated in the defense of the territory, blocking insurgent attacks.[58]

Tacón's military strategy consisted in blocking the northern rebels' constant attempts to make contact with Quito's forces in order to increase their strength.[59] This was especially the case after Quito formed a second junta that tried to create an alliance with the autonomists from Cali and Santa Fe. Quito's second junta emerged when the Junta Central was dissolved in Spain and the Regency formed in its place, on January 29, 1810. Under the leadership of Carlos Montúfar, who had arrived from Spain as the representative of the Regency, Quito's Junta Superior was formed on September 19, 1810. Much like the 1809 junta, it had pretensions to establishing autonomy from Lima and Santa Fe, as well as to ruling over the other cities in the kingdom. But this junta was less authoritarian, trying to gain the respect of Quito's neighboring cities by inviting them to form their own juntas and collaborate with the government in the capital. Once more those plans did not go well. The cities of Cuenca, Guayaquil, Pasto, and Popayán did not accept the legitimacy of the junta, and there was a renewal of military confrontations. The Regency in the peninsula worried that Montúfar was creating conflicts and decided to send a new person to serve as president of the Kingdom of Quito, General Joaquín Molina, who arrived in Cuenca in 1811. Montúfar's constant wars against Quito's enemies, including Molina, ended in his removal from the presidency. Between late 1811 and early 1812, the Junta Superior radicalized its goals, declaring a government autonomous of the Regency, which recognized only the authority of Fernando VII. Internal rivalries weakened the junta to the point where a new attack from General Toribio Montes gave it a final blow in November of 1812.[60]

In spite of the fact that Tacón had mobilized a large sector of the population to his side and that Indians, slaves, and free blacks represented

[58] Archivo General de la Nación (hereinafter AGN) Archivo Anexo/Historia, I.17,13, D. 75, fols. 574r–575v. April 15, 1812.

[59] "Oficio del Gobernador de Popayán, don Miguel Tacón, al Virrey del Perú, Almaguer, August 11, 1811," in *Documentos Importantes*, ed. Restrepo, 26.

[60] Rodríguez, *La independencia*, 263–64; Abascal, *Memoria*, 149.

an important royalist military force, his tactics did not keep him from defeat.[61] He was driven from Patía to Barbacoas and Iscuandé where the insurgent forces from Cali forced him to flee by sea to Guayaquil. From Guayaquil he went to Lima, where Viceroy Abascal recognized his merit in the campaigns against the Popayán insurgents and put him in charge of the royalist army in Upper Peru.[62] Although Tacón left Popayán defeated, Toribio Montes' rise to power in Quito in late 1812 was a positive turning point for the Pacific royalists from New Granada and Peru. Finally, there was a stable royalist government in place between Pasto and Lima, enabling better communication, fostering political coherence, and permitting unified military action against the Cauca Valley and Santa Fe rebels. Montes represented the liberal project taking shape in the peninsula and implemented the decrees of the Cortes and the Constitution of Cádiz, promulgated in March 1812.

After reconquering Popayán in June 1813 with the support of Tacón's Indian and black allies, Montes appointed the Spanish colonel Juan Sámano as governor of Popayán. Thus, the period that followed Montes' arrival to power in Quito initiated the shift to a liberal government within the royalist regions of southwestern New Granada. However, at the same time, Popayán entered a phase in which the government was led by a military governor whose priorities were to maintain an army. Sámano tended to alienate even the most loyal in the province with forced collections of money. In numerous instances the priorities of enacting imperial legislation were mediated by military interests on the ground. Conflicts between the representatives of military power and those that aimed to uphold the constitutional framework were common thereafter.[63]

---

[61] Archivo Nacional Militar (hereinafter ANM), "Hoja de Servicios del Mariscal de Campo Don Miguel Tacón," November 29, 1815.

[62] According to Juán Pérez de la Riva's "Introduction" to *Correspondencia reservada del Capitán General Don Miguel Tacón con el gobierno de Madrid, 1834–1836* (La Habana: Consejo Nacional de Cultura, 1963), Tacón's experience as a veteran of the independence wars won for him the position of Captain-General in Cuba (1834–38).

[63] "Representación del Presidente de Quito, don Toribio Montes, ante el Secretario de Estado, sobre actuaciones de su gobierno en las pasadas convulsiones, desde que tomó posesión del mando," in *Colección de documentos para la historia de Colombia: Época de la independencia*, ed. Sergio Elías Ortiz (Bogotá: Academia Colombiana de Historia, 1964), 79. Hamnett, "Popular Insurrection and Royalist Reaction." An interesting analysis of the clash between constitutional and military interests in Venezuela can be found in Inés Quintero and Ángel Rafael Almarza, "Autoridad militar vs. legalidad constitucional: El debate en torno a la Constitución de Cádiz (Venezuela 1812–1814)," *Revista de Indias* LXVIII, 242 (2008), 181–206.

Citizenship and constitutions after 1810

The Cádiz constitutional debates posed a challenge for the juntas in New Granada, and the insurgent territories swiftly turned to their own legislative project, writing constitutions. Along with Río de la Plata, New Granada pioneered in the creation of confederated regimes based on provincial representation that attempted to secure rule over the provinces that had previously been under a common viceregal government.[64] Between 1811 and 1815, seventeen constitutions were proclaimed in the territory of the Viceroyalty of New Granada. The first was proclaimed in April 4, 1811, by the *Colegio Electoral* in Santa Fe, with the goal of creating the Kingdom of Cundinamarca (alluding to the pre-Hispanic name given to this area by the Muiscas).[65] This constitution preceded the Cádiz charter, making it the second written constitution in the Hispanic world after that of Bayonne.[66] But the New Granada elites' widespread search for constitutional legitimacy did not guarantee stability, and conflict ensued across the territory.[67]

In fact, although separated by a growing difference in loyalties, changes to political language and institutions developed in a parallel way in the royalist territories and in those under insurgent control. In the territories controlled by both factions, war was a constant, shaping

---

[64] For Río de la Plata, see Geneviève Verdo, *L'indépendance argentine entre cités et nation (1808–1821)* (Paris: Sorbonne, 2006).

[65] Hans-Joachim König, *En el camino hacia la nación: Nacionalismo en el proceso de formación del estado y de la nación en la Nueva Granada, 1750–1856* (Bogotá: Banco de la República, 1994); Margarita Garrido, *Reclamos y representaciones. Variaciones sobre la política en el Nuevo Reino de Granada, 1770–1815* (Bogotá: Colección Bibliográfica del Banco de la República, 1993).

[66] Soon after occupying Spain, Napoleon directed the writing of a Constitution, the 1808 Constitution of Bayonne, which was institutionalized during Joseph's reign. The Spanish opposition grew with such force that the newly named monarch's strength was reduced, his illegitimacy revealed, and his plan of government destabilized, hampering the efficient application of the Constitution of Bayonne. However, the 1808 Constitution was undoubtedly significant in that it granted the American kingdoms of Spain the right to representation, establishing a precedent that the Spanish Cortes later imitated. Jordana Dym, "Napoleon and the Americas" (unpublished manuscript), 32; Guerra, *Modernidad e Independencias*, 115–44; Gutiérrez, *Un Nuevo Reino*, 239. Cundinamarca alone produced two constitutions between 1811 and 1812. See Calderón and Thibaud, *La majestad de los pueblos*, 35.

[67] Gutiérrez, *Un Nuevo Reino*, ch. 6. Clément Thibaud, *Repúblicas en Armas: Los ejércitos Bolivarianos en la guerra de independencia en Colombia y Venezuela* (Bogotá: Planeta/IFEA, 2003), deals with the intersection of politics and war at the level of the individual, analyzing the connection of military participation to the rise of citizenship.

political dynamics and possibilities. The turn to constitutional rule was an innovation, on both sides. But for the royalists it became a tool that represented simultaneously the sovereignty of the king and of the nation. The juntas, and later the congresses that were the product of attempts to unify those juntas, pledged allegiance to Fernando but also wrote constitutional texts as obvious foundational gestures. The first constitutions in New Granada were intended not only to legislate but also to "constitute" the government and societies they represented. Creole constituents made efforts to claim that their laws were legitimate, even transcendent, by maintaining a link with Catholicism and claiming that "the people" were the incarnation of a providential plan.[68] The Cádiz charter, which was publicized in every town under royalist control and sworn to by all of its subjects, held a special symbolic power during Fernando's captivity. Because it represented the king in his absence, the constitution retained the aura of solemnity and majesty that only the king possessed.[69]

Spanish liberals conceptualized the Spanish monarchy as a nation – albeit one existing in two separate hemispheres. The insurgent territories of New Granada, meanwhile, struggled to give shape to a new government that would allow them to combine the old and the emergent jurisdictions into a republican form. The erratic process of trial and error that characterized the functioning of local governments across New Granada speaks of the importance of association for restoring sovereignty. But restoring sovereignty was challenging because associations between local governments oscillated between centralist and federalist forms.[70]

Given the reality of insurrection on the ground, in 1812 the Viceroyalty of New Granada was abolished and was turned, instead, into a Captaincy General with its seat in the *Audiencia* of Panama, where it remained until 1816. The Cádiz Constitution was published in March 1812, but it took time to arrive in the Americas, more specifically in the territories that continued to be under royalist control. In New Granada,

---

[68] Calderón and Thibaud, *La majestad de los pueblos*, 130–38.

[69] Federica Morelli, "La publicación y el juramento de la constitución de Cádiz en Hispanoamérica: Imágenes y valores (1812–1813)," in *Observation and Communication: The Construction of Realities in the Hispanic World*, ed. Johannes-Michael Scholz and Tamar Herzog (Frankfurt am Main: Vittorio Klostermann, 1997), 135–49. Scott Eastman argues that Spanish liberalism produced an ideology of nationalism that was "inherently Catholic." Eastman, *Preaching Spanish Nationalism*, 41.

[70] Garrido, *Reclamos y representaciones*, 314. A comparative example of the role of cities in the search for sovereignty during this period can be found in Jordana Dym, "La soberanía de los pueblos: ciudad e independencia en Centroamérica, 1808–1823," in *Revolución, independencia y las nuevas naciones de América*, 309–38.

the charter was received first in Panama on August 1, 1812. It was then sent to Quito from where President Montes dispatched it to Pasto in May 1813, along with orders to formally swear allegiance to it in Pasto and the Province of Los Pastos. This was done in the city of Pasto in July, but, in the Province of Los Pastos, the war delayed the process.[71]

Thus, although unevenly applied because of the existing context of war, the Cádiz charter had repercussions at the level of the legal and political categories of membership in the monarchical community. While citizenship was not an entirely new category in the Hispanic lexicon, before 1812 it had been linked to *vecindad*, which simultaneously denoted being an active member of the political community, a Catholic, and eligible to serve in municipal posts. By definition, women were excluded as well as Indians and people of African ancestry. Both categories, citizen and *vecino*, had a local connotation that linked people to a city or town. In granting citizenship to Indians, Cádiz boldly modified the juridical division between Spaniards and Indians that had been so fundamental to colonial society since the fifteenth century. This redefinition of the legal composition of the monarchy was a gesture toward instituting equality and the dissolution of social divisions between estates.[72]

By granting citizenship to the Indian population, the Cádiz Constitution undoubtedly impacted the politics of indigenous communities throughout Spanish America. It was a catalyst for the incorporation of Indians into municipal bodies, since as citizens with the right to vote, they now could gain access to positions from which they previously had been marginalized. In Pasto the issue of tribute payment affected the consequences of the arrival of liberal decrees. The Cortes abolished tribute, sparking contradictory dynamics on the ground. On the one hand, such a liberal measure was appealing to some sectors of indigenous society but, on the other hand, it was largely opposed by the caciques and colonial authorities who depended on tribute to sustain the war. Therefore, the shift to liberalism in the royalist territories was a trigger for the conflicts

---

[71] Guillermo Sosa, *Representación e independencia, 1810–1816* (Bogotá: Instituto Colombiano de Antropología e Historia, 2006), 112–13; Jairo Gutiérrez, "La Constitución de Cádiz en la Provincia de Pasto, Nueva Granada, 1812–1822," *Revista de Indias* LXVIII, 242 (2008), 216.

[72] Marta Irurozqui, "De cómo el vecino hizo al ciudadano y de cómo el ciudadano conservó al vecino: Charcas, 1808–1830," in *Revoluciones, Independencia y las nuevas naciones de América*, 451–84; Cristóbal Aljovín, "Monarquía o república: 'ciudadano' y 'vecino' en Iberoamérica, 1750–1850," *Jahrbuch für Geschichte Lateinamerikas* 45 (2008), 31–55.

and transformations within Indian communities that characterized the decade of 1810 to 1820.[73]

The logic underlying Cádiz's privileging people of Spanish and indigenous ancestry for citizenship was highly politicized, as seen in the Cortes debates. Part of this logic referred to the traditional understanding of purity of blood that regarded *castas* as impure and Indian and white as core racial categories. However, there was also an innovation involved in the exclusion of people of African descent from citizenship between 1810 and 1812. The exclusion was grounded on a more recent tendency to equate blacks with slaves, in the context of the rise of the slave trade in the Caribbean colonies. Between the late eighteenth and early nineteenth centuries, with the advent of an increase in the number of plantations and Spain's incursions into the slave trade, racial connotations of people of African descent turned away from the previous tolerant model that had characterized Spanish American contexts, when the crown had created avenues for free people of color to assimilate and mobilize socially. In other words, the liberalism of the Cádiz constitutional debates was complicit with slavery's expansion. And slavery and race were essential political issues in Cádiz inasmuch as they impacted the incorporation of the charter in the American territories. The exclusion of the *castas*, who accounted for a large percentage of the population across Spanish America, was also a means of reducing the number of American deputies in Cádiz.[74]

Between March and April of 1811, an important debate that dealt with the abolition of the slave trade and slavery took place within the Cádiz constitutional assembly.[75] That debate about African slavery in the Hispanic world as well as the developments in English legislation favoring

---

[73] Jaime Rodríguez, *La revolución política durante la época de la independencia: El reino de Quito, 1808–1822* (Quito: Universidad Andina Simón Bolívar, Corporación Editora Nacional, 2006); Steinar Saether, "Independence and the Redefinition of Indianness around Santa Marta, Colombia, 1750–1850," *Journal of Latin American Studies* 37 (2005), 70–72; Marcela Echeverri, "Popular Royalists, Empire, and Politics in Southwestern New Granada, 1809–1819," *Hispanic American Historical Review* 91, no. 2 (2011), 237–69. The regions where Cádiz was not applied also abolished tribute. See Sosa, *Representación e Independencia*, 105–12; Marixa Lasso, "Población y Sociedad," in *Colombia: Crisis Imperial e Independencia*, Tomo I (1808–1830), ed. Eduardo Posada Carbó (Madrid: Taurus, Fundación MAPFRE, 2010), 224–25.

[74] Rieu-Millan, *Los diputados americanos*, 152–73; Schmidt-Nowara, *Slavery, Freedom, and Abolition*, 111; Lasso, *Myths of Harmony*, 36–43; Josep Maria Fradera, *Gobernar Colonias* (Barcelona: Ediciones Península, 1999), ch. 2.

[75] Manuel Chust, "De esclavos, encomenderos y mitayos: El anticolonialismo en las Cortes de Cádiz," *Mexican Studies/Estudios Mexicanos* 11, no. 2 (1995), 187.

abolition were reflected in local political events in the Caribbean, including Cuba.[76] The racial underpinnings of the debate about representation also became central to the way in which the peninsular liberal regime was perceived in Caribbean New Granada. Cartagena had a very large population of free blacks who felt directly excluded from the early Cádiz debates. The Cartagena elites questioned such an exclusion and allied with free blacks in their critique of Spanish liberalism. That alliance catalyzed divisions between Americans and Spaniards, which in turn triggered an independence movement that was supported by a substantial number of free blacks or *pardos*. After 1810 the independence project in Cartagena was infused with ideals of racial equality. Of course, it is important to keep in mind that this was not always the case. As an example, in Venezuela, east of Caracas, enslaved and free people of color in the haciendas and towns around Barlovento mobilized as early as 1811 to challenge the first junta in Caracas, which did not espouse ideas of racial equality.[77] Moreover, as a result of the pressure exercised by American deputies in the Cortes, Article 22 of the Cádiz Constitution ultimately did leave an avenue open for people of African ancestry to gain their citizenship in cases that merited it. Military duty was one way to prove that merit.[78]

In Popayán, where slavery was still a very significant force in society in the nineteenth century, racial equality – either as a legal project or a

---

[76] Aside from the ones taking place in Cuba, in the year 1811 several slave rebellions or conspiracies occurred in New Orleans, Santo Domingo, and Martinique. See Robin Blackburn, *The Overthrow of Colonial Slavery, 1776–1848* (1988; London and New York: Verso, 2000); David P. Geggus, "Slavery, War, and Revolution in the Greater Caribbean," in *A Turbulent Time: The French Revolution and the Greater Caribbean*, ed. David B. Gaspar and David P. Geggus (Bloomington and Indianapolis: Indiana University Press, 1997), 1–50.

[77] Lasso, *Myths of Harmony*; Blanchard, *Under the Flags of Freedom*, 23. See also Marcela Echeverri, "Race, Citizenship, and the Cádiz Constitution in Popayán (New Granada)," in *The Rise of Constitutional Government in the Iberian Atlantic World: The Impact of the Cádiz Constitution of 1812*, ed. Scott Eastman and Natalia Sobrevilla Perea (Tuscaloosa: University of Alabama Press, 2015), 91–110.

[78] However, a caveat in Article 22 stated that subjects aiming to become citizens claiming that they deserved it as recognition of their loyalty had to be of legitimate birth and to have been born of free parents. *La Constitución de Cádiz (1812) y Discurso Preliminar a la Constitución*, ed. Antonio Fernández García (Madrid: Editorial Castalia, 2002), 97. For Panama, see Sosa, *Representación e Independencia*, 105–12; for Santa Marta, see Saether, *Identidades e Independencia*, 200–01; for Yucatan, see Melchor Campos García, *Castas, feligresía y ciudadanía en Yucatán* (Mérida: Universidad Autónoma de Yucatán, 2005), 102; for Cuba, see Landers, *Atlantic Creoles in the Age of Revolutions*; Sartorius, *Ever Faithful*.

nationalist trope – faced big hurdles. During the eighteenth century, when the crown created certain openings for free blacks to ascend the social ladder through membership in the militias, the Popayán elites hindered that particular development. The Creole elites clung to racial privilege in spite of – or perhaps because of – the growth of a free black population in the province. However, the monarchical crisis gave great latitude for action to a royal official such as Governor Tacón who was open to extending new privileges to free and enslaved blacks in exchange for military service. Tacón's bold move to incorporate people of African descent in the army reflected his perception that it was a decision consistent with the crown's integrationist policy of the previous century. Even though the governor acted with caution when mobilizing the slaves, for the local elites that intervention constituted a threat.

Tacón's innovation in the southwest had long-lasting consequences in the region and in the territory of New Granada at large. For instance, in 1813 Antonio Nariño, the president of Cundinamarca, sought to counter the situation in Popayán by also offering freedom to slaves who joined his army. The most immediate results were slave rebellions in the mining zones to the west. Subsequently, in Antioquia Juan del Corral advocated the gradual abolition of slavery in order to pacify the slaves.[79] Slavery also became a central issue for Simón Bolívar's military campaign and republican project. Clearly, if legislation in the emergent republics was strategically aligned with the interests of free and enslaved blacks, those republican projects had a better chance of gaining the support of a considerable amount of the population. The significance of the priorities of free and enslaved blacks throughout the wars and, as a consequence, during the political and legislative process of state formation was unquestionable. But, in particular, the problem of slavery and race in the context of war played out as a factor of military expediency. This was apparent in the aforementioned examples of legislation that aimed to mobilize the population toward supporting one of the two competing political poles. It was also the case when, although realizing that military victory could depend on the black troops, Bolívar removed the *pardo* caudillos (or leaders) Manuel Piar in 1817 and José Padilla in 1828 from

---

[79] Hamnett, "Popular Insurrection and Royalist Reaction," 309–10; Peter Blanchard, "Slave Soldiers of Spanish South America: From Independence to Abolition," in *Arming Slaves: From Classical Times to the Modern Age*, ed. Christopher Leslie Brown and Philip Morgan (New Haven, CT: Yale University Press, 2006), 263; Peter Blanchard, *Under the Flags of Freedom*, 34; Daniel Gutiérrez, "Las políticas abolicionistas en el Estado de Antioquia (1812–1816)" (unpublished manuscript).

their positions because of their alleged ambitions to claim equality for all and abolish racial distinctions.[80]

The dynamics of political radicalization among New Granada insurgents implied the circulation of a language of liberation that was very powerful yet also ambiguous. In propaganda and political debates, liberation and emancipation were explicitly opposed to enslavement, a term used to denote colonial oppression. Enslaved communities were receptive to those ideas, but they also perceived the contradictions intrinsic to the way that Creole elites used that language, which continued to promote the exclusion of people of African descent. These contradictions, in fact, were very costly to the insurgent project in southwestern New Granada, because free and enslaved blacks preferred to support the royalists when they had a choice. The consequences of this were not only that the insurgents' project did not intersect with the interests of people of African descent but also that by embracing royalism and mobilizing to defend the crown's cause, people of African descent also sought to expand and radicalize the potential of the royalist project in a way unexpected by the royalist elites. Even though the Popayán royalists did not abolish slavery, enslaved people sought emancipation from their status as slaves by claiming the right to become free vassals as a reward for their loyalty.

Free and enslaved Africans were part of an informal Atlantic information network that between the late eighteenth century and the first decades of the nineteenth spread increasingly common rumors regarding emancipation. Indeed, during the Age of Revolution, in many cases slaves contested slavery's legitimacy, inspired by ideas circulating across the Atlantic that freedom would come as a result of the French Revolution, the abolition of the slave trade, and antislavery ideology. In the Spanish Atlantic, the promulgation of the *Instrucción* or Spanish Slave Code in 1789 (see Chapter 3) and the Cádiz constitutional debates were triggers for slave unrest. During the independence wars, rumors of freedom gained traction in relation to the legal and military dynamics on the ground.[81]

---

[80] Lynch, *The Spanish American Revolutions*, 210–12; Helg, *Liberty and Equality*, ch. 6.

[81] Marcela Echeverri, "'Enraged to the Limit of Despair': Infanticide and Slave Judicial Strategies in Barbacoas, 1789–1798," *Slavery and Abolition* 30, no. 3 (2009), 403–26; María Eugenia Chaves, "Esclavos, libertades y república: Tesis sobre la polisemia de la libertad en la primera república antioqueña," *Estudios Interdisciplinarios de América Latina y el Caribe* 22, no. 1 (2011), 88; David Geggus, "The Caribbean in the Age of Revolution," in *The Age of Revolutions*, ed. Armitage and Subrahmanyam, 85–88; Wim Klooster, "Le décret d'émancipation imaginaire: Monarchisme et esclavage en Amérique du Nord et dans la Caraïbe au temps des révolutions," *Annales Historiques de la*

1814–1820: The monarchical restoration and "reconquest"

In Spain the Napoleonic army finally succumbed to peasant guerrilla warfare across the peninsula and the allied forces in Vitoria on June 21, 1813. The paradoxical turn of events that followed once again put the entire monarchy at stake. When he returned to the throne, King Fernando VII rejected the liberal premises of the resistance regime that had flourished during his absence. Repression was the order of the day as Fernando embarked on a crusade to purify the government of any links with liberal and constitutional creeds, language, and institutions. Unraveling the constitutional monarchy may have been a clear statement of the monarch's disapproval of the philosophical and economic underpinnings of the nationalist form that the liberals had worked so hard to give the monarchy. But it was not a politically wise gesture from a king whose transatlantic territories were in revolt, with those who remained loyal to Spain now tied to liberalism and the constitution as much as to the king himself.[82]

In early 1815 Fernando VII sent an army – known as the *Costa Firme* Expeditionary Army – from Cádiz to Spanish America for the purpose of putting a halt to the uprising that was spreading across the region. Led by Pablo Morillo, the 10,500 soldiers arrived on the Caribbean coast of New Granada and went directly to Venezuela, Santa Marta, and Cartagena. Although it was one of the largest forces sent from Spain since the outbreak of the wars, it was certainly not sufficient, so the royalist forces continued to rely on the local population.[83] Morillo and his army quickly pacified New Granada and Venezuela's Caribbean regions, where cities and towns swore loyalty to Fernando VII. Cartagena, considered one of the most important military objectives, succumbed to a siege that lasted over three months and left the city in ruins.

In the months after Morillo's reconquest began, the New Granada insurgent military forces were not difficult to overcome, and by July 1816 New Granada was under royalist control. Following the reconquest

---

Révolution Française 1 (2011), 111–28; Schmidt-Nowara, *Slavery, Freedom, and Abolition*, 90–93; Cristina Soriano, *Tides of Revolution: Information and Politics in Late Colonial Venezuela* (Albuquerque: University of New Mexico Press, forthcoming).

[82] See Anthony McFarlane, *War and Independence in Spanish America* (New York and London: Routledge, 2014), 284–338.

[83] José Semprún and Alonso Bullón de Mendoza, *El ejército realista en la independencia Americana* (Madrid: Editorial MAPFRE, 1992), 144; Thibaud, *Repúblicas en Armas*, 262.

of Cartagena, the *audiencia* was relocated there between July of 1816 and January of 1817. During this period the viceroyalty was reinstituted, and Francisco de Montalvo, who until then had been the Captain General of the Captaincy whose center was in Panama, was promoted to viceroy of New Granada. But in spite of the military strength of the royalists, the sources of authority that now ruled over New Granada were clearly divided between the military power represented by Morillo and the civil government of Viceroy Montalvo. For the former, exemplary punishment and the waging of war were the only viable methods for achieving military victory, the goal of his pacifying crusade. For the viceroy, on the other hand, pardon and conciliation made sense, given the number of people who had been involved in the insurgency and the need to restore trust in the king. Those differences translated into divergent policies, generating inconsistencies and confusion.[84]

Thus 1816 was a turning point for this turbulent period, the year in which royalism became the official discourse and an imperative. Because of the repressive nature of Morillo's campaign, royalism depended on a negative mechanism that sought to eradicate the supporters of independence, punishing them so that treason would not be attempted again. To a large extent, the model was borrowed from the *juntas de purificación* that Fernando had established in the peninsula to eradicate *afrancesados* and liberals from the government. But the tribunals in New Granada were also grounded in the Inquisition, which Morillo reinstituted soon after he arrived in Santa Marta. Not only were the church and the clergy thus expected to take part in the investigations against suspect insurgents, religion and traditional religious values became central to the project of reclaiming obedience to the crown and its ministers "as a matter of conscience."[85] At another level the *Consejo de Guerra Permanente* or Permanent Court-Martial became very unpopular for trying civilians and often determining that execution was a fit punishment for accusations of *infidencia* (treason), leaving little time for appeals. In Santa Fe, the council collected information that involved the most prominent families and applied the death sentence to many who had been involved in the juntas such as Jorge Tadeo Lozano, Camilo Torres, and Francisco José de Caldas.

[84] Real Academia de la Historia (hereinafter RAH), 9/7653 Leg 10 a, fol. 55; Rebecca Earle, *Spain and the Independence of Colombia, 1810–1825* (Exeter: University of Exeter Press, 2000), Part II.

[85] Brian Hamnett, "The Counter Revolution of Morillo and the Insurgent Clerics of New Granada, 1815–1820," *The Americas* 32, no. 4 (1976), 600.

Morillo's impolitic campaign affected public perception of the crown's rule, as even Viceroy Montalvo claimed, and the rise of military officers to power gave the official administration a tinge of repression. But for some time the insurgency was unable to envision a clear alternative. Some important members of the independence military campaign in New Granada escaped, including the prominent Venezuelan general Simón Bolívar, who took refuge first in Jamaica and then in Haiti. On the mainland, small groups of guerillas began to regroup in the eastern Llanos of Venezuela.[86] In regions such as Santa Marta and Popayán that had remained under royalist control throughout the previous years, the strong hand of the royalist reconquest generated new opportunities for recognition. Royalists from all classes sought rewards for their loyalty and even cities, such as Pasto, continued their search for benefits. In Popayán, the new governor, Juan Sámano, applied the stringent policies of reconquest to insurgent elites from the Cauca Valley region, forcing them to pay great sums of money.[87]

Eventually the insurgency reemerged. After 1815 Simón Bolívar's strategy shifted significantly, in part because he had traveled to Haiti, where he received conditional aid from Alexandre Pétion, head at that time of the southern republican area of Haiti (the northern part was a kingdom ruled by Henri Christophe). Pétion extended his support to proindependence families from Cartagena and Caracas that required asylum during Morillo's reconquest and provided supplies and soldiers for Bolívar's expeditions. However, in exchange, he expected to see the independence project on the mainland take on the cause of antislavery.[88] This alliance with Latin America's first independent state and first black republic radicalized the anticolonial struggle. It must be recalled that during the First (1811–13) and Second (1814) Venezuelan republics, Bolívar had, in fact, maintained a suspicious and far from conciliatory attitude toward people of African descent, free or enslaved, who were a majority in Venezuela. That factor alienated blacks, who tended to side with the royalists, as in the famous cases of Coro and the Llanos, where

---

[86] Lynch, *The Spanish American Revolutions*, 242–43; Thibaud, *Repúblicas en Armas*, 236.

[87] Hamnett, "Popular Insurrection and Royalist Reaction," 307; Saether, *Indentidades e Independencia*, 197–207.

[88] Ada Ferrer, "Haiti, Free Soil, and Antislavery in the Revolutionary Atlantic," *American Historical Review* 117, no. 1 (2012), 60–61; Sibylle Fischer, "Bolívar in Haiti: Republicanism in the Revolutionary Atlantic," in *Haiti and the Americas*, ed. Carla Calarge, Raphael Dalleo, Luis Duno-Gottberg, and Clevis Headley (Jackson: University Press of Mississippi, 2013), 25–53.

they joined forces with the Spanish royalist Tomás Boves, causing serious problems for the republican project.[89]

In fact, it was partly because of the complicated association between popular fury and blackness that characterized Boves' movement prior to Morillo's arrival that the leader of the new Expeditionary Army was initially apprehensive of arming locals and, particularly, of arming slaves. But after assessing the situation, Morillo made moves to facilitate the transition of enslaved people who were fighting for the insurgents into his army and also to grant freedom to those that had previously remained loyal to the king. What is more, aware of the risk that the black majorities would be attracted to the insurgent side, in Venezuela the royalists considered reintroducing the liberal policy of granting of citizenship to free blacks who could prove merit.[90]

In 1818, after a successful campaign in Venezuela, Bolívar turned again to New Granada. His army included large numbers of blacks, many of whom had been brought in from the Caribbean. But he also sought to recruit slaves and free blacks on the mainland. He famously called for the enlistment of slaves from Cauca (Popayán), hoping to reduce the numbers of slaves available to the royalists. Simultaneously, Bolívar conceived of the recruitment of slaves as a punishment to them for having traditionally been on the king's side. In Cauca slave owners were not effusive in their response to the Liberator's call. After a decade of war, the slave- and landholding elites' power was waning, their properties and wealth having been hit hard by growing demands from the state and the armies. Many slaveholders hid their slaves, trying to preserve what was left of their estates. The slaves themselves responded with caution. In 1819, after Bolívar called for the recruitment of 5,000 slaves into his army, the Minister of the Interior José Manuel Restrepo noted in his diary:

the slaves were happy, *although most of them in the province [of Popayán] are royalist*, quite a strange thing given that we proclaimed legal equality and since the first republic all have been born free.[91]

---

[89] On the alliances of slaves with royalists in Venezuela during this period, see Blanchard, *Under the Flags of Freedom*, ch. 2; and Blanchard, "Slave Soldiers," 262–65.

[90] Clément Thibaud, "De la ficción al mito: Los llaneros de la independencia de Venezuela," in *Mitos políticos en las sociedades andinas: Orígenes, invenciones y ficciones*, ed. Germán Carrera Damas et al. (Caracas: Instituto Francés de Estudios Andinos, 2006), 327–42; Blanchard, *Under the Flags of Freedom*, 30–31; James King, "A Royalist View of the Colored Castes in the Venezuelan War of Independence," *Hispanic American Historical Review* 33, no. 4 (1953), 526–37.

[91] Restrepo, *Diario político y militar*, Vol. 1, 54. Entry for April 9, 1819.

Indeed, in spite of the fact that the brutality of Morillo's reconquest made it difficult to rebuild support for the Spanish government, in Popayán enslaved people of African descent as well as indigenous people continued to constitute important segments of the royalist army. This was partly due to the almost absolute exclusion of blacks from the local insurgent forces, particularly in Cali, where most mine- and slave-owning insurgents were zealous protectors of their economic interests and the racial barriers needed to support them. Many slaves identified the republican project with the attempt of their owners to curb the king's authority and consistently sought to obtain personal and collective gains by defending the crown's sovereignty. Specifically, when claiming their right to freedom in return for their loyalty, slaves envisioned that freedom would include being granted the privileges stemming from the category of vassals of the king. Moreover, the slaves who lived in the Pacific lowland mining districts were able to remain in that territory enjoying close to absolute autonomy for almost a decade during the course of the wars. They appropriated the mines and their communities flourished, while also welcoming runaway slaves from the region. Most importantly, after Morillo arrived, some of these slaves sought to legalize their de facto freedom in court, which not only points to their awareness of a political context favorable to them but also suggests that they had an interest in acquiring the legal status of free people.

Antiroyalist propaganda remarked on the fanaticism of people from Pasto who defended the king, especially if they were Indians. These were said to blindly follow royalist priests who terrified them about the implications of the sinful action of turning their back on the king. As with other propaganda, it was a simplified representation of the situation on the ground regarding the priests.[92] They were not exclusively involved on the royalist side. In fact, in Cali the Franciscans had been the leading force behind the first junta in 1810. Church officials had important incentives for supporting the insurgency given the Bourbon attack on their regalist privileges, which they sought to reclaim in exchange for their support for the independence project.[93] Indigenous communities were far from

---

[92] Restrepo, *Historia de la revolución*, perfectly illustrates this. See also Bolívar's 1813 "Decreto de guerra a muerte," RAH 9/7649 Leg 6 a, fol. 9. A complete study of the role of the clergy in the Spanish liberal revolution dealing with Spain and New Spain is Eastman, *Preaching Spanish Nationalism*.

[93] Alfonso Zawadzky, *Clero insurgente y clero realista: Estudio de los Informes Secretos del Obispo de Popayán doctor Salvador Jiménez al Rey de España sobre la actuación de Sacerdotes de su Diócesis durante la Guerra de Independencia* (Cali: Imprenta

irrationally following the religious or colonial elites. Just as the liberal context induced indigenous commoners in the royalist army to seek tribute reduction, the monarchical restoration context encouraged caciques and priests to reclaim the privileges that had tended to become eroded under Cádiz rule.

In the following chapters, we will look more closely at the political worlds of Indians and slaves before and during the wars of independence. A detailed analysis of the transformations underway during Bourbon rule will illustrate the dynamic interaction between their legal position, community politics, and internal conflicts among indigenous people in Pasto and the enslaved in the Pacific lowlands. After 1808, the emergence of a sustained conflict between royalists and insurgents in Andean South America reveals a process in which sovereignty changed its shape and meaning over the course of legal experiments and war. The cross-class and multiethnic appeal of royalism in Popayán cannot be explained in terms of resistance or opposition to innovations. Portraits of royalism as backward do not account for the multiple transformations of royalist discourse and practice during the period of the crisis.[94] When Indians and slaves sought an alliance with the empire, they did so based on their informed sense of the opportunities it might give them to defend their interests. At the same time, they entered the military arena in the context of the wars because the revolutionary age offered a volatile environment in which to expand the realm of political possibilities with their struggles.

Bolivariana, 1948); Zawadzky, *Las ciudades confederadas*; Hamnett, "The Counter Revolution."

[94] The profile of Pastusos as resistant to innovations throughout the previous century of Bourbon reformism as an explanation for royalism can be found in Hamnett, "Popular Insurrection and Royalist Reaction," 292–326; and Earle, "Indian Rebellion and Bourbon Reform in New Granada," 123.

2

Indian politics and Spanish justice
in eighteenth-century Pasto

On the afternoon of Monday, May 19, 1800, around three hundred Indians armed with stones and sticks met in the plaza of the Indian town of Túquerres in the Province of Los Pastos to protest an impending tithe increase. Some of them had traveled for a day from the towns of Chantán and Guaytarilla. From the plaza the Indians went to the *aguardiente* (cane liquor) distillery that also was the home of the *corregidor* (Spanish magistrate), Francisco R. Clavijo, demanding to speak with him and his brother, the tithe collector, Atanacio R. Clavijo.[1] The group of Indians turned increasingly impatient when the Clavijo brothers failed to come out to face them and began tearing down the distillery. When the building had been set on fire and was burning, armed with spears the Clavijos escaped and ran toward the church at the center of the town plaza, soon to be followed by the crowd. The priest, Ramón Ordóñez de Lara, attempted to pacify the Indians and keep them from entering the church, and he kept watch over it throughout the night. But early on Tuesday morning, Julián Carlosama, an Indian porter from Túquerres, broke into the church, followed by a group of men. Inside they found the Clavijo brothers hiding behind the altar. Ramón Cucas Remo, an Indian from Túquerres, jumped on top of the altar and killed the *corregidor* with his own spear. The Indians then dragged his brother Atanacio toward the front of the church and killed him also.

---

[1] The Clavijos' first last name was Rodríguez, but their contemporaries knew the brothers as "los Clavijo." Alberto Montezuma Hurtado, "Los Clavijos y la casa de los muertos," *Boletín Cultural y Bibliográfico* 9, no. 8 (1968), 15–16.

On the morning of May 20, right after the killings, more Indians arrived from Sapuyes and Imués to join the protest in Túquerres. The Túquerres cacique, Pablo Dias, organized an Indian guard around the ruins of the *aguardiente* distillery to keep it from being looted. Meanwhile other Indians destroyed the buildings of the tobacco and gunpowder monopolies, as well as a food and clothing store that Francisco Clavijo owned. The protest continued throughout the week in other towns in the Province of Los Pastos, where Indians also rebelled and destroyed more royal property linked to the *aguardiente* monopoly. Sometime in June the disturbances began to abate but did not definitively end until Popayán Governor Diego Antonio Nieto arrived to begin the criminal inquest. One year later seventeen participants in the revolt were convicted: six women were exiled, seven men were sent to jail, and all were sentenced to public flogging. The remaining three were sentenced to death: the Indians Ramón Cucas Remo, Julián Carlosama, and Lorenzo Piscal. The first two had been involved in the killings, while Piscal was accused of participating in the destruction of the distillery and of instigating the protests with his drums. One of the convicts, Marcelo Ramírez, agreed to act as executioner in exchange for the pardon of his eight-year sentence in prison. On November 20, 1802, two and a half years after the revolt, the three culprits faced death in Túquerres.[2]

Atanacio Clavijo's attempt to change the traditional arrangements of tithe collection led to the collective protests that turned into the rebellion of May 1800. The priest Bernardo Erazo had announced during mass in Guaytarilla the proposed tithe increase the day before the insurrection. The Indians immediately complained because Atanacio Clavijo "tried to charge tithe against custom, of chickens, *cuyes* (guinea pigs), eggs, vegetables, and even of their very children."[3] Indeed, the tithe increase broke with customary arrangements for tithe collection in Pasto: the amount had been fixed at 3 *reales*, and certain animals raised for consumption were exempted. The *Recopilación de las leyes de Indias*, a compendium of laws for Spanish America published in 1680, recognized the importance of custom in the collection of tithe. This gave the Indians an argument for

---

[2] The main sources for the trials were published in Ricardo Oviedo, *Los Comuneros del Sur: Levantamientos Populares del Siglo XVIII* (San Juan de Pasto: Editorial de Nariño, 2001). See also ANE Criminales 179, doc. dated September 26, 1800; AGN Colonia, Miscelánea, t. 100; AGN Colonia, Empleados Públicos del Cauca, t. 4, fols. 914r–979v. The most extensive treatment of the revolt is Williams, "Acomodación, negociación y el actuar político."

[3] "Declaración de Salvador Ojeda," in Oviedo, *Los Comuneros*, 82.

the protection of previous arrangements, and they denounced as illegitimate Atanacio Clavijo's attempt to change them.[4]

But the tithe increase was only one factor that sparked the unrest. The Indians' killing of the Clavijo brothers and the destruction of royal property linked to the *aguardiente* monopoly that Francisco Clavijo had administered in the province since 1794 were the result of the deeper excesses that the *corregidor* and the tithe collector had been committing against customary, and indeed legitimate, terms of resource extraction in the region. The disruption of the tenuous balance of interests on three fronts – the *aguardiente* monopoly, cacique appointments, and land tenure – led to the violent Indian protest in Los Pastos against the Clavijos.

The Túquerres revolt was not the only Indian mobilization in southwestern New Granada in the late eighteenth century. In this region, which included the Kingdom of Quito, a number of small-scale Indian revolts broke out that share traits with contemporary Andean revolts as well as some that took place in New Spain. In most eighteenth-century instances of mobilization, Indians were reacting to the creation of monopolies, especially of liquor, and the deepening of extractive measures that transformed customary tribute collection practices. The revolts were also the result of shifting alliances among *corregidores*, priests, and ethnic authorities in the context of the Bourbon reforms. Thus, although it was one of the largest indigenous rebellions to take place in the late eighteenth century in New Granada, the Túquerres revolt was not unique. It was framed within a larger Spanish-American reaction to the Bourbon reforms.[5]

Yet the Túquerres revolt and other Indian protests in New Granada are not comparable in size and reach to the ones that shook the central Andes in the 1780s. While the Túpac Amaru rebellion and others linked to it in the Viceroyalty of Peru developed anticolonial goals, in New Granada the rebellions – Indian rebellions in the southwest and the multiethnic Comunero revolt around Santa Fe – sought redress for abuses committed by government officials, without expressing anticolonial interests.

[4] Ley 13, título 5, libro 6, *Recopilación de las leyes de los reynos de las Indias*; Earle, "Indian Rebellion and Bourbon Reform in New Granada," 115. As a unit of currency, 8 *reales* amounted to one silver *peso*.

[5] Moreno Yáñez, *Sublevaciones indígenas en la Audiencia de Quito*, describes and analyzes eleven insurrections between 1730 and 1803. For Guatemala, see Greg Grandin, *The Blood of Guatemala: A History of Race and Nation* (Durham, NC: Duke University Press, 2000), ch. 2.

This distinction is crucial for eliminating independence teleologies from a political reading of revolts in late-eighteenth-century New Granada.[6]

The Túquerres crisis conforms to another Spanish-American pattern: it was entwined with a history of legal politics in which Indians negotiated their rights and reacted to abuse. Many historians have explored the dialectic between legal and violent action, and it seems evident that they were two of the main expressions of indigenous people's political engagement in colonial Spanish America.[7] To illustrate the centrality of monarchic justice to Indian juridical identity and politics, my focus here will be on how Indian elites deployed the rhetoric of paternalism that defined Indians as "miserables" and classified indigenous people along with minors.[8]

During the investigation that followed the death of the Clavijos, the caciques of the towns involved in the uprising (Túquerres, Guaytarilla, Sapuyes, Imues, and Chantán) were in charge of defending the Indians. Their legal defense attempted to explain the reasons for the revolt and to plead for leniency for the Indians involved in the rebellion by professing

[6] The first to write about New Granada's Comunero rebellion against anticolonial readings was John Phelan in *The People and the King*. Analyzing Cuzco, Charles Walker in *Smoldering Ashes: Cuzco and the Creation of Republican Peru, 1780–1840* (Durham, NC: Duke University Press, 1999), esp. ch. 2 and p. 117, proposed that the Túpac Amaru revolt should be understood as a protonational movement. Sinclair Thomson, *We Alone Will Rule: Native Andean Politics in the Age of Insurgency* (Madison: University of Wisconsin Press, 2002), 124, also identifies anticolonial goals in the La Paz rebellion. See the two most recent works on the south-Andean insurrections: Sergio Serulnikov, *Revolution in the Andes: The Age of Túpac Amaru* (Durham, NC: Duke University Press, 2013); Charles Walker, *The Tupac Amaru Rebellion* (Cambridge, MA: Harvard University Press, 2014).

[7] Especially important here is Sergio Serulnikov's analysis of legal action and violent action as part of the spectrum of Indian politics in Chayanta. See Serulnikov, *Subverting Colonial Authority*; Serulnikov, "Andean Political Imagination in the Late Eighteenth Century," in *Political Cultures in the Andes, 1750–1950*, ed. Jacobsen et al., 272. See also Walker, *Smoldering Ashes*, 56. The classic study of this process in colonial Mexico, accounting for similar patterns of legality and violence, is William B. Taylor, *Drinking, Homicide & Rebellion in Colonial Mexican Villages* (Palo Alto, CA: Stanford University Press, 1979), esp. ch. 4. For the Andes, see the volume edited by Steve Stern, *Resistance, Rebellion, and Consciousness in the Andean Peasant World* (Madison: University of Wisconsin Press, 1987).

[8] Owensby, *Empire of Law*, 56; José María Ots y Capdequí, *Manual de Historia del Derecho Español en las Indias y del Derecho Propiamente Indiano* (Buenos Aires: Instituto de Historia del Derecho Argentino, 1943); Bartolomé Clavero, *Derecho indígena y cultura constitucional en América* (Mexico: Siglo XXI, 1994); Lauren Benton, *Law and Colonial Cultures: Legal Regimes in World History, 1400–1900* (New York: Cambridge University Press, 2002).

their loyalty to the king and gathering evidence of the Indians' respect for the royal monopolies. To that end, the caciques wrote a "memorial" and a series of questionnaires that explained the destruction of the royal property, stating that the target of the insurrection had not been the royal distillery but the Clavijos' home.[9]

The trial records, read critically against other sources, reveal class divisions within the Indian communities. Following the story of the Túquerres cacique Pablo Dias closely, we will see how he was both a beneficiary of Clavijo's tyranny and an architect of the defense of the Indians who killed him. By using his defense to appeal to the wretchedness of the indigenous people, Dias was able to distort his role in the course of the legal dispute and advance his own interests.

Insofar as the legal dimension of the Túquerres revolt revealed the tensions intrinsic to "Indianness" at the turn of the nineteenth century, it also allows us to see the interdependence between the Indian commoners and their caciques. At critical junctures in 1800 and beyond, it was clear that although Indians in the north Andean region of Pasto were not monolithic in their actions, Indian elites and commoners adapted to the challenges of political conflict.[10]

AGUARDIENTE REFORM, INDIANS, AND LOCAL POLITICS

Two years after he became *corregidor*, in 1794 Francisco Clavijo was granted the rent of the *aguardiente* distillery in Túquerres in the amount of 25,000 pesos over eight years (3,125 pesos a year). This monopoly was among the least popular reform elements in southwestern New Granada and the Quito *Audiencia*.[11] In the transformative context of the eighteenth century, the Bourbon reforms targeted liquor production and consumption as two crucial aspects of the existing economy that could yield much-needed revenues for the crown to finance years of continuous war

---

[9] "Memorial" was a written document requesting mercy and detailing the grounds for such a request.

[10] Earlier analyses of the revolt treated Indians as a monolithic group. See Earle, "Indian Rebellion and Bourbon Reform in New Granada." Earle's study of the late colonial riots, as well as her brief statement about Indian royalism during independence, portrays "Indians" as homogeneous. This limits the understanding of political processes that should be studied with attention to the internal dynamics of the communities and the distinct interests of Indian elites and Indian commoners, which were certainly in conflict during the years 1780–1820.

[11] Williams, "Acomodación, resistencia y el actuar político," 23.

and defense projects.[12] Viceroy Pedro Messía de la Cerda regarded New Granada cities in the south and the Kingdom of Quito, which had been recently made part of New Granada, as important sources of income for the protection of Cartagena. The creation of the *aguardiente* monopoly had different phases. Before 1750 the monopoly was leased to different producers. In the decade between 1750 and 1760 the policy tended to unify production around one exclusive producer. The third phase completed the establishment of the monopoly, turning the production and distribution of *aguardiente* over to direct administration by the state, as in Clavijo's case.[13]

Clashes surrounding the establishment of this monopoly in the viceroyalty were constant since the conception of the idea and its early implementation in the 1750s. *Hacendados* (hacienda owners) throughout New Granada rejected Bourbon intrusion into local *aguardiente* production. Cane growers who extracted the juice from the cane (*hacendados cosecheros de miel*) were quick to express their discomfort with the plan to monopolize production, because it would result in lower prices for cane juice.[14] However, consumers as well as small-scale producers also were unhappy with the measure.[15] Protests broke out against the institution of the monopoly in every city from Honda (in today's Tolima department) in 1738 and Tunja (in Boyacá) in 1752 to the urban areas of Quito in the 1765 Rebellion of *Los Barrios* and Hato de Lemus (Cauca) in 1781.[16]

Aguardiente reform took long to arrive to southwestern New Granada, and until the 1780s the *cabildo* of Pasto expected distillers to pay a share of the fixed tax of approximately 500 pesos.[17] The reform to Pasto's system of the manufacture and sale of liquor symbolized a rough transformation that would increase the price of *aguardiente* and attack any

---

[12] John Fisher et al., *Reform and Insurrection in Bourbon New Granada and Peru* (Baton Rouge: Louisiana University Press, 1990); Adolfo Meisel Roca, "¿Situado o contrabando?: La base económica de Cartagena de Indias a fines del Siglo de las Luces," *Cuadernos de Historia Económica y Empresarial* 11 (2003), 17.

[13] Gilma Lucía Mora de Tovar, *Aguardiente y conflictos sociales en el Nuevo Reino de Granada durante el siglo XVIII* (Bogotá: Universidad Nacional de Colombia, 1988), 217.

[14] Mora de Tovar, *Aguardiente y conflictos sociales*, 38–39.

[15] Tamar Herzog, "De la historia y el mito: las rebeliones de Quito (1592–1765)," *Reflejos* 7 (1998), 72–80; Earle, "Indian Rebellion and Bourbon Reform in New Granada," 104.

[16] Anthony McFarlane, "The Rebellion of the *Barrios*," in *Reform and insurrection in Bourbon New Granada and Peru*, ed. Fisher et al., 214. The news of rebellion in Quito inspired the popular rejection of the monopoly in and around Cali also in 1765, see Gustavo Arboleda, *Historia de Cali desde los orígenes de la ciudad hasta la expiración del periodo colonial* (Cali: Imprenta Arboleda, 1928), 441.

[17] Earle, "Indian Rebellion and Bourbon Reform in New Granada," 103.

illegal producers of the liquor. It was unwelcome in Pasto as well as in neighboring Tumaco where people protested in 1781. In Pasto, a revolt in mid-1781 against the *aguardiente* monopoly and a rumor about a possible uprising of neighboring towns against this same monopoly in Túquerres were important regional precedents of the 1800 insurrection in Túquerres, when the Clavijos were killed.

In 1781 Indians in the city of Pasto revolted against Josef Ignacio Peredo, the lieutenant governor of Popayán, who was in charge of establishing the *aguardiente* monopoly in the district of Pasto. Peredo accomplished his task in Cali, Popayán, and Túquerres, but when he arrived in Pasto on June 22 during the Feast of Corpus Christi, a large assembly of Indians from nearby towns who were expected to pay tribute on St. John's Day, two days later, confronted him. Shortly after this incident, some Indians began complaining about taxes, and the crowd declared that they would calm down only if the monopoly were suppressed and Peredo left the city. Witnesses to the protest described "a crowd of Indians and plebeians armed with sticks and stones raising a red flag, screaming, and throwing stones, and saying that if the *estanco* (monopoly) was established there would be war and if it wasn't then there would be peace."[18] Peredo hid in a church and later escaped, but when he arrived at Catambuco (southwest of the city of Pasto, see Figure 1.1), Indians there beat him and his guards to death.

The subsequent exchanges between officials in Santa Fe and those in Popayán strongly condemned the actions of the local elites in Pasto. According to those views, they were responsible for the popular unrest; the popular classes were stripped of responsibility, indeed of political interests. But, paradoxically, at the same time that the management of the riot during and after the upheaval reflected the tensions between Bourbon officials and local elites, it also provides evidence of Indian rejection of the monopoly.

That the Indians were not comfortable with the establishment of the *estanco* is also clear from the rumors that circulated five years after the death of Peredo. In July 1786, then-*corregidor* Miguel González del Palacio wrote to the governor of Popayán, Pedro de Becaria, requesting armed support to prevent an Indian uprising targeting the *aguardiente* distillery located in Túquerres.[19] González del Palacio was informed of

---

[18] Archivo Central del Cauca (hereinafter ACC) Colonia, MI 6j 7848, fol. 110.

[19] ANE Popayán 204, doc. dated July 3, 1786. In the Province of Los Pastos the royal distillery was located in Túquerres, and the *estanquillos* or authorized selling points were established in Ancuya, Carlosama, Cumbal, Guabo, Guachucal, Guaytarilla, Ipiales,

this potential unrest by the cacique of Túquerres, Pablo Dias, who insisted he had heard the rumors from two other Indians in the town. The rumors announced that "the Indians around the city of Pasto united with those of the Province of Los Pastos are conspiring to destroy the house of the royal distillery of *aguardiente* ... kill its employees and burn the building." According to González del Palacio, the rumors included circulation of ideas (*especies*) about the imminent "return to the old liberty."[20]

Officials in Popayán denied the existence of the conspiracy. An advisor to the governor reviewed González del Palacio's letter and decided that the situation did not merit sending troops to Túquerres, as the *corregidor* had requested, because the advisor considered the rumors to be simply a consequence of an "individual unhappy with the royal revenues." With that explanation, Popayán's governor rejected the supposition that "Indians would have an organized and premeditated rebellion" planned. He supported his argument saying "their natural rusticity would not allow them any prudence to conceal any kind of wicked plans and these would be public by now."[21]

The denial that the monopoly was unpopular among Indians both obscured and reflected the underlying tensions between local elites, regional elites, and Indians. At play here was the Hispanic discourse of Indian rusticity. Denying political agency to Indians, the discourse played a crucial role in local politics and it was linked to their juridical status as "miserables."[22] As we will see in the following, these assumptions also were visible in the defense's strategic deployment of Indian loyalty to the crown during the trial of the Indians convicted for participating in the 1800 destruction of the royal distillery in Túquerres.

Notwithstanding the fact that the governor discredited the letter from Pasto's officials, other evidence indicates that in the years following the killing of Peredo in Pasto, Indians did reject the *aguardiente* monopoly and the officials in charge of it in the Province of Los Pastos. According to

Pastas, Puerchag, Pupiales, Sapuyes and Túquerres. Earle, "Indian Rebellion and Bourbon Reform in New Granada," 103.

[20] ANE Popayán 204, doc. dated July 3, 1786.   [21] Ibid.

[22] Serulnikov, *Subverting Colonial Authority*, speaks of a "colonial discourse" to refer to this depiction of native peoples as lacking a sophisticated understanding of political contexts. Derek Williams analyzes the "hidden hand" theory prevalent among elites in Santa Fe and Quito, who suspected Creole involvement in every protest or conspiracy, as was the case in their view of the 1800 Túquerres revolt. See Williams, "'Who Induced the Indian Communities?' The Los Pastos Uprising and the Politic of Ethnicity and Gender in Late-Colonial New Granada," *Colonial Latin American Historical Review* 10, no. 3 (2001), 293.

the witnesses who answered questions about the rumors, the Indians of
Pasto had convoked between three and four hundred Indians from the
towns of Catambuco, Cumbal, Imbues, and Obonuco to tear down the
distillery and "kill all the whites and the workers in the royal distillery."
Salvador Asmasa, governor of one of the towns, declared that Indians
from Obonuco had specifically said:

they thought the Indians from Túquerres were ridiculous (*unos malucos*) because
they had not destroyed the royal distillery and if they did not do it soon then those
from Obonuco would come to destroy it, and if on their way to accomplish it the
Indians from Túquerres did not help them, then they would kill them too.[23]

Considering that the 1800 rebellion in Túquerres took place with the participation of Indians from Los Pastos and not from Pasto, it is interesting to
pause and reflect on the discrepancy in the content of these rumors. Certainly
Túquerres had become a target of criticism and potential violence from
surrounding towns given that the distillery was located there, yet the rumors
that circulated referred to different alignments and antagonisms among the
Indians. While Asmasa's declaration implied a division between the Indians
in Pasto and Los Pastos, in contrast, the rumor that Dias and González del
Palacio were concerned about mentioned that the Indians in Pasto and Los
Pastos were going to mobilize to destroy the distillery together. In other
words, the first rumor presumed discord and the second, unity. Whether the
monopoly caused divisions or alliances among Indians, in both cases the
rumors stand as recorded indications of the Pasto Indians' persistent hostility
toward the *aguardiente* monopoly in the two decades prior to the revolt.[24]

As *corregidor* and administrator of the monopoly in the 1790s, Clavijo
had a conflictive relationship with the Indian communities. Moreover, he
tried to make changes in the government of the Indian communities that
touched the political interests of the Indians in Pasto, thus magnifying his
antagonism to local customs and traditions that the Indians defended and
valued as rights.

CHANGES TO INDIAN GOVERNMENT IN THE LATE EIGHTEENTH CENTURY

Although in theory indigenous people had a fundamental right to self-
government through the figures of the Indian caciques, colonial relations

---

[23] ANE Popayán 204, doc. dated July 3, 1786.
[24] Williams, "Who Induced the Indian Communities?"

made this difficult to carry out in practice. As the main source of tribute and labor, these communities lay at the intersection of royal and private interests, which gave their legal autonomy a relative value. The *corregidor*'s role in overseeing colonial resource extraction very easily slipped into the sacrifice of the protectionist aspect of Hispanic rule, which aimed to keep Indians from exploitation and abuse. Especially during the late eighteenth century, the way the *corregidores* carried out their duties diverged significantly from the legal expectations that the post initially entailed. As the Spanish magistrate in charge of the Indian communities, the post of *corregidor* had been designed by law to be held by a peninsular who did not have stakes in the local community.[25] But in the 1790s it became available to local entrepreneurs, *hacendados*, and merchants, who used the position for their own benefit and disregarded their role as Indian advocates.

In the Province of Los Pastos throughout the centuries, Indian communities had actively defined the terms of their economic contribution, such as taking a count of the Indian population for determining tribute payments and negotiating with priests for determining tithe payments. However, in the last decade of the eighteenth century, the appointment of Francisco Clavijo to the position of *corregidor* by Viceroy José de Ezpeleta in February 1792 created great tension with these communities.[26] Clavijo (who was born in Cartago, north of Popayán) was the owner of La Cofradía, one of the largest estates in Los Pastos. Thus he had direct economic interests as a landowner and also as someone who traded meat to the Pacific lowlands mining region. Although in Pasto there was not a *repartimiento de mercancías* (also known as *reparto*, forced sale of goods to Indians), Clavijo owned the only store that sold clothes and food in the Province of Los Pastos.[27] As *corregidor* he used his power to obstruct Indian access to justice and to accumulate resources in the region of Los Pastos, things he was able to do because of his role as an intermediary between the Indians and the colonial justice system. Conflicts with the *corregidor* Clavijo emerged around the issues of changes in tribute extraction and the succession of caciques, land appropriation by whites and

---

[25] Laura Lewis, *Hall of Mirrors: Power, Witchcraft, and Caste in Colonial Mexico* (Durham, NC: Duke University Press, 2003), 50; Stern, *Peru's Indian Peoples*; Calero, *Chiefdoms under Siege.*

[26] Williams, "Who Induced the Indian Communities?," 290.

[27] AGN Colonia, Aguardientes del Cauca 1, fol. 297v.

mestizos (of mixed white and Indian descent), and the communal defense of Indian entitlement to communal territories (*resguardos*).

The hierarchy of caciques and commoners structured the Indian communities and was fundamental to their articulation within the colonial government and society in the northern Andes. As native authorities the caciques stood above the commoners as a class. The caciques also oversaw the communities' tributary responsibilities and administered local resources, a double role that defined cacique legitimacy in relation to both indigenous and Spanish channels. A visible consequence of this structural organization of indigenous communities was the ambiguous position of native elites vis-à-vis the communities' most pressing interests, and for that reason the political dynamics and conflicts within Indian communities were the reflection of broader imperial changes.[28]

In the context of Bourbon fiscal reform, the Indian communities around the city of Pasto, and elsewhere in Spanish America, became the focus of multiple adjustments that sought to increase the crown's income. When Bourbon officials attempted to tighten control over tribute collection, they turned their attention to the crucial role of cacique authority and fiscal responsibility. Ultimately Bourbon interest in increasing revenues through tribute led to questioning earlier arrangements that had allowed the Indian communities to maintain a degree of control of tribute payment, particularly its collection in kind rather than in cash.

Indeed, before the reforms, Indian communities in Pasto and Los Pastos held a firm grip on the terms of tribute collection, paying mainly with textiles (*capisayos*) produced by women in the communities. In the centuries-long process of adjusting to colonial rule, Indians were successful in setting the terms of tribute collection according to the material and cultural coordinates of the communities, as opposed to the interests of *asentistas* (contractors) and the Royal Treasury.[29] The traditional system

---

[28] See Thomson, *We Alone Will Rule*, 43–44; Karen Spalding, *Huarochirí: An Andean Society under Inca and Spanish Rule* (Stanford, CA: Stanford University Press, 1988); Yannakakis, *The Art of Being In-between*; Garrett, *Shadows of Empire*.

[29] The long efforts of Indians in Pasto and Los Pastos to control the terms of tribute collection and payment began in the sixteenth century, with the impositions of Tomás López and García de Valverde, the *visitadores* sent from Peru. In the 1550s López prepared a list of twenty different items to be accepted as tribute payment, which "proved to be a burden to collect." In 1570, García de Valverde simplified tribute to gold pesos, *chaquira* (beads), cotton cloth, and chickens. See Calero, *Chiefdoms under Siege*, 74; ch. 4 in part 1 of William's "Acomodación, resistencia y el actuar político," 110–160; Alejandro Bernal, "La circulación de productos entre los pastos en el siglo XVI," *Revista Arqueológica del Área Intermedia* 2 (2000), 135; Frank Salomon, *Native Lords of Quito*

of collection in the Viceroyalty of New Granada and the *Audiencia* of Quito before 1780 was based on "asientos" (contracts), meaning that a local "asentista" (generally *corregidores* but also private contractors) paid for the right to collect tributes for a period of three years.[30] This type of contract was beneficial to the Indians, who took advantage of the fact that the *asentistas* did not intend to keep a full count of tributary Indians, since by underreporting the tributary population to the royal treasury, they were then able to make a profit from the amount they actually collected. It was a system that Jorge Juan and Antonio de Ulloa denounced as highly corrupt and, in particular, "harmful for the royal treasury."[31] This system was also convenient for the crown, however, since it guaranteed a stable income based on prior payment levels and freed state officials from the complications of collecting the tribute and in many cases, particularly in Pasto, of converting tribute payment in goods into cash.[32]

Yet during the Bourbon era, fiscal and administrative reforms aggressively targeted such pivotal customs, seeking to adjust tribute in two ways: First, as a means of strengthening political control in rural areas, and second, as a way of increasing royal revenue.[33] The *corregidor* Clavijo was a central figure in this shift. As tribute administrator he had an interest in seeing that the tribute quota would be met. Heading the reform of the tribute system, Clavijo decided to appoint in every town new caciques who would collaborate closely with the tribute administrator. Conflicts ensued as the traditional practice of hereditary succession of caciques fell victim to the caciques' crucial role in the collection of tribute.[34]

In 1797 Clavijo appointed Manuel Getial to the post of cacique of Yascual, generating controversy with other Indian caciques and with Nieto, the governor of Popayán. The Indians of the town denounced Getial "on account of the excesses he committed with the Indians and because being dependent (*adicto*) to the *corregidor* he mistreated them too much, forcing them to irregular services." To these accusations Clavijo

in the Age of the Incas: The Political Economy of North Andean Chiefdoms (New York: Cambridge University Press, 1986), 112.

[30] Moreno Yánez, *Sublevaciones indígenas en la Audiencia de Quito*, 104; Williams, "Acomodación, resistencia y el actuar político."

[31] Jorge Juan and Antonio de Ulloa, *Noticias Secretas* (1826; Bogotá, Banco Popular, 1983), 234; Williams "Acomodación, resistencia y el actuar político," 115, 118.

[32] Williams, "Acomodación, resistencia y el actuar político," 119.

[33] This also happened in Peru. See Serulnikov, *Subverting Colonial Authority*, 139.

[34] ANE Popayán 156, doc. dated October 26, 1775.

responded that he had named Manuel Getial "because he seems to suit the needs of *apadronamiento de indios* (Indian counts) and timely extraction of tributes."[35] In other words, Clavijo expected that the caciques he appointed would produce new, accurate lists of the tributary Indians and thus increase revenues.

Then, in 1798 Clavijo named Pablo Dias cacique of Túquerres. Clavijo's report on Dias' appointment noted:

Now that the royal treasury is collecting Indian tribute on administration, it is necessary to reduce all complications that resulted from the previous method, in which the multitude of tribute collecting Indian governors who most of the time were badly behaved or ineffective Indians, we name don Pablo Dias cacique of this town for life with all the faculties that the law concedes him and the duty to *apadronar* (count) the Indians and present them in the house of collection to pay tribute.[36]

In fact, Dias had been cacique since around 1786. He was an important protagonist in the conflicts unleashed by the expansion of haciendas onto Indian lands. During his initial tenure at least two judicial cases were filed against him in Túquerres, where Indians from the community denounced his use of communal lands for private purposes.[37] For example, Guaytarilla commoners (Guaytarilla being the *anexo* or satellite village of Túquerres) denounced him for making private use of their communal plot of land called "El Manzano," while outsiders invaded community lands and demographic pressures increased.[38] He also was charged with promoting the sale of Indian lands to benefit white or *mestizo vecinos* (*despojo*). These conflicts with the Indian communities indicate that Dias played a crucial role in the transformations of landed property underway in the last two decades of the eighteenth century, when a major infringement on Indian lands took place on the Túquerres plateau.[39]

Thus aside from disrupting the pillars of native autonomy – the mechanisms of cacique election and tribute collection – Clavijo's tenure as *corregidor* saw an increase in the dispossession of Indian lands. Moreover, the alliances between the *corregidor* and the caciques he elected gave

[35] ANE Popayán 249, doc. dated March 10, 1797, fols. 3, 5.

[36] AGN Colonia, Tributos, t. 2, doc. dated November 12, 1798.

[37] ANE Popayán 209, doc. dated December 31, 1787; ANE Popayán 242, doc. dated January 1, 1795.

[38] ANE Popayán 239, doc. dated August 23,1794.

[39] Williams, "Acomodación, resistencia y el actuar político," 89; Benhúr Cerón and Rosa Isabel Zarama, *Historia socio espacial de Túquerres, siglos XVI–XX: De Barbacoas hacia el horizonte nacional* (San Juan de Pasto: Universidad de Nariño, 2003), ch. 4.

Chantán, who produced a memorial and presented other evidence to the governor of Popayán in the Indians' defense. Legal mediation was mandated for commoners, and the internal communal hierarchy gave the caciques the responsibility for drafting and presenting petitions and for engaging in litigation to defend the communities. It is likely that the *protector partidario de indios*, Francisco Martínez de Segovia, gave juridical advice to the caciques on the format and terms that the defense should contain. The Indians' corporate identity (based on the legal category of "miserable") made them vassals of the king with the right to royal protection and legal representation by a *protector de naturales*. Thus, in the north Andean region of Pasto, as in other places in Spanish America, collective and multiethnic decisions – taken by the caciques and the *protector* – influenced how to best represent native interests in court.[50]

Let us look closer at the memorial, in which the caciques accepted the seriousness of the crimes committed by the Indian rebels and yet tried to obtain mercy for them. The defense presented two central arguments: One, the Indians were ignorant and, therefore, incapable of being conscious of the existence of the law and its consequences, and two, the circumstances of the attack on the *corregidor* should be taken into account as an explanation for the Indians' actions and in mitigation of their punishment. These judicial developments following the Túquerres uprising indicate that in seeking redress from the legal system for the Indian prisoners, the legal arguments of the caciques were aided by the ambiguities embedded in the Indians' double-edged social status.

The caciques' defense of the rebels underscored the character (*calidad*) of the delinquents – "ignorant and rustic pitiful Indians" who lacked the capacity to understand the consequences of their actions – to explain their lack of malice when committing the crime. Indians had been educated "wildly (*selváticamente*)" and oppressed by their masters. Furthermore, the defense stated that the oppression of the Indians by their masters and "their masters' extreme egoism" generated the conditions for the uprising. Denouncing the situation of oppression thus blurred the Indians'

---

[50] Yanna Yannakakis, "*Costumbre*: A Language of Negotiation in Eighteenth-Century Oaxaca," in *Negotiation within Domination: Colonial New Spain's Indian Pueblos Confront the Spanish State*, ed. Ethelia Ruiz Medrano and Susan Kellogg (Boulder: University Press of Colorado, 2011), 147. There is no evidence that an Indian scribe drafted the documents. For the significance of Indian scribes in Cuzco, see Kathryn Burns, "Making Indigenous Archives: The Quilcaycamayoc of Colonial Cuzco," *Hispanic American Historical Review* 91, no. 4 (2011), 665–89.

responsibility for their actions.[51] Significantly, the caciques put at the forefront the rhetoric of rusticity, which represented the Indians as incapable of acting judiciously.

By denouncing Clavijo and exposing the iniquity of a colonial official who had not complied with his duty, the Indian caciques of the pueblos involved in the uprising upheld the colonial principle of the Indians' need for protection against Creole oppression. Yet the caciques expanded the language of wretchedness, a legal status that appertained to the Indians, with the language of rusticity that presumed their inferiority and irrationality. Otherwise stated, as well as serving as arguments by the Indians' legal intermediaries in court, their combination of the categories of "rústicos" and "miserables" suggests that legal concepts acquired particular meanings through reinforcing the everyday life perception about the Indians' social inferiority.[52]

Invoking the singularity of the Indian peoples and of their position in society, defined by certain privileges that at the same time reflected their oppression, the defense crafted an argument to assert that the violence of the Indians during the insurrection was predictable. The Indian authorities and the *protectores* were able to use this aspect of the legislation that dealt with the indigenous population to mitigate the responsibility of the convicted Indians for certain crimes while at the same time demanding their right to protection as vassals of the crown. The defense's judicial appeal emphasized their "miserable" character and actively denounced the conditions of oppression that Clavijo had institutionalized in the region. By doing so they directly appealed to royal justice for mediation. Thus, a second argument laid out by the defense in the aftermath of the uprising in Túquerres was that the circumstances of the attack on the *corregidor* should be taken into account to explain the Indians' actions, thereby reducing their guilt and subsequent punishment.

With a long exposition of the abuses that as *corregidor* Clavijo had committed in the region, in the memorial the caciques used a rationale that allowed them to take to the tribunals an image of the *corregidor* as a tyrant and of the Indians as victims in need of royal protection. According to the defense, these were the circumstances of the crime: the *corregidor*

[51] AGN Colonia, Empleados Públicos del Cauca, t. 4, fol. 915; Oviedo, *Los comuneros*, 41.

[52] Cañeque clearly summarizes the logic of colonialism vis-à-vis Indians saying that the construction of Indians as wretched persons, paired with the authorities' obligation to protect them, was a "project of domination hidden behind the discourse of protection." See Cañeque, *The King's Living Image*, 192. See also Owensby, *Empire of Law*, 88.

Clavijo was a "despot, a tyrant, a tormenter of these towns." He was a selfish figure who only wanted to enrich and expand his property by excessively oppressing the Indians, dispossessing them, and "sucking up their last drop of blood and exposing them to hunger and misery." He also was accused of inventing crimes that Indians had not committed in order to attack them and to attain outcomes positive to him at trial through the use of his political power. According to the memorial, Clavijo had several times forced Indians to sell their properties below their true value. The denunciation highlighted that Clavijo always wanted what was not his and tried to get it through the use of violence and force – this was how the legitimacy of his position as a crown official was put into question.[53]

But the communities had not remained silent in the face of Clavijo's excesses. The second part of the memorial drafted by the caciques took a very different approach to the uprising. The counterpart to their argument about the rustic character of the Indians (which, in this case, essentially corroborated their miserable legal status) was the account of the continuous abuses of Clavijo. They backed this up with extensive evidence of Indian complaints against the *corregidor* that had been presented to the *audiencia* during the decades preceding the revolt, complaints in which they had claimed protection under the law as vassals of the king.

The communities' long legal battle against the *corregidor* expressed their belief in the legitimacy of the king's law and their hope in its effectiveness, which they knew and used as a moral resource.[54] The defense's document in the Túquerres case stated that long before the uprising the Indians had "cried out" to the authorities by denouncing the *corregidor*. They had complained "a thousand times" to higher authorities, without having been heard, and had had to return home to the same "tyrannical domination."[55] According to the defense, it was disheartening experiences such as these that had led the Indians to see that their "unjust" persecutor was winning and that his triumph was irreversible. But who constantly ignored the voices of the Indians? The "ministers whom the king appointed to serve for the consolation of his vassals and to

---

[53] AGN Colonia, Empleados Públicos del Cauca, t. 4, fol. 915v; Oviedo, *Los comuneros*, 42.
[54] Owensby, *Empire of Law*, 88. As Charles Walker has put it for the case of Cuzco, Indians considered abusive conduct as illegitimate and "knew that they could gain the ear of the colonial officials" by denouncing such behavior. Walker, *Smoldering Ashes*, 35.
[55] AGN Colonia, Empleados Públicos del Cauca, t. 4, fol. 916; Oviedo, *Los comuneros*, 42.

protect them from their tormenters."[56] Highlighting this, the text made clear that, in order to plead their case, the communities had previously gone through the channels of Spanish authority created to protect the Indians as vassals of the king. Because they had not been protected, and they saw themselves "dispossessed from the favor of the law," they asserted that the responsibility for the crisis in Túquerres rested with the colonial officials who had betrayed their duty when they ignored the Indians' appeals for justice. The language is very explicit: the absence of royal justice forced them to act to free themselves from the tyranny by their own hands.[57] This implied that the Indians were better subjects of the crown than was Clavijo, an agent of the crown.

To support this claim, during the juridical inquest conducted by Popayán governor Nieto, the Túquerres cacique Pablo Dias added new evidence to the case in support of the Indians. It took the form of documents from the year 1795 (that is, before the uprising) containing the declarations of witnesses who had been asked eighteen questions relative to the *corregidor*'s behavior. All of the testimony characterized Clavijo as an abusive *corregidor* who made Indians work without paying them wages and gave evidence of cases in which Indians were physically mistreated by him.[58] Those documents presented proof of earlier efforts to manage the conflict with Clavijo, thus backing up the defense's important statement about Clavijo's excesses and the lack of response from the judicial authorities to the Indians' ongoing complaints.

The caciques' defense presented in the memorial defined justice as something that should be realized in the courts, but might end up having to be realized outside the courts. In the years preceding the insurrection, the conditions to which the Indians were exposed went beyond the just and legitimate terms of government. In the years leading up to 1800, the Indians perceived the measures introduced by the Clavijo brothers, such as increasing the tithe, as abusive because they were clearly selfish. The uprising stood as a means to remedy, through violence, the ongoing

---

[56] AGN Colonia, Empleados Públicos del Cauca, t. 4, fol. 916; Oviedo, *Los comuneros*, 42. Although there is evidence of multiple complaints made by Indians against Clavijo in the years previous to the insurrection, the argument also stands as a discursive strategy used by the protector. In Walker's terms it was a commonly employed "Habsburgian notion of state and society in which authorities were understood to be guardians of Indians, which was part of a pact between crown and subjects." Walker, *Smoldering Ashes*, 79.

[57] AGN Colonia, Empleados Públicos del Cauca, t. 4, fol. 917v; Oviedo, *Los comuneros*, 45.

[58] AGN Colonia, Empleados Públicos, t. 23, fols. 937–38.

injustice and abuses, an alternative that materialized once the higher courts had failed to respond to the Indians' pleas presented through institutional royal channels.[59]

Just as the second part of the defense argued, in the decade before the insurrection the Indians actively used judicial strategies in their struggle against the *corregidor* Clavijo by submitting their complaints to the *audiencia*. It is noteworthy that a contradiction seems to emerge between, on the one hand, the evidence of Indian judicial activity, including the evidence they presented to the court in the 1790s, and, on the other hand, the emphasis placed on the ignorance and incapacity of Indians to understand juridical thinking. Such a contradiction reveals to us the tension between colonial representations of the Indian and the Indians' actual juridical and social practices.[60] In other words, although the Indians' legal activities were extensive and recurrent, as the defense in Túquerres argued and proved, in their legal strategy the caciques mobilized deep-seated Spanish prejudices based on Hispanic legal discourse about Indians. These were the same prejudices that justified the caciques' mediation in Indians' judicial representation.

To be sure, the caciques' defense of the communities was as much a denunciation of Clavijo as it was an idyllic portrait of community politics. In the acknowledgement that Indians had sought redress from the *corregidor*'s excesses by resorting to the courts, the caciques failed to mention the cacique Pablo Dias' conflicts of interest, which the Indians of Túquerres had also denounced. The caciques used the legal sphere to side with the communities and to erase their own responsibility (which had in large part entailed obstructing the law, and in some cases implied being allied with the *corregidor* at the expense of the commoners' interests). In that regard, although the caciques represented and defended the communities in court, the legal strategy of the defense was partially separated from the actual politics of the people involved in the revolt. At the turn of the nineteenth century, Indian authorities such as Dias were in fact complicit in the economic, political, and legal crises that had brought about the violence in the first place.[61]

---

[59] As Sergio Serulnikov has argued in his study of the case of Chayanta, Indians "constituted themselves as political actors in the very process of using both law and force successfully." Through these two means, Indians expressed and enforced their definition of legitimate conditions of rule and their expectation of justice from the king and the king's officials. Serulnikov, *Subverting Colonial Authority*, 5.

[60] Serulnikov, *Subverting Colonial Authority*, 138.

[61] Although the language used in the defense produced after the revolt resembles the one analyzed by Owensby for seventeenth-century Oaxaca, differences among Indians across

THE DISCOURSE OF INDIAN LOYALTY

As we have seen, the Indian defense presented evidence intended to bring to the fore the concept of an Indian that would conform with the juridical principle that affirmed the crown's duties to protect its "miserable" indigenous vassals. The defense also described the excesses and abuses of the *corregidor*, using multiple examples that pointed out Clavijo's lack of legitimacy with regard to both customary arrangements and the precepts of Hispanic justice. Finally, the defense prepared a questionnaire that allowed it to affirm, very explicitly, the Indians' deference to the government. The responses the witnesses gave made a distinction between Clavijo and the royal government. This was an astute strategy that obscured the history of tensions stemming from the *aguardiente* monopoly, the creation of the distillery, and the establishment of regulations and taxes linked to commerce in cane liquor analyzed earlier in this chapter.[62]

In February of 1801 the cacique Dias made preparations for an interrogatory to question the *corregidor*'s reputation and to demonstrate that Clavijo was an illegitimate administrator of the royal monopoly.[63] One of the questions dealt with the way in which Clavijo lived in the *aguardiente* distillery building and, specifically, if it was possible to know whether it was royal property or a private establishment. It went on to ask if the Indians had burned down Clavijo's house because they perceived him to be an illegitimate agent, without having intended to destroy royal property. This was precisely the core of the witnesses' testimony, that the *corregidor* always pursued his private interests to the detriment of the community. All of the people interrogated asserted there was no sign that the *aguardiente* distillery was royal property. Clavijo lived there with his brothers and some friends, so it had appeared to be his home. Most likely, part of the reasoning behind such a question was that it allowed the Indian defense to affirm the importance of upholding the common good, a value intimately linked to Hispanic notions of justice, one that the Indians had appropriated for use in their own legal lexicon. To be sure,

---

class lines in Túquerres make it impossible to assert that during the revolt Indians were acting uniformly against non-Indians who were "chok[ing] off the channels of legal redress so important to the king's most vulnerable vassals." Owensby, *Empire of Law*, 283.

[62] AGN Colonia, Archivo Anexo/Justicia, t. 6, fol. 377. Owensby suggests that this was a widespread Indian legal strategy. See his interesting analysis of the Oaxaca uprising in ch. 5 of *Empire of Law*, esp. 282–83.

[63] AGN Colonia, Empleados Públicos, t. 22.

by showing that Clavijo's unruly behavior was a danger to the common good, the case could be made that he was also challenging the king's authority.[64] These arguments implied that the Indian rebels were actually acting on the king's behalf, in defense of his interests, rather than against them.

Another question referred directly to the Indians' loyalty. It inquired whether there was evidence that prior to the insurrection the Indians might have spoken of the royal monopoly in a degrading manner or if, on the contrary, the Indians were known for their loyalty to the king. Pablo Reyes, a *vecino* from Túquerres, said:

The deponent is certain that since the establishment of the royal monopoly, the Indians in this town manifested no hatred whatsoever against it, but instead they have always been obedient and loving toward our monarch.[65]

To the same question, Gerardo Mera, another *vecino* from Túquerres, replied, "that he is certain that all the Indians in this town have accepted ... the royal taxes, with pleasure and great submission ... to our monarch." All the witnesses said Clavijo treated the Indians badly, and Mera specifically said, "that if the royal distillery was destroyed it was because of the mortal hatred they had for Clavijo and his family, whom they feared because they were so prejudiced." Reyes also said "that they revolted and destroyed the distillery because of the hatred they felt for the *corregidor* and not out of hatred of our King."[66]

The strength of the statements that portrayed the Indians as loyal subjects to the king increased over time. In mid-March 1801, the *protector* Martínez de Segovia interrogated other witnesses about whether the Indians had stationed a guard outside the ruins of the royal distillery on the night of the insurrection, in order to protect royal property. The declarations repeatedly affirmed that "in benefit of the royal interests" a group of Indians was delegated to look after Francisco Sarasti, the tribute collector, whom they escorted to the house of the priest where he slept that night.[67] Those declarations conveyed that the Indians, after setting the distillery on fire, wanted to protect the space and people who were linked to royal interests, and they reiterated the argument that the Indians

---

[64] On the common good, see Owensby, *Empire of Law*, 74.
[65] AGN Colonia, Empleados Públicos, t. 22, fol. 921.
[66] AGN Colonia, Empleados Públicos, t. 22, fol. 921.
[67] AGN Colonia, Empleados Públicos, t. 22, fol. 934.

had attacked the *estanco* building because it represented Clavijo and his abuses and not the royal government.

The declarations of other witnesses emphasized the complexity of the paths of participation in the revolt. Melchor Paz, an Indian, was accused of stealing items from the ruins of the distillery. He remarked that although he did try to steal a ham from the house, he was unsuccessful because a group of Indians who were standing at the door took it from him and threw it into the fire saying, "there is nothing there to be stolen, but everything should be destroyed in the fire."[68] Paz commented on other cases similar to his, where it had not been possible for individuals to rob the factory or the *corregidor*'s house.

Here it is important to recall that it was precisely the cacique Pablo Dias who had set up guards around the distillery after the insurrection to protect what was royal property.[69] Paz's declaration indicates that the cacique Dias attempted to strengthen the uprising's symbolic character by making it apparent that the Indian rebels were not driven by material gain. Dias disciplined the Indians, making sure that participation in the revolt would not include robbing and looting the distillery for personal profit. Having achieved control over the insurgents during the critical hours of the revolt, Dias made sure to include references to his prudent actions in the public record during the trial. The cacique's defense of order prevailed over the commoners' far more radical behavior. This example of disciplined behavior during the insurrection expressed the capacity for coercion of an "insurrectional political culture" that reflected a "communal ethos."[70]

At the heart of the testimony that Dias presented in 1801 was the argument that the insurrection had sought to solve a problem of extreme abuse and injustice, which implied that the Indians' violence constituted a political – not a criminal – action. In the absence of royal protection, justifiable violent action followed. Indeed, the Indian defense's narrative also rationalized the Indians' violent actions, by claiming that the target of Indian violence had been Clavijo and not the crown, thus attesting to Indian loyalty to the crown and portraying the *corregidor* as a tyrant and illegitimate holder of his post. Moreover, according to the defense, the

---

[68] "Declaración de Melchor Paz," in Oviedo, *Los Comuneros*, 122.

[69] Williams, "Acomodación, resistencia y el actuar político," 222–23.

[70] In the words of Felix Patzi, "Rebelión indígena contra la colonialidad y la transnacionalización de la economía: Triunfos y vicisitudes del movimiento indígena desde 2000 a 2003," in *Ya es otro tiempo el presente. Cuatro momentos de insurgencia indígena*, ed. Forrest Hylton et al. (Bolivia: Muela del Diablo Editores 2003), 208.

insurrection was not the action of an individual Indian. It was the collect-ive political expression of a group of Indians who were opposed to the prerogatives of royal officials in the government of the communities and who wanted to limit official abuses. In denouncing the abusive authority of the *corregidor,* the caciques, in their roles as legal intermediaries, demonstrated that the Indians' position as miserable vassals of the king entitled them to royal protection.

It is interesting to read this counternarrative of Indian respect for the "rentas reales" (royal taxes) against the evidence that indigenous people around Pasto had not been in favor of the *aguardiente* monopoly since its inception in the 1780s. Clearly, the court was a space that required the use of loyalist arguments for the Indians' defense; it was a place where they could act upon their right to make pleas and present complaints as vassals of the king. But the elaborate defense of the Indians who had killed two royal officials, the *corregidor* Francisco Clavijo and the tithe collector Atanacio Clavijo, illustrates the way monarchic discourse was employed by the caciques (and probably by the *protector,* too) to fulfill their duty to look after the community's needs and also to maintain good standing as ethnic authorities in the aftermath of the revolt.

PUNISHMENT AND NEGOTIATION

In spite of the fact that during the trials the caciques and the *protector* actively defended the violence perpetrated against the Clavijos in May 1800, the *audiencia*'s decision after two years of Governor Nieto's investi-gation was to execute three men found guilty of the killings and destruc-tion of the royal *aguardiente* distillery. Julián Carlosama, Ramón Cucas Remo, and Lorenzo Piscal were all hanged and dismembered in Pasto on November 20, 1802. Reports of their punishment were dispatched to surrounding towns, warning people about the consequences of rebellious actions against crown property and officials. In addition, the caciques of the five towns involved in the revolt – Túquerres, Guaytarilla, Sapuyes, Imués, and Chantán – were expected to be present for the execution, and their towns were held responsible for paying the crown for the damages to the *aguardiente* distillery.[71] But all of the Indians in positions of authority, that is, the caciques, were declared free of any charges of rebellion or

[71] Ortiz, *Agustín Agualongo,* 51–52.

leadership of the revolt. The legal defense had convinced the lawyers in the *audiencia* that the caciques were not responsible for the disorder.

Although in New Granada Spanish justice had been permissive and forgiving with insubordinate subjects, as in the case of the Comunero rebellion in and around the highlands of Santa Fe, in coming to a decision about the Túquerres killings, the Quito *Audiencia* followed the advice of the fiscal Juan de Roxas. According to Roxas, "it [wa]s necessary to proceed with the ultimate rigor and with no indulgence in judging the participants."[72] During the judicial deliberations, he argued that impunity would leave the door open to other insurrections. He specifically used the case of Josef Ignacio Peredo, who had been killed in the 1781 riot in Pasto when attempting to institute the *aguardiente* monopoly in the Pasto district, as an example of what can happen when culprits are not punished. Roxas argued that the mistake of having responded with mercy at that time (when no punishment had been declared against Peredo's killers) had led to the insubordination of the Indians in May 1800. According to Roxas, it was obvious that the rebels had supposed that their actions would go unpunished this time around too. From the prosecutor's perspective, then, that earlier mistake on the part of the government should be avoided by firmly applying the law and punishing those guilty in order to set an exemplary precedent.

Meant to be a respect-inspiring legacy, the *audiencia*'s exemplary punishment left relations between the local government and the communities in a state of tension. The *audiencia*'s decision to punish the culprits with death sought to claim authority for the Bourbon project of reform. Yet, on the other hand, that symbolic statement did not prevent the local government from conceding to Indian interests in the matter of the fiscal reform. From the commoners' perspective, Clavijo's abuses and his alliances with the caciques were concrete expressions of Bourbon politics. Through the rebellion the communities had demonstrated their collective strength to act upon their grievances and oppose fiscal changes. Thus, among the positive effects of the revolt in the region was the eradication of Clavijo's control and the de facto abolition of the *aguardiente* monopoly.

Within the communities change would be much slower as long as the caciques continued to control access to the law and to stand in as the legal voice of the commoners vis-à-vis the state. The caciques were trained to use, and did employ, legal language to represent their indigenous vassals

---

[72] "Acusación en forma, February 1, 1801," in Oviedo, *Los Comuneros*, 172–75.

in the political realm of justice. The Túquerres case suggests that the caciques used judicial spaces to further critiques of colonialism that were grounded in the defense of native rights. This meant that the commoners depended on the caciques for a political voice. In defending the Indians, however, the caciques were simultaneously trying to prove to colonial authorities that they were in control of the Indian commoners.[73] The Indian authorities had a special interest in ensuring recognition of their legitimacy and prestige. The Túquerres cacique Pablo Dias was particularly involved in erasing any traces of abuse that could reveal how, once caciques like himself had become compromised and beholden to Bourbon royal officials such as the *corregidor*, commoners could no longer rely on legal means to redress their grievances and were forced to turn to violence.[74]

THE POLITICS OF "INDIANNESS" IN PASTO

As a gateway to understanding Indian politics in Pasto at the turn of the nineteenth century, the Túquerres rebellion shows that Indians represented an important sector of southwestern New Granada society. Given the significance of indigenous communities in regional dynamics, they were central to Bourbon reformism as sources of revenue, and the communities represented a space where state control could be expanded over Indian people's lives. At this time, when the Bourbon Crown was especially interested in the existence of cohesive communities, the ethnic authorities of Pasto had an incentive to demonstrate that they held authority and maintained control. All of these factors were visible in the

---

[73] In her study of indigenous intellectuals in Peru, Alcira Dueñas found that "whereas educated Indian elites described themselves as capable and deserving of their autonomy and power, they portrayed their 'fellow' Indian commoners for the most part as weak and inferior and projected onto them the colonial perceptions of the state and the church vis-à-vis Indians at large as wholesale minors in need of paternalistic protection." Thus, in the Southern Andes, too, the indigenous intellectuals appropriated legal culture to emphasize, and justify, the subordination of Indian commoners to the native elites. See Dueñas, *Indians and Mestizos in the Lettered City: Reshaping Justice, Social Hierarchy, and Political Culture in Colonial Peru* (Boulder: University Press of Colorado, 2010), 202.

[74] For comparative examples of cacique litigation, see Alcira Dueñas, "Ethnic Power and Identity Formation in Mid-Colonial Andean Writing," *Colonial Latin American Review* 18, no. 3 (2009), 407–33; John Charles, "More Ladino than Necessary: Indigenous Litigants and the Language Policy Debate in Mid-Colonial Peru," *Colonial Latin American Review* 16, no. 1 (2007), 23–47; Gabriela Ramos and Yanna Yannakakis, eds., *Indigenous Intellectuals: Knowledge, Power, and Colonial Culture in Mexico and the Andes* (Durham, NC: Duke University Press, 2014).

alliances that the *corregidor* established with Indian caciques across Los Pastos, most importantly with the Túquerres cacique Pablo Dias.

The rebellion of 1800 was a critical moment indicative of the conflicts that emerged from such alliances, which the Indian commoners suffered and rejected. In the aftermath of the rebellion, the caciques had to account for the conflicts in the Indian towns and attempt to reduce their responsibility for these events. Indeed, it is clear that with the changes brought by Bourbon reformism to community governments, the caciques had ample room in which to maneuver and control the communities, given their privileged access to legal tools. For this reason, the caciques' mediation was a crucial factor in the Indians' continued claim to the validity of the legal logic about the native peoples' need for a separate authority and their entitlement to protection. This Janus-faced ideology ultimately confirmed the commoners' subjection to their caciques.

In this regard, the 1800 insurrection clearly points to the power of representation that the caciques held over the Indian commoners, or the communities, seen as a collectivity. Yet speaking for the Indians as a class reinstated their communal identity in a way that perhaps obscured their individual motives and ambitions. As individuals, Indians were vulnerable to punishment for their crimes, while the caciques' defense of the collective mobilization against the *corregidor* provided an explanation that made extensive use of legal evidence, referring to legal precedents that the caciques and the *protector* could display in court. The testimony of the Indian prisoners during the trial contained details about the location of each individual commoner at the moment of the revolt. But the commoners also tended to speak in terms of the group, which provided a political basis for their grievances and actions.

No wonder, then, that there are fewer written records of commoners' voices. But we do get glimpses of their aspirations through their actions. An obvious one comes from the recorded actions of the Indians who participated in the revolt in order to denounce and correct the Clavijos' abusive power. In the years prior to the revolt, the stories about the Indians' rejection of the *aguardiente* monopoly suggest that the Indians contested the terms of colonialism and did not accept at face value the changes imposed by the government. Moreover, throughout the centuries Indian commoners had contested the terms of "reciprocal" relations in the way they practiced them, such as when they manipulated official taxation rules to benefit their communities. This illustrates the Indians' active maneuvering to shape colonial relations.

Thus the Túquerres revolt, seen in its legal dimension, reminds us of the complexity of the Indians' double-edged legal status: as "miserable" subjects in need of protection and as political actors claiming their rights and participating in setting limits to the power of colonial officials. Indians adapted to their legal position as minors and used it consistently to advance their interests. Moreover, when seeking lenient treatment from the authorities, they also took advantage of their representation in colonial political discourse as "rustic," which amounted to their relative ignorance or irrationality.

One question that remains is how to understand the resilience of Indian corporate identity in southwestern New Granada in the midst of intracommunity conflicts. Clearly the concept of "Indianness" was a longstanding product both of colonial society within the Spanish empire and of the fact that Indian politics was able to adapt to change. In terms of the first, the legal dimension of "Indian" identity was a salient product of Spain's colonizing project in the Americas. The production of such a category could not have been possible without the active engagement of natives with the moral and legal terms of colonialism, which intersected with practical and philosophical questions about how to incorporate natives into the monarchy. For that purpose, the urban native elites swiftly sought to learn the essential elements of Spanish law and used them to articulate their political power in order to rule and simultaneously to defend the natives' interests within the institutional machinery of the Spanish "Empire of Law."[75]

From having to deal with a wide variation in native societies and cultures, one that pre-dated Spanish colonialism in the Americas, the imperial project evolved into a dialectic between Atlantic politics and local dynamics. The establishment of "Indians" as a category of vassalage clearly disavowed ethnic differences, but over time – in one of the exemplary processes of empire formation – natives throughout Spanish America adjusted to this common identity and incorporated the principles of Spain's "unwritten constitution" into the practices of their community governments. This was an ongoing negotiation. In other words, native peoples' varied engagement with the rhetoric of "Indianness" to protect their changing interests resulted in transformations in indigenous society. By the late eighteenth century, for example, native structures of authority had tended to weaken, but the institution of *cacicazgo* continued to be central to community government and politics.[76]

---

[75] Owensby, *Empire of Law*.
[76] See Grandin, *The Blood of Guatemala*, 65–67, for an analysis of a similar question about why community identity thrived while communal relations fractured in Guatemala during the same period.

Thus Indian identity was also in constant flux. Cacique authority in Pasto evolved within a tension between carrying out its role as the representative of Indian ethnic interests and rights and having to deal with the day-to-day dynamics that were transforming the ground of its legitimacy in the face of economic and political change. Toward the end of the eighteenth century, Bourbon rule aggressively redefined state–Indian relations, and the role of cacique shifted. Their contradictory interests in some cases brought commoners in confrontation with their caciques. Given the caciques' privileged position as spokesmen for the communities, implicit in political and legal cacique activity during this period was a forward-looking interest in intervening in favor of Indian legal status, something on which their position as native rulers depended. During the course of exceptional circumstances such as rebellions, caciques negotiated their rule and sought to reassure their legitimacy in the eyes of both the communities and the crown.

The fact that Indian politics was based on the discourse of royal justice is also relevant for understanding the simultaneous display of critique and loyalty embedded in late-colonial insurrections. Manifesting loyalty was crucial to the proper codification of indigenous grievances in a language appropriate for appealing to a political voice. And that was not just a formal requirement: loyalty had different connotations since the understanding of the relationship between the crown and the Indians was a changing concept. Therefore, in the specific context of Bourbon rule, although certain economic measures were potentially detrimental to the communities' well-being, the state also protected the interests of the Indian communities that had a social profile acceptable to eighteenth-century reformist visions of the empire. Indians were as much aware of those changing standards of participation as they were of the vulnerabilities of the local government. In Túquerres, this led to the revolt against the Clavijo brothers and the subsequent composition of a legal defense of the Indians involved in the revolt that highlighted both the insufficiencies of state protection for Indian vassals and the public rejection of the Clavijos for being a threat to both the common good and royal interests.

Though the revolt of 1800 did reflect deep tensions and sought to remedy the extremes of colonial oppression, it was not anticolonial in the sense of seeking to overthrow the Spanish monarchical system. Yet the timing of the insurrection has led some historians to suppose that it was a precursor of the independence movements. According to a nationalist narrative, the Indians who had rebelled against Bourbon reformism and colonial abuse would have had substantial motives to join the Creole attack against Spain during the independence wars.[77] But neither in the late colonial context nor during the independence process did Indian politics conform to those historiographic expectations. Pasto Indian ideological and military support proved crucial to the royalist government in the area, which poses a challenge to the "age of revolution" narrative that equates political action with anticolonialism in the nineteenth century.

The fact that Indian politics in Pasto was not anticolonial should not lead us to believe that Indians were static. As the recorded evidence of the Túquerres crisis suggests, Indian politics was embedded within the changes that were part of imperial reforms during the eighteenth century. The revolt expressed conflicts affecting the Indian communities in the late eighteenth century: the ongoing changes in cacique authority and tribute collection, both of which were pivotal to Indian identity. The legacy of these social antagonisms within the communities was the single most important factor in Indian politics in the nineteenth century. When the monarchy imploded ten years later, the fissure between Indian commoners and the caciques deepened, making more explicit the coexistence of contradictory notions of "Indianness" within the Indian communities.

---

[77] See, for example, Lidia Inés Muñoz, *La última insurrección indígena anticolonial* (Pasto: Imprenta Departamental, 1982); Javier Laviña, "La sublevación de Túquerres de 1800: Una revuelta antifiscal," *Boletín Americanista* 28 (1978), 189–96; Oviedo, *Los Comuneros del Sur*, 19–39.

3

The laws of slavery and the politics of freedom in late-colonial Popayán

In the decade between 1788 and 1798 authorities in Quito grew concerned about the conflicts in the mines of Marcos Cortés, a powerful man who administered five gold mines in the Telembí River, in the district of Barbacoas. The Quito *Audiencia* was alarmed about the lack of control over the slave *cuadrillas*, or work gangs, in Cortés' mines. These were said to be in "total libertinage," a premonition of danger that the *audiencia* said could affect not only Cortés himself but also the whole region. These uneasy remarks by officials in the *Audiencia* of Quito were voiced after hearing the numerous judicial cases reflecting recurrent disturbing events in the mines. The *audiencia*'s attention was initially called by infanticides committed between 1788 and 1789 by slaves in the mines of Guinulté, Boasé, and Teranguará, where five children were killed in the span of nineteen months.[1] These infanticides were expressions of the violence at the base of slavery, reproduced by the slaves themselves. They were not, however, simple barbaric or anarchic acts. The declarations of the slaves who committed the infanticides suggest that they linked their aspiration to leave the mine with the means of having access to judicial expression. Once taken prisoner and brought to court, slaves denounced their master, the miner, and the conditions inflicted on them. Slaves were acting to free themselves from the harsh situation in which they lived in Cortés' mine.

---

[1] According to the *Diccionario de Autoridades* (1732) *infanticidio* or infanticide is the homicide or violent death inflicted upon a child. The definition does not, however, specify a relation between the killer and the child, nor does it imply that the term only applies to the killing of babies. Following this eighteenth-century definition, I use the term infanticide to refer to the killings of five children, between the ages of seven months and eight years, in the Barbacoan mines.

Through actions that evinced their desperation, slaves transformed how local authorities in Barbacoas and regional powers in Quito thought of Cortés; authorities first put him under their vigilance and ultimately ordered him to follow Hispanic legislation for the treatment of slaves.[2]

These infanticides, along with a sixth attack recorded in September 1798, were crucial precedents to the investigation of "excessive cruelty" begun on December 3, 1798, against Casimiro Cortés, Marcos Cortés' son who administered the mines after his father's death in 1791.[3] The case began with the declarations of two of his slaves, Bernardo and Manuel Salvador, who fled the mine of Guinulté for the city of Barbacoas to denounce the situation of oppression their *cuadrilla* was suffering. Manuel Salvador, captain of the mine, said in his deposition to the judge that he came

to complain against his master [Casimiro Cortés], the executor (*albacea*) [of Marcos Cortés' will], representing the impiety and lack of charity with which they are treated ... the slaves in the said mine are enraged to the limit of despair and disorder because the life they live is simply impossible to suffer[,] and together they *unanimously* collaborated in a single agreement to send him to lodge the most rightful complaint in the tribunals of the city [of Barbacoas] in name of the group (*cuadrilla*).[4]

In their declarations, both Manuel and Bernardo mentioned the high risk of outbreaks of violence in the mine at that time, because the miner, Manuel Ferrín, put slaves in living and working conditions that were not acceptable. They also stated that if they did not receive proper care the killings of previous years might happen again at the mine.

The slaves' legal and political identity was shaped by their interactions with the colonial judicial system since the sixteenth century. At the end of the eighteenth century, the publication of the *Instrucción sobre la educación, trato y ocupaciones de los esclavos* in 1789, in particular, was significant for shaping ideas of justice and rights in the context of Hispanic government among the enslaved.[5] These cases in the span of

---

[2] AGN Colonia, Negros y esclavos del Cauca, t. II, doc. 13. Echeverri, "Enraged to the Limit of Despair," 403–26. Marta Herrera explains the infanticides in economic and not political terms. By considering their consequences individually, Herrera concludes that they are part of a "destructive" dynamic. Here I argue that it is possible to see a "productive" use, which, in later years and in the context of the *Instrucción*, slaves made of the process of violence. See Herrera "En un rincón de ese imperio en que no se ocultaba el sol: Colonialismo, oro y terror en Las Barbacoas. Siglo XVIII," *Anuario Colombiano de Historia Social y de la Cultura* 32 (2005), 31–50.

[3] ANE Religiosos 46.

[4] AGN Colonia, Negros y esclavos del Cauca, t. II, doc. 13, f. 770r. My emphasis.

[5] As Laurent Dubois has argued for the French Caribbean, the intellectual history of the enslaved and the political culture within slave communities were tied to the slaves'

ten years illustrate that the controversy initiated by the royal decree in 1789 is crucial for understanding Bourbon-era tensions between the government, slave owners, and slaves in their ongoing negotiation of rights and duties. The slaves' recognition of royal institutions as part of their social and political environment is clear during the period of Bourbon legal reforms, when slaves relied on the state's protection to defend themselves from abuse. Moreover, at the end of the eighteenth century, the slaves' political appeal for justice in the nonplantation mining region of Popayán combined violent and legal action.

Until recently, few scholars have explored the legal strategies employed by the mining slaves in Popayán, because of two converging commonly held notions. One dealt with the particularity of southwestern New Granada. Historians of slavery in the mines of Popayán commonly characterized the region as remote, tending to support the views of Spaniards and Creoles, who considered the western lowlands to be inhospitable. These scholars further argued that "Spanish legislation and law regarding slavery was not generally known" in the Pacific mining area.[6] Yet the region was not as isolated as these historians portrayed it, nor was it economically or politically marginal. The Province of Popayán was an intermediary in the slave trade between Cartagena and Quito and therefore central to the Caribbean-Andean economic axis of New Granada. Slaves had to be imported through the Cartagena slave markets and then sold in places as far away as Peru and Chile. Thus, the ocean was a gateway for people, goods, and information traveling legally or illegally along the Pacific coast between Panama, Guayaquil, Lima, and Chile. Indeed, as active commercial centers fully integrated into the Atlantic economy and culture, Popayán and the Pacific lowlands were not isolated from news and knowledge about transatlantic political events or changes in legislation.[7]

---

engagement with legal reasoning, which was "a key strand of political discourse" in the prerevolutionary Atlantic. Dubois, "An Enslaved Enlightenment: Rethinking the Intellectual History of the French Atlantic," *Social History* 31, no. 1 (2006), 4, 13. The links between slaves' knowledge and uses of the law and their political strategies challenges the views of scholars who ascribed the slaves' judicial appeals to their mystical perception of a protective king. See Soulodre-La France, "'Los esclavos de su Magestad,'" 183, 201.

[6] William F. Sharp, *Slavery on the Spanish Frontier: The Colombian Chocó, 1680–1820* (Norman: University of Oklahoma Press, 1976), 128. These conditions were interpreted to mean that enslaved people in the Pacific lowlands were isolated, with one scholar speaking of a situation of "incarceration." Romero, *Poblamiento y sociedad*, 106–07.

[7] Inspired on the Tannenbaum thesis that African slavery in Ibero-America was "relatively mild," Norman Meiklejohn explored the issue of whether the "humane legislation"

Aside from misconstruing the mining region as a backwater and a periphery, studies of slavery in New Granada – as in Latin America more broadly – have focused on revolts and marronage as the means to access the political interests and goals of the enslaved.[8] This was a product of the assumption that the institution of slavery legally disabled enslaved individuals, an idea which obscured the fact that slave politics cannot be properly treated as a realm separate from imperial law. Recent historiography that recaptures slaves' legal strategies aids our understanding of slaves' engagement with Spanish judicial concepts.[9]

governing slavery in Spanish America had been applied in New Granada. In spite of the problematic argument that formed the basis of Meiklejohn's research – which tended to hamper the potential of the historical question about the relationship between slave politics and the law – his work did provide crucial evidence about the specific legal culture of slavery in New Granada. Norman Meiklejohn, "The Observance of Negro Slave Legislation in Colonial Nueva Granada," (PhD diss., Columbia University, 1968), i, iii, 1; Norman Meiklejohn, "The Implementation of Slave Legislation in Eighteenth-Century New Granada," in *Slavery and Race Relations in Latin America*, ed. Robert Brent Toplin (Westport, CT: Greenwood Press, 1974), 176–203. See Tannenbaum, *Slave and Citizen*, 65, 69, 93, 100. Some works representative of the debate that followed the publication of *Slave and Citizen* are Stanley Elkins, *Slavery: A Problem in American Institutional and Intellectual Life* (Chicago, IL: University of Chicago Press, 1968); Eugene Genovese, "Materialism and Idealism in the History of Negro Slavery in the Americas," in *Slavery in the New World: A Reader in Comparative Perspectives*, ed. Laura Fones and Eugene Genovese (Englewood Cliffs, NJ: Prentice-Hall, 1969), 238–55; Marvin Harris, *Patterns of Race in the Americas* (New York: Walker and Co., 1964); Herbert Klein, *Slavery in the Americas: A Comparative Study of Virginia and Cuba* (Chicago, IL: The University of Chicago Press, 1967), 37–38. For a more recent iteration of the debate, see the forum in *Law and History Review* 22, no. 2 (2004), including articles by Alejandro de la Fuente, María Elena Díaz, and Christopher Schmidt-Nowara.

[8] Jaime Jaramillo Uribe, *Ensayos de Historia Social* (1989; Bogotá: Ediciones Uniandes, 2001); Helg, *Liberty and Equality*, 66. Moreover, massive slave rebellions like the ones that characterized plantation societies in the Caribbean and Surinam were not common in Popayán. A few rebellions and conspiracies were recorded in Chocó. See Bernardo Leal, "Pido se me ampare en mi libertad. Esclavizados, manumisos y rebeldes en el Chocó (1710–1810) bajo la lente colonial y contemporánea" (MA Thesis, Universidad Nacional de Colombia, 2006), 119–31.

[9] While studies of resistance engendered very transformative questions about the nature of slave agency, the framework has evolved to require more historically specific analyses of politics. In this regard, Walter Johnson's critique of the empty and ultimately teleological notion of "slave resistance" and his call to allow more specific, local, and diverse experiences to permeate our research and analysis exemplifies an important shift in focus. Stemming from studies of slavery in the United States, Johnson's insight has relevance to the broader Atlantic context, because the diversity of imperial practices did have an effect on the particular political options available to the enslaved. Walter Johnson, "On Agency," *Journal of Social History* 37, no. 1 (2003), 118. See also David Scott, *Conscripts of Modernity: The Tragedy of the Colonial Enlightenment* (Durham, NC: Duke

This means that slave protests and politics were closely entwined with changing legal contexts.[10]

As in other places across Spanish America, in the Pacific lowlands mining region of Popayán, slaves had practical knowledge of their rights within slavery. By the eighteenth century, enslaved people had found commonalities that bridged their ethnic differences and acquired cultural knowledge crucial for their survival. They positioned themselves as interlocutors with the church, the crown, and their masters by developing the ability to claim certain rights.[11] Further, legal principles were essential for and shaped the politics of freedom in Popayán, mediating the slaves' access to manumission and freed people's prospects for civil recognition and rights.[12] In this sense, Spanish law and legal institutions were part of the shared repertoire of knowledge and skills of slaves and free people of African origin and descent in Popayán, particularly given the practical – indeed, foundational – importance of those limited rights granted and acquired over time that helped slave communities across the region to endure. The growing maroon and legally free black populations in

University Press, 2004), 122–23, who speaks about the "metaphysical assumption of a slave Will to Freedom" that characterizes the historiography of slavery.

[10] Within the British social history approach to slave resistance, Anthony McFarlane wrote "*Cimarrones* and *Palenques*: Runaways and Resistance in Colonial Colombia," *Slavery and Abolition* 6, no. 3 (1985), 131–51, mentioning cases of slaves who ran away to appear in court to seek colonial justice. A practical approach to slaves' uses of the law can be found in Sherwin Bryant, "Enslaved Rebels, Fugitives, and Litigants: The Resistance Continuum in Colonial Quito," *Colonial Latin American Review* 13, no. 1 (2004), 8; Alejandro de la Fuente, "'Su único derecho': los esclavos y la ley," *Revista Debate y Perspectivas* 4 (2004), 7–21; Díaz, *The Virgin, the King*, chs. 2 and 11; Brian P. Owensby, "How Juana and Leonor Won Their Freedom: Litigation and Liberty in Seventeenth-Century Mexico," *Hispanic American Historical Review* 85, no. 1 (2005), 39–80; Javier Villa-Flores, *Dangerous Speech: A Social History of Blasphemy in Colonial Mexico* (Tucson: University of Arizona Press, 2006); Michelle McKinley, "Fractional Freedoms: Slavery, Legal Activism, and Ecclesiastical Courts in Colonial Lima, 1593–1689," *Law and History Review* 28, no. 3 (2010), 749–90; Manuel Barcia, "Fighting with the Enemy's Weapons: The Usage of the Colonial Legal Framework by Nineteenth-Century Cuban Slaves," *Atlantic Studies* 3, no. 2 (2006), 159–81; Gloria García, *La esclavitud desde la esclavitud* (La Habana: Editorial de Ciencias Sociales, 2003).

[11] Herman L. Bennett, *Africans in Colonial Mexico: Absolutism, Christianity, and Afro-Creole Consciousness, 1570–1640* (Bloomington: Indiana University Press, 2003), 13; John Thornton, *Africa and Africans in the Making of the Atlantic World, 1400–1800* (1992; New York: Cambridge University Press, 1998), chs. 3 and 4.

[12] The ability of enslaved people to attain freedom through self-purchase in the Pacific lowlands of Popayán contrasts with Frank Proctor's recent assessment of manumission in New Spain. See Frank T. Proctor III, *"Damned Notions of Liberty": Slavery, Culture, and Power in Colonial Mexico, 1640–1769* (Albuquerque: University of New Mexico Press, 2010), 183.

Popayán also sought recognition as communities; thus imperial law was as important to negotiating freedom as it was to shaping rights within slavery.

THE LAWS OF SLAVERY

Slavery was regulated in *Las Siete Partidas* of Alfonso X, which dates from the thirteenth century; they were based on early Roman legal codes and were promulgated well before the Spanish came to America.[13] After the sixteenth century, the Laws of the Indies (*Leyes de Indias*) sporadically dealt with particular issues addressing the new forms of African slavery, but in general it was Castilian law (the *Partidas*) that regulated this widespread and quotidian aspect of the Hispanic world. Although within the framework of the *Partidas* slaves were treated as chattel or property, an important provision in Title XXI, Law VI, of *Partida* IV noted that slaves could make complaints before a judge if their owners mistreated them.[14] In 1680, a collection of laws, the *Recopilación de las leyes de Indias*, compiled decrees specifically related to the Indies. Even in this reinterpretation, the fundamental rights of slaves continued to be based on the ancient legal precepts for the protection of slaves laid out in the *Partidas*, which gave them access to the courts.

Slaves had some knowledge of the rights regulated by positive law, and such rights had important practical consequences because slaves used them both in their daily lives and when they found themselves in court.[15] It is notable that the flexible character of Hispanic law and the casuistic basis by means of which each legislative dispute was evaluated allowed slaves to present their complaints in contexts and at critical moments when jurisdictional tensions between their masters and the institutions of the church or the state could benefit them. During these legal proceedings,

---

[13] Robin Blackburn, *The Making of New World Slavery: From the Baroque to the Modern, 1942–1800* (New York: Verso, 1997), 51; Jose Andrés-Gallego, *La esclavitud en la América española* (Madrid: Ediciones Encuentro y Fundación Ignacio Larramendi, 2005); Manuel Lucena Salmoral, *Sangre sobre piel negra: La esclavitud quiteña en el contexto del reformismo borbónico* (Quito: Centro Cultural Afroecuatoriano, Ediciones Abya-Yala, Colección Mundo Afro 1. 1994); Abelardo Levaggi, "La condición jurídical del esclavo en la época hispánica," *Revista de Historia del Derecho* 1 (1973), 83–175.

[14] Robert Burns, ed., *Las Siete Partidas*, trans. Samuel Parsons Scott, vol. 4 (Philadelphia: University of Pennsylvania Press, 2001), 979.

[15] De la Fuente, "Su único derecho," 15.

the notaries, lawyers, and judges involved became crucial mediators of the slaves' search for justice.[16]

In the eighteenth century, the Bourbon administration's interest in creating more specific legislation dealing with slavery was linked to their desire to mimic the economic success of French Caribbean plantations.[17] This ambition required importing greater numbers of African slaves to boost production capacity. In 1789 King Charles IV published a royal decree giving incentives to Spanish and foreign traffickers of slaves by granting them free trade rights for two years. In 1791 the policy was extended for another six years, with the main goal being to promote agricultural production in the Spanish Caribbean.[18] Assuming that the French had gained their success not only because of the technical and economic development of colonies such as Saint-Domingue, the Spanish court put together a legislative proposal to back the economic experiment with new mechanisms of control. Indeed, in order to guarantee positive results and to promote ongoing investment, plantation slavery required a wide array of provisions to carefully handle massive numbers of slaves.

When drafting the codes they imagined necessary to accompany the Bourbon project, the Spanish monarchy drew on the example of the French *Code Noir* of 1685, which had been in operation for over a century.[19] After two different sets of *Ordenanzas* were put into effect in Santo Domingo, the *Instrucción sobre la educación, trato y ocupaciones de los esclavos* was printed in Madrid as a decree issued in Aranjuez on May 31, 1789. It was then immediately sent to all of the *audiencias* in

---

[16] Bennett, *Africans in Colonial Mexico*, 130; Victor Tau Anzoategui, *Casuismo y Sistema* (Buenos Aires: Instituto de Investigaciones de Historia del Derecho, 1992); Benton, *Law and Colonial Cultures*, 33. A similar argument about the importance of locality in the functioning of legal institutions in the post-Revolutionary U.S. South can be found in Laura F. Edwards, "Enslaved Women and the Law: Paradoxes of Subordination in the Post-Revolutionary Carolinas," *Slavery and Abolition* 26, no. 2 (2005), 309. For the importance of lawyers and judges as mediators in the legal politics of slaves, see Premo, "An Equity Against the Law."

[17] Lucena Salmoral, *Sangre sobre piel negra*.

[18] The *Real Cédula* dated November 24, 1791, extended for six years the concession of freedom of trade of Africans given in 1789, and it now included the viceroyalties of Santa Fe and Buenos Aires, in addition to the *Capitanía General de Caracas*, and the islands of Santo Domingo, Cuba, and Puerto Rico. The decree was justified in this way: "This commerce is supported to promote agriculture." Archivo General de Indias (hereinafter AGI) Santafe 549, doc. without number, fol. 3.

[19] In Louisiana the *Code Noir* was in effect between 1724 and 1800. Manuel Lucena Salmoral, *Los códigos negros de la América española* (Ediciones Unesco/Universidad de Alcalá, 1996); Lucena, *Sangre sobre piel negra*; Andrés-Gallego, *La esclavitud en la América*.

America.[20] This *Instrucción* incorporated relevant concepts from Hispanic laws on slavery from the time of the *Partidas*, from Roman Law, and from the elements borrowed from the *Code Noir*. For example, chapter 2 of the *Instrucción* spoke of the need to give good treatment to slaves, in particular by feeding and dressing them well, and reasserted providing Christian education as an essential duty of slave owners.

Within the absolutist project, the *Instrucción* also had specific innovative goals. Along with the government's explicit objective of exercising control over slavery, the *Instrucción* dictated that agents of the crown should directly watch over the treatment slave owners gave to their slaves. Just as in the French colonies the application of the *Code Noir* heightened a conflict of sovereignties between metropolitan and local governments, in the Spanish context, several of the central elements of the *Instrucción* were perceived as intrusive.[21] Slave owners manifested generalized discomfort about the loosening of discipline that chapters 8 and 19 pointed to, especially the reduction of the number of lashes (twenty-five) that could be applied as punishment and the stipulation they only use "a soft instrument." Slave owners also protested the idea that an external authority, "the justices of cities and villages" (chapters 2 and 3), would decide the needs and obligations of slaves. Clearly these new decrees took the overall management of the plantations, mines, and haciendas away from the hands of the owners and placed it within a mediated governing arrangement that would not only slow decision making but also take a great deal of discretion away from the slaveholders.

This legislation reflected the Bourbon crown's growing desire to guarantee state participation in and responsibility for the economic endeavors that it was promoting. So even though, as in the French case a century earlier, the purpose of the law was to create conditions for the better long-term functioning of an enslaved labor force, the planters and miners did not seem to back the crown's interest in sharing sovereignty over these spaces.[22] Among the many and diverse complaints the legislation aroused in America, we

---

[20] Two codes were drafted in Santo Domingo, where the transformation was being planned and directed according to local interests. One, the *Código de Santo Domingo*, was published in 1768 and the other in 1784. Lucena Salmoral, *Los códigos negros*, 49. The *Instrucción* can be found in Richard Konetzke, *Colección de documentos para la formación social de Hispanoamérica 1493–1810*, III:2 (Madrid: CSIC, 1962), 643–52.

[21] An interesting discussion of the political issues at stake in French colonial contexts in relation to slave law can be found in Malick W. Ghachem, *The Old Regime and the Haitian Revolution* (New York: Cambridge University Press, 2012), especially chapter 1.

[22] Ghachem, *The Old Regime and the Haitian Revolution*, 121.

know that in Barbacoas, the southwestern center of gold mining in the Viceroyalty of New Granada, the region's slave-owning elite promptly manifested strong negative reactions.[23] The menace inspired by Bourbon ideals and the slave owners' powerful reaction against the Spanish monarchy resulted in the demise of the *Instrucción* in all of the American territories. On March 17, 1794, a resolution of the Council of the Indies suspended the "effects" of the *Instrucción*. It made reference to the complaints of the municipal councils of Caracas, Havana, Louisiana, Santo Domingo, and Santa Fe, all of which had been sent to the Council for a final judgment.[24]

The main threat was founded, the Council suggested, on the slaves' potential interpretation of the *Instrucción*. It was argued that *negros* were likely to interpret the text with "bad intelligence." Indeed, all this concern should be understood in the context of the ongoing uprisings in the French colony of Saint-Domingue, a clear example of the risks that slaves represented if not controlled properly. On these grounds, specific reference was made to the "*negros* [of the French colonies] who began a revolution, linked to the general disorder and the mistaken ideas of its unhappy metropolis, and [our] municipalities fear that in its imitation, their slaves could also be disturbed."[25] For all these reasons, Council members determined that the *Instrucción* was not, and would not be, necessary to guarantee the good treatment of slaves.

However, as we will see in the following, events in the gold mines of Marcos Cortés in Barbacoas during the decade following the initial publication of the *Instrucción* show that, even after the law was revoked, slaves made appeals based on its provisions, and it continued to influence royal officials in Quito and Barbacoas when they had to deal with slave complaints.

SLAVERY AND FREEDOM IN LATE EIGHTEENTH-CENTURY POPAYÁN

Based on slave labor since the seventeenth century, gold mining in New Granada's Pacific lowlands had evolved into the most productive sector of Popayán's economy. Gold extraction in Popayán was done by enslaved

---

[23] In February 1792 Diego Antonio Nieto, governor of Popayán, presented an appeal document (*representación*) to the Viceroy in Santa Fe in which he explored the risks of applying the decree in his jurisdiction. See Echeverri, "Enraged to the Limit of Despair," 414.

[24] "Consulta del consejo de las Indias sobre el reglamento expedido en 31 de mayo de 1789 para la mejor educación, buen trato y ocupación de los negros esclavos de América." Published in Konetzke, *Colección de documentos*, 726–32.

[25] Ibid.

Africans who lived in the Pacific lowlands, a humid forest territory that runs parallel to the Pacific coast and where the rivers carry gold. Thus, just as the Brazilian expansion toward Minas Gerais to the west of Rio de Janeiro was driven by the search for gold, the Spanish colonization of western New Granada was fueled by an interest in exploiting these rivers. Originally, the city of Barbacoas was the most important mining center in this region, which included the Telembí and Patía rivers. During the eighteenth century, pacification of the local Indians took place in the northern region, and the mining frontier expanded to include the mines along the rivers Micay, Timbiquí, Saija, Naya, Cajambre, Raposo, and Yurumanguí, with population centers in the towns of Guapi, Micay, and Iscuandé.[26]

Significant particularities of the slave trade along the Pacific coast and in adjoining inland areas of South America marked the region's demographic profile. Colombian historiography has highlighted the progressive natural growth and emergence of an Afro-Creole population in Popayán, which guaranteed that the slave economy would continue to thrive. The evidence we have suggests that in Popayán and along the Pacific littoral, arrivals of Africans had become less common by the eighteenth century. This fact has to be put into perspective when considering the important differences between Caribbean and Brazilian slavery, on the one hand, and mainland slavery, on the other hand, starting in the seventeenth century with the sugar boom. With the rise in cane production, and with plantation slavery as a corollary, slave trafficking changed its focus and began to privilege the Antillean context to the detriment of the mining economies of the South American continent. To counter this phenomenon, slave owners in New Granada stimulated a demographic policy to increase birth rates among the slave population. This was certainly true in Popayán, where the profitability of the mining economy was achieved by maintaining an internal market of creole (American-born) slaves.[27]

---

[26] See Bryant, "Finding Gold, Forming Slavery," 110; McFarlane, *Colombia*, ch. 3; Sharp, *Slavery in the Spanish Frontier*; West, *Colonial Placer Mining*; Caroline Williams, *Between Resistance and Adaptation: Indigenous Peoples and the Colonisation of the Chocó, 1510–1753* (Liverpool: Liverpool University Press, 2004).

[27] Jaime Jaramillo Uribe and Pablo Rodríguez argue that, by the end of the eighteenth century, Popayán had a "self-sufficient" internal market that did not depend on new imports. See Jaramillo Uribe, *Ensayos*; Pablo Rodríguez, "Aspectos del comercio y la vida de los esclavos: Popayán, 1780–1850," *Boletín de Antropología* 23 (Universidad de Antioquia, Medellín, 1990), 13. See also Colmenares, *Historia económica y social*, II, ch. 3; Sharp, *Slavery on the Spanish Frontier*, 124; David Chandler, "Health and Slavery in Colonial Colombia" (Dissertations in European Economic History. New York: Arno Press, 1981). Further research on the illegal arrival of Africans in Popayán throughout the

We lack a precise count of the slave population for this region like the ones available for Brazil, the Caribbean, or the United States, and the persistence of contraband makes official data insufficient, adding to the difficulties of outlining the demographic profile of the enslaved population in southwestern New Granada. Moreover, like most places in Spanish America, except for the Caribbean, the slave trade between Africa and Popayán was long-lasting, beginning in the sixteenth century. This means that the provenance of the captives varied throughout the centuries, generating deeply mixed and heterogeneous communities of people of African origin and descent.[28] However, as scholars of the African diaspora have shown, even when the enslaved population was ethnically and linguistically diverse, Africans never arrived at their destinations entirely isolated from one another. Across the Americas, Africans formed polycultural communities that articulated the multiple African legacies with the social and cultural dynamics that marked their lives in the context of slavery.[29] Likewise, in the cities and towns of Popayán, as well as in the Pacific lowlands and other rural areas in the province, enslaved and free people of African origin and descent formed communities.

The Pacific gold mines were generally run by on-site managers while the mine owners lived in the cities. Gold was extracted mainly through placer mining: the workers built pools and canals to get access to the river waters and to have places to wash the gravel and search for gold. To perform that type of labor, the managers organized the enslaved in

---

eighteenth century is needed, but we can assume that the continuous threats of flight and high mortality rates also contributed to a contraband market for slave imports.

[28] Luz Adriana Maya, *Brujería y reconstrucción de identidades entre los africanos y sus descendientes en la Nueva Granada, siglo XVII* (Bogotá: Ministerio de Cultura, 2005), 193, 194–95; Williams, *Between Resistance and Adaptation*, 160–62; Kris Lane, "Gone Platinum: Contraband and Chemistry in Eighteenth-Century Colombia," *Colonial Latin American Review* 20, no. 1 (2011), 61, 63–64; Alex Borucki, David Eltis, and David Wheat, "Atlantic History and the Slave Trade to Spanish America," *The American Historical Review* 120, no. 2 (2015), 433–61.

[29] Philip Morgan, "The Cultural Implications of the Atlantic Slave Trade: African Regional Origins, American Destinations and New World Developments," *Slavery and Abolition* 18, no. 1 (1997): 122–45; Herman Bennett, *Colonial Blackness: A History of Afro-Mexico* (Bloomington: Indiana University Press, 2010), 61; Gwendolyn Midlo Hall, *Slavery and African Ethnicities in the Americas: Restoring the Links* (Chapel Hill: University of North Carolina Press, 2005); Thornton, *Africa and Africans*, 197. The term "polycultural" is from Gomez, *Exchanging*, 10. Jane Landers speaks of "cross-cultural accommodations that made both resistance and accommodation into the Spanish world possible." See Landers, *"Cimarrón and Citizen*," 119.

cuadrillas or slave gangs, with sizes that ranged from ten to a hundred people, depending on the capacity of the mine owner to invest in slaves.[30]

Thus, while the ethnic component of the *cuadrillas* varied significantly and was related to shifts in the slave trade between the sixteenth and eighteenth centuries, as social structures, *cuadrillas* were the foundation for the emergence, over time, of communities composed of enslaved Africans and their descendants.[31] The most important role in the *cuadrilla* was that of captain, which was performed by a male slave who was especially trusted by the mine owner and the manager. The captains' duties included collecting gold on a weekly basis, administering the provision of food, and disciplining the group. In the Pacific lowlands, captains were slaves who spoke Spanish and could help other enslaved laborers learn the language. Especially in the late eighteenth century, they were generally slaves who had been born in the region and could be mediators in the socialization of any captives arriving from Africa. As in other places across the Atlantic world where African slavery prevailed, in the Pacific lowlands that leading role had a special impact on the growth of a society among the enslaved.[32] Notably, the structures of authority that were established around labor shaped the political channels within slave communities, giving the captains responsibilities vis-à-vis other slaves as well.

In Popayán many slaves found routes to freedom: some took advantage of the legal right to self-purchase and bought their freedom by participating in the cash economy that gold mining offered. Free life flourished in the Pacific lowlands, in the semiurban areas around the haciendas near Popayán and Cali and in other frontier territories across the province, where fugitives formed maroon settlements. In all these cases, which resembled patterns found in other Spanish American settings, free blacks looked for ways to acquire land, sought economic and

---

[30] Not all of the slaves in a *cuadrilla* were employed in mining since there were other tasks, such as growing food, that also had to be done by slaves. And many times *cuadrillas* included indigenous people from nearby, who could be hired to build houses for the slaves, using their knowledge of local materials and techniques. See West, *Colonial Placer Mining*, 86.

[31] See Del Castillo, *La llave de las Indias*, 289–96; Borucki, Eltis, and Wheat, "Atlantic History and the Slave Trade to Spanish America." Colmenares, *Historia económica y social*, II, 49–52; Romero, *Poblamiento y Sociedad*, ch. 3.

[32] Romero, *Poblamiento y Sociedad*, 74; George Reid Andrews, *Afro-Latin America, 1800–2000* (Oxford: Oxford University Press, 2004), 14. For Chocó, see Sharp, *Slavery on the Spanish Frontier*, 132; Eric Werner Cantor, *Ni aniquilados, ni vencidos: Los Emberá y la gente negra del Atrato bajo el dominio español. Siglo XVIII* (Bogotá: Instituto Colombiano de Antropología e Historia, 2000), 161.

political inclusion, and, in the process, shaped the emergence of colonial society in Popayán.[33]

In the context of the Pacific mines, one comparable to the situation in the Brazilian gold-mining region of Minas Gerais, the rise of a significant free population was facilitated by the fact that the enslaved had the possibility of mining independently during their free time and thus amassing the gold necessary for purchasing their freedom. It was also very common for family members who were already free, or even still enslaved, to purchase the freedom of someone in the family. On the other hand, the difficulties of sustaining the enslaved population in the Pacific region became an incentive for mine and slave owners to allow their slaves to work for themselves for certain periods of time in exchange for a settled sum that the slave paid to the manager. This practice was beneficial for the mine and slave owners who were then not responsible for the slaves' subsistence during these periods of time, while also giving the enslaved a margin of profit that they could then use toward self-purchase.[34]

Slaves also sought freedom extralegally, and flight was typical across the Pacific lowlands. Some escaped slaves traveled as far as the cities while others formed maroon communities, or *palenques*, along the margins of the mining region.[35] The most important *palenque* that was formed within the jurisdiction of Popayán was located east of the Pacific mines, in the Patía River Valley. This *palenque* was significant because it evolved into a town that, as we will see in later chapters, was central to the royalist defense of Popayán during the wars of independence. Runaways settled in

---

[33] This trend was analyzed by Herbert Klein and Ben Vinson III, *African Slavery in Latin America and the Caribbean*, 2nd ed. (New York: Oxford University Press, 2007), ch. 10; and Herbert Klein, "The African American Experience in Comparative Perspective: The Current Question of the Debate," in *Africans to Spanish America*, ed. Bryant et al., 206–22.

[34] Orián Jiménez, "La conquista del estómago: Viandas, vituallas y ración negra. Siglos XVII–XVIII," in *Geografía Humana de Colombia*, ed. Maya, 232, 235. This practice was common in the cities as well. For Buenos Aires in the eighteenth century, see Johnson, *Workshop of Revolution*, 42–43. For Minas Gerais and its free population of African descent, see Laird Bergad, *Slavery and the Demographic and Economic History of Minas Gerais, Brazil, 1720–1888* (New York: Cambridge University Press, 1999), 103, 115; Mariana Dantas, *Black Townsmen: Urban Slavery and Freedom in the Eighteenth-Century Americas* (New York: Palgrave MacMillan, 2008), chs. 5 and 6; Kathleen Higgins, *"Licentious Liberty" in a Brazilian Gold-Mining Region: Slavery, Gender, and Social Control in Eighteenth-Century Sabará, Minas Gerais* (University Park: Pennsylvania State University Press, 1999); Herbert Klein and Francisco Vidal Luna, *Slavery in Brazil* (New York: Cambridge University Press, 2010), ch. 9.

[35] McFarlane, *Cimarrones* and *Palenques*, 136–45.

a place called "El Castigo," taking advantage of the frontier area around the Patía River Valley north of Pasto and east of Barbacoas, which was not colonized by the Spanish until the 1720s. By then, when exploration of the area and land titling began to take place, the *palenque* was populated mostly by renegade whites and runaway slaves from the mines of Barbacoas and Iscuandé and from the haciendas in the Cauca River Valley. During this period Spanish colonial officials unsuccessfully attempted to conquer or destroy this *palenque*.[36]

Yet, as occurred in the neighboring *palenques* of Esmeraldas and Baudó, and in other runaway communities in colonial contexts, the inhabitants of El Castigo sought the presence of representatives of the church in the territory.[37] Between 1731 and 1732, they sent three messengers to the city of Pasto to request that a priest visit Nachao and Nalgua, two towns they had established, each of which had built a church within its boundaries. This request exposed their strategy of aligning their community with the Catholic precepts that were central to social and political life in Popayán.[38]

The Quito *Audiencia* tried to take advantage of the maroons' interest in the church, attempting to co-opt the *palenque* into establishing civil government in the area in exchange for a pardon from the state. The runaway community resisted the *audiencia*'s attempt to include them within its jurisdiction (*reducción*) but succeeded in securing a permanent priest for their settlement. Moreover, the Popayán municipal council conceded their right to name two people from the *palenque* to "administer justice in the name of His Majesty to all the individuals who currently are congregated in those towns," with the condition that they not admit any new runaways to the community, detaining these fugitives and

---

[36] In January 1729 the Quito *Audiencia* sent a group of soldiers to capture the runaways. See Bryant, *Rivers of Gold*. This case contrasts with those studied by Stuart Schwartz in Brazil, where the communities of fugitives were attacked and destroyed by representatives of the Portuguese government. See Schwartz, "Rethinking Palmares: Slave Resistance in Colonial Brazil," in *Slaves, Peasants, and Rebels: Reconsidering Brazilian Slavery* (Chicago: University of Illinois Press, 1992), 103–36.

[37] Orián Jiménez, *El Chocó: un paraíso del demonio. Nóvita, Citará y El Baudó, siglo XVIII.* (Medellín: Editorial Universidad de Antioquia, 2004), 52; Rocío Rueda, *Zambaje y autonomía: Historia de la gente negra de la provincia de Esmeraldas, siglos XVI-XVIII* (Quito: Ediciones Abya-Yala, 2001); Patrick J. Carroll, "Mandinga: The Evolution of a Mexican Runaway Slave Community, 1735–1827," *Comparative Studies in Society and History* 19, no. 4 (1977), 492–93; Richard Price, *Maroon Societies: Rebel Slave Communities in the Americas* (1973; Baltimore, MD: Johns Hopkins University Press, 1996).

[38] Francisco Zuluaga, *Guerrilla y sociedad en el Patía: Una relación entre el clientelismo político y la insurgencia social* (Cali: Universidad del Valle, 1993), 34–35.

informing the Popayán authorities of their presence.[39] Thus, the maroons in Patía not only used religion for the purpose of community building; they also seem to have preferred to establish a relationship with the church rather than with the civil authorities.

In the Hispanic context, the crown promoted a corporate organization of society, and thus collective rights could be secured to a greater extent than individual rights. This constituted an incentive for enslaved and free blacks to link their legal strategies to the colonial corporate logic. Indeed, the politics of freedom and community building among free people of African descent pivoted around the struggle to gain recognition, acquire political rights, and overcome the racist assumptions of the larger society. During the eighteenth century, those goals coincided with the crown's interest in integrating the maroons into society – to "reduce" the communities of runaways to legitimate towns – by negotiating and extending certain concessions in exchange for their professed loyalty. The integration of free blacks into civil life in this and other contexts reminds us that maroon communities were forged within the colonial world and not outside of it.[40]

In Popayán, free and enslaved people of African origin and descent upheld justice through their underlying pattern of engagement with imperial legal institutions. This was visible in instances when, as in Patía, maroons negotiated their conditions of integration into colonial society. It was also clear when the enslaved sought freedom legally and, once freed, formed communities that sought the crown's protection. Yet legal freedom was not the only goal of the enslaved. As we will see next, in the Pacific mining region, garnering greater rights within the institution of slavery may have been their most realistic goal.

INFANTICIDE AND SLAVES' STRATEGIES FOR JUSTICE IN BARBACOAS

The gold mines in the province of Barbacoas were known by the slaves to be the harshest of places to be an enslaved worker, especially those located in the southwestern region of Popayán and the area north of

---

[39] Zuluaga, *Guerrilla y sociedad en el Patía*, 40.

[40] Beatty-Medina, "Between the Cross and the Sword"; Landers, "*Cimarrón* and Citizen," 111–45; Yuko Miki, "Fleeing into Slavery: The Insurgent Geographies of Brazilian Quilombolas (Maroons), 1880–1881," *The Americas* 64, no. 4 (2012), 511; Carolyn Fick, *The Making of Haiti: The Saint Domingue Revolution from Below* (Knoxville: University of Tennessee, 1990), 57.

Quito. Mine work was hard in the hot and humid forest regions, but, in addition to these two difficulties, Barbacoas had a negative reputation among slaves for the lack of "justice" that prevailed in this area. María Mazo, an enslaved woman from Quito, had rebelled when faced with the possibility of being taken to work in Barbacoas and later testified that she feared going to those mines because there "*negros* are tyrannized."[41] In 1799, another two slaves who were pleading to leave Barbacoas spoke of their "martyrdom" in the mines, where they were constantly punished with excessive cruelty. They further commented that it was useless to seek assistance from the authorities because in Barbacoas "deaths and other crimes are constant without any justice being done."[42]

In such circumstances, however, enslaved individuals searched for extreme means to denounce their conditions. On May 9, 1788, Mónica de la Cruz, one of Marcos Cortés' slaves who worked at the Teranguará mine, was interrogated for killing her own daughter, María Merced (aged four to five), with a machete. Mónica said that when she killed her daughter, she cried out loud, "This is what the captain gets for all the violence he inflicted on me!" Mónica had been sick and had not received any special treatment for her illness. Instead, she had been forced to work by the mine captain (another slave), who had threatened to take her with him to the mine "even if it should be by dragging [her] forcefully." Choosing to recall the words she cried out when attacking her child, and thus explicitly blaming the captain for her mistreatment, Mónica stood strong in her desire to speak of the circumstances that had influenced her actions. Moreover, Mónica said she knew her conduct would have consequences, perhaps even that of her own death, yet she "decided it was better to die in the hands of justice" than to bear the violence of the captain.[43]

Three months later on July 16, also in the Teranguará mine, Marcelino Pirio killed Juana, a small seven-month-old black girl. The day before Marcelino, a black enslaved worker, had been punished with twenty-five lashes and put in the stocks for not following the captain's order to go to the mine of Boasé to confess to a priest, along with the other slaves in the group. In the trial Marcelino said "he realized he was going to suffer [in the stocks], so he would be better off going to suffer in jail one year[,] and

[41] Quoted in Bernard Lavallé, "'Aquella ignomiosa herida que se hizo a la humanidad': El cuestionamiento de la esclavitud en Quito a finales de la época colonial," *Procesos* 6 (1994), 43.
[42] Ibid.   [43] AGN Colonia, Negros y esclavos del Cauca, t. II, doc. 13, fols. 788r–789v.

only with this reflection" he killed the little girl.[44] The interrogators did not ask Marcelino whether or not the precedent of Mónica killing her daughter had influenced his "reflection." Nevertheless, like Mónica, in court he did not plead for forgiveness but instead justified his action, adamantly denouncing the manager. Punishment in the mines was clearly worse than what Marcelino expected to get from the authorities in Barbacoas.

The following year, on March 15, 1789, Gregorio, another slave in the Teranguará mine, was brought to the city of Barbacoas, along with the body of Anselmo, an eight-year-old boy he had killed by giving him a "serious and cruel wound in the stomach."[45] During the interrogation Gregorio was asked why he decided to "hurt a little innocent creature" in such a way. Gregorio replied he had originally hoped to kill the manager, but because this was not possible, he had instead killed the black boy to escape from the mine. This confession of his intention to kill the manager suggests that Gregorio was not pleading for forgiveness, stating that his actions had been misled or irrational; instead, he gave testimony of how killing the child was the displaced result of his enraged desperation.

From the record of the trial it is not possible to know what the final decision was regarding Gregorio's case. However, another document reveals that both Marcelino and Gregorio escaped from jail during their times of imprisonment. Mariano Landázuri, the mayor of Barbacoas, writing as the representative of Marcos Cortés, his father-in-law, emphasized that great care should be taken to punish the slaves for their crimes as a way to prevent the risk of a "bad example infesting" other mines in the province.[46] Landázuri pointed out the "no fewer than three homicides committed by one black woman and two black men" owned by Marcos Cortés and stated that "until today those convicts remain unpunished, and worse, they escaped from prison and probably are going around seducing others to a general tragedy." To strengthen his point, Landázuri wrote about the fear that this situation had provoked among mine and slave owners like himself, who were now afraid to be around the slaves. The mine managers, said the mayor, had begun speaking of leaving their jobs in the mines because of their terror of the insubordinate slaves. For slave owners such as Landázuri and Marcos Cortés, this was a problem that required a strong reaction from colonial officials. Justice in the form of court-regulated punishments, such as imprisonment or death, would be

[44] AGN Colonia, Negros y esclavos del Cauca, t. II, doc. 13, fol. 793v.
[45] Ibid., fols. 796r–799r.   [46] Ibid., fol. 799r.

the only means to make a statement to slaves in the mines about the singular consequences such criminal behavior would have. Landázuri wrote the petition while bringing another slave to court for committing an infanticide, this time in the mine of Boasé. The culprit was Domingo Gómez, an enslaved *zambo*,[47] who on July 8, 1789, had killed a seven-year-old enslaved boy named Anastasio.

The prosecutor (*fiscal*) recounted the tragic events in his legal advice to the court, saying Domingo had confessed that, "fed up with slavery and the rigor with which the manager mistreated him ... he decided to act upon the idea that by killing he would be freed from being Cortés' slave, and with the desire to better die hanged" he committed the crime.[48] In response to the call of the anxious slave owners in Barbacoas, the court did just what the prosecutor recommended. They sentenced Domingo to be "shot with a firearm before being hanged," and his right hand to be cut off and exhibited in the mine, for everyone there to see.[49] However, the prosecutor had also added a note that implicated the mine owners as well. He wrote:

Notice will be given to the *Real Audiencia* about this case and the many other homicides executed by the slaves of the mines of Cortés on their children and *compañeros*, which are *attributed to the rigor with which the mine manager treats them* and he is from now on *ordered to treat them gently*, as he should, giving them the necessary food and care, and in the opposite case he will be punished.[50]

The legal motion following this fourth infanticide case is significant because, while the case was resolved with a strong verdict that sentenced Domingo to death, the judges in Barbacoas signaled that the recurrent killings merited the attention of a higher authority, the *Real Audiencia* in Quito, to investigate the excessive cruelty of the manager and owner. They also commanded managers and slaveholders to treat their slaves well, threatening them with punishment if evidence proved that they had acted with cruelty or disregard for their slaves' well-being.

After evaluating the case, on February 27, 1790, the *audiencia* responded, calling attention to the depositions of slaves arrested for previous murders of children, who all "equally express that they killed the little creatures to rid themselves of servitude." The *audiencia* asserted that the harsh circumstances influencing the slaves' desperate actions must be real, because in the *cuadrillas* of other mine owners, infanticides were not

---

[47] *Zambo* is a term that denotes racial mixture between an African descendant and an Indian.
[48] Ibid., fol. 802r.   [49] Ibid., fol. 802v.   [50] Ibid., fol. 802r. Emphasis added.

common. Additionally, the *asesor* (advisor) from the *audiencia* asked the justices of the district of Barbacoas to investigate and take measures regarding the treatment of the slaves in the mines of Cortés. For the *audiencia* the solution was not simply to punish the slaves, as mine owners had recommended. The lawyers in Quito added, "The laws and royal ordinances should be observed, taking into account the last royal decree published on the issue," referring for the first time to the *Instrucción*, which had been published the previous year in late May. The remark on the relevance of the new legislation to the infanticide cases reveals that the *Instrucción* had already been received in Quito. It also suggests that the new regulation had been incorporated into a framework for the treatment and control of slaves and was being applied as an essential element of the policies coming from the peninsula in the context of the Bourbon reforms.[51]

The last of the five initial infanticides in the mines of Cortés took place two months later in the mine of Guinulté on November 10, 1789. Francisco, who had killed a little boy called Adriano, explained that he "killed him when he found himself tired of slavery and the torments of hunger and whippings that he continuously suffered, and he realized that by these means he would free himself from slavery, preferring to die [by being] hanged."[52] Francisco confessed he had planned to kill the manager, José Guzmán, but, after thinking it over that night, he realized that it would be impossible and instead killed the black boy. Francisco's case was complicated because of his age. During the first interrogation, he said he was younger than twenty-five but older than fourteen, which led the lawyers to argue in his favor, saying he was still too young to be sentenced to death. If he had been a minor, the punishment for this crime would have only been imprisonment for ten years in Cartagena, a victory for Francisco, who would then have been away from Barbacoas, alive and, in his view, safer. Other documents dating from 1791 show that further inquiries into Francisco's age led to the conclusion that he was in fact twenty at the time of the crime, and thus he was condemned to death.[53] However, it seems significant that a note was added to the verdict telling

---

[51] Ibid., fol. 802r–v. This counters Sharp's statement that Spanish legislation was not known in Pacific New Granada. See Sharp, *Slavery on the Spanish Frontier*, ch. 8.

[52] Ibid., fol. 804r. In the original: "lo mató de verse aburrido de la esclavitud y martirios de hambre y azotes, que continuamente padece, y haciéndose cargo que por este medio se libraría de la esclavitud, apeteciéndole más el morir ahorcado."

[53] ANE Popayán 227. Verifying ages of criminals was an important part of any criminal case, as the benefits of legal minority were jealously guarded by court officials. See Premo, *Children of the Father King*, 115–19.

the mayor in Barbacoas to be alert and prevent "slaves [from being] punished inhumanely and cruelly in the mines."[54]

Through the act of murder, these five slaves living in the Telembí River mining camps had proved the manager's excessive cruelty, demonstrating to royal officials that their recourse to the murder of innocent children only reflected the extremes to which they had been driven. These infanticides are historical evidence of how the slaves combined their actions with judicial arguments in order to denounce abuse. The infanticides were the means whereby slaves denounced mistreatment and "excessive cruelty." On one level, the actions of the slaves pointed directly to the problem they were desperately reacting to: a violation of their rights. On another level, these depositions made by slaves in court addressed issues of mistreatment and injustice in the mines, and as a result, the manager and owner were held accountable for these irregular situations.[55] The slaves also explicitly argued that they preferred to face royal justice than to have to put up with the arbitrary violence imposed on them in the mines. Their appeal to justice in this context was clearly a strategy that enslaved individuals were exercising, which speaks of their conscious request for protection under the law. The slaves in Barbacoas were challenging the physical violence and imprisonment that were essential elements in the slave owners' and mine managers' domination of their workers. Cortés' slaves sought access to the courts, which traditionally in Hispanic law represented the possibility of speaking about mistreatment and abuse. That enslaved individuals such as Mónica, Gregorio, and Francisco committed infanticide to gain access to the court – one of the basic rights of slaves according to the law – suggests they were in extreme desperation. Instead of ending their suffering by taking their own lives, they opted for a violent and dramatic act to catalyze the justices' attention. While knowing that they could be punished with death, these slaves thought the city court was a place where they would be heard and protected, even if they had been responsible for committing crimes.[56]

---

[54] AGN Colonia, Negros y esclavos del Cauca, t. II, doc. 13, fol. 805v.

[55] The sources in question do not reveal any suspicion at the time that African religious practice was involved. We have ruled out this possibility for these reasons: two of the killings were committed in public, and in all the cases, according to court testimony, immediately after the attacks the killers were taken to the city to be jailed and judged. Additionally, the bodies of the dead children were taken to a forensic doctor for examination. For a contrasting case in which slaves confessed to ritual practices involving child killings, see Maya, *Brujería y reconstrucción de identidades*, 697–705.

[56] Javier Villa-Flores' work is laudable for bringing to our attention the controversial risks that slaves took in extreme situations of abuse and desperation. As his work on the case of colonial Mexico shows, the slaves' transgression of Christian speech regulations through

There was a difference between the first murder, carried out by Mónica, and the four other murders, carried out by male slaves unrelated to their victims. The first infanticide, which a mother committed in despair, was framed by the authorities in the legal terms that guaranteed women special rights. Although the local officials in Barbacoas initially studied the case and sentenced Mónica to death, her defender at this point intervened in favor of Mónica, arguing that the sentence should be lessened. The appeal was to the law that stated punishment should be "softer for a weak woman and for those who are rustic (*rústicos*) [and not] wise." It was added that, particularly in this case, the penalty should be reduced because it would cause Mónica sufficient pain to "recognize her mistake and mourn bitterly the death of her little daughter." With these arguments taken into consideration, the verdict was changed, and Mónica was sold to another owner as a way of expelling her from the province.[57] Although this decision was certainly beneficial to her owner, who was reimbursed for the loss of his slave (instead of having to bear the economic loss that would have occurred if she had been punished with death), it was also a successful outcome for Mónica, who was liberated from the terrible conditions of slavery in Cortés' domain.

Mónica's case might have spurred other slaves to consider that committing murder would not necessarily result in severe punishment, but perhaps could instead lead to their escape from the mines. It is therefore noteworthy that, seemingly following her example, it was young men who committed the rest of the killings. Each and every one of them expressed a history of conflict with the manager or captain who had recently punished him severely. They also mentioned having considered killing the children in a moment of desperation and vulnerability, reacting to their own inability to kill the manager (an adult) or to flee the mine. Yet the courts did not express similar sympathy in the four men's cases, and

blasphemy was a strategic action that aimed at creating further conflict, removing the slave from the authority of the owner, and placing him or her under the authority of the Holy Office – then turned into a "protective shield" – where he or she might be treated with mercy. See Villa-Flores, *Dangerous Speech*, ch. 5, esp. 131.

[57] ANE Popayán 221. In her study of infanticide and abortion in nineteenth-century Argentina, Kristin Ruggiero found that straightforward sympathy for women who killed their offspring led to the pardoning of the accused in cases of both abortion and infanticide. See Ruggiero, "Not Guilty: Abortion and Infanticide in Nineteenth-Century Argentina," in *Reconstructing Criminality in Latin America*, ed. Carlos A. Aguirre and Robert Buffington (Wilmington, DE: Jaguar Books, 2000), 149–66.

their treatment in court was ultimately less lenient than what Mónica received.[58]

In spite of these differences along gender lines in motive and treatment, the development of the cases studied here shows that both sides of the criminal proceedings – defense and prosecution – were persuaded by the slaves' arguments about cruelty. Even if in some cases a harsh punishment was given to dissuade other slaves from committing infanticide, the documents that circulated among the authorities in the courts stated the need for control over slaveholders such as Cortés. In this sense, the actions of the slaves had consequences for the relations between slave owners and judicial authorities. Further, the repeated horrendous consequences of the desperation of these slaves left a clear mark on the history of slavery in Barbacoas.[59] Between 1788 and 1789 officials became increasingly interested in the conditions of the slaves working in the mines of Cortés; the effect of court records documenting the persistent infanticides permeated the different levels of the judicial institutions, establishing precedents for actions to protect slaves.[60]

SLAVES AND THE LAW "IN FAVOR OF SERVITUDE"

Although legal strategies had informed the local customary practices of slaves since Habsburg times, historians have argued that the possibility of allying with the Bourbon regime shortened the distance between the slaves and the crown, the ultimate source of justice.[61] In the cases studied

---

[58] Another interesting example of the privileges women enjoyed in the legal proceedings surrounding infanticide is Jane Landers, "'In Consideration of Her Enormous Crime': Rape and Infanticide in Spanish St. Augustine," in *Sex and Race in the Early South*, ed. Catherine Clinton and Michele Gillespie (Oxford: Oxford University Press, 1997), 205–17.

[59] In the case of the antebellum U.S. South as studied by Walter Johnson, slaves forced their "critique of slavery ... into the public record." Johnson, *Soul by Soul: Life Inside the Antebellum Slave Market* (Cambridge, MA, and London, England: Harvard University Press, 1999), 30.

[60] I agree with de la Fuente and Bryant, who note that the slaves' appearances in court were precedents that determined local and regional slaves' and officials' legal practices over time. See de la Fuente, "Slaves and the Creation of Legal Rights in Cuba," 664; Bryant, "Enslaved Rebels," 21.

[61] Hermes Tovar, *De una chispa se forma una hoguera: Esclavitud, insubordinación y liberación* (Tunja: Nuevas Lecturas en Historia, 1992); see María Eugenia Chaves, *Honor y Libertad: Discursos y recursos en la estrategia de libertad de una mujer esclava (Guayaquil a fines del período colonial)* (Gothenburg: University of Gothenburg, 2001), which offers a poststructuralist analysis that emphasizes the role of eighteenth-century legal discourse, which allowed slaves to use the strategy of the enunciation of

here, slaves in a frontier town such as Barbacoas appealed to their right to denounce their mistreatment, even if they did so through the extreme means of infanticide to gain the attention of the courts. A sixth attack on an enslaved infant in 1798 and the declaration of the perpetrator in court illuminate the ways in which a changing legislative context conditioned the slaves' arguments as well as their struggle for an amelioration of their condition. In addition to the issue of excessive violence, the sixth case included protests about the problems of lack of food and poor care to which slaves in Cortés' mines were subjected. Three months later, two slaves from Guinulté ran away to Barbacoas and lodged a complaint against Casimiro Cortés, Marcos Cortés' son, who administered the mines after his father's death in 1791, providing detailed declarations about the problems with food, clothing, and spiritual care in the mines. A transformation is visible between the two 1798 cases as regards the particular tactics the slaves used to pose their claims: the second case suggests a strategic intention to gain support from the courts, thus placing judicial action above violent action. Most importantly, the collective form that this judicial action took, with the two slaves arriving in Barbacoas as "representatives" of their group, is evidence that even though the gold mines kept the slaves in harsh conditions, this did not eliminate their capacity to engage in the communal assertion of their rights.[62]

On September 1, 1798, nine years after the last infanticide, a similar crime was denounced in the court of Barbacoas. Manuel Santa Fe, a black slave in the mine of Guinulté, had wounded a boy named Pablo, eight to ten years of age, striking him several times with an ax. In this interrogation questions were asked about the motives and circumstances of the crime. One question was whether or not Manuel Santa Fe wanted to kill the boy when he attacked him. Santa Fe said he had wanted to "rid him of the sorrow, [and] he considered it best that the little boy did not suffer as he did, and be free [of slavery] once and for all now when he was young." He added that by wounding Pablo,

---

their rights in court. As Sherwin Bryant notes in his study of black litigants who "employed tactics that foreshadowed those used by litigants in the late colonial period," historians have interpreted the evidence of the increase in the number of cases found in the archives to mean that the use of the courts by slaves heightened in this period. Bryant rightly argues that this should not lead us to think that slaves did not pursue legal strategies prior to the eighteenth century. See Bryant, "Enslaved Rebels," 7–46.

[62] Previous interpretations of the situation in Barbacoas link isolation with a consequent incapacity of the slaves in the gold mines to build a community. See Romero, *Poblamiento y sociedad*, 107–14.

the little boy would leave the mine with his family, along with [Manuel Santa Fe] himself; [And] *perhaps with the novelty of the attack they might all be taken to the city and be sold* ... tired as they were of the tyranny of the manager Manuel Ferrín and the great needs they have in the mine.[63]

Manuel Santa Fe spoke of those needs, for example, about the food they were given, six plantains a day and a pound of meat a week, which was not much, especially considering that they were expected to work very hard. The court asked whether or not those conditions were also imposed on other *cuadrillas* in Cortés' mines; his answer was that indeed it was widely known that conditions in Cortés' mines were especially harsh. In this declaration Santa Fe stated two points that were central to showing why he had proceeded as he had. On a practical level, perhaps knowing that a decade earlier Mónica had been sold to a different owner, Manuel Santa Fe thought that he could obtain a similar outcome from a violent act, one which might also yield benefits for the child and his mother. On a symbolic level, his remark about "freeing" the child is very significant. In his declaration Santa Fe spoke directly to the issue of liberation. This is an aspect of infanticide among slaves that has been widely documented in the historiography and one that can be applied to the intentions behind the violent actions of some slaves in Barbacoas.[64]

The two slaves who fled the mine on December 3 to denounce Cortés' "excessive cruelty" were clearly reacting to the crime recently committed by Santa Fe. They traveled to Barbacoas to make accusations against Cortés and to prevent further damage to their *cuadrilla*. Manuel Salvador said they had come to denounce

the sad state in which they are found, lacking spiritual and temporal care, and [to say] they did not want to remedy it as they did in the past in the said mine, *killing one another under the influence of desperation* from the bad life they are given, [but] denouncing everything they go through and suffer so that *opportune remedy will be taken to prevent the decisive upheaval that the master's excessive violence can cause.*[65]

With this choice of action, they not only rejected violence as a response to their critical situation but also chose to defend their community while still living within the confines of slavery, and not in marronage. Due to the

---

[63] Ibid., fol. 808v. Emphasis added.
[64] Various references can be found in Renée Soulodre-La France, "Por el amor! Child Killing in Colonial Nueva Granada," *Slavery and Abolition* 23, no. 1 (2002), 87–100; see also Johnson, *Soul by Soul*, 33.
[65] AGN Colonia, Negros y esclavos del Cauca, t. II, doc. 13, fol. 770r. Emphasis added.

harshness of mining slavery, many slaves fled, mostly looking to join the *palenque* of El Castigo near the Patía River just north of Barbacoas. Although this would have been an option for escaping slavery and the mine for good, the two slaves, Manuel Salvador and Bernardo, were seeking justice and developed a tactic from which they and their *cuadrilla* would all benefit.[66] The purpose of their accusation was to seek justice by representing the group before the colonial officials. Bernardo highlighted this point in his declaration. When confronted with Manuel Salvador's testimony, he said:

All that the captain Manuel Salvador has declared is true and known, and subject to desperation, the rest of *the* negros *with one voice asked him to come to lodge a complaint* and ask for justice from the *señor* lieutenant, and then he accompanied him, but not having even a canoe in which to travel, they were exposed to the great risk of drowning, riding on a couple of sticks of corkwood because they had no canoe and in fact they were at great risk of losing their lives in the horrible current called *cabezas* in which even the most secure canoes are in danger, but God freed them equally [from this and] other river currents, until they were able to set foot in this city and *present themselves before the face of justice.*[67]

Both slaves sought the crown's protection, which was what justice meant to them, in order to be granted their rights within the institution of slavery. Their aim was not necessarily to become free, which is what they would have hoped for if they had left the mine to live a life of marronage. Claims to the collective protection and rights of the *cuadrilla* were at the heart of the politically strategic action of these slaves, the *capitán* and his partner. To pursue this plan, first and foremost they based their strategy on the history of the previous violent actions of slaves in the mines, and although they now rejected such violence, they used potential violence as a threat.[68] It is significant that the captain was in charge of denouncing the injustice, which reflects the political structure and dynamics within the *cuadrilla*.

Although, in their recorded testimonies, the two enslaved men did not explicitly mention knowledge of the *Instrucción*, this *cuadrilla*'s framing of their appeal for justice as "unanimous" was a strategic use of language in the complaint. Among the slaves, information circulated that was

---

[66] As in the cases described by McFarlane, "rather than a flight *from* the justice of slave owners or the state, this was a flight *to* justice." See McFarlane, "*Cimarrones* and *Palenques*," 148.

[67] AGN Colonia, Negros y esclavos del Cauca, t. II, doc. 13, fol. 774v. Emphasis added.

[68] As Bryant states, "At times the enslaved verbalized the threat of violence," since slaves' suits were "almost always connected to – and enhanced by – other, more radical forms of resistance employed by the enslaved." See Bryant, "Enslaved Rebels," 10–11.

related, more or less directly, to what was regulated in positive law. It was not necessary for them to have had direct contact with the written legal texts because oral channels were fundamental for this transfer of knowledge.[69] A look at the detailed court declarations of the two slaves provides positive evidence of this process. Manuel Salvador opened his remarks by saying that at the mine they "lacked spiritual and temporal care."[70] The emphasis on the spiritual needs of the slaves resonates with laws mandating the proper education of slaves through religious agents (chapter 1 of the *Instrucción*). In the long statement he made against Cortés, Manuel again referred to religion, saying that twenty-five months had passed without them being able to confess to a priest, nor they had attended mass or "heard the word of God." Furthermore, in two years no priest had visited the mine to bring oils for baptizing the children, and for this reason, "at least twenty [children] can be counted lacking such an essential requirement for Christians."[71]

Both Manuel Salvador and Bernardo also carefully described the rations of food they were given, which they said were not enough: barely six plantains for women and eight for men, plus one pound of meat per week, and a woman's portion was not different if she had children. However, the biggest problem seemed to lie in the arbitrariness of its distribution, which depended on the mood of the manager. Additionally, according to Manuel Salvador, the manager had instituted a "law" which said that if the slaves did not sweat while they worked, they would be punished. This had led to a series of constant violent punishments; one example was the *negra* Dominga who "was left with a scar below her back for the rest of her life."[72]

According to the *Instrucción*, another crucial duty of slave owners was to provide clothing (chapter 2). The slaves declared that in addition to being almost naked, their master had prohibited them from making purchases in the city, forcing them to buy the goods they needed from him at the prices he wanted. A final, striking point the slaves made was that women were forced to carry weights "disproportionate" to their strength while engaged in their work, and in some cases pregnant women had even given birth to their children prematurely, trying to comply with

---

[69] de la Fuente, "Su único derecho," 15. An interesting study of the relation of slaves to written culture can be found in José Ramón Jouve Martín, *Esclavos de la ciudad letrada: Esclavitud, escritura y colonialismo en Lima (1650–1700)*, (Lima: Instituto de Estudios Peruanos, 2005), ch. 4.

[70] AGN Colonia, Negros y esclavos del Cauca, t. II, doc. 13, fol. 771v.

[71] Ibid., fols. 772v–773r.   [72] Ibid., fols. 771v–772r.

the rules of the manager. This violated chapter 3 of the *Instrucción,* which said that the daily work of slaves should be determined "*in proportion* to their ages [and] strength."

Aside from these claims, the slaves announced the risk of a resurgence of infanticides, speaking also of the possibility of an insurrection. In this way, they made conscious juridical and political use of the history of the infanticides, adding them to their petitions for good treatment. This threat was effective in generating pressure because it drew on widespread fears of slave uprisings in the context of the massive slave rebellion in Saint-Domingue, which had been ongoing since 1791. Once the slaves had made their complaints and demands in a tribunal, antagonism between the slave owners and the colonial authorities grew. In a document dated December 24, 1798, prosecutors from Quito's *Audiencia* wrote: "Given the interest of this province in the particular calm of each part, it follows that all of it is at risk in the turbulence of each one."[73] This recognition meant that the danger of a crisis breaking out in Cortés' mine could have repercussions in the entire mining region, a risk that had to be properly addressed. Consequently, the colonial authorities perceived the situation as described by the enslaved black men as evidence of a violation of the laws stipulated by the crown, giving way to an official request in the case against Casimiro Cortés that he follow the norms promulgated by the crown in earlier years. The lawyers wrote:

The *negros* have complained about the excesses with which they are treated, so this should be remedied opportunely following the royal *cédula* [decree] given in Aranjuez on May 31, 1789, *in favor of servitude (servidumbre)*[.] Equally the Royal *Audiencia* of the district has ordered its judges to watch the good behavior and treatment of [Cortés] with the *cuadrillas* in his care given the repeated deaths executed in this mine in [past] years and the present caused by the rage and desperation in which they suffer.[74]

The royal officials in Quito were interested in protecting slaves from extreme abuse, mainly as a means of preventing disorders.[75] Yet the *audiencia* officers mentioned the *cédula* as legislation that was given "in favor of servitude," and they sided with the slaves, making reference to the tension between the precepts in the legislation and Cortés' reluctance to cooperate with these procedures. Their appeal to the decree of May 31 and their use of language in favor of the slaves and against Cortés

---

[73] Ibid., fol. 785r.   [74] Ibid., fol. 785r. Emphasis added.
[75] French slave law was fundamentally oriented toward reducing the risk of slave insurrections and marronage. Ghachem, *The Old Regime and the Haitian Revolution.*

became an opportunity for the latter to cunningly reject their recommendation and disregard the validity of the legislative framework. In his reply Cortés said, "You leave no doubt about the royal *cédula* of His Majesty related to servitude, but up to now I have not seen it publicized as it should have been for it to be observed."[76] In addition, following his repudiation of his duty to apply the law, Cortés transformed the terms of the problem, establishing that as the defendant in the trial, he expected to receive more information about the case, asking to have all of the declarations of his slaves sent to him. He also sent numerous excuses to prevent the other slaves called to testify from appearing in court in Barbacoas, complicating the development of the case. Given his reluctance to cooperate, the lawyers of the *audiencia* decided to include copies of all the cases of infanticide in Cortés' file, those from the years 1788–89 and the more recent attack on a child in 1798. They used the evidence to illustrate the risk of heightened violence to which the slaves Manuel and Bernardo had called attention, and as proof of the excessive cruelty with which Cortés and the managers treated his *cuadrillas*. In a decree dated January 11, 1799, the local court asserted its role as magistrates who were "[put] in charge by the government [in the *audiencia*] to aid and protect slaves in their condition as miserable people, to hear their pleas and resolve them, and all the more so under these circumstances."[77]

The recurrence of infanticides in the gold mines in Barbacoas had become a visible sign of the agitation generated by Cortés' cruel dominion over his slaves and of the potential "disorder" that his mistreatment of them might provoke. These judicial cases of infanticide reveal that through their violent actions, the slaves sought to utilize the colonial courts to denounce the injustices committed against them, while at the same time injuring the reputation of the master and the manager. A decade later, the slaves' understanding of their rights under the new law enabled them to make practical use of their collective identity, a remarkable development given the adverse circumstances of slavery in Barbacoas. While in the years previous to the publication of the decree, the slaves had resorted to violence – in 1788 and 1789 when infanticides were a radical strategy for attracting juridical attention – after 1789 their

---

[76] AGN Colonia, Negros y esclavos del Cauca, t. II, doc. 13, fol. 786r.

[77] Ibid., fols. 786v–787v. This antagonism between masters and judges on the matter of uses of the Carolinian *Instrucción* proves that, in Premo's words, "the edict ... had more of an edifying effect on litigants and judges than on masters." Premo, *Children of the Father King*, 217.

awareness of the new juridical framework was an incentive for them to reject self-destructive violence and express their complaints and pleas in court, as a means of seeking the crown's protection of their communal rights.

COMMUNITY AND AUTHORITY IN SLAVERY AND FREEDOM

In the nonplantation context of Popayán, slaves carved out spaces in which to build their lives and sought an understanding of the institutional avenues that could be useful for shaping the world according to their interests. Moreover, communities prospered among people of African descent. This was a process that entailed a deep knowledge of the environment, and across Popayán slaves and free blacks were active colonizers of the territory. Some of these communities were framed within slavery while others were created in freedom, either illegally, by those who had escaped slavery, or legally, by freed people.

Slavery was a relationship mediated by the king's authority and power; the legal rights of slaves as well as those of freed people were circumscribed in imperial institutional contexts. During Bourbon rule the change in legislation that regulated slavery was a turning point that affected the slaves' perception of new ways to claim protection and request freedom. Those changes in the eighteenth century symbolized pathways for enslaved people to expand their communities by relying on the crown's protection. Moreover, as in the case of Manuel Salvador and Bernardo in Barbacoas, collective priorities gained relevance over individual ones. Like the slave communities, those of free blacks relied on the law and other Hispanic political precepts as tools for seeking integration into the colonial economy and society. In Popayán, towns of free blacks (including maroon settlements) sought the church's and the crown's recognition of their right to own land and to enjoy self-rule. This process was facilitated by the interest of Bourbon officials in ensuring the loyalty of the region's inhabitants and expanding their control of de facto colonized areas.

We still lack knowledge about the organization, lives, and views of the men and women who formed communities while living in slavery. Yet it seems clear that the structures common to the enslaved communities were linked to privileges derived from the slave regime and from the access that gang captains had to relevant legal knowledge, which they used to represent the groups' interests. The captain was in a privileged position to mediate between the power and authority of the mine owner and the manager and the rest of the members of the *cuadrilla*, on their behalf. His access to relevant information regarding economic conditions and political events would have also given him the possibility of exercising control over the enslaved by selectively handling the diffusion of this information. For that reason, the captains developed a significant role as representatives of the *cuadrilla* or community in legal settings. That privilege was a corollary of their authority being recognized by the other members of the group as much as by the colonial officials.

Despite the paucity of documentation about the internal workings of these communities, it is possible to imagine that the decision to approach the legal authorities at certain times was strongly influenced by the captain's own interests. It is also possible that, ultimately, the captains did not necessarily represent the views of the entire *cuadrilla*, as conflicts within the group were also common – such as we saw with Mónica in Barbacoas, who complained about the captain's treatment of her and blamed him for her recourse to violence. The captains were accountable to the manager for other people's behavior, which, in some situations, must have given them incentives to exercise their authority at the expense of the others' interests.[78]

For these reasons, the figure of the captain was marked by an ambiguity similar to the role of the cacique among indigenous people. On the one hand, slave owners picked the most Hispanized slaves and relied on them to help educate the recent arrivals about their duties and to impart discipline. On the other hand, slave captains were entrusted by the community to represent them, and this was a crucial aspect of the intersection between the conditions of enslavement and the rise of figures of authority among the slaves. This aspect of community politics continued to be important during the independence wars.

Although there were few rebellions in the Pacific mining region, in the cases studied here we have seen that violence was also part of community life. Violence permeated the communities in abusive conditions at the mine or in conflicts among the enslaved. Significantly, the resolution of these conflicts in the legal arena linked the slaves' actions to the local and imperial contexts that regulated their political voice. This means that the conflicts that sprang up between owners and slaves or among the slaves were defined by larger legal contexts that simultaneously gave meaning to the social position of individuals and framed their sense of justice in terms of rights and duties. In the Hispanic context, the imperial legal framework

---

[78] AGN Colonia, Negros y esclavos del Cauca, t. II, doc. 13, fols. 788r–789v.

functioned in tandem with the notion that the king was the administrator of justice. This was clear to enslaved Africans, who appreciated the power embedded in the figure of the king and claimed protection by invoking him. Far from being a "mystification," this was a practical understanding of the monarchical political structure of which enslaved people were a part.

4

Negotiating loyalty

Royalism and liberalism among Pasto Indian communities (1809–1819)

In 1809, a local junta formed in Quito under the leadership of Juan Pío Montúfar, Marqués de Selva Alegre, put forth a proposal to Popayán that was not in the least an attempt to subvert the monarchic order. In principle, it was a project to "safeguard our independence and the rights of our religion against the common enemy [i.e., Napoleon]."[1] But as was the case in all of Spanish America, the fear of a French invasion that so dominated the imagination of elites as well as of the Indians and people of African descent in southwestern New Granada fueled internal strife. Common languages and goals, based on loyalist premises, were displayed to validate a confrontation between historic rivals. Popayán Governor Miguel Tacón reacted to Quito's invitation by publicizing the danger of what he feared could become a definite alliance between the Quito junta and the French. To confront that danger, he organized an army, calling upon all town residents (vecinos), local Indians, and slaves to support him.[2] As the Quito nobles received news of Popayán's reluctance to join their plans, they too armed a militia, which they sent to pacify the north with a similar argument: that the reluctance of Popayán to join their junta expressed seditious plans and pro-French interests.[3]

Although there was no evidence that either city had an actual alliance with the French, the way both Quito and Popayán seized on and publicized

[1] John Carter Brown Library (hereinafter JCBL) Archivo Restrepo, Fondo I Vol 25, fol. 54.
[2] Santiago Arroyo y Valencia, "Memoria para la historia de la revolución de Popayán," *Revista Popayán* 5 (1910), 486.
[3] Manuel María Borrero, *La revolución quiteña, 1809–1812* (Quito: Editorial Espejo, 1962), 63–89.

rumors of such links with France dramatically signaled the severity of the monarchy's current crisis to local actors in Spanish America. For New Granadans these dangers included the whole Spanish empire's vulnerability to takeover by the French expansion, a takeover further associated with images of French revolutionary culture, a culture that had been officially repelled in Hispanic circles up to that date.[4] Second, news in the Americas about the Napoleonic invasion of the peninsula was conflated with stories involving profanities committed against religious authorities and of violent repression of the people. The abduction of the Spanish king, publicized in Pasto by late September 1808, included an official call to the defense of the sovereignty of the king throughout his territory.[5]

In a proclamation dated August 21, 1809, and made public throughout cities in the province, Tacón blamed Quiteños for being "rebels, imitators of the French, who aim to violate our religion, unsettle our rights, and commit the disorders that sedition can bring." Tacón appointed Gregorio Angulo, a Creole, as Captain of the Militias in Barbacoas to carry out the much-needed resistance to Quito's invasion – he was given one hundred men from the local militias and the few bullets and gunpowder they could round up. On August 30, Tacón ordered that all privately owned weapons be delivered to the municipal council and that all the men who enlisted be properly trained, so as to prepare them for the "glorious and sacred cause" they were to defend. Each man was offered a salary and was covered by the legal privileges of military jurisdiction.[6] Posts for the defense of the province were established in the Indian towns of Túquerres, Sapuyes, and Guaytarilla.[7]

The militias organized in Quito and Popayán faced each other in territory that, as Governor Tacón noted, was "especially interesting."[8] The Andean region of Pasto was home to numerous Indian communities, encompassing eighty Indian towns. To the west, bordering the Pacific Ocean, were the important mines of Barbacoas and Iscuandé, a region

---

[4] Gerardo León Guerrero, *Pasto en la guerra de independencia, 1809–1824* (Bogotá: Tecnoimpresores, 1994), 25. Responses to the French Revolution in Spanish America were mixed. The fear of disorder as implied by references to Haiti inspired largely negative expectations. See, Guerra, *Modernidad e Independencias*, 36–42; Renán Silva, *Prensa y Revolución a finales del Siglo XVIII* (Bogotá: Banco de la República, 1988), 130–46. For Peru, see Claudia Rosas, "El miedo a la revolución: Rumores y temores desatados por la Revolución Francesa en el Perú 1790–1800," in *El miedo en el Perú: Siglos XVI al XX*, ed. Claudia Rosas (Lima: Universidad Católica, 2005), 139–68.

[5] Guerrero, *Pasto en la guerra*, 18.

[6] Archivo Histórico Nacional (hereinafter AHN) Consejos 21674, exp. 1, doc. 5.

[7] Guerrero, *Pasto en la guerra*, 26.   [8] AHN Consejos 21674, exp. 1, doc. 5.

characterized by the large numbers of slave gangs that worked at gold extraction. The region encompassed between Pasto, the Patía River valley (midway between the mountains and the coast), and Barbacoas was the main gold-mining area, one important reason why it was a contested space, one fought over by the powers in Quito and Popayán.

On September 28, 1809, armies of Indians from the district of Quito attacked the district of Los Pastos, located at the southernmost point of the province of Popayán. Governor Tacón had reached Pasto with his army to prevent the invasion of these troops. Captured in combat by Tacón in the town of Funes in late 1809 and subsequently transferred to Cumbal, Antonio Espinoza Ibarra explained Quito's motives for attacking Pasto. He said that his army had come to "contain the *vecinos* in Pasto who wanted to rise in revolt."[9] This suggests that at this point Quito's soldiers saw themselves as exercising legitimate authority and assumed that their role was to suppress the rebellion that they saw forming in the province of Popayán. Espinoza Ibarra announced that Quito military leader Manuel Zambrano had arrived in the plaza of Tulcán to address the soldiers who had been summoned by proclamation, and Zambrano put a white flag displaying the king's arms on a saber and asked each one to swear to the defense of religion, Fernando VII, and the fatherland. Once this demonstration of loyalty was concluded, he exhorted the priest José Riofrio, who was the chaplain of honor in Quito's junta, to encourage the men to be brave.[10] Around six hundred and thirty men armed with rifles and spears and led by Zambrano and Riofrio were ordered to fall on Pasto with the strategic goal of preventing the diversion of vital goods into the gold mines of Barbacoas. For Quito, gaining control of the mining lowlands was the main objective that guided it in the early period of the confrontation.

The Pasto authorities interrogated another prisoner, eighteen-year-old Miguel Carrasco, who had enlisted in the village of Ibarra, about why he was serving the interests of an "illegitimate" junta, such as the one led by Quito. He replied that "he did not know who the authors of the turbulence were, and when he heard a junta was established in Quito, he thought it was a regular meeting of the municipal council."[11] Carrasco supposed the purpose of the meeting was to commemorate the coronation of "His Majesty," but was not aware of its actual purpose, given that "he was a man who was always away, on and dedicated to his *chacra* (plot of land) and rarely visited the village." This man (possibly an Indian) argued

---

[9] JCBL Archivo Restrepo, Fondo I Vol 25, fol. 113.   [10] Ibid.
[11] JCBL Archivo Restrepo, Fondo I, Vol. 25, fol. 115.

that he was ignorant of the reasons why he was being called to military action and stated that he did not support it but rather "found the expedition repugnant."[12] Carrasco and others added that they found the dangers from desertion were too great and thus had participated against their will.

The declarations of prisoners of war from the first military confrontation to take place in New Granada are very significant and must be read carefully. For scholars who have argued that peasants and Indians were generally drawn into the independence wars in spite of their "parochial" worldview and interests, some of these men's declarations can support this point of view deceptively well.[13] For example, Carrasco and other prisoners argued that they were unaware of the reasons why they had been drafted and supported this claim by saying they were simple peasants, workers of the land.[14] Yet it should be noted that these statements were produced under threat of violence from the army interrogating the prisoners, in this case the army led by Governor Tacón. The idea that by living "simply" on his plot of land, a peasant was disconnected from political events in the village or town, the province, viceroyalty, or monarchy cannot be taken for granted. I would argue, rather, that this was in many cases a strategic display of the rhetoric about apolitical peasant views that would help the prisoners seem harmless. Furthermore, as the documents suggest, this was a credible claim to the authorities, and it helped prisoners gain pardon for having served on "the wrong side."[15]

Testimony added by other soldiers shows that when drafted, the men went to fulfill their duty to conquer Pasto, whose inhabitants were supposedly "in favor of Bonaparte." Moreover, the soldiers said they had enlisted in the name of the defense of the king, religion, and the *patria*. According to Elías Bolaños, the company took a ritualized oath in the

---

[12] Ibid.

[13] Jairo Gutiérrez, "'El infame tumulto y criminal bochinche': Las rebeliones de los indios de Pasto contra la República (1822–1824)," in *Independencia y transición a los estados nacionales en los países andinos: Nuevas perspectivas*, ed. Armando Martínez (Bucaramanga: Universidad Industrial de Santander, 2005), 373; Van Young, *The Other Rebellion*, 114.

[14] JCBL Archivo Restrepo, Fondo I, Vol. 25, fol. 115.

[15] As discussed in Chapter 2, colonial discourse about Indians and plebeians had a component that portrayed these groups as apolitical and incapable of understanding legal and juridical language. See Serulnikov, *Subverting Colonial Authority*, 138. Eric Van Young remarked on the common argument of war prisoners during the Mexican struggle for independence (1810–21) who claimed not to be conscious of their political involvement in the war. See Van Young, *The Other Rebellion*, ch. 1.

town's plaza, in which they swore to pacify Pasto because "if they let the French enemies penetrate ... they would commit profanities in their temples, rob their houses and families, and enslave them with chains."[16] These latter declarations suggest that recruitment involved the circulation of propaganda about the origin of the crisis in the peninsula and the particular risks that the elites, Indians, and slaves attributed to a potential French invasion. The enlistment ritual, led by a local parishioner and performed displaying the symbols of royal authority, was a crucial process of political socialization. Such evidence of transatlantic political awareness and use of interimperial references for Indian mobilization vitally demonstrates that their participation in the war was guided by political principles rather than by their ignorance.[17]

Tacón's decision to turn to Indian communities in the context of Quito's attack suggests that the loyalty of Indians to the crown and royalist elites was not assumed. On the contrary, for the colonial elites in Popayán, the precedent of the 1781 and 1800 Indian rebellions in Pasto and the Province of Los Pastos, respectively, signified that natives could pose a grave threat to the authorities in the context of a crisis. Therefore, Tacón's need to secure the Indians' loyalty drove him to break with the policy of control and repression of the communities that had been dominant in the aftermath of the late-eighteenth-century revolts.[18] He instead proposed attractive terms of negotiation to the Indians and thereby prevented them from being tempted to join the rebellion against the government. As we will see in detail in the following, in 1809 Indians were mobilized by their caciques, who responded to the call to defend the monarchy in search of rewards.

ROYALISM AND INDIAN TRIBUTE, 1809–1810

In 1809, reacting to the news about the "revolt" in Quito, Tacón wrote to the viceroy in Santa Fe, "The most interesting issue about this province of Popayán is the district of Los Pastos because it borders on [Quito's rebel

---

[16] JCBL Archivo Restrepo, Fondo I, Vol. 25, fol. 116.

[17] As Alejandro Cañeque and other scholars have shown, ritual was a fundamental aspect of the performance of rule in the Spanish empire. See Cañeque, *The King's Living Image*; Linda Curcio-Nagy, *The Great Festivals of Colonial Mexico City: Performing Power and Identity* (Albuquerque: University of New Mexico Press, 2004); Stanley Brandes, *Power and Persuasion: Fiestas and Social Control in Rural Mexico* (Philadelphia: University of Pennsylvania Press, 1988).

[18] See Chapter 2.

territory] and because of the large number of Indians who inhabit it, who are exposed to a risk of seduction that the rebels might attempt."[19] At this juncture the geographic location of Los Pastos was more vulnerable than the city and district of Pasto, which were protected or enclosed by the natural frontier of the Guáitara River (see Figure 1.1). Marching north, the Quiteño armies set out to invade the Province of Los Pastos and block the entrance to Barbacoas. This signaled the geopolitical importance that the province of Los Pastos had during the confrontation of Quito with Popayán, which ultimately put the Indians in Los Pastos at the center of the dispute. The representatives of the Quito junta invaded the towns of Túquerres and Guaytarilla and attempted to negotiate with the Indians by offering them a tribute reduction as they organized their quarters along the western margins of the Guáitara River. Although it is unclear whether or not the Indian communities in Los Pastos mobilized in favor of the Quito junta, the offer of tribute reduction to Indians in exchange for their loyalty and military service expresses the centrality of tribute as a means of negotiation with indigenous peoples across the Andean region.[20]

Gregorio Angulo, the militia captain that Tacón charged with defending Pasto, knew that to defend the city from an attack from Quito, he first had to call to arms the Indians who lived in the communities on the eastern side of the Guáitara River. On September 13 Angulo wrote to Tacón reassuring him "that all the Indians in this district remain faithful and loyal, wishing to be employed in defense of the crown, and they offered to mobilize, with slings and other weapons that they use."[21] He added that "in order to keep them in such good disposition and so it serves as a stimulus for others in the province (who I am informed have the same enthusiasm), I have considered it convenient to lower tribute by

---

[19] AHN Consejos 21674, exp. 2, doc. 18, fol. 2. Similar arguments were used in ongoing communications from Governor Tacón to the viceroy, found in AHN Consejos 21674, exp. 1, doc. 5.

[20] "Representación del Cabildo de Pasto," in Guerrero, *Documentos históricos*, 41–47. For Charcas, see Maria Luisa Soux, *El complejo proceso hacia la independencia de Charcas (1808–1826): Guerra, ciudadanía, conflictos locales y participación indígena en Oruro* (La Paz: Instituto Francés de Estudios Andinos, 2010), chs. 3 and 5; René Danilo Arze, *Participación popular en la independencia de Bolivia* (La Paz: Fundación Cultural Quipus, 1987); José Luis Roca, "Las expediciones porteñas y las masas altoperuanas (1811–1814)," *Historia y Cultura* 13 (1988), 111–38. In this region tribute was a contested issue from the perspective of Peru royalists and of the insurgents from Buenos Aires. For Quito, see Federica Morelli, *Territorio o Nación: Reforma y disolución del espacio imperial en Ecuador, 1765–1830* (Madrid: Centro de Estudios Políticos y Constitucionales, 2005), 144.

[21] AHN Consejos 21674, exp. 2, doc. 18, fol. 7v.

one-third or one-half." Angulo decreed such a dispensation (*gracia*) for Indians who remained firmly loyal and who provided help either with their bodies or with donations of weapons. As a result of this offer, "all the Indian authorities in the district presented themselves [to Angulo] ratifying their disposition to collaborate." On September 18, Angulo notified Tacón that Miguel Díaz, the Indian cacique of Buesaco (a town to the north of the city of Pasto, near the Juanambú river), had offered to go with him on the march toward the south with other Indians from his town. Angulo thanked him but took only one Indian with him to be used in case new forces had to be called to join from Buesaco, and "to use his help for encouraging other Indians along our path to join us."[22] Indians from the towns of Obonuco and Jongovito as well as from Catambuco were also decisive in the defense of Pasto against Quito in the battle of Funes. According to the official description of the battle, the Indians from the town of Funes "fully expressed their loyalty" by mobilizing with their priest José Palacios and were "ready to sacrifice for our cause." After this battle the Quiteños returned southward, defeated, and Tacón's troops took control of Los Pastos and Barbacoas, thereby restoring the integrity of Popayán Province.[23]

The overtures of Tacón and Angulo toward the Indians, who were seen simultaneously as potential allies and as threats, proved successful. This success was linked to the history of tribute in Pasto, because the negotiation took place using the language of reciprocity between the Indian communities and monarchic power. The political dynamics in 1809 were based on older monarchical logics of power, as evidenced by the fact that the first card that the government played was always a display of magnanimity. Granting dispensations in recognition of worthy behavior secured loyalty and ongoing alliance in this "economy of favor."[24] Tacón's gesture was legitimate in the eyes of the Indians, because it followed the rules of royal patronage and "liberality." The careful negotiations undertaken by Popayán's government, based on the reduction of tribute, were successful and assured that the Indians would become fundamental supporters of their cause, contributing with men, weapons, and their strategic knowledge of the territory.

---

[22] AHN Consejos 21674, exp. 2, doc. 18, fol. 8.
[23] Guerrero, *Pasto en la Guerra*, 29; Guerrero, *Documentos históricos*, 39, 46.
[24] See the discussion on transatlantic political practices of the Spanish monarchy in terms of an "economy of favor" in Cañeque, *The King's Living Image*, ch. 5; and Antonio Hespanha, *La gracia del derecho: Economía de la cultura en la Edad Moderna* (Madrid: Centro de Estudios Políticos y Constitucionales, 1993).

In this way, Tacón and Angulo's offer to lower the fiscal burden of Indian communities in exchange for their participation in the early confrontations in southwestern New Granada set the terms for subsequent attempts by royalists to recruit indigenous soldiers throughout the following decade of war. The link between tribute reduction and military service transformed political dynamics within Indian communities as well as their relationship with Spanish colonial officials and priests. And these two elements (tribute payment and military service) were crucial factors, both material and symbolic, that gave meaning to royalism from the perspective of the Indian communities in Pasto.

What is perhaps more significant is that in July 1810, the caciques in the district of Pasto declared that they would donate to the king the tribute waived by military officials in 1809 as a reward for their alliance against Quito. In a letter written by the Indian caciques of Pasto, twenty-nine towns (*pueblos*) referred to their involvement in the early conflicts between Popayán and Quito, saying, "We Indians offered to serve the just cause [of the king] with our own persons and lives, for no other reason than our loyalty to and love for our unhappy, beloved King Don Fernando VII." The letter recalled that the captain of the royalist militias, Gregorio Angulo, had rewarded their actions by "promising to forgive one-third of the tribute payment *to those who served in his armies*. … We," the caciques wrote, "remit to His Majesty this tribute, the portion which had been promised to be forgiven. Although we could have claimed this clemency, far from doing so, considering the wants and afflictions that our King and natural Lord suffers because of the treachery and evils the French [have committed], and feeling our own poverty – which provides us nothing with which to save him – we would be so happy if we could aid our beloved sovereign with the cost of our own lives."[25]

Is this decision of the Indian communities of Pasto to give up the financial reprieve Tacón had granted them an example of their irrationality or naïveté? On the contrary, I would argue it actually reflects the strategic interests of the Pasto caciques, as it relates to their alliance with

[25] Printed in Guerrero, *Documentos históricos de los hechos ocurridos en Pasto*, 52–53. Emphasis added. The governors that signed the letter were from the following towns: Jongovito, Obonuco, Catambuco, Botanilla, Gualmatán, Buesaquillo, Pejendino, Mocondino, Jamondino, Males, Canchala, Puerres, Aranda, Tescual, Pandiaco, Anganoy, Chapal, Genoy, Matituy, Mombuco, Matacunchuy, Tambo, Chachagü, Buesaco, Monte, Yacanquer, Tangua, Funes, and Sibundoy.

the royalist elites and the complex internal politics within Indian communities. The exemption of a third of their tribute was certainly appealing to Indians from the Pasto towns in 1809 when they chose to join the armies of Governor Tacón in the name of King Fernando VII. That proposal was based on the particularities of the Indians' communal rights, which were put into practice through the traditional recognition of reciprocal authority between the king and the caciques, who had initially mobilized their communities to fight in the war.[26]

The nature of the caciques' proposal to Tacón in 1810 went a step further. The Pasto caciques had become aware of changes in the power relations within the monarchy, and they used this information to attempt to secure a positive outcome for themselves and their communities by strategically displaying their loyalty to the Spanish king. In this exchange, the caciques revealed an awareness of political relationships and opportunities, as well as their ability to transform their strategies and relations to monarchic and local powers.

Traditionally, Indians had been able to negotiate the terms of their fiscal burden for the benefit of their communities, such as when they resisted the monetarization of tribute and continued paying in textiles during the eighteenth century. This type of negotiation over tribute in 1809 enabled Tacón and Angulo to successfully secure the allegiance of the Indians in Pasto to the cause of the king. In 1810, however, the caciques of these communities dynamically changed the content and meaning of tribute payment in order to legitimize – in a new way – their authority and that of the king. The caciques' reestablishment of the tribute quota was more than an economic contribution; it was also a symbolic statement of Indian loyalty to the king and the royalist elites. The "donation" of the traditional tribute for the king's fiscal benefit was intended to gain a privileged position in the local political context.[27] Indeed, it had its desired effect. Governor Tacón received the offer "with great satisfaction," responding in a public decree: "These loyal Indian towns should be aware that their [gift to the sovereign king] will from now on always be taken into account

---

[26] On the pact of reciprocity see Platt, "Liberalism and Ethnocide"; Platt, *Estado Boliviano y ayllu andino*; Brooke Larson, *Cochabamba, 1550–1900: Colonialism and Agrarian Transformation in Bolivia* (1988; Durham, NC: Duke University Press, 1998); Larson, "Explotación y economía moral"; Larson, *Trials of Nation Making*.

[27] Saether, "Independence and the Redefinition of Indianness," 70–72. In Saether's study of Indian royalism around Santa Marta, it is clear that the military role of Indians who allied with peninsular officials "gave them a moral capital which they actively used to gain influence."

and translated into the considerate treatment that they deserve as loyal vassals of Don Fernando VII."[28]

This maneuver shows a high degree of politicization among the Indians across the Pasto district, and it illuminates the fact that Indian politics was neither static nor ahistorical, but rather susceptible to constant flux. The monarchic crisis allowed these communities to redefine their relationship with the Spanish Crown, particularly as they were reasserting their loyalty to the king through military service. The communities' vision of the monarch's authority was always mediated through their understanding of the crown's obligation to protect them as vassals. The Indians' rights were secured through their commitment and response to different types of service, such as tribute payment and the provision of labor. In Pasto, the caciques were able to negotiate the terms of that relationship to the extent that, by adding to the burdens of the communities an obligation to participate in military service, Indians were now entitled to be recognized for their crucial role in the defense of the territory. Once the caciques decided that the communities would continue paying the reprieved portion of the tribute, they in fact were securing extra recognition of the fundamental role the Indian vassals in Pasto had played. This recognition would be acknowledged by the local authorities as well as by the king in coming years.

It is necessary to note, however, that in the context of the crisis (not yet the "independence" wars), the caciques, who historically had been agents for the collection of tribute, sought new bases of power. As brokers of tribute payment, on one hand, the caciques received part of their income through the tribute itself. On the other, their authority as well as their standing derived from the traditional role that they played as overseers of the crown's fiscal interests and as representatives of their communities before the state. In deciding that their communities would continue paying tribute, the Pasto caciques benefited from the added income and, by guaranteeing that their communities would provide much-needed resources for the war, defended their privileges and authority as ethnic elites. The action of the Pasto caciques should not be surprising. Scholars of Peru and Upper Peru have shown that during the Túpac Amaru rebellion and on through to independence, the Indian elites were among the most fervent in their loyalty to the monarchy and the dynamics of vassalage. With their actions in support of the king's cause, the caciques

[28] Guerrero, *Documentos históricos de los hechos ocurridos en Pasto*, 54.

in Pasto applied a measure that risked overburdening their communities –
who now had both to pay tribute and to perform militia service – but the
caciques expected that, in return, the Spanish crown would protect their
particular privileges as native elites.[29]

More to the point, that the caciques highlighted in their representation
to Governor Tacón that Angulo had promised to lower the tribute payment of "those who served in his armies" also suggests that the caciques
were concerned that such a change would be introduced unevenly into
community politics and financial institutions. Tribute payment among
Indians traditionally had been determined by categories in the communities, such as age and land-holding status. From the perspective of the
Indian authorities, introducing a change in the individual tribute quota of
many groups of Indians (based on the government's contingent military
plan) could well have generated problems for them in terms of their rule
and authority. Additionally, this measure was a potential source of differentiation among the Indian commoners, which the caciques rejected
because it could have generated conflicts among Indians in their communities. The tribute reduction was a threat for the caciques, particularly
because it could have vested men (especially young men who proved
successful as warriors) with a separate source of status, thus calling into
question their subordination to the caciques.[30]

That this letter was written by the Indians from the Pasto district and
did not include any Indian towns from Los Pastos suggests that, at this
point, the two jurisdictions were acting independently. It is hard to know
what the position was of the Indians in Los Pastos during the 1809 invasion from Quito. In fact, it seems that the mobilization and military
involvement of indigenous people was confined in particular to the Pasto
district; that is, to the jurisdiction governed by that city, encompassing the
Indian towns south of the Juanambú River and east of the Guáitara River.
Taking this into account, it seems possible that the caciques of the Indian
towns across Pasto were also attempting to gain particular favors by
differentiating themselves from the Indians in Los Pastos.

Moreover, events in Los Pastos took a different turn when Carlos
Montúfar created a second junta in Quito on September 19, 1810. The

---

[29] Garrett, *Shadows of Empire*, 1; see also Thomson, *We Alone Will Rule*, 168–69; Walker, *Smoldering Ashes*, 52.

[30] See Calloway, *The American Revolution in Indian Country*, 175, for a comparative example of how Shawnee elder chiefs lost authority to a new generation of Indian warriors.

corregidor in Los Pastos, Francisco Sarasti, accepted Quito's invitation to proclaim independence from the Junta Central in Spain. From the town of Ipiales, Sarasti drafted a declaration accepting Santa Fe's decision to form a junta and ignore the authority of Spain's Junta Central. Los Pastos' search for autonomy from the city of Pasto had a deep history that explains the division that took place in 1811 between the Creoles of Pasto and Los Pastos. Los Pastos was directly connected to Barbacoas geographically and was therefore one of the most economically dynamic regions in Popayán. However, since it was governed by Popayán, it did not have its own *cabildo*, and its elite resented Popayán's intervention in its local affairs.[31] It seems likely that these were the reasons for Sarasti and others to embrace ideas of autonomy, a reaction that resembled the territorial fragmentation, based on previous confrontations, that was taking place on a larger and smaller scale all across Spanish America during the absence of Fernando VII. Los Pastos' support of Quito's second junta was short-lived: by mid-1811 Tacón was in control of Los Pastos again.[32] It is unclear whether or not the Indians from Los Pastos were aligned with Sarasti and the other elite men who signed the declaration. If there ever was a confrontation between the indigenous communities on both sides of the Guáitara, or if the Indians from Los Pastos did indeed support the ideas of the elites to separate from the jurisdiction of Pasto and Popayán, it is not evident in the documentation available. Nonetheless, years later, during the 1822 revolt against Bolívar (to be treated in Chapter 6), the Indians from Los Pastos were very active, and their towns, such as Sapuyes, were the ground where the royalist rebellion was fought.

THE PROTECTOR AND INDIAN POLITICS, 1811–1815

Royalist Indians were not "conservative" insofar as they were not interested in perpetuating relationships that did not benefit them. Negotiation with local officials was not simply a part of maintaining traditional political and social relations. Depending upon their class position, the Indians who were loyal to the crown promoted important changes in their rights and duties based on their changing understanding of the larger monarchical context that itself underwent drastic transformations after 1809. Indian commoners, in particular, imbued the royalist struggle with

---

[31] Minaudier, "Pequeñas patrias," 158–59.   [32] Ortiz, *Agustín Agualongo*, 112–19.

their interests and notions of justice, which could challenge, for example, the authority of caciques and local priests.

A fundamental figure in the relationship of Indian communities to the monarchy was the *protector partidario de naturales*. During the crisis of government that occurred after 1809, the *protector partidario* played a crucial role in guaranteeing the loyalty of Indian communities to the king and the royalist cause, and his support of the Indian interest in lowering tribute payments in exchange for their military service generated important conflicts as well as transformations in the relationship between the Indians and their caciques. Over time, the situation resulted in the politicization of the post of protector in an unprecedented way because some Indians from the towns in the district of Pasto relied more strongly on the protector to represent their interests than on the ethnic authorities who had been appointed to govern them.

That caciques and commoners were divided, and the latter allied with the protector, is clear in a document that the *protector partidario de naturales* of the city of Pasto, Juan Díaz Gallardo, wrote in December 1814 to the municipal council of the city in the name of the "Indian commoners of the Pasto district." Gallardo requested a copy of the concession (*gracia*) that Governor Tacón made public in 1811, which stated that Indians "should pay only four *pesos* of tribute from then on."[33] The document, dated May 2, 1811, was signed by Gallardo's predecessor, Francisco Martínez de Segovia, who had called for the execution of a royal decree for the reduction of Indian tribute. In the concession Martínez de Segovia contended that the Indian communities in Pasto deserved recognition for their loyal services to the king during the 1809 revolution in Quito. He also recalled their "generosity when, [in 1810] in favor of His Majesty, they renounced the tribute reduction that Gregorio Angulo conceded." Based upon such meritorious actions, the *Protector partidario* Martínez de Segovia pleaded for the municipal council to "reduce perpetually for *all those Indians and towns* an amount of tribute payment that you consider advisable."[34]

After an internal evaluation of the 1811 proposal, the municipal council asked the tribute collector, Tomás Miguel Santa Cruz, to deliver an annotated list of the amounts (*tasa*) paid by each type of Indian to

---

[33] ANE Popayán 342, doc. dated December 13, 1814, fol. 1.
[34] ANE Popayán 342, doc. dated December 13, 1814, fol. 1v. In the original: "se digne hacer una rebaja perpetua de la cantidad que estimare conveniente *a todos aquellos indios y pueblos*." Emphasis added.

determine the possible reduction to be applied. Interestingly, the council's ruling acknowledged a royal decree on the matter and a recent announcement by the viceroy mandating that the tribute be lowered in Pasto. The *cabildo* recognized that a set of new regulations had been on its way, but it was declared lost given that the insurgent government was, at the time, occupying the capital (Santa Fe, which formed an autonomist junta in July 1810). Although neither the council nor the *protector* specified which decree they were referring to, it is very likely that the allusion was to the Cortes' decree of March 13, 1811, which abolished tribute throughout the Spanish monarchy.

The abolition of tribute by the Cortes was one of the early expressions of the liberal spirit of the constituency in Cádiz. Although the Cortes were acting in the name of the abducted king's sovereignty, they were also promoting a series of preliminary arrangements that had the goal of dismantling the seigniorial regime according to which jurisdiction over all Spanish territory (in the peninsula as well as in America) was granted to the king. In other words, the Cortes was embarking on a process of nationalization of the territory and its economy. The ultimate logic behind the Spanish Cortes' abolition of *encomiendas*, *mitas*, the *reparto*, and tribute payment was the creation of the Spanish nation as the culmination of the revolution promulgated by the liberals.[35]

Of course, conditions in the American territories at the time did not allow for complete execution of the Cortes' decrees. Not only were some of the cities controlled by insurgents, but also the royalist authorities sometimes responded to the liberal mandates by questioning their viability. For example, Peru's viceroy José de Abascal famously opposed the alleged authority of the Spanish Cortes, especially given the liberal thrust of their rule. Abascal commented that the abolition of tribute was the product of "either the most incredible ignorance or the bad faith of the government that decreed it."[36] Tribute amounted to a fundamental part

---

[35] Chust, "De esclavos, encomenderos y mitayos," 183; Cesáreo de Armellada, *La Causa Indígena Americana en las Cortes de Cádiz* (Caracas: Universidad Católica Andrés Bello, 1979); Portillo, *Crisis atlántica*, esp. ch. 4.

[36] Cited in Heraclio Bonilla, "Clases populares y estado en el contexto de la crisis colonial," in *La independencia en el Perú*, ed. Bonilla and Karen Spalding (Lima: Instituto de Estudios Peruanos, 1981), 68. Discussions of the consequences of the Cádiz resolutions on tribute in Peru can be found in Mark Thurner, *From Two Republics to One Divided: Contradictions of Postcolonial Nationmaking in Andean Peru* (Durham, NC: Duke University Press, 1997), 21–25; Víctor Peralta, *En pos del tributo. Burocracia estatal, elite regional y comunidades indígenas en el Cuzco rural (1826–1854)* (Cuzco: Centro de Estudios Andinos Regionales, 1991); Walker, *Smoldering Ashes*, 93–97.

of the revenue of the royal treasury, and it was also a particularly important source of income for local administrators, such as parish clergy, the caciques, and the *corregidores*.[37] In many colonial regions, the measure could not be applied as liberally as the Cortes expected, given the exigencies of war and the need to maintain troops in various parts of the Americas, which were paid for mainly by tributary income. Pasto was part of the Pacific royalist block, which had a center in Lima but was governed from Quito by Quito president Toribio Montes, a liberal. Paradoxically, Montes made sure that the Cortes' decree on tribute was not enforced because it threatened to "introduce a disturbing novelty to good order."[38]

Historians have recently suggested that in Pasto in 1811, Governor Tacón and the Pasto *cabildo* ignored the Cortes' decree abolishing tribute because of the pressing need to maintain the royalist troops. However, the significant fact that *Protector* Gallardo requested a reduction in the tribute of one peso per Indian in exchange for their military support of the royalists in 1814, and his success in securing such a reduction as a consequence of the previous negotiations between the communities and Tacón, suggest otherwise. It is my contention that the 1809 process had crucial significance for subsequent negotiations with indigenous communities to gain their military support. Indeed, in 1811 *Protector partidario* Martínez de Segovia was appealing for the tribute reduction because a new "revolutionary junta" had been created in Quito, and that alarming development required that Pasto gain reassurances of Indian loyalty. The tone of the response given by the *cabildo* and by Governor Tacón on June 15, 1811, expressed this very clearly. The members of the *cabildo* agreed to reduce Indian tributes since the "will of the King was oriented to the alleviation of Indian tribute," added to the fact that the communities in Pasto "deserve such a reduction, having participated in the defense of the city during the last insurrection of Quito, *and they are ready to do it again in the present situation.*" Therefore, rather than ignoring the decree of the Cortes, the governor and the *cabildo* combined an argument in favor of

---

[37] During the Cádiz debates, the Cortes confronted the issue of how to obtain funds to pay parish clergy once tribute was abolished. See De Armellada, *La causa indígena Americana*, 34–40.

[38] ANE Tributos 25, doc. dated July 23, 1812. Montes cited in Morelli, *Territorio o Nación*, 170–171. See also "Representación del Presidente de Quito, don Toribio Montes, ante el Secretario de Estado, sobre actuaciones de su gobierno en las pasadas convulsiones, desde que tomó posesión del mando," in *Colección de documentos para la historia de Colombia*, ed. Ortiz, 80.

the tribute reduction with the justification that it was the "will of the King" (referring to the Cortes' decree).

The other, more pragmatic reason, based on the history of negotiation between themselves (the local government) and the Indian communities, was the importance of providing recognition of the Indians' "fidelity and patriotism." Reducing tribute was a way to make it clear to the Indians that "the government [was] pleased (*satisfecho*) with their loyalty and love for His Majesty."[39] In his report to the *cabildo*, the tribute collector in Pasto had stated in May 1811 that the payment was the same for the Indians considered to be "oriundos o estipendarios" (Indians residing in their places of birth) and for those called "forasteros o anacondas [sic]" (Indians living away from their village of origin), all of whom paid five pesos.[40] The reduction that the government agreed upon in June was one peso per Indian, starting in mid-1811.[41]

It is not accurate to say that the local Spanish and Creole elites had complete autonomy when it came to making decisions about their relationship to the Indian communities, especially when they urgently needed to guarantee both the Indians' loyalty and their military service. That *Protector partidario* Gallardo begged for the reduction in Indian tribute again in 1814 also merits our attention in another sense. If in 1810 the caciques had officially decided to continue paying the entire tribute quota for the benefit of the king, why was Gallardo later requesting a tribute reduction? As mentioned earlier, the caciques manifested their unconditional loyalty to the king by giving up the tribute reduction, yet this was a decision that first and foremost benefited them as indigenous authorities. The *protector partidario*'s later plea for a tribute reduction reflects the important relation that existed between him and Indian commoners, who, in contrast to the caciques' view, thought that the tribute reduction was in

---

[39] ANE Popayán 342, doc. dated December 13, 1814, fol. 3. Emphasis added.

[40] *Forasteros* are also known as *Yanaconas*. In the Andes, Indian migration was linked to the consolidation of royal power and the decline or transformation of the *cacicazgo*. As research for Quito and the southern Andes has shown, originally Indians left their communities seeking to avoid tribute and labor services. These *forasteros* or *vagamundos* eventually became integrated into communities and acquired tribute obligations but generally paid less than *originarios*. Although more research is needed on the history of migrations in and around Pasto, from the tribute categories in 1811 it is clear that *forasteros* were integral to indigenous society in that region. It is especially significant that they paid tribute and, further, the same sum as the *originarios*. See Powers, *Andean Journeys*, 15, 89–90, 101, 120.

[41] ANE Popayán 342, doc. dated December 13, 1814, fol. 2v.

their best interests, particularly given their participation in the war as soldiers or performing other services.

Gallardo's plea, once it reached the *audiencia* in 1815, sparked a controversy among the magistrates (*oidores*), who manifested their doubts about the legitimacy of Tacón's decree of 1811. They argued that only the king was allowed to make such a concession and passed the request to the king for his determination of the case. Restored to his throne, King Fernando VII's response to Gallardo's request was positive (dated May 15, 1817). He "lower[ed] the tribute perpetually by one peso to the [Pasto] Indians," wishing that "they be told how satisfied He is of their exemplary loyalty and services."[42] Additionally, the king decreed that more tangible symbols of his gratitude should be made, granting "that the caciques of such meritorious towns have the privilege of wearing a silver medal with the bust of the King, and written on the back: Fernando Séptimo for the fidelity of the caciques in Pasto."[43] Although historians of the period have repeatedly written in an ironic tone about this event, saying that the medal never reached the Pasto caciques, therefore diminishing the actual gains of the Indians in exchange for their support of the royalists, the king's decree was received at the *Audiencia* in Quito, and the document included a certificate of its publication by a *pregonero* (town crier) as well as a notification that the royal decree had been received by Gallardo.[44] Once the protector received such news, it is very possible that he informed the Indians about the king's decision, adding to his merits as a *protector partidario* in the eyes of the Indian commoners.

THE DUTY OF MILITARY AND LABOR SERVICE

After collecting the appropriate documentation from 1809 to 1812, Gallardo then elaborated a memorial, which he attached to his petition for tribute reduction; in this memorial, he recounted the "difficult

---

[42] AGI Santa Fe 765, fol. 1r; ANE Popayán 350, doc dated January 9, 1819, fol. 52v.

[43] ANE Popayán 350, doc. dated January 9, 1819, fol. 52v. These medals would later be used to show the king's benevolence towards the caciques of Santa Marta in the aftermath of the independence wars, and were awarded by Pablo Morillo to the Indians in Venezuela for their loyalty. For the award of the caciques in Mamatoco, Santa Marta, for their service, see AGI Santafe 632 and Cuba 749, and Saether, "Independence and the Redefinition of Indianness," 73. Medals to the Indians of the pueblos of Pilar, Caigua, San Miguel, San Francisco, Clarines, and Piritu in Venezuela were given by Pablo Morillo in 1819, see RAH Colección Morillo 9.7664, fols. 287–287v.

[44] Such is the interpretation of Ortiz, *Agustín Agualongo*, 354; Urresty, *Las guerras de Pasto*, 23.

situation in which the *naturales* find themselves at present."[45] The *protector partidario* highlighted the "Indians' unalterable fidelity and love for the king since the revolution debuted in these provinces and stressed the useful *services* they had performed since the beginning in support of the just cause." He was referring mainly to Indian participation as soldiers in the royalist army, having "fought in many of the battles with the enemies, some with their slings and sticks, others with their shotguns."[46]

Gallardo also testified about how the communities surrounding the city of Pasto and its province were "central actors in the defense" of the cause of the king and that, throughout the military conflicts, the Indians were, in Gallardo's words, "the pack mules (*las mulas de acarreo*) for the transportation of everything necessary for the defense and subsistence of the troop."[47] Indians in this region had generally worked as *cargueros*, hauling goods from the Pasto plateau to the mines of Barbacoas.[48] But the *protector partidario* noted that, in the context of the war, Indians were not even being paid the customary one peso for their role as *cargueros* of goods and artillery. They, however, did not falter in their support even though this service required them to abandon their families. On the contrary, their families "brought food to those who were performing service," even if they were not being paid for it.[49]

Although Gallardo was possibly exaggerating the abuse of the Indians during the war, in order to get the tribute reduction, further attention should be given to his description of the way Indians were accompanied by their families while they were "performing service." The description resembles the conditions of *mita* labor, a system of labor extraction instituted in the region, which had evolved, particularly in the Andes, from a pre-Hispanic form of labor draft. In early colonial Huamanga, for example, men (called *mitayos*) who were drafted into the *mita* were generally accompanied by their relatives during their labors, and these relatives contributed to the men's work with resources, mainly food. Although the communities suffered greatly from the way the institution

---

[45] ANE Popayán 342, doc. dated December 13, 1814, fol. 4. The memorial is dated December 13, 1814.

[46] Ibid. Emphasis added.   [47] ANE Popayán 342, doc. dated December 13, 1814, fol. 4v.

[48] On the role of *cargueros* as a form of service and as inheritors of the pre-Hispanic *mindalaes*, see Rosa Isabel Zarama, "Consolidación de Túquerres al final del periodo colonial, 1750–1810," in *Historia socio espacial de Túquerres, siglos XVI–XX: De Barbacoas hacia el horizonte nacional*, ed. Behur Cerón and Rosa Isabel Zarama (Pasto: Universidad de Nariño, 2003), 141–56.

[49] ANE Popayán 342, doc. dated December 13, 1814, fol. 4v.

of the *mita* was transformed during the colonial period, as it threatened the social and ecological balance of Andean territorial groups' economies (*ayllu*), what is interesting for us to note here is that a certain communal structure of support had remained in place, as well as an understanding of the *mita* as part of the service required by Indians to secure certain rights, or privileges, from the Spanish king.[50]

A similar practical response to and understanding of service was visible among the Pasto communities during the war. While Gallardo remarked on the abuses that were committed against the Indians, his account also reveals the strategies that were the basis for Indian participation in the war, during which, as part of their commitment to serving the king, Indians mobilized social and economic resources to fulfill their service.[51]

The resemblance between Indian participation in the war and in the *mita* as porters also resonates with the military service that some ethnic groups had performed for the Inca before the Spanish arrival. After the conquest, some of these groups maintained the tradition of celebrating their participation in the *mita* for some time, because it resembled the rituals of their military service for the Inca.[52] Therefore, though Indians did not have an official role in the local militias in the context of colonial rule, being part of the royal army or performing military service had a

[50] Stern, *Peru's Indian Peoples*, 80–96; on the *mita* in Peru, the historiography is extensive, see also Luis J. Basto Girón, *Las mitas de Huamanga y Huancavelica* (Lima: Editora Médica Peruana, 1954); Jorge Basadre, "El régimen de la mita," in *El virreinato del Perú*, ed. José Manuel Valega (Lima: Editorial Cultura Ecléctica, 1939), 187–203; Guillermo Lohmann, *Las minas de Huancavelica en los siglos XVI y XVII* (Seville: Escuela de Estudios Hispano-Americanos, 1949); Enrique Tandeter, *Coacción y mercado: La minería de la plata en Perú colonial, 1692–1826* (Buenos Aires: Editorial Sudamericana, 1996). For Colombia, see Germán Colmenares, *Historia Económica y Social de Colombia, 1537–1719* (1973; Bogotá: TM Editores, 1997), 190–97; Heraclio Bonilla, "La economía política de la conducción de los indios a Mariquita: La experiencia de Bosa y Ubaque en el Nuevo Reino de Granada," *Anuario Colombiano de Historia Social y de la Cultura* 32 (2005), 11–30. On the establishment of the *mita* in the Pasto plateau, see Calero, *Chiefdoms under Siege*.

[51] Claudia Guarisco, *Los indios del valle de México y la construcción de una nueva sociabilidad política, 1770–1835* (Zinacantepec: El Colegio Mexiquense, 2003), ch. 5, mentions that Indians in the parish of Zumpango (Citlaltepec) composed their own companies within the royalist armies "which became defensive associations of a territorial-ethnic character" (158). This example suggests that Indian communities gave a particular meaning to military service in terms of defending their territory.

[52] As stated in "El memorial de los Mallku y principales de la provincia de los Charcas," in Tristan Platt, *Qaraqara-Charka: Mallku, Inka y Rey en la provincia de Charcas (siglos XV-XVII): Historia antropológica de una confederación aymara* (La Paz: IFEA, Plural Editores, University of St Andrews, University of London, IAF, Banco Central de Bolivia, 2007), 841–42 (fol. 8v).

political value.[53] At the time of the crisis of the monarchy, which began with the Napoleonic invasion of the peninsula and the abduction of the monarch, enlisting in the armies of the king represented an honor for Indian communities. Yet this honor and interest in participating in the war should not be interpreted as a naïve notion of Indian service or of their "pact" with the king. Such participation along with their positioning themselves as political and military allies of the royalists could be profoundly strategic and brought about important benefits to the communities as well as put them in a privileged position vis-à-vis the royalists in southwestern New Granada.[54]

To be sure, the memorial drafted by Gallardo is rife with images of Indian submission. With the goal of gaining the tribute reduction, Gallardo used an important account to highlight the unconditional support of Indians for the king's cause. He said that Indians "currently suffer worse hostilities from the royal army who are around the [Indian] towns. They fell their crops, take away their goods, animals, hit them and abuse them ... yet these unhappy people are willing to serve humbly and happily in benefit of the just cause."[55] Furthermore, the "miserable Indians" had not been able to produce enough crops given their involvement in the war and therefore were unable to pay the entire tribute quota. This added to the motives for the need of a tribute reduction or at least a waiver of the most immediate payment until their condition improved.

Hence, although the *protector partidario* was appealing to the Hispanic legal framework within which Indians were considered "miserable," the petition for tribute reduction reflected a very concrete and important conjuncture of events. Indians were participating in the war with broad forms of military service (including supplying provisions and

---

[53] See Ben Vinson and Matthew Restall, "Black Soldiers, Native Soldiers: Meanings of Military Service in the Spanish American Colonies," in *Beyond Black and Red: African-Native Relations in Colonial Latin America*, ed. Matthew Restall (Albuquerque: University of New Mexico Press, 2005), 23–24.

[54] Ary R. Campo Chicangana, *Montoneras, deserciones e insubordinaciones. Yanaconas y Paeces en la guerra de los Mil Días* (Cali: Secretaría de Cultura, Archivo Histórico, 2003), 34, argues that the indigenous communities of Yanaconas and Paeces in Cauca understood their participation in the War of a Thousand Days (1899–1902) as a "minga." In the northern Andes, the "minga" was a communal gathering, generally convoked by the Indian authorities, to labor for the service of tasks required by the community. Campo argues that Indians perceived participation in the war as a "minga" both because the indigenous authorities dictated it and because military defense was a way of "safeguarding the community's interests."

[55] ANE Popayán 342, doc. dated December 13, 1814, fol. 4v–5.

transport), yet a limit had been reached where they could no longer fulfill the dual positions of tribute payment and military service. Gallardo, then, was representing the interests of Indian commoners who saw the conditions of their loyalty and service stretched to an unbearable limit. This means that in the context of the war the Indians did not support royalists unconditionally; furthermore, while the caciques expected their communities to fulfill both obligations, an alliance grew between the communities and the *protector partidario* to guarantee that the interests and needs of the commoners also be met. In other words, royalist Indian communities were not without internal conflict. Their unprecedented empowerment through the alliance with the royalist elites also created definite shifts of power that were reflected in the conflict between common Indians and their caciques.

"THE RUIN OF RELIGIOUS AND PIOUS CUSTOMS"

There is no doubt that Gallardo increased his power among the Indian communities by providing support for the process of securing a tribute reduction with the *cabildo* and the *audiencia*. For this reason, among the Indian elites and some colonial officials, Gallardo became a controversial figure. An important document has survived that explains why Gallardo was replaced in 1817 by another *protector partidario*, Ramón Medina, captain of the militias of Pasto's royalist army.[56] The controversy around Gallardo's replacement as *protector partidario* reveals that he and his political maneuvers were not welcomed by everyone in Pasto, especially not by the caciques, priests, and Quito's *Audiencia*. Nonetheless, Gallardo challenged the *audiencia*'s decision to remove him from his post and complained to the *Audiencia* in Quito, stating that he had been unfairly and unjustly removed as *protector partidario*. After all, he had "advised the Indians to remain faithful and loyal to the king's cause, even fighting by the Indians' side in the combats." This particular argument aimed at justifying Gallardo's positive relation to Indian royalism in the eyes of the government, which should have valued Gallardo's role as a leader among the Indian communities. Cast in traditional colonial terms, Gallardo had

---

[56] ANE Popayán 350, doc. dated January 9, 1819, fol. 31. The *fiscal* in Quito declared on February 22, 1819, that Medina's military title made him "very recommendable" for the post of protector.

performed his role of "treating Indians like his children, always caring for them and defending them."[57]

In his attempt to regain his position, Gallardo played up his popularity with the Indians, who, he stated, were happy with him as *protector partidario* because of his committed defense of their interests. Indeed, the post of *protector partidario* had become profoundly politicized during the war. This was due, first, to the leading role it played in committing Indians to the royalist cause. Additionally, precisely because he was now so influential in promoting and enabling their active participation in the military, the *protector partidario* became a symbol of authority for the communities, while at the same time acquiring unprecedented duties. Among those, and most evident, was his role in obtaining the reduction of tribute payments.

In the remainder of this chapter, I will show why such overtly political accomplishments by Gallardo in favor of Indian commoners were not equally welcomed by the Creole and indigenous elites in Pasto. However, to understand the particularities of Gallardo's politicization in the context of the war, we should recall the specific ways in which the post of *protector* was in itself political in Spanish America. Attention has been given to the rise of the office, particularly in Peru and Mexico, and even in Quito (which included Pasto).[58] As a religious and civil position for imparting justice, the post had had a political dimension since its inception because the *protector* embodied the crown's mandate to protect its Indian vassals. The ability of the *protector* to mediate between the major sectors of colonial society (the colonists, the church, and the Indians) was essentially a political role inasmuch as the law was a political arena in the Spanish empire. Furthermore, it is well known that the *protectores* were

---

[57] Gallardo accompanied the Indians of the town of Catambuco during their military confrontation in the year 1812. ANE Popayán 350, doc. dated January 1, 1819, fol. 77v.

[58] Borah, *Justice by Insurance*; Cutter, *The Protector de Indios*; Diana Bonnett, *El protector de naturales en la Audiencia de Quito, siglos XVII y XVIII* (Quito: FLACSO, 1992); Bernard Lavallé, "Presión colonial y reivindicación indígena en Cajamarca (1785–1820) según el Archivo del Protector de Naturales," *Allpanchis* 35–36 (1990), 105–37; José de la Puente Brunke, "Notas sobre la Audiencia de Lima y la 'protección de los naturales' (siglo XVII)," in *Passeurs, mediadores culturales y agentes de la primera globalización en el Mundo Ibérico, siglos XVI–XIX*, ed. Scarlett O'Phelan Godoy and Carmen Salazar-Soler, 221–48 (Lima: PUCP-Instituto Riva-Agüero-Instituto Francés de Estudios Andinos, 2005); Carmen Ruigómez, *Una política indigenista de los Habsburgo: el Protector de Indios en el Perú* (Madrid: Ediciones de Cultura Hispánica, 1988); Renzo Honores, "La asistencia jurídical privada a los señores indígenas ante la Real Audiencia de Lima, 1552–1570" (Paper presented at the 2003 Latin American Studies Association meeting, unpublished).

not free from getting involved in local conflicts, for example, having confrontations with the *encomenderos* and *hacendados*, with the church (priests or missionaries), and with government officials. Additionally, the *protectores* could end up in antagonistic relationships vis-à-vis the caciques, given that the role of *protector* included regulating not only the Indians' relationship with the Spaniards but also relationships within their communities. The *protectores* did not have legislative or executive powers, but that did not reduce their ability to have an impact on local politics. In fact, by being responsible for keeping the indigenous people informed of their rights, at different levels and in every context, and for staying informed of any abuses committed against Indians and denouncing them, the *protectores* were central to the power struggles common in every locality.[59] These involved issues of authority as much as material disputes over land and other resources. As has been described here, tribute payment amounted to one of the most contentious points that the *protectores* oversaw.

Thus, it is clear that the post of *protector partidario* had always been highly politicized, from the sixteenth century through the nineteenth century, when the independence wars began. Before the monarchical crisis broke out, the *caciques* had had a monopoly on Indian representation, and they had exercised that privilege in alliance with the protector. But in the context of the independence wars, the arrival of liberal legislation from the government in Cádiz increased the Indian commoners' unprecedented ability to negotiate the terms of their loyalty to the crown, transforming the protector's position and making it more controversial.

This shift in the protector's role began after 1809 when, as we have seen, the reduction of tribute payment was not to everyone's satisfaction in Pasto. Aside from the caciques, other local figures who clearly disliked the measure were the priests. In fact, the *protector general de indios* in Quito's *Audiencia* said he had received numerous complaints against Gallardo from caciques and priests, who pleaded for Gallardo's removal.[60] The *audiencia* also actively rejected Gallardo's political alliance with the Indian commoners; this went hand-in-glove with the

---

[59] Caroline Cunill, "Tomás López Medel y sus instrucciones para defensores de indios: una propuesta innovadora," *Anuario de Estudios Americanos* 69, no. 1 (2012), 541, 556; Benton, *Law and Colonial Cultures*, 33, 84.

[60] ANE Popayán 350, doc. dated January 9, 1819, fols. 15–16. The *protector general* said he based his decision on the report of sixteen Indian governors from the Pasto district added to the three representations from priests. The offensive against Gallardo came from the Indian governors of Jongovito, Catambuco, Obonuco, Botanilla, Mocondino,

reestablishment of the absolutist policy of the Spanish government, which took place after 1814. The arguments against Gallardo also had an explicit racial connotation. Some of the priests who criticized him referred to him as a "dark man (*hombre oscuro*)," "of humble origins," and a military officer who testified against him said he should be removed on account of the law of *Recopilación*, where it was stated that *mestizos* could not be *protectores partidarios*.[61]

The conflicts with parishioners in the Indian towns surrounding Pasto were the result of the challenges that Indians had mounted over their obligation to perform certain types of personal service for the priests, challenges that Gallardo seems to have endorsed. In 1818, while Gallardo was in Quito lodging the complaint about his removal from the post of *protector partidario*, Ramón Medina provided new evidence of Gallardo's unsuitability for the post. It included representations written by the caciques of Obonuco and Botanilla and the Indian leaders of the parish of Jongovito, all of whom were highly concerned about certain aspects of Gallardo's role in previous years. Aside from noting that Gallardo had not fulfilled his duties of defending the Indians, they said that the *protector partidario* had "promoted discord, division, and revolt in our towns." Indians from the towns of Obonuco, Botanilla, and Jongovito were said to have declared themselves against the priest, refusing payment for his services (such as mass, burials, and marriages), and some even had "given up attendance at the sacred sacrifice of the mass."[62] The caciques stated their fear that Indian commoners "having lost the veneration and respect for a distinguished priest, what can we expect to happen with the unhappy and powerless caciques and community authorities?" In conclusion, these authorities from Obonuco, Botanilla, and Jongovito stated that, given the existing threat, they would rather give up their *varas* or staffs of authority "until our pueblos are *reconquered*."[63]

It is noteworthy that in their complaint the caciques resorted to the language of wretchedness to refer to their situation, terminology that was generally ascribed to the Indian commoners who were socially and politically beneath the ethnic elites. This might have been a strategy on the part of the caciques to magnify their powerlessness. The complaints lodged by the indigenous authorities in these towns in the Pasto district suggest that,

Buesaquillo, Pejendino, Jamondino, La Laguna, Aranda, Males, Puerres, Jesquial, Pandiaco, Anganoy, and Matachunchuy.
[61] ANE Popayán 350, doc. dated January 9, 1819, fols. 20, 22, 141v.
[62] ANE Popayán 350, doc. dated January 9, 1819, fol. 25v.   [63] Ibid. fol. 27.

among the royalist Indians, Gallardo had sided with Indians from the town who were contesting their traditional subjection to the priests and the caciques. Such a challenge was supported by the liberal transformations that the Cádiz Constitution was promoting in terms of the treatment of Indians by priests and other Spanish authorities, a thrust that Gallardo was clearly taking to its ultimate conclusions.[64] The Indian elite felt threatened by the transformations that some Indians in the town were seeking, and they saw the need to immediately resolve the problem by removing Gallardo from his post of *protector partidario*.

That this change in the role of the *protectores partidarios* took place in the years after the restoration of the monarchy is significant, because in 1814 Fernando VII reinstituted the basic tenets of absolutism and in doing so forcefully attempted to erase all traces of the changes instituted while the liberals had been in power. Clearly, the authority that Gallardo had amassed during his years as protector, through the mobilization of the Indians in favor of royalism and particularly through his support of the interest of nonelite Indians in change, became untenable once the political context shifted and absolutist values were again being officially enforced. The changes in social and political relations that certain commoners had been putting into effect were halted by an alliance between the Indian elites and the *audiencia*, made possible through the mediation of Ramón Medina, who was expected to guarantee the preservation of a traditional order, something that was in the interest of the Indian authorities as well as that of the priests.

The context that explains Gallardo's ousting from the post of *protector partidario* is the king's decree of April 29, 1817, received in Quito on January 8, 1818, which was a reaction to the complaints about the

---

[64] Beginning with the early sessions in the Cortes of Cádiz, the deputies debated the need to address the afflictions of the Indians. One of the champions of this cause was Dionisio Inca Yupanqui, who represented the Viceroyalty of Peru. His speech on the need to protect the Indians, given on December 16, 1810, resulted in a decree that can be found in Archivo del Congreso de los Diputados (ACD) Sección General Legajo 7 n. 27; the printed copy of the decree dated February 10, 1811, is in Legajo 6 n. 89. The decree stated that "prohibiendo con todo rigor que bajo de ningún pretexto por racional que parezca persona alguna constituida en autoridad eclesiástica, civil o militar, ni otra alguna de cualquier clase o condición que sea, aflija al indio en su persona, ni le ocasione perjuicio el más leve en su propiedad, de lo que deberán cuidar todos los magistrados y jefes con una vigilancia la más escrupulosa." See also De Armellada, *La causa indígena Americana*, 13–14. Pascual Temaran, a commoner from the town of Catambuco, declared that Gallardo promised to enact the royal mandate to reduce Indian service to priests. ANE Popayán 350, doc. dated January 9, 1819, fol. 130.

insubordination of Indians toward the religious authorities and recalled the need to reempower priests to punish Indians. The *cédula* reinstated an absolutist framework, one that had been espoused by the Quito *Audiencia* in the latter part of the first decade of the nineteenth century, and it criticized the "disorders caused in the *pueblos de indios*" as a result of the Cádiz Constitution and other resolutions of the Cortes.

The declarations of witnesses in favor of Medina and against Gallardo, most of them from priests and caciques, are evidence of the empowerment of these authorities in a renewed absolutist context. In particular, the use of the language of "reconquest" at once was suggestive of the caciques' desperation in view of the disempowerment they were facing and also revealed their awareness of and connection with the larger political project of the *audiencias* in Santa Fe and Quito known as the *reconquista*.[65] The reference to "reconquering" the Indian towns partially alluded to the importance of exercising military force against the Indians in Obonuco, Botanilla, and Jongovito and also compared the conflictive situation in the towns with subversion or revolution.

It seems paradoxical that such complaints of disorder or subversion were coming out of towns known for their unalterable royalism. It well could be that the representation of the Indian authorities was exaggerated and that, aside from the explicit challenges that priests had been exposed to during the liberal phase of government, the Indian governors had other problems with Gallardo's interference in their towns. For example, when called upon to confirm his testimony in the collective representation presented by Medina to the *audiencia*, the cacique of Jongovito admitted that "because of the appeals made by Gallardo [when he was protector], the Indians were willing to serve in anything they were called to do for defending the rights of the king." Yet he added that the reason why Gallardo had been removed from the post of protector was "probably because of the resentment of some priests, given that Gallardo was interested in restraining their abuses of the Indians in their services as *pongos* and *platucamas* and contributions of wood and herbs, and for the

---

[65] As we saw in Chapter 3, Pablo Morillo and his army arrived from the peninsula in 1815 as envoys of king Fernando VII to "reconquer" Venezuela and New Granada. The effects of the politics of this military offensive on revolutionary territories were brutal. This period is traditionally represented as the turning point for the alienation of large numbers of royalists, who were not in favor of the strategy of the peninsula recovering sovereignty in the Americas. See Garrido, *Reclamos y representaciones*; Saether, *Identidades e Independencia*.

moderation he tried to achieve in the punishment of the Indians who did not follow Christian doctrine."[66]

Similarly, the cacique of Matituy said he thought Gallardo had been removed from the post because he "defended the rights of the Indians and did not give preference to whites."[67] A *mayor* or elder from the town of Matacunchuy, Francisco Botina, defended Gallardo, acknowledging his active defense of Indians as, for example, in the reduction of punishments given by *hacendados* as well as by priests. He additionally denounced the new *protector partidario* Medina for attempting to reverse such measures and provided testimony of Medina's alliances with scoundrels (*pícaros*), such as the Indian Andrés Pianda from the town of Anganoy. Botina said Medina enraged people in the town when he named Pianda cacique. Some opposed Medina when he attempted to take the staffs of authority (*varas*) from the caciques of Anganoy and depose them. Significantly, Botina said Medina had received money from the people in the towns of Anganoy and Matacunchuy, after promising them that he would "stand in their favor to get their yearly tribute reduced by one peso."[68] Such complaints against Medina were taken further by Jesús Botina, a *regidor* (town-council member) from Anganoy, who said Medina charged them five pesos, "making fantastic promises such as that he would raise the salary of *conciertos* [Indians subject to long-term labor contracts] and put into practice other policies favorable to the Indians, which would be hidden from the *cabildo*."[69] Here the *regidor* was probably referring to the April 29 decree of the king in which he ordered that attention be paid to the situation of Indians on haciendas.

These confrontations between Gallardo and Medina and the different factions that supported each suggest that, while the city of Pasto remained under royalist rule and the Indians from nearby towns assured the authorities of their loyalty to the king, some people within the Indian communities were able to transform the terms of their subjection, creating a credible threat to the local authorities. These conflicts and transformations are noteworthy because they reveal that royalism was not singular or static and that the legitimacy that commoners acquired by demonstrating their loyalty within the royalist faction also allowed them to undertake daring actions and projects, challenging their immediate authorities, namely priests and caciques.

---

[66] ANE Popayán 350, doc. dated. January 9, 1819, fol. 81v, *Pongo* was a name given to the Indian who performed service for a hacienda owner or a civil or ecclesiastical authority. It is unclear to me what the meaning of *platucama* was.

[67] Ibid. fol. 83v.   [68] Ibid. fol. 85v.   [69] Ibid. fol. 88v.

Interpretations of Indian royalism have generally attributed popular support of the king's cause in the independence period to the influence of priests or religious fanaticism.[70] However, the complaints of the priests of Sibundoy, Pandiaco, and Aganoy presented to the *Audiencia* in Quito suggest otherwise. Royalist communities took advantage of the outbreak of the war and a changing political context to challenge the relationship of domination that the priests had over them. As *protector partidario*, Gallardo had access to the incoming liberal decrees that benefited the Indians. Although he had to mediate those mandates in view of the decisive obstacles to them existing in Pasto-Quito, he was able to press for the new rights in favor of the communities. Clearly not all Indians, and particularly the Indian caciques, were interested in such change. The conflicts that ensued between the religious authorities and the communities in Pasto reveal the complexity of Indian royalism. By siding with the royalist government in the second part of the decade (1815–20), the Indian communities were not necessarily conforming to the rule of the "two pillars of government" – God and king – but they were actively transforming the nature of colonial rule and power in relation to their communities.[71]

IMPERIAL CHANGE FROM BELOW

Spanish policy since the mid-sixteenth century had excluded Indians from serving in militia companies, and Indians were not part of imperial armies during the late eighteenth century, when Spain first created standing militias in almost every town. But throughout the history of the monarchy, in critical moments the government chose to regard alliances with Indians as an opportunity, reassured that introducing native troops into the armies would not threaten the needs of defense.[72] Indians, for their part, took advantage of their importance to the government's needs, welcoming beneficial offers from local authorities and taking the opportunity to actively redefine their political relation to the crown. The rise of hostilities across Spanish America in 1809 and 1810 was a critical juncture that forced colonial officials to search for a negotiated incorporation

---

[70] This view was first proposed and is best represented by Restrepo, *Historia de la Revolución*; see also Garrido, *Reclamos y representaciones*, 272; Guerrero, *Pasto en la guerra*, 53; Lynch, *The Spanish American Revolutions*.

[71] For the two pillars of government, see Cañeque, *The King's Living Image*, chs. 2 and 3.

[72] Vinson and Restall, "Black Soldiers, Native Soldiers," 23.

of Indians into their armies.[73] Compared with prior attempts, when the crown searched for an alliance with natives in order to expand frontier areas through the support of local indigenous groups, the case of Pasto provides evidence of an unprecedented alliance between colonial officials and Indian communities in the northern Andes, one that sought to repress a Creole insurrection.

This reevaluation of the terms of the relationship between the government and the Indian communities in Pasto in turn transformed the very nature of loyalty and royalism. The participation of Pasto Indian communities in the royalist faction reveals how Indians articulated their political interests in relation to the monarchy. Because of the centuries-long lack of a consistent policy regarding Indian inclusion in militia companies, historians of Spanish America have had few sources with which to interpret royalist Indian military mobilization within a native historical, symbolic, and political framework. Further, the complex negotiations during the monarchical crisis with Indians regarding tribute payments have been completely omitted from an independence narrative that long assumed that Indians obediently participated as royalists, and always on disadvantageous terms.[74] Yet the context of Pasto allows us to gain insight into the meanings that Indians gave to military service, as well as the ways native communities transformed themselves by taking on the military defense of the sovereignty of the Spanish king.[75]

The idea that royalism represents a sort of backward or conservative choice fails to acknowledge the dynamic transformation of the crown and the multiple meanings that loyalty acquired throughout the first two decades of the nineteenth century. That the Indians had an antagonistic relationship vis-à-vis the elites and other social sectors in colonial society was the starting point for mid-twentieth-century social historians, who

---

[73] Kuethe, *Military Reform and Society in New Granada*, 29. As Ben Vinson and Matthew Restall have shown, since the conquest and throughout the centuries of Spanish rule, in Spanish America both natives and people of African descent had played military roles in varied contexts and for multiple reasons. See Vinson and Restall, "Black Soldiers, Native Soldiers." For Quito after 1809, see Morelli, *Territorio o Nación*, 138–52.

[74] As Rebecca Earle has argued, assumptions about Indian royalism permeated propaganda from both royalists and insurgents in the context of the wars of independence. See Earle, "Creole Patriotism and the Myth of the 'Loyal Indian,'" *Past and Present* 172 (2001), 125–45.

[75] Vinson and Restall refer to the way "military service could be wholly transformative for blacks and natives" because "the state's perception of these individuals could change radically when they were employed as militiamen," from oppositional or subordinate to allies. See Vinson and Restall, "Black Soldiers, Native Soldiers," 23–24.

integrated class analysis into the study of independence.[76] The history of the Indians in Pasto provides evidence that allows us to produce a more complex understanding of "Indianness" and of Indian politics rather than a rigid scheme that supposes that interests or mental structures are the reflection of social structures.[77]

Royalism among the Indians in Pasto was far from a conservative or "naïve" attitude. It was a political choice that benefited them along class lines within their communities. Such a choice was first and foremost determined by the changing political context that entitled Indians to redefine the content of royalism, to pursue new benefits, and to attempt to transform their position in society. As a consequence of the active participation of Indians in royalist politics throughout the first decade of conflicts in southwestern New Granada, the relationships that defined "Indianness" were transformed, both inside the communities and outside, with priests and government officials. While this change was very much embedded in the particular circumstances of this juncture in the independence period, and linked to the transformation of royalism from an absolutist to a liberal imperial framework, change was not intrinsically new to Indian politics. Between 1809 and 1819 adjustments continued to pivot on the issue of tribute and cacique authority, so central to community politics, and expanded to include military service as an expression of Indian loyalty. This new dimension of Indian vassalage during the decade had long-lasting consequences as it opened up new possibilities for belonging to the monarchy and to the community, for leadership and participation, for expressing allegiance and claiming rights.

The tensions between the absolutist and liberal discourses that were characteristic of the decade following 1810 clearly manifested themselves in antagonism among the members of the indigenous communities in the district of Pasto. As commoners engaged with the liberal project to abolish tribute, caciques saw their privileged position threatened. The caciques advocated a pacification of the Indians and a return to an earlier

---

[76] Brian Hamnett, *Revolución y contrarrevolución en México y el Perú. Liberalismo, realeza y separatismo* (México: Fondo de Cultura Económica, 1978), 63; Bonilla and Spalding, "La independencia en el Perú," 95.

[77] Arze, *Participación popular en la independencia de Bolivia*; and Roca, "Las expediciones porteñas y las masas altoperuanas," assume that the interest of the oppressed class (the Indians) was emancipation. Two authors that challenge the structural equivalence between social position and political consciousness are: Nuria Sala i Vila, "El levantamiento de los pueblos de Aymaraes en 1818," *Boletín Americanista* No. 39–40 (1990), 224; Méndez, *The Plebeian Republic*, 146–53.

order while the commoners sought alliances with the *protector de naturales* in order to pursue their interests with the municipal council and to make appeals to the king. These latent conflicts between caciques and commoners defined royalist priorities in the region, and the conflicts reveal that royalism among north-Andean Indian communities was not monolithic. Moreover, royalism was not antagonistic to liberalism but, on the contrary, both were in constant dialogue through the Indians' political practices.

To make a comparison with events in another area, it is important to note that in Peru, where the abolition of tribute was put in effect, once Fernando VII returned to the throne and attempted to reverse that liberal measure, the Indian communities revolted. The unpopularity of Fernando's reinstatement of tribute resulted in the Indians joining the insurgents' anticolonial struggle against the crown. In contrast, in Pasto there were no revolts to protest changes in tribute; instead, the colonial officials' negotiation of tribute payment was crucial for Indian support of the royalists.[78]

The commoners whose military service for the crown transformed their social position had a vision of the changes they sought to see enacted and that vision did not simply derive from liberal legislation. In fact, the Indian communities in Pasto had been experiencing fissures since the eighteenth century. They were mainly linked to the abuses of power that caciques and colonial magistrates had perpetrated against the commoners in the context of Bourbon reform. While the commoners viewed their condition of vassalage as linked to the crown's protection of their rights, they needed to have access to channels of justice that would uphold their interests. In the context of the war and the royalist government in Pasto, the Indian commoners sought the support of the protector and, by doing so, challenged the rights of the caciques to govern, represent, and control them.[79] Facing that situation, aside from trying to curb the alliance of the protector and the commoners, with the support of the *audiencia*, the

[78] On the Aymara rebellions against tribute reinstatement in Peru, see Sala i Vila, "El levantamiento de los pueblos de Aymaraes en 1818," 203–26. See also Christine Hünefeldt, "Los indios y la Constitución de 1812," *Allpanchis* 11–12 (1978), 33–57; Soux, *El complejo proceso hacia la independencia de Charcas*, 267–71.

[79] In the late 1810s the similarity between the conflict surrounding the *protectores* in Pasto and in Sonora suggests that both inside and outside New Granada, the instability of the monarchy was creating conflicts with the *protectores* and adding a new layer to the conflicts that characterized the institution. In Sonora, as in Pasto, the rhetoric deployed against the *protectores de indios* was explicit about the risk of insurrection among the Indians as a result of their relationship with the current protector. See José Refugio de la Torre Curiel, "Un mecenazgo fronterizo: el protector de indios Juan De Gándara y los

caciques had to adjust to the changing context and assume that their authority was less linked to the collection of tribute than it was to their role in the military mobilization of the communities.

As central actors in the political theater, the Indians always established alliances that involved non-Indians, in relationships that were not necessarily oppositional.[80] The vertical alliances that royalism enabled had a history in the ongoing engagement of Indians with royal officials. The *protector partidario de naturales* is a case in point. The *protectores partidarios* had the responsibility to protect the Indians' rights and interests, and over time they became profoundly immersed in local native politics. The alliances of Indian commoners with the *protector* Gallardo reveal his strategic position as mediator of their interests in the changing political and legal landscape.

It should not be surprising that in this decade the *protector de naturales* played such a central role in the politics of the indigenous people in Pasto. The Indians mobilized militarily, expecting rewards from the crown. This was not simply a misguided calculation; the viceroy in Santa Fe instructed Tacón to promise recognition of their loyalty to all vassals, and Tacón was quick to offer a tribute reduction to guarantee the Indians' support for the royalist cause. The protector was the legal advocate who could defend the interests of the Indians and ensure that their efforts were justly rewarded. The protector was a mediator whose role became vulnerable to the conflicts arising from the sharp division between the Indian authorities and the commoners. The protector's ability to influence decisions at the level of the municipal council, the *audiencia*, and even with the king, once he returned to the throne, and his knowledge of imperial legislation made the protector the preferred ally of Indian commoners who were seeking to transform their position in the communities and in relation to the priests.

Historians have found evidence from Mexico, Central America, and Cuenca about the centrality of the redefinition of Indians as citizens with voting rights, and have come to conclusions about the radical impact of the Cádiz Constitution on the integration of indigenous communities into national politics on an imperial scale.[81] Yet the evidence suggests that in

---

ópatas de Opodepe (Sonora) a principios del siglo XIX," *Revista de Indias* LXX, no. 248 (2010), 185–212.

[80] A study that focuses on these alliances in Guatemala is Grandin, *The Blood of Guatemala*, esp. ch. 2.

[81] For Quito and Cuenca, see Rodríguez, "Las primeras elecciones constitucionales en el Reino de Quito"; and Morelli, *Territorio o Nación*. For Cuenca, see Silvia Palomeque, "El sistema de autoridades de 'pueblos de indios' y sus transformaciones a fines del período colonial: El partido de Cuenca," *Memoria Americana* 6 (1997), 10–47. For Mexico, see Antonio

Pasto elections did not influence the communities in the same way as they did in Mexico, where there was a proliferation of municipal councils representing indigenous society. The Cádiz Constitution arrived in Quito and Pasto in 1813 under the presidency of Toribio Montes, who decided to apply it selectively. Montes was wary about having elections in the context of a polity of largely indigenous communities. In the absence of the monarch, military needs gave Montes room to exercise discretion, taking into account local conditions and his own views.[82]

Nonetheless, the impact of Spanish liberalism on indigenous people was more diverse than the electoral focus suggests. Across the Quito *Audiencia*, as much as in Pasto, indigenous people took advantage of the liberal constitutional experiment to question their traditional obligations vis-à-vis the church. Indigenous people interpreted the liberal creed to their advantage, and the incidence of similar conflicts in the regions of Quito and Popayán suggests that Indians shared information regarding the political transformations of the period.[83]

Finally, by looking at the case of Pasto, where Indians saw connections with their own struggles and the first manifestations of Hispanic liberalism that came out of Cádiz after 1810, it is clear that periodization is essential for understanding the political dynamics of indigenous people during the independence process. Historians have supposed that emergent

Annino, "Cádiz y la revolución territorial de los pueblos mexicanos," in *Historia de las elecciones en Iberoamérica, siglo XIX* (Buenos Aires: Fondo de Cultura Económica, 1995), 177–226; and Guarisco, *Los indios del valle de México*. For Peru see Víctor Peralta, "Los inicios del sistema representativo en Perú: Ayuntamientos constitucionales y diputaciones provinciales (1812–1815)," in *La mirada esquiva: Reflexiones históricas sobre la interacción del estado y la ciudadanía en los Andes (Bolivia, Ecuador y Perú), siglo XIX*, ed. Marta Irurozqui (Madrid: Consejo Superior de Investigaciones Científicas, 2005), 65–92. For Guatemala, see Alda, *La participación indígena*; and Jordana Dym, *From Sovereign Villages to National States: City, State and Federation in Central America, 1759–1839* (Albuquerque: University of New Mexico Press, 2006). For Tlaxcala, see Marco Bellingeri, "Sistemas jurídicos y codificación en el primer liberalismo mexicano, 1824–1834," in *Dinámicas de Antiguo Régimen y orden constitucional: Representación, justicia y administración en Iberoamérica, Siglos XVIII–XIX*, ed. Bellingeri (Turin: Otto Editore, 2000), 367–95; and Raymond Buve, "La influencia del liberalismo doceañista en una provincia novohispana mayormente indígena: Tlaxcala, 1809–1824," in *La trascendencia del liberalismo doceañista en España y en América*, ed. Manuel Chust and Ivana Frasquet (Valencia: Generalitat Valenciana, 2004), 115–35.

[82] "Representación del Presidente de Quito, don Toribio Montes, ante el Secretario de Estado, sobre las actuaciones de su Gobierno en las pasadas convulsions, desde que tomó posesión del mando," in *Colección de documentos para la historia de Colombia*, ed. Ortiz, 80.

[83] For the case of Quito, see Rodríguez, *La revolución política*, 122–23.

nation states used liberalism to attack the Indians and have thus explained royalism as a reaction against the threat that independence represented. However, as we have seen here, in the decade of the wars in New Granada and Peru that took place between 1810 and 1820, liberalism and royalism were intertwined. And during this phase neither independence nor liberalism meant an offensive against Indian lands.[84] Indians were "positively" drawn to royalism because specific political dynamics on the ground, in Popayán, Pasto, and Quito, offered important opportunities to caciques and commoners alike. Some opportunities derived from military participation in the war, but others also resulted from the imperial shift toward liberalism that, although somewhat contested in the region from Peru to Popayán, allowed for important appropriations by Indians of the possibilities ushered in by the 1812 charter. After Fernando VII returned to the throne in 1814, though the king recognized the loyalty of indigenous people in Pasto, the region experienced a regression in terms of the expanded rights granted to commoners by the Cádiz Constitution. Yet the story does not end there. Once Simón Bolívar proclaimed the Colombian Republic in 1820, Indian royalism continued to change.

---

[84] Juan Friede, *El indio en lucha por la tierra: Historia de los resguardos del macizo central colombiano* (1944; Bogotá: Editorial La Chispa, 1972); Christine Hünefeldt, *Lucha por la tierra y protesta indígena. Las comunidades indígenas del Perú entre Colonia y República, 1800–1830* (Bonn: Estudios Americanistas de Bonn, 1982); Robert Jackson, ed., *Liberals, the Church, and Indian Peasants: Corporate Lands and the Challenge of Reform in Nineteenth-Century Latin America* (Albuquerque: University of New Mexico Press, 1997); Larson, *Trials of Nation Making*; Fiona Wilson, "Reconfiguring the Indian: Land-Labour Relations in the Postcolonial Andes." *Journal of Latin American Studies* 35 (2003), 221–47.

5

Slaves in the defense of Popayán

War, royalism, and freedom (1809–1819)

In 1809, in his desperate attempt to defend the region from the insurgents advancing from Quito, Governor Miguel Tacón decided the situation merited the mobilization of slaves from the haciendas and mines in Popayán. It should not be surprising that colonial officials in Popayán approached the enslaved in the province during the crisis that began in 1809. These types of alliances between imperial powers and people of African descent – meant as a means of controlling the population and increasing manpower – were typical throughout the revolutionary Atlantic. Yet the significance of the study of the specific contexts that enabled negotiation between slaves and the representatives of the Spanish crown in Popayán lies in gaining a fuller understanding of the ways in which the politics of the enslaved shaped the political process underway. The particularities of those encounters reveal that for slaves it was not just a matter of taking advantage of the emergency situation into which imperial rivalries and internal tensions had led the colonial power. Enslaved people forged these alliances from the standpoint of the goals of their previous activism: to create families, to gain legal recognition of their communities, to procure themselves rights within the monarchical context, and to expand their control of the territory in which they lived. And the military mobilization of enslaved people of African descent in this region was intricately related to their social organization and political goals.[1]

---

[1] One interpretation of slave mobilization during the independence wars that privileges the moment of opportunity at the expense of understanding the depth of enslaved peoples' politics in Spanish America is Blanchard, *Under the Flags of Freedom*.

The cases of the slaves in Popayán who defended the crown invite us to rethink the nature of slaves' struggles for political inclusion and community protection during this revolutionary age. The politics of the enslaved intersected with the opportunities that the monarchical crisis offered at this juncture. The crucial development of alliances in the Pacific-Andean region that lay between Popayán, Quito, and Lima gave enslaved blacks the possibility to act on their interests by joining the royalist struggle. Located in a strategic military frontier zone that connected Popayán, by means of an ocean route, to the viceregal capital of Lima, throughout a decade slaves transformed their relationship to the colonial power and gained unprecedented autonomy. Their actions further shaped the military process of the war by consistently blocking the advance of insurgent forces from across New Granada.

"TO ENJOY THE SAME LIBERTY AS LOYAL VASSALS, WITH SUBORDINATION ONLY TO HIS MAJESTY"

In 1810 the tension heightened within Popayán Province because of the opposition of the northern city of Cali and adjacent towns to Miguel Tacón's absolutist government and military defense strategies. Questioning the legitimacy of the new organs of government in place on the peninsula – first the Junta Central, the Regency, and later the Cortes – these southwestern insurgents aligned with Santa Fe, where on July 10, 1810, the Creole-led autonomist junta had expelled the Spanish government, including the viceroy. Cali proceeded to ask Santa Fe for authorization to create a junta, which at the time was the symbol of a secessionist attitude. The main supporters of the junta, which was to become a confederation of cities in the Cauca Valley, were Creole land and mine owners. The mine- and slave-owning elite, along with other *hacendados* from Popayán, backed Cali's plan and openly opposed the war politics of Tacón. They questioned the way he had forcefully been collecting provisions from them for defense purposes since 1809 when Quito had formed the first junta in the region. In particular, they contested what they saw as a risky measure – the governor's decision to arm Indians and slaves in the province. Tacón reacted militarily to Cali's secessionist plans and defended his alliance with enslaved people by arguing that they, too, were against their masters' revolutionary plans.[2]

---

[2] AGI Quito 386. On the confederation of the cities of the Cauca Valley, see Zawadzky, *Las ciudades confederadas*.

The controversy sparked by Tacón's alliance with the slaves reached critical proportions during Cali's march toward the city of Popayán. Facing the threat of an invasion, the Popayán municipal council agreed to offer freedom to those slaves who would take up arms in defense of the royalist party. The council drafted those plans in the minutes of a meeting that took place on March 10, 1811, noting that, at that time, the situation involving the thousands of slaves in the province was already complicated by the fact that insurgent slave owners were going around making public affirmations that "the time had come to break the chains of slavery, tyranny, and despotism . . . and of recovering freedom," causing the slaves to revolt.[3]

The Popayán *cabildo* was concerned about the crisis at the mine of Yurumanguí, which was owned by the Valencia family. The *cabildo* was informed that once the slaves there "understood the aggression" that the Confederated Cities of the Cauca Valley planned against the capital city of Popayán – because they wanted to separate from Popayán's jurisdiction and deny Spanish sovereignty – the slaves rebelled, claiming

They, insofar as they had remained enslaved to their masters while these were vassals of the king, [and the king] *guaranteed the slaves protection against excessive violence and cruel treatment*, should not continue in their [masters'] dominion and servitude but rather *enjoy the same liberty as loyal vassals* with subordination only to His Majesty and His ministers, under whose dominion and authority they insisted they would remain.[4]

In other words, the slaves promised to remain faithful to the king and to turn against the insurgents of Cali and Popayán. The argument they used highlighted the protections that the enslaved received from the king as the mediator in their relationship of servitude with the slave owners. As we have seen for the Indians of Pasto, at play here was the centrality of "legal reasoning" and legal practice to the slaves' ongoing political strategies, something that was not exclusive to the slaves in Popayán but also was shared with enslaved people across Spanish America and the Caribbean.[5]

---

[3] AGI Quito 386.

[4] AGI Quito 386. Emphasis added. Original: "Ellos, que en tanto eran esclavos en cuanto sus amos habían sido vasallos del Rey, que los amparaba y dispensaba su real protección cuando la imploraban contra la sevicia y crueldad con que los trataban, no debían continuar en su dominio y servidumbre sino gozar de la misma libertad que los vasallos fieles con subordinación únicamente a Su Majestad y a sus ministros, bajo cuyo dominio y autoridad protestaban permanecer."

[5] On legal reasoning and for the French Caribbean, see Dubois, "An Enslaved Enlightenment," 13.

In different contexts of the imperial crisis across the Atlantic world, slaves appropriated the ideologies of the contending sides to justify rebellion against their masters. For example, in 1793 during the French Revolution, a slave revolt took place on the island of Guadeloupe. Once the white troops who had been sent to pacify the revolt encountered the slaves, they explained that they "rose in defense of the Republic against their royalist masters."[6] While we could suppose that the statement of the Yurumanguí slaves was merely a utilitarian deployment of royalist language to calm the royalist authorities, this evidence needs to be put into perspective given the history of the slaves' uses of the law and their appropriation of the Spanish discourse of justice. Their emphasis on the king's role as protector suggests that the slaves had brought the accumulated experience of their earlier negotiations with Spanish colonial officials and their knowledge of Spanish law to their self-interested evaluation of the possibilities opened up by the insurgency. As we will see throughout this chapter, the slaves in the Pacific lowlands sought to bridge the distance between their de facto freedom (achieved through revolting against their masters) and a legalized freedom that would be the outcome of the reward for their loyalty (if they were men) or their self-purchase (if they were women or children). The slaves were not merely uttering royalist sentiments instrumentally; their royalist positioning at the time was consistent with their belief in the king's justice and their interest in becoming free vassals of the Spanish king.[7]

The royalist slave and mine owners who confronted the revolting slaves tried to persuade them to end their seemingly "loyal" insurrection, given that they, as royalists, had not given up their respect for the legitimate authorities. The slaves then responded that other slave gangs had threatened them, and that they were obliged to continue defending their freedom because "if they did not pursue their freedom, they would be persecuted and treated as enemies."[8] The slaves might have been using this as a convenient excuse, but it is clear that the geographical scope of the insurrection went beyond the mines of Yurumanguí. The slaves in Micay and Raposo were also in revolt.[9] Across the Pacific lowlands,

---

[6] Laurent Dubois, "Citizen Soldiers: Emancipation and Military Service in the Revolutionary French Caribbean," in *Arming Slaves*, ed. Brown and Morgan, 237.

[7] The interpretation of slave royalism as instrumental can be found in Oscar Almario, *La invención del suroccidente colombiano: Independencia, etnicidad y estado nacional entre 1780 y 1930* (Medellín: Universidad Pontificia Bolivariana, 2006), 115–40.

[8] AGI Quito 386.

[9] For Micay see ACC Independencia CIII 2g 6596. For Raposo, see Zawadzky, *Las ciudades confederadas*, 109, 128–29, 134–35.

slaves destroyed the machinery and infrastructure that made the mines productive and took over the territory to produce their own goods. Such an alliance between slave gangs in the mining region – presented to the elites as a menace and backed up with royalist arguments – was how the enslaved seized the opportunity to impose their numerical force and show their strength and ability to pursue their common project of controlling the lowlands.

Clearly, the rise of conflicts between the Cali and Popayán elites and the government of Tacón – of which the slaves became immediately aware – catalyzed a movement among the slave communities in different mines, and they were able to unify, using these conflicts as a legitimate argument. It was particularly possible to take advantage of this situation in the mining region, so distant from the city, because the mine owners had left their properties to join the insurgent armies. The slaves were also aware of the weakness of the government at the time, as it did not have the military capacity to undertake the pacification of the slave gangs because of the multiple offensives it was facing in the cities.

Hence, the royalist slave owners approached Tacón to ask for his support in attempting to implement a strategy of control that consisted of the "soft" measure of meeting with the "captains and leaders of the mine" to "listen to them."[10] The conciliatory attitude of the royalists is remarkable but also consistent with the government's interest in maintaining a negotiated relationship with the enslaved rather than treating them as enemies. The fact that the conversation was established with the "captains and leaders" reasserts the importance of the gang captains as representatives of the slave communities. However, it is unclear whether the term "leaders" implied that, in the context of the rebellion, new men and women were taking the leading role in organizing the community and communicating with the government. It is very likely that, at this critical juncture in the transformation of authority structures throughout Popayán, the authority of the captains was being challenged, but at this time we do not have the means to explore the changes taking place within the community.

In March 1811, the municipal council of Popayán argued that, for the purpose of recruiting large numbers of men in preparation for a confrontation with the Cauca Valley insurgents, the most practical tactic would be to approach the slaves and co-opt them by offering them their freedom.

---

[10] AGI Quito 386.

This would be better, it was argued, than waiting for "the loss of all the slave gangs" who might in an "unexpected situation join the enemy's destructive force." The municipal council proposed that Tacón

> invite slaves to voluntarily enroll for the defense of the city [of Popayán] assuring them that if they perform such defense with honor, loyalty and *patriotismo* ... presenting themselves with their arms and horses, if they have any, such important service to religion and to the state will be rewarded with *la libertad*, which they will be granted in the name of the king; a full and certain freedom so that they never again can be reduced to servitude nor be appraised because they were previously slaves, compensating their owners (those who can prove to have remained loyal and not contributed to the crisis of the legitimate government) for their fair value by account of the royal treasury.[11]

In addition, the slaves were to be promised that they would henceforth be treated as loyal and brave vassals of the king and receive the same treatment as other Catholic Christians, all at the expense of the royal treasury.

The municipal council members hoped that Governor Tacón would publish such a decree, posting it in the usual places and sending copies to the captains of every slave gang. In short, their hopes were that before the insurgent slaveholders could gain control of the enslaved in the province, such an offer would induce the slaves to ally with the royalist side. To have the slaves "follow the call of their [insurgent] masters or their own inclinations" would mean the ruin of Popayán. But apparently Tacón did not go as far as to publish the decree, but, instead, negotiated the promise of freedom on a case-by-case basis, which speaks of the governor's deliberate and strategic approach to arming the slaves.

Even if the decree were not published, the fact that the Popayán council considered offering freedom to the slaves was quite an innovation, causing conflict among the elites and commotion among the enslaved. In taking the step of considering an alliance with the slaves, the colonial authorities were overstepping slaveholder opposition that was – as in other contexts where the imperial power did not own slaves – one of the critical obstacles to mobilizing the slaves militarily.[12] But the *cabildo* members' motives contrast with the way in which, for example, the French reacted to the possibility of arming their slaves on the island of Guadeloupe. There, the administrators were open to arming the slaves because they recognized they could become valuable citizens through

---

[11] AGI Quito 386.
[12] For a comparative discussion, see Christopher Brown, "The Arming of Slaves in Comparative Perspective," in *Arming Slaves*, ed. Brown and Morgan, 348.

performing military service.[13] In Popayán the generous offers that the municipal council considered were inspired mostly by the fear that the municipal council members had that the enslaved might side with the insurgents, and it is not clear what type of treatment the slaves would have received as "loyal and brave vassals of the king." Nonetheless, what is clear is that the council members were taking advantage of the fact that the enslaved had positioned themselves against their masters (the insurgents). As a result, the government made offers to comply with the slaves' interest in being recognized as vassals of the king, a promise that, as we will see, would not be so easy to keep.

Days later, on March 28, 1811, the first battle between Tacón's royalist troops and the army of the Confederated Cities of the Cauca Valley took place in Palacé. The king's troops were defeated, and the triumphant colonel Antonio Baraya captured part of the royalist army. Tacón escaped to the south, first entering Pasto and then moving into Patía to secure men and recover strenght. Meanwhile the insurgents took control of the provincial capital, Popayán, instituting a junta there. Neither Pasto nor Barbacoas participated in the elections to the junta, confirming their royalist stance and Tacón's control over those cities.

One of the priorities of the insurgent junta in Popayán was precisely to stop the "scandalous" plan of the municipal council. In April the new government sent notices to the councils in Iscuandé, Barbacoas, and Cali to inform them of the decision of Popayán's royalist *cabildo* to arm the slaves. Responding to this call, in May 1811, Manuel Olaya, the mayor of Iscuandé, wrote to the superior junta of the Cauca Valley to inform it that Tacón and his lieutenant in Micay, Manuel Silvestre Valverde, were expecting a shipment from Guayaquil of "sabers and fire arms, gunpowder, and shrapnel *to arm the province's blacks and Indians,*" in order to more effectively resist the insurgents.[14] Olaya planned to intercept the arrival of the weapons, take over the coastal zone of Iscuandé and Micay, and institute a provisional government that would allow the Caleños to regain control of the Pacific area. When Olaya and his twenty-five poorly armed men arrived in Micay, a patrol of *zambos* attacked them, yet soon after Olaya was able to capture Valverde, who was taken by sea to Cali, where he was to be imprisoned. However, Olaya stopped on the beach close to the Yurumanguí River late at night, and the slaves in the mines there, who were acting autonomously yet were still "subordinate" to the

---

[13] Dubois, "Citizen Soldiers," 236–37.
[14] ANE Popayán 341, doc. dated November 17, 1813, fol. 1. Emphasis added.

royalists, came out to save Valverde from his captors, proving that the slaves' rebellion was not inconsistent with their loyalty to the royalist authorities.[15]

The Creole insurgents were not interested in incorporating slaves into their armies because they saw this as possibly leading to a threat of widespread rebellion and as a physical risk for whites in the coastal areas. Olaya condemned Tacón's arming of the slaves, characterizing him as "a monster, an enemy of men" who could cause "a total ruin with the revolting slave gangs who can finish off the few whites who live in this coast."[16] Popayán's municipal council (now composed of insurgents) equally denounced Tacón for promoting the general insurrection of the slaves who would cause nothing less than "sedition and a butchery." Insurgent slave owners certainly saw slaves as dangerous, savage brutes, and they feared that "thirty thousand beasts deluded with freedom would quickly destroy Barbacoas, the coast, and Chocó."[17] Part of their concern reflected the fact that the entire wealth of the province was based on slave labor, particularly in the mines. Olaya's words also illustrate perfectly the whites' fear of a race war, and the slave owners presumed that the ultimate goal of enslaved black people was to exterminate their oppressors.[18] Yet, as we have seen, the alliances of the slaves with the royalist officials were of a sophisticated nature, involving the slaves' perception of slavery as a relationship that was mediated by the king. In the slaves'

---

[15] ACC Independencia CIII 2g 6598; ANE Popayán 341, doc. dated November 17, 1813. It is unclear why Olaya called the patrol *zambos*. This would imply that they were offspring of Indians and blacks, which was a possibility in the Pacific region where there were free communities of blacks who created families with Indians. But it could also be that he used it as a derogatory term.

[16] ANE Popayán 341.   [17] AGI Quito 386.

[18] As with the historiographical representations of Tomás Boves in Venezuela, the alliance of a royalist leader with groups of slaves could be stigmatized in situations where looting was an incentive as well as a systematic practice, one that often led to extreme violence. Yet all of the troops of all races on both sides of the conflict were violent and rapacious in their looting. Germán Carrera Damas, *Boves: Aspectos socioeconómicos de la guerra de independencia* (Caracas: Ediciones de la Biblioteca de la Universidad Central de Venezuela, 1972), 51. One of the main narratives that gave an imbalanced picture of this situation is José Manuel Restrepo's *Historia de la Revolución de Colombia*. As noted by Carrera Damas, in his history of the independence wars Restrepo made sure that whenever the royalist troops put in an appearance, as in the case of Popayán, they were portrayed as ferocious savages or, its complement, as ignorant and fanatic. See Restrepo, *Historia de la Revolución*, Vol. I (1969), 327. Another example can be found in "Diario de las noticias y hechos ocurridos que nos dieron los senores limeños, desde el 1 de octubre de 1813 hasta el 15 de enero de 1814," *Boletín Histórico del Valle* 23–24 (1934), 450.

view, freedom was linked to attaining the status of vassal. It was that aspect of the slaves' politics and political vision that the insurgents could not recognize and that they rather obscured by labeling the blacks as "beasts."

Barbacoas, in contrast to Popayán, remained faithful to Tacón. Once the city received the insurgent *cabildo*'s notice denouncing the Popayán royalists' plans to give freedom to slaves in exchange for service, the *cabildo* wrote to inform Tacón about the profound injury that the insurgents wished to cause to the governor's image, respectability, and power. Because the Barbacoas *cabildo* members knew that the governor had not published the decree of freedom after all, they suggested that the governor improve his image by proving that loyal owners had in fact voluntarily given some slaves to the government. Following this advice, the governor drafted a document that confronted some of the most serious accusations leveled by the insurgent *cabildo*, including the claim that Tacón was a tyrant who had confiscated property by freeing slaves. The governor's goal was to prove that in the royalist Popayán *cabildo*'s original proposal, serious account had been taken of the need to compensate slave owners in the event that some of their slaves were taken for military purposes and later freed. Additionally, Tacón clarified that he was not offering freedom to all the slaves who joined his army but only to those who "distinguish themselves through a heroic action."[19]

The questionnaire elaborated by Tacón and designed to provide evidence of such important matters indicates the role that slavery and slaves played in the confrontations between royalists and insurgents. Twenty of the thirty-six slaves who had joined Tacón's army, who hailed mainly from the haciendas near Popayán, were questioned, as were five slave owners who had ceded their slaves to the army. The slave owners were asked if the governor had forced them to provide slaves, while the slaves were asked if they had been promised freedom by the governor or if they had chosen to join the army voluntarily. The testimony of the slaves shows clear evidence that the scribes fit their words into a pattern that highlighted the legitimacy of the government and the slaves' voluntary decision to join the royalists. Yet the slaves' testimony also reveals important details about the reasons that slaves from nearby Popayán were interested in defending the cause of the king as well as information about their relationships to their masters and their insurgent project. The

[19] AGI Quito 386.

slaves who lived in cities or on haciendas near Popayán were in a different situation from those in the mines. The former were less able to ensure their freedom by sheer numbers or by rebelling. Some of the urban slaves fled toward the lowlands, where they found refuge, or joined the militias in the Patía Valley. Yet most of them were attracted by the royalists' promises of freedom and joined the royalist army as a means of escaping slavery.[20]

All twenty of the slaves interviewed noted that they had left their masters because they had found out about their owners' rebellious plans and had feared that their masters would force them to collaborate with the insurgents. As a result, they had preferred to join the governor's army. José Ilario Caldas testified: "The cause that the Caleños are defending is unjust while the one that the *señor* governor defends is legitimate because his highness was appointed by our king, but the deponent has not heard that His Majesty has put the Caleños in the government." Similarly, Victorino Sarasti said that he knew about his owner don Agustin Ramón Sarasti's plans to aid insurgent troops with the gunpowder, bullets, shotguns, and pistols he had collected for precisely such a purpose. He told "his *compañeros* what he knew about the treason that was being prepared, that it was not fair that the *señor* governor and the city were going to be sacrificed like that," and as a loyal vassal of the king, he decided to denounce the situation, with the others following him "voluntarily." Damasco Hurtado declared that once he realized that his owner don Marcelino Hurtado was accommodating the troops from Cali on his hacienda San Joaquín, he decided "he would prefer to give his blood defending the legitimate government, not going back to his owners because they are traitors."[21]

Another important point that was common to the testimony of the slaves is that they had to clarify that their actions were not intended to be a rebellion against their masters. Hence Cayetano Sarasti declared that he had joined the government's troops, not informing his owner, "without the intention of acting against him but to defend the city from the enemies ... and because the *negro* captain told them that their owner was making a prison to secure them and prevent them from running away to defend the governor ... and they decided they preferred to die defending the law and not in those prisons." Felipe Mosquera said he

---

[20] Significantly, male slaves almost always made such decisions in groups. At present, however, we have little information about the situation or choices of enslaved women in urban settings. ACC Independencia MI 3j 6384.

[21] AGI Quito 386.

had not asked permission from his owner, Maria Josefa Hurtado, to enlist in the governor's army "not because I wanted to act against her but to defend the law of god, the authority of the king, and the city."[22]

It is easy to imagine that the scribe who wrote the declaration adjusted Felipe Mosquera's statement to fit a pattern of royalist language that would present the slaves as loyal subjects.[23] Yet beyond the language of loyalty, there is another underlying commonality in the slaves' declarations: the affirmation that they were either tired of their owners' treatment of them or fearful of punishment. Salvador Caldas, for example, noted that "he had come [to the camp] to serve the king and because his master don Rafael Caldas constantly mistreated him." Mauricio Hurtado said he fled because his owner "tried to punish him and send him off to be sold" for having decided to collaborate with the governor. Cayetano Sarasti had come "to serve the legitimate government and because he feared that his master would punish him for having denounced him." Likewise, Francisco Hurtado argued that he had joined the royalist army not because anyone forced him to but because he "thought that was the way to proceed and he came looking to be under the protection of the government fearing that his master would take his life because of what he had done."[24]

Roque María Hurtado mentioned that his owner had threatened him with one hundred lashes for having joined the camp of the governor and for that reason, "and to serve the king," he had left to follow the "legitimate" government. Dionicio Hurtado, too, said his owner told him he would "whip him to death," and so he "fled in defense of the just cause." Dionicio mentioned that he had not intended to rebel against his master, but that in the event that he saw him among the enemies "he would not hesitate to attack him." His declaration suggests that although the slaves were openly defending the royalist cause, they were also seizing an opportunity to avenge themselves – not only by the act of fleeing their masters, but also through the possibility of confronting them in combat. Slaves such as José Ilario, Cayetano, and Roque included in their testimony complaints of mistreatment and abuse, which expressed the antagonism that existed between the slaves and their masters. They all called the government legitimate and said they were searching for its protection. Ultimately, it seems possible to argue that the slaves saw the government

---

[22] AGI Quito 386.

[23] On the role of scribes in creating written statements, see Kathryn Burns, *Into the Archive: Writing and Power in Colonial Peru* (Durham, NC: Duke University Press, 2010).

[24] AGI Quito 386.

and the king as providing them with protection from their oppressors, and that they trusted that following the royalist cause would eventually translate into benefits for them. That this might or might not mean freedom is suggested in the declaration of Mauricio Hurtado, who said that once in the camp, "The governor told them that those who performed a brilliant action when they attacked the enemies would get their freedom in the name of the king."[25]

The bulk of the testimony was probably useful to Tacón for the purpose of clearing his name of the accusations made by the insurgent elites that he was responsible for the "agitated (*alterados*) slaves." In December 1811 Tacón drafted a letter to the secretary of the Universal Office of the State (*despacho universal del estado*) that included this report in an effort to prove that he had used "good sense and care to guarantee the subjection of the slave gangs [resulting in the] state of respect toward royal authority in which those [from Popayán] and the ones from the provinces of Iscuandé, Micay, and Raposo are found."[26]

After the battle of Iscuandé (January 1812), in which the royalist troops were defeated, Tacón escaped by sea to Guayaquil and from there went to Lima. In the Peruvian capital he was well received by his ally Viceroy Abascal, and was later decorated with the cross of Isabel the Catholic Queen in recognition of his efforts to defend Popayán Province. From Lima, Tacón wrote to Benito Pérez, viceroy of New Granada, that

> The blacks on the coast and in the district of Popayán were never in favor of their masters because they considered them enemies of the King and, on the contrary, they always offered to defend the government, and if it had not been for the difficult political circumstances that stopped me, I would have welcomed and armed them a long time ago. ... When the [insurgent] troops from Cali went to the Anchicayá River to control the slave gang in Yurumanguí, [the slaves] rejected them and declared, with other slave gangs, to be resolved to first fulfill their duties as Christians and faithful vassals than of slaves.[27]

To protect his image and defend his reliance on slaves as allies, Tacón made use of the evidence that the slaves in the mines had legitimated their revolt for freedom in royalist terms. But he conveniently silenced the consequences of the slave revolts, and he did not report to Pérez the fact that since 1810 the Pacific lowlands had been out of the control of royalists and insurgents alike. What was taking place in this region was

[25] AGI Quito 386.   [26] AGI Quito 386.
[27] "Oficio del gobernador de Popayán, don Miguel Tacón, al Virrey don Benito Pérez," in *Documentos Importantes*, ed. Restrepo, 75.

a large-scale rebellion in which the enslaved were able to win unprecedented freedoms. A closer look into the situation of the slaves at the mine of San Juan will allow us to see how enslaved people in the mines envisioned their freedom and the reasons that royalism was compatible with their search for autonomy.

RUMORS OF FREEDOM IN SAN JUAN

As had happened previously in Yurumanguí and Raposo, in 1810 there was a slave revolt at the San Juan mine on the Micay River, which was owned by Gerónimo Torres. According to a letter that Torres wrote to governor Tacón, the slaves had revolted because "a black queen had arrived to the Americas bringing freedom to the slaves, and slave owners were trying to hide her." For that reason, Gerónimo Torres explained, the slaves "began meeting at night in juntas to take measures to reject obedience."[28] The words of slave-owner Torres are sparse. He gives no description of the political organization the slaves reportedly established (composed of the juntas) for achieving their goals. When Torres said the slaves "began" meeting in juntas, was he implying that the slaves' meetings were something new? It is very likely that the enslaved in the mines actually had a tradition of social gatherings that were permitted and not considered dangerous. Thus it seems that Torres' use of the term "junta" in fact signaled a concrete change in the nature of the slaves' meetings.

This change was perhaps linked to the creation of Creole juntas that enjoyed autonomous rule in southwestern New Granada. Significantly, the junta created in Quito in August 1809 had attempted to take control of the Pacific lowlands as a way of contesting Popayán's economic power. Then, as we have seen, during the year 1810, multiple juntas were set up by the municipal councils of almost every city across New Granada, leading to increasing conflict in the Pacific-Andean region. Of course, it is plausible that Torres labeled the slaves' meetings "juntas" but that the enslaved themselves were not using that term to define their gatherings. But the alternative possibility – that Torres had correctly reported the word the slaves in San Juan were using for their organizations – is particularly interesting because it indicates that the communities in the Pacific lowlands were informed and aware of the implications of the changes in government structures in many cities in the Kingdom of Quito

---

[28] ACC Independencia CIII 2g 6596, fol. 1.

and Popayán. If this were the case, Torres' use of the term "junta" hints at the slaves' appropriation of the emergent institutional language to legitimate their rebellion.

This does not mean that, by using the term that was central to Spanish and Creole politics at the time, the slaves' political imaginations or organizations were corollaries of the Hispanic world. On the contrary, it is fascinating to ponder and it makes sense to suppose that the enslaved gave institutional value to their overtly political meetings by equating them to the juntas that Creoles had formed in the city to govern in the name of Fernando VII. After all, in that particular context and at that moment, the juntas were symbols of contested political sovereignty. Thus the fact that the mine-owner Torres called the slaves' meetings "juntas" could mean that he acknowledged that the slaves constituted a political organization with de facto rights to common deliberation and representation.

Moreover, the content of the rumor on which the slaves acted did not reference the Creoles' justification for demanding autonomous rule at the crucial 1810 juncture but instead explained that a black queen had brought freedom to slaves in the Americas, a freedom that they claimed to deserve. The slaves' pursuit of freedom based on rumored declarations of emancipation had been frequent in the Atlantic world since the eighteenth century.[29] The variety of news circulating among the enslaved in different settings is evidence of the flow of oral information, the "common wind" that connected African diasporic communities across the Atlantic world. The Pacific lowlands, although relatively distant from the urban centers in Popayán, were filled with merchants who arrived in the region from many places: they came by land from Quito, Los Pastos, Cali, and Chocó and by sea from Panama, Guayaquil, and Lima (and other places in Peru); in the independence period even some pirates from Buenos Aires were seen in the area.[30] These were all possible places from which information reached the enslaved in Popayán. But where the rumor about a black queen who was granting freedom to slaves in 1810–11 originated cannot be easily or satisfactorily explained.

---

[29] Geggus, "Slavery, War, and Revolution"; Klooster, "Le décret d'émancipation imaginaire."

[30] Biblioteca Luis Angel Arango (hereinafter BLAA) Archivo de Emiliano Díaz del Castillo, Caja 8, Carpeta 85, fol. 101; Fray Juan de Santa Gertrudis, *Maravillas de la Naturaleza*, Vol. II (1799; Bogotá: Empresa Nacional de Publicaciones, 1956), 158; Julius Scott, "The Common Wind: Currents of Afro-American Communication in the Era of the Haitian Revolution" (PhD diss., Duke University, 1986).

To make an informed inference and envision the source of the rumor, the question to be answered is whether the reference to the black queen was historically contingent (related to a specific event) or if the reference was in fact part of the circulating African diasporic imaginary alluding to mythical figures, such as Nanny or Queen Nzinga from Kongo.[31] Beyond that we can only say for certain that the very fact that the people in San Juan based their revolt on the rumor and on the expectation that a black queen had liberated them reflects the intellectual and political world of the slaves in San Juan as well as their interests. Moreover, the reference to the black queen "arriving" in the Americas (from Africa?) is qualitative evidence that hints at the vitality of diasporic cultural references among the enslaved in the Pacific region, surely a subject that merits further research.[32]

With the evidence available, interpretation must remain at the level of analyzing the rumor. It is telling that the story shares two fundamental elements with other emancipation rumors circulating among enslaved people at that time. First, the slaves said that the slave owners and local authorities were hiding the black queen, which resembles the notion that the ones preventing justice were the local white elites. Second, the fact that

---

[31] In some cases, rumors can be traced to events. See Ada Ferrer, "Speaking of Haiti: Slavery, Revolution, and Freedom in Cuban Slave Testimony," in *The World of the Haitian Revolution*, ed. Geggus and Fiering, 236–37. In Barbados, following the "Bussa Rebellion" of 1816, slave testimony mentioned that in 1815 "there was a report that the negroes were to be freed, and that their freedom was to be given them through a black woman who was a Queen, for whom Mr. Wilberforce acted in England." See *Report from a Select Committee of the House of Assembly Appointed to Inquire into the Origins, Causes, and Progress of the Late Rebellion* (Barbados: House of Assembly, 1818), 27.

[32] It might be possible that the slaves were referring to an actual black female leader who was promoting ideas of emancipation among enslaved black communities. Or it could be a reference to an African or an otherwise black royal personage who had arrived somewhere in the Americas and who represented hopes of freedom for enslaved blacks. Another possibility is that the rumor circulating was linked to or resembled the eighteenth century legends about Nanny that were so central to maroon society in the Jamaican northeast. In one version of Nanny's origin, she was not a slave but an Asante queen who traveled to Jamaica to help free her people. It is difficult to know whether this was an idea that circulated between the Caribbean and the Pacific coast. But the active (although largely illicit) commerce between New Granada and Jamaica involved trade in slaves, and these captives could likely have ended up crossing to the Pacific coast to work in gold mining and bringing news and knowledge. Jessica Krug, "Social Dismemberment, Social Remembering: Contested Kromanti Identities, Nationalism, and Obeah, 1675–Present" (MA thesis, University of Wisconsin, 2007), 9; Ernesto Bassi, "Between Imperial Projects and National Dreams: Communication Networks, Geopolitical Imagination, and the Role of New Granada in the Configuration of a Greater Caribbean Space, 1780s–1810s" (PhD diss., UC Irvine, 2012), 119.

this was a rumor about a black queen suggests that monarchy was in itself a symbol of justice. This means that emancipation and freedom were not exclusive of monarchic symbolism or imagination in the minds of the slaves.

Across the revolutionary Atlantic, rumors – particularly rumors of emancipation – were a crucial expression of the political visions of the enslaved. Through rumor, moreover, slaves shaped the political realities of the world that surrounded them and participated in "the broader transformation in the legal and political order of the Atlantic world."[33] This entanglement of the notions of freedom, justice, and monarchism should come as no surprise. It is useful to remember that Africans who arrived enslaved in the Americas were generally coming from kingdoms and brought with them a political imagination that conceived of sovereignty as linked to justice and law. These ideas were not far removed from the Spanish understanding of the monarch as the fountain of justice. In the long term, throughout the centuries and across Spanish America, these enslaved people had learned about the possibility of appealing to the king's justice through the legal system to claim protection of their rights.[34]

Thus by the early nineteenth century, the politics of the enslaved population was rooted in the power of political symbolism and the institutional effectiveness of legal-discursive recourse to the crown. The rumor of the black queen suggests that Spanish-American political culture, to which the discourse of royal justice was central, coexisted among the enslaved in Popayán with the royalist view that included references to black kings and queens, just as it did in other places across the diaspora, such as Brazil and Haiti.[35] Yet in contrast to Saint-Domingue, where, on the eve of the Haitian Revolution, two-thirds of the slaves had been born and raised in Africa, in Popayán, by the 1800s the slave communities had a majority of locally born slaves.[36]

---

[33] Laurent Dubois, "Calling Down the Law: Prophetic Rumor and the Coming of Emancipation in the Caribbean, 1789–1848," unpublished manuscript, 42. See also Ada Ferrer, *Freedom's Mirror*, 78.

[34] For an analysis of the slaves' royalist political culture in Saint-Domingue, see Ogle, "The Trans-Atlantic King."

[35] For Haiti, see Thornton, "I am the Subject of the King of Kongo," *Journal of World History* 4, no. 2 (1993), 183; and Fick, *The Making of Haiti*, 231. For Brazil, see Elizabeth Kiddy, "Who Is the King of Congo? A New Look at African and Afro-Brazilian Kings in Brazil," in *Central Africans and Cultural Transformations in the American Diaspora*, ed. Linda M. Heywood (New York: Cambridge University Press, 2002), 153–82.

[36] Thornton, "I am the Subject of the King of Kongo," 183.

Historians have acknowledged the existence of a monarchical imaginary among the maroon communities, often labeling it as "restorationist" (i.e., backward). The case of Saint-Domingue/Haiti has become a benchmark for understanding slave politics at the turn of the eighteenth century. The slaves' massive participation in the making of Haiti was used by scholars to divide "traditional" or restorationist revolts from forward-looking revolutions, a perspective that wrote off the significance of the participation of royalist slaves in the context of an "independence revolution."[37] Similarly, the category of "slave revolt" does not allow for inclusion of royalist revolts.[38] Yet, along with other situations discussed recently by historians, the case of Popayán – one in which slaves appealed to royal decrees in order to legitimate their freedom or laid claim both to the authority of the king and to the promises of republican rights – shows that across the Americas enslaved subjects were acting according to their political choices and the possibilities available.

For example, in Cuba in 1811, the Aponte Rebellion drew on rumors about decrees from the Cádiz Cortes, as well as from the kings of Spain, England, Kongo, and Haiti (Henri Christophe, crowned in June). By invoking these decrees, the slaves justified their insurrection against the colonial elites, who were presumably delaying freeing the slaves. These cases illustrate the political awareness of slaves and their sophisticated understanding of political institutions and authority, as well as of their legal condition in a slave society. By appealing to the legitimacy of freedom granted by a monarch, slaves were recognizing royal authority, which allowed them to legitimize their own pleas and struggles – even if they had to achieve their goals through revolt.[39]

The contest over political knowledge was thus an important element of the conflicts in the mine of San Juan. There, the slaves revolted again in 1811, this time inspired "by the false news of [Tacón's] declaration of freedom for slaves," in the words of the mine owner, Torres. The slaves

---

[37] Eugene Genovese, *From Rebellion to Revolution: Afro-American Slave Revolts in the Making of the Modern World* (Baton Rouge: Louisiana State University Press, 1979), esp. ch. 3. When referring to maroon involvement in the Saint-Domingue revolution, Fick, *The Making of Haiti*, 151, also critiques Genovese's use of overly simplified categories, which does not allow for understanding or even accessing "a highly fluid, rapidly changing, and richly diverse situation."

[38] See Geggus, "Slavery, War, and Revolution," 5–6, 46–49.

[39] See Dubois, "An Enslaved Enlightenment," 11; and Matt Childs, *The 1812 Aponte Rebellion in Cuba and the Struggle against Atlantic Slavery* (Chapel Hill: University of North Carolina Press, 2006).

claimed that two deserters had informed them about the new decree of emancipation. Yet it is clear that Governor Tacón had intended a radically different outcome when, in 1809–10, he set out to defend the region from the attack from Quito's junta. As we have seen, Tacón promised to free those slaves who joined his army as a reward for their services, but he did not intend to promote any widespread manumission of slaves or law of emancipation. Exactly what version the two deserters told the slaves is lost to us. But, in any case, such a rumor permitted the slaves in San Juan to open an important path – one that was both symbolic and practical – one leading to the emancipation of the whole slave gang in January 1811. They drew strength from the idea of the governor's promises of freedom to slaves and proceeded to enact and defend their own freedom by sending an announcement to their masters in the city, "advising them that they should no longer count on their slaves or the mine because the mine was now theirs and they were free."[40]

What happened was similar to the events of a year earlier that had been inspired by the rumor of the black queen. The slaves justified their insurrection against their masters, who were presumably delaying freeing the slaves, by invoking the governor's call for slaves to join him in defending the king's sovereignty in Popayán province, all of which resulted in their declaring their freedom.[41] Although the slave owner, Gerónimo Torres, complained to Tacón and sought his help to straighten out the situation, the governor implicitly recognized a certain degree of responsibility for the situation and did not find the slaves' actions criminal or rebellious. That the government interpreted the slaves' actions as a misunderstanding also reflected the success of the slaves' strategy.[42]

In the San Juan mine, the promise of the governor of Popayán to grant the slaves freedom became an important precedent for the relations between the slaves and the opposing factions of royalists and insurgents. The politics of the slaves was framed within the royalist alternative because, at the time, it offered the most promising avenue for ending slavery. Additionally, the slave owners' reaction to Tacón's policy evinced their fear of armed slaves as well as their reluctance to give up their

---

[40] ACC Independencia CIII 2g 6596, fol. 1v.

[41] Peter Blanchard makes reference to this case in his recent book, yet he does not analyze the contingencies of the process through which Tacón negotiated with slaves in southwestern New Granada. Blanchard, *Under the Flags of Freedom*, 20. See also Roger Pita Pico, *El reclutamiento de negros durante las guerras de independencia de Colombia, 1810–1825* (Bogotá: Academia Colombiana de Historia, 2012), 94–99.

[42] Childs, *The 1812 Aponte Rebellion in Cuba*, 160.

property (horses, weapons, and slaves) as a response to what they saw as a violent misappropriation by the government. In view of the radicalization of the slave owners in Cali and Popayán, who had rebelled against the government because, among other things, of their disagreement with the policy of arming and freeing slaves in the region, it became evident to the slaves that freedom would not arrive from or be delivered by the revolutionary faction. Eventually, the contradictions of the insurgents' talk about freedom and liberation became all the more clear to them. In this regard the paradoxes underlying the emergence of the liberal concept of freedom were clearly exposed in Popayán when the Creoles sought to break free from the imperial power, equating anticolonialism with freedom but still seeking to maintain their rights to hold slaves and their racial privileges.[43]

"MOVED BY THE JUDGMENT OF THEIR CONSCIENCE"

If the slaves in San Juan drew on rumors of freedom to justify their rebellion at the outset of the war, they also sought to legalize their freedom once the king was restored to the throne and the royalists had regained control of the government. In August 1816, Camilo Torres, the slave captain in the mine of San Juan, presented a "memorial" or written request in name of his *compañeros* (twenty-three men) that accounted for the services they had performed for "our sovereign" and asked that they be rewarded their freedom. Torres' request included a questionnaire asking witnesses to describe their loyal actions in which they "repressed the insurgents on two occasions when their expeditions attempted to pass along the San Juan road," and to confirm that they served "without being afraid of the risk and other dangers that this could bring because of the reduced forces they had to defend the entrance" to San Juan.

Another question was intended to prove the slaves' "obedience to the orders and rulings of the judges who have followed and protected the just cause of the King, as well as to the priests who have followed the same just system." The following question noted that the slaves in San Juan had assisted the royalist troops commanded by Colonel Francisco Delgado, supplying them with provisions during the four days of their trip toward Micay. Additionally, the slaves' questionnaire mentioned the fact that

---

[43] For the tensions of liberalism in slaveholding Jamaica, see Thomas Holt, *The Problem of Freedom: Race, Labor, and Politics in Jamaica and Britain, 1832–1938* (Baltimore, MD, and London: Johns Hopkins University Press, 1992).

their owners had attempted to make them join the insurgent party, yet the slaves had not followed those orders but kept the insurgents outside the mines. Finally, Torres requested that the lieutenant governor of the province of Micay, Manuel Silvestre Valverde, certify that Camilo Torres had – in the name of his community – recently written a letter to him offering the services of the slave gang to fix the road between Nahita and Playa Rica and to build huts in different places so that mail could be transported easily along that coast, "without causing any cost to our sovereign but with the intention to offer such service to him."[44] The slaves clearly had the means to write such a letter and were well advised about the best way to present statements and witnesses to the court to make their case. What is remarkable about their intention to fix the road is that the slave community in San Juan considered that, living in freedom, their labor was an asset they could utilize to manifest their loyalty to the king. They envisioned a different type of "service" that was within their reach and had particular value in the context of the war. This suggests that these slaves' royalism went beyond the military arena, which until now has been the one privileged by authors studying the period.

In 1816, Camilo Torres' plea in favor of his *compañeros* indicates that in 1811, once Tacón had officially informed the slaves that their loyalty was the requisite for earning their freedom, the slave gang proceeded to maintain a positive and fruitful relation with the royalists and devised a legal strategy to secure their freedom over time. In fact, although the governor attempted to bring the slaves back to a state of subordination, once they learned that one of their owners, Ignacio Torres, had joined the insurgents, they instead continued living independently, taking the mine's profits for themselves. According to Gerónimo Torres, after 1811 they "strengthened their libertine state, affecting other slave gangs on the coast with their behavior and became an asylum for every fugitive slave, and from that time on turned absolutely indifferent, governing themselves and laboring only for their comfort and benefit."[45]

If the accounts of the mine owner Torres portray an insubordinate slave gang during this period, how can we reconcile such a representation with the witnesses' testimony that the slave gang's appeal for freedom was based on their loyalty to the king? All the witnesses who were called to testify and respond to the questionnaire drafted by the slave captain Camilo Torres were (presumably white) royalist military men. For

---

[44] ACC Independencia CIII 2g 6598, fol. 1.
[45] ACC Independencia CIII 2g 6596, fol. 1v.

example, the captain of the militias, Vicente Parra, said that it was publicly known that the *negros* of the mine of San Juan had "remained strong in favor of the cause of the king." He added that they had obeyed the orders of the legitimate ministers of the king, as when, in charge of a contingent at the Cuchilla del Tambo, he received a letter from Camilo Torres, the captain of the slave gang, "in which he offered all his people and weapons, such as machetes and blowguns (*vodoqueras*), to defend the sites under his charge."[46] José María Zúñiga declared that the *negros* of San Juan blocked the entrance of the insurgent troops into Micay, "absolutely refusing to turn against the king."[47] Valverde, the lieutenant of governor in Micay, certified that the *negros* in the mine had been

in favor of the cause of the King since the beginning of the horrifying revolution that this kingdom has suffered, and with that purpose have contributed by defending the [entrance to Micay,] always being subject and obedient to the legitimate authorities, informing us about the situation in the area *and requesting advice on how to govern themselves, fulfilling the orders they received.* It is also true that the captain Camilo wrote to me offering to fix the road as service to the King ... which I accepted and I have no doubt they will perform this.[48]

Valverde is an interesting figure because of his alliance with slave gangs in the Pacific lowlands, those in Yurumanguí, and those in San Juan. As Governor Tacón's representative, Valverde promoted political relations with slave gangs during the time when mine owners had abandoned their properties (throughout most of the decade of the 1810s, either because they were participating in the wars or because of the slaves' "insubordination"). Evidence of this was Camilo Torres' letter to Valverde stating that his gang would fix a road as service to the sovereign. This implies that the royalist elites maintained relations with the slaves and guaranteed their – at least partial – control of their communities. Through these alliances the royalists in Popayán did not simply address shortages of manpower; they also made loyalty the government's main goal in negotiating with the slaves.[49]

Even more striking is the defense presented in February 1818 by the state attorney (*síndico procurador general*) of Popayán, Manuel Alonso de Velasco, in support of the cause of the twenty-three slaves. Based on

---

[46] ACC Independencia CIII 2g 6598, fol. 2. Borrowing from a native practice in the region, blowguns were used to attack with darts infused with venom.

[47] ACC Independencia CIII 2g 6598, fol. 2v.

[48] ACC Independencia CIII 2g 6598, fols. 4–4v. Emphasis added.

[49] Brown downplays the importance of loyalty in the process of arming slaves. See Brown, "The Arming of Slaves in Comparative Perspective," 337.

the information presented by Camilo Torres, Velasco argued that the enslaved men should be declared "free of the yoke of servitude" in light of three legal precedents. First, Miguel Tacón had "tacitly promised the liberation of those slaves who conducted a heroic action in the defense of the holy cause." Second, Tacón had "explicitly conceded freedom in the name of the king to the *mulato* Joaquín" in Popayán. Finally, the slaves of San Juan deserved their freedom because it was the will of the sovereign who, having returned to the throne, with his liberal hand had rewarded the "merit and virtue" of any of his loyal vassals who in any way had sustained his rights.[50]

The case of the *mulato* José Joaquín Sánchez had taken place in 1811 during the early controversy around recruiting slaves. He joined the royalist army when the Colegio de San Camilo, who owned him, "voluntarily" gave him to Tacón. He distinguished himself when he ran to seize an enemy cannon during the entrance of the insurgent troops into Popayán. He was valued at four hundred and fifty pesos, which the royal treasury paid to the priests to grant José Joaquín his freedom.[51] As was proved by the attorney Velasco's use of the case, this became a legal precedent, and it was also a clear example to follow for those slaves who learned about the *mulato*'s reward.

The attorney believed not only that the testimony included in the report was truthful, having been offered by men who were defenders of the holy cause, but also that the San Juan slaves' rejection, on two occasions, of the attempts of the armed troops to attract them to the revolutionary cause was an action that proved their merit. Even more notably, those troops were led by none other than the mine and slave owners, who urged the slaves to reject the obedience to the king that religion prescribed. Additionally, if their object had been to shake off slavery, the gang clearly could have run away, either to another port or to any island in the Pacific Ocean. After all, Velasco added, many other slaves had escaped during this "damned revolution without forming a defense corps." His interpretation of the slaves' choice to be obedient and collaborate with the cause of the king was that "undoubtedly, the *negros* of the mine of San Juan have acted heroically, moved by the judgment of their consciences."[52] It is noteworthy that the lawyer used such words to imply that since the beginning of the war in 1810, the slaves had been exposed to political alternatives that allowed them to

---

[50] ACC Independencia CIII 2g 6598, fol. 6.   [51] AGI Quito 386.
[52] ACC Independencia CIII 2g 6598, fol. 7v.

make unprecedented choices, which were of crucial importance to the contending sides. Slaves, he said, were not merely property, as the insurgents, who denied that the slaves had stakes in the war, wanted them to remain. He added that they were not simply being *seduced*, which was the expression that insurgents generally used to portray the relation between slaves and royalists.[53] The defense that the attorney prepared for the liberation of the twenty-three slaves in San Juan was based on the crucial decision they had made in favor of the king.

Finally, after "proving their fidelity and services" so that they would be granted their freedom as a reward for their services, Velasco pleaded that purchase prices for the enslaved men's women and children, who had contributed to the defense of the king's holy cause, "be calculated by taking into account the low price of slaves today and with the equity that these slaves deserve for their merit," so their husbands and fathers could purchase them. This final point of Velasco's request for freedom of the slave gang in San Juan is interesting because it points to the fact that slave prices had dropped significantly during the independence wars. Partially because of the chaotic situation in the bulk of the mining economy, prices for slaves had fallen during the decade from 1810 to 1820.[54] At the same time, although it had not been explicitly stated in Camilo Torres' "memorial," it seems likely that they had also strategically arranged for the attorney to request the valuation of their families as part of his plea for a just reward for their royalist services. This suggests that the slaves' judicial strategy was complex, since it took into account pricing issues, and it also suggests that Valentín, Lázaro, Apolinario, and the other slaves probably had enough funds to cover the expenses of purchasing the freedom of their families. It also reveals the gendered nature of the political, juridical, and economic routes to freedom that royalist slaves took. While military service would necessarily privilege men, as targets and also as potential beneficiaries of the reward of freedom, women were only vaguely mentioned as having

---

[53] ANE Popayán 341; ACC Independencia MI 3j 6384. José Manuel Restrepo will also write that the royalists were able to *seduce* the slaves due to their ignorance. See Restrepo, *Historia de la Revolución*.

[54] Rodríguez, "Aspectos del comercio," 16, says, "the most radical fall in prices took place during the years of the war and hardship, when no property offered security, particularly slaves"; Juan Ignacio Arboleda, "Entre la libertad y la sumisión: Estrategias de libertad de los esclavos en la gobernación de Popayán durante la independencia, 1808–1830" (Bogotá: Universidad de Los Andes, 2006), 20; Germán Colmenares, "Castas, patrones de poblamiento y conflictos sociales en las provincias del Cauca, 1810–1830," in *La Independencia: Ensayos de Historia Social*, ed. Germán Colmenares et al. (Bogotá: Instituto Colombiano de Cultura, 1986), 151.

contributed to the holy cause "in their capacity," indirectly or partially. Yet they were included in the specific strategy that slaves devised to pay for their families' liberation (see Figure 5.1).

The means of paying for their families' freedom would have been saved up by the slaves, who were able to maintain an internal economy of their own during the nine years when the mine was not inhabited by whites or officially exploited in favor of the mine owners or the king's treasury. In a letter Gerónimo Torres sent to the governor of Popayán Pedro Domínguez in 1820, he explicitly mentioned that upon his arrival at the mine, he found that the slaves had "worn out all the tools [and] divided the land for their own plots (*sementeras*) and personal work."[55] Torres also described their hunting practices, which they used to complement their sowing of plantains and sugar cane. Given the fragility of Torres' economic situation after having lost control of the mine, which implied a great financial loss, he highlighted the fact that while the slaves produced enough on their plantations to survive and were even trading plantains and cane (which explains why they did not want to work for him in the mine), he had been forced to buy plantains from them for his survival. All this suggests that the slaves, having "divided the mine and hacienda among themselves" between 1811 and 1820, had developed a subsistence economy that allowed them to project profits and savings that would make it possible for them to pay for the liberation of the women and children in their community, once the men were granted their freedom.

What is striking is the decision of the slaves to recur to a legal strategy of appealing for manumission even after having lived in a de facto situation of freedom for years. Such a choice reveals the slaves' continued belief in legal or juridical strategies as viable means for securing their freedom. It may have been a product of their ongoing relationship with royalist authorities, who could have advised Camilo and the others to plead for their freedom in court, on the basis of their services to the royalist cause. Certainly the evidence of a sustained working relationship between the slaves and the royalist military authorities during the period when the former were not subject to their masters suggests their strategic interest in negotiating with the government, such as when they attempted to be liberated in 1816. Additionally, the timing of their legal request was a calculated one because, once the king had returned to his throne, it was during those years that Pablo Morillo was promoting an intense policy of persecution of

[55] ACC Independencia CIII 2g 6596, fol. 1.

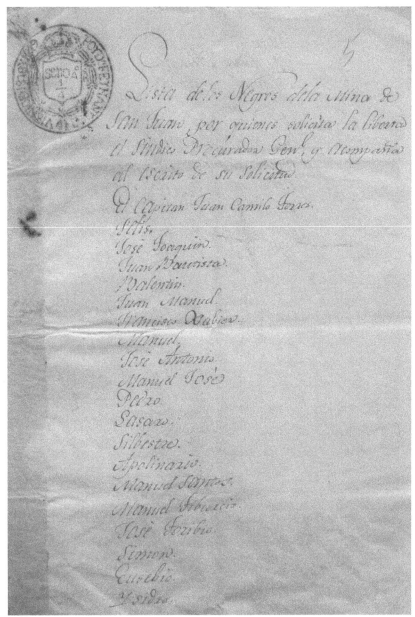

FIGURE 5.1 *Lista de negros de la mina de San Juan por quienes solicita la libertad el síndico procurador general* (List of *negros* from the San Juan mine for whom the state attorney requests freedom).
Archivo Central del Cauca, Independencia, CIII 2g 6598, fols 5–5v.

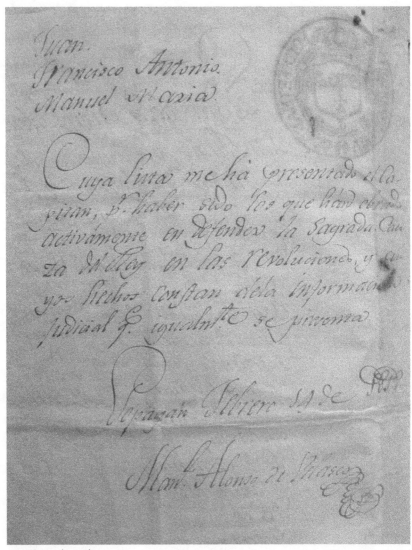

FIGURE 5.1 *(cont.)*

revolutionaries in New Granada. For the slaves this may have seemed like the perfect moment to prove their loyalty and be rewarded for it.[56]

---

[56] Saether notes that, for Indians and powerful whites alike, "those who fought for the royalist cause had acquired the right to distinctions and favors." Saether, *Identidades e Independencia*, 203.

Although the outcome of the request for the manumission of the twenty-three slaves in San Juan is not clear, the final comment by José Joaquín Sanclemente, the legal representative of the Torres family, suggests that conceding freedom to the slaves was not a simple task. In his written brief in 1818, Sanclemente diminished the merits of the slave gang and said that if they had defended the monarchy during the years of war it was simply the fulfillment of their duty as vassals of the king. He also pointed to the high price that the royal treasury would have to pay for the freedom of those many slaves, because the manumission would have to be backed up by royal funds. Finally, Sanclemente added a counterargument to those testimonies that pointed out the obedience and fidelity of the slaves in San Juan, saying he had not received such a positive response when calling upon the slaves for "matters concerning the service of the king" in the year 1813. Hence, it is very probable that the request for liberation of the slaves of San Juan was not fulfilled in February 1818. And the consequences that this would have for slave political action in that mine are apparent from the developments in 1819–20, when Gerónimo Torres traveled there.[57]

LIBERTINE BEHAVIOR: "THE SLAVES ACT AS IF THEY WERE FREE"

In July 1819, Gerónimo Torres decided to travel to his mine given that during the previous months the royalist government had devised a campaign against the insubordinate slave gangs of San Juan and neighboring Saija. Although the government's offensive led to apparent victory, after eleven months at the mine, Torres had to draft a letter pleading for help because of the difficult situation he had encountered. Torres' 1820 letter to the governor of Popayán noted that the "scandalous insubordination [of the slaves in the mine] demands that public authority aid the masters to subject and correct them."[58]

Torres had arrived thinking he would find "the slaves weakened, submissive, and willing to repair all of the damages they had caused their masters." Instead he was shocked when all he found in the slaves was "pride, arrogance, insubordination, and neglect." The description that

---

[57] ACC Independencia CIII 2g 6598, fol. 10. Almario notes that "the denial by the royal authorities of the blacks' request [for freedom] turned the region in a serious problem of social order." Almario, *La invención del suroccidente colombiano*, 125.

[58] ACC Independencia CIII 2g 6596, fol. 1. The letter is dated June 20, 1820.

Torres provides in his letter is interesting and certainly serves as an exceptional source of information. He notes that in the months he spent among what he considered to be his slaves, they rejected his orders, forcing him to tolerate their disorder and disrespect. Particularly noteworthy is that Torres said that whenever he attempted to scold a slave, the parents and family of the slave being punished would soon arrive at Torres' house to challenge him. Additionally, he recounted that he constantly received threats from the slaves, who used the hunting spears they possessed to warn him, "if I punished them they would kill me with their spears." Finally, Torres noted that he was particularly bothered because they "have organized dances in my house without my permission, insulting me even in their songs," and "the slaves act as if they were free."[59]

Torres decided to leave the mine given that it was impossible for him to keep the slaves under control, since he had no authority over them, and in view of the "innate, and impossible to overcome, hatred that the slave has for his master, which he immediately applies at the moment when he does not feel the master's authority over him." From this statement it seems that Torres acknowledged his slaves had expressed their will not to be dominated by him nor to obey him. This was possible for the slaves – now closer to ex-slaves – largely because during the past nine years they had made the mine their own and, at the time of his return, were armed (with spears and knives); thus, they did not feel threatened by a single white mine owner attempting to return them to slavery. They were not receptive to his multiple attempts to negotiate with them, through such measures as giving them new work tools, allowing them to continue working their plots, decreasing the working day (*jornal*) by one-half, treating them for their illnesses, and distributing clothes and goods to them free of charge.[60]

During the nine years in which the slaves had remained on their own, their relations with outside political and economic powers seem to have been ambivalent. On the one hand, the slaves had maintained good relations with the royalist authorities, who may have delegated to them the control of the region in the face of insurgent threats. This was an alternative tactic for the royalists who were not able to provide cover for all of the province's territory because of a lack of manpower. By negotiating with the slave gang in San Juan (and presumably also with the slaves in Yurumanguí and Saija), the royalists acquired something akin to irregular soldiers. The slaves, on the other hand, took the opportunity

[59] ACC Independencia CIII 2g 6596, fols. 1–2.
[60] ACC Independencia CIII 2g 6596, fol. 1.

to remain in an effective state of marronage – they were able to do this because they had formed a free community and also welcomed fugitive slaves from surrounding areas – while guaranteeing for themselves the approval of the authorities, albeit not that of their masters.

In January of 1819, Governor Domínguez planned an expedition to apprehend the eighty slaves in the mines along the Saija River who had revolted against their masters, "some of them denying slavery" (*otros negando la esclavitud*), and formed a *palenque*. Dominguez sent Lieutenant Valverde to "attack and undo such a gathering," which could have very negative consequences. Obviously Governor Dominguez had distanced himself from the earlier practice of negotiating with the slaves in the mines, and for that very reason, in 1819, he sent Valverde to pacify them, a man who had previously been crucial to the government's efforts to maintain amicable relations with the *cuadrillas*.

From Valverde's report of the expedition, it is clear that the slaves were unwilling to give up or negotiate. The lieutenant first sent a black man to try to speak with them, but they insisted that Valverde and his men enter their territory to meet them. This proved to be an ambush, since, when Valverde was heading out to meet them, he and his men were attacked with poison darts. Valverde went back to secure more forces and was eventually able to penetrate into the place where the *palenque* was located. Then he proceeded to enter the mining area to destroy the cultivated fields (*sementeras*) and burn the houses in order to force the local residents to come out in search of provisions. However, Valverde noted that it was highly possible that the fugitives were receiving aid from Indians and other slaves in the nearby mines.[61]

In spite of the fact that the royalist government tried to recover the mines, probably as a means to undoing the results of the crisis that Tacón's original negotiation with the slaves in Popayán had generated, and to attempt to maintain good relations with the slave owners, throughout the decade, the effects of the slaves' appropriation of the territory were visible and difficult to overcome. Although the slaves' political goals between 1809 and 1817 (at least until their request for emancipation was turned down) showed a fundamental interest in expressing their loyalty to the Spanish king and being embraced by the category of (free) vassals, it is clear from their struggle against Dominguez's expedition and their

---

[61] Document transcribed in Pedro H. González Sevillano, *Marginalidad y exclusion en el Pacífico colombiano: Una visión histórica* (Cali: Editorial Universidad Santiago de Cali, 1999), 57–59.

treatment of their previous owner that they were not willing to give up their de facto freedom and return to servitude.

Torres' letter to Domínguez describes the slaves' behavior "as if they were free" in terms of what was most striking to himself. Living in his house, disregarding his orders and offers, and even threatening him – although not hurting him – all signaled unacceptable transgressions against the logic of the system of slavery that Torres aimed to restore. They were statements of the community's pride in its accomplishment of having regained sovereignty over their bodies, families, and community, even if they would have to be defended by force. We hear almost nothing about the type of society the ex-slaves had built in the Pacific lowlands, or what type of authority emerged among the slaves. However, the fact that in 1816 Captain Camilo claimed the right to freedom for the whole gang suggests that, at least formally, the authority of the captain continued to be relevant for the purpose of making pleas and negotiating with the government.

We can also assume that the community had expanded during this time to include slaves who had escaped from other places and free blacks and that it sustained relations with other mines across the Pacific lowlands that were in a similar situation. In fact, the process that had begun during the independence wars in this region, whereby free and enslaved blacks appropriated mines and territory, was ultimately irreversible. During the last years of the war, in 1820 and 1821, the slaves continued to claim control of the mines between Raposo and Barbacoas. Although Bolívar's representatives attempted to get the region back under republican control after 1822, they did not have enough manpower to accomplish that goal. In the early days of the republic, the mining economy became marginal to the republican project, and enslaved people in the Pacific lowlands were able to continue living in a state of autonomy or eventually were able to buy their freedom, as their owners preferred that to continuing to suffer financial losses.

FREEDOM, RIGHTS, AND LOYALTY IN THE AGE OF REVOLUTION

The evidence for the specific events that took place in the mine of San Juan gives us a good idea of the situation in the Pacific lowlands of New Granada during the wars of independence. This case is crucial for understanding the concepts that slaves in the region held of slavery and servitude, their perception of the war and of its contending sides, the underlying interests and principles that guided their choice to support the royalists, and the structures of authority in the black communities during the war. As we have seen, as soon as the war broke out and the slaves became aware that the majority of their masters were turning against the crown, they revolted to earn their freedom. The slaves in the mines of the Pacific lowlands could benefit from their relative isolation and the fact that, due to their numbers, they could intimidate the authorities and force them to negotiate on the slaves' terms. Two arguments underlay their collective movement: one, the assumption that a decree of freedom entitled them to receive emancipation and two, on a different note, that they were not willing to continue being enslaved under masters who denied the authority of the king. Both arguments were based on royalist political culture, and each one reveals important elements of the slaves' perception of their opportunities to end slavery at the beginning of the war. The first one, as mentioned earlier, represents a strategic intention to uphold their legal right to freedom in a context where slave owners allegedly flouted the authority of the king. The second represented the slaves' vision of the institution of slavery as a relationship between them and their masters, which they respected only insofar as it was mediated by the king's justice. The slaves expressed their will to be free and to remain subject to the king's sovereignty, an argument that secured the royalist elite's confidence in their support for the king's cause.

The case of the slaves in San Juan also reveals the centrality of the *capitanes* to the political organization within the communities throughout the independence wars. The *capitanes* continued to mediate the relations of the communities with the government: colonial officials approached them with any information they needed or any orders they had to give, and they, in turn, communicated the communities' decisions or interests to the government. For example, the fact that Camilo Torres wrote letters to lieutenant Valverde clearly indicates that either the captains themselves or someone else among the free and enslaved people who lived in the lowlands was literate. In addition, they had a good sense of how to procure legal advice and prepare the case for legalizing their de facto freedom.

The events studied here suggest that the enslaved black communities of Popayán were doing what many across the Americas had tried to do before them to secure freedom – that is, take advantage of new opportunities that the moment provided. In a significant way, they attuned their project to the offerings that the royalist party made to those slaves who remained loyal. The slaves maintained contact with the royalist authorities and played a role in the defense of the territory against the insurgents.

Such military action was also a defense of their own freedom, which, in the case of the San Juan mine, meant appropriating the enterprise, producing gold for themselves, and perhaps trading it. Even though in practice they had secured their freedom – which distanced them profoundly in social and political terms from their previous owners' authority – during the years of the monarchical restoration and Reconquest (between 1814 and 1819), once the royalist government seemed about to achieve a certain victory, the slaves appealed to the law as an institutional arena in which they would be able to legitimate their de facto freedom.

The slaves were not automatically driven to the insurgent side, as some nationalist narratives would have it. The historical choices of enslaved people in Popayán during this period challenge us to put aside assumptions about the association between enslaved and free blacks and liberal-republican agendas.[62] In the Spanish colonial context, militia service radically changed the position of marginal people in relation to the government.[63] And across New Granada insurgent slave owners were reticent about arming their slaves during most of the period of the independence wars. In Colombia, the republican project neglected to address a transformation of slave society, especially in places such as Popayán, until 1852. Thus, to write a history of enslaved peoples' freedom strategies and struggles, we need to be flexible enough to move beyond the liberal narrative of anticolonialism.[64] As we have seen here, the actions of the royalist slaves in Popayán were determining factors that weakened the institution of slavery in the region. By turning slave and mine owning into

---

[62] See Steinar Saether, *Identidades e Independencia*, 201. Saether is one of the few authors who aims to portray a complex picture of the participation of Indians and blacks in Colombia's wars of independence. His work focuses on the Caribbean provinces of Santa Marta and Riohacha, the other pole of popular royalism in New Granada.

[63] Vinson and Restall, "Black Soldiers, Native Soldiers," 23–24. See also Jane Landers, "Transforming Bondsmen into Vassals: Arming Slaves in Colonial Spanish America," in *Arming Slaves*, ed. Brown and Morgan, 120–45.

[64] Alfonso Múnera and Marixa Lasso have shown the importance of *pardo* politics in Cartagena during independence as well as the links that existed between republicanism and the discourse of racial equality; yet neither of these authors engages the problem of slavery in relation to the region of their study. Cartagena's case was different from that of Popayán. See Alfonso Múnera, *El fracaso de la nación* (Bogotá: Banco de la República, El Ancora Editores, 1998); Lasso, *Myths of Harmony*. Helg, in *Liberty and Equality*, includes slaves in her narrative but, as Steinar Saether has pointed out, Helg, Múnera, and Lasso provide a rather essentialist view of racial politics. Saether instead argues that "the fact that people were Indian, black, white or *mestizo* had less to do with their political affiliation than the nature of the conflicts and political tensions in each locality." Saether, *Identidades e Independencia*, 202.

a risky and ultimately unprofitable business, the black communities of the Pacific helped make New Granada's and Colombia's dependence on gold unsustainable during the nineteenth century.

It is important to restate here that slave royalism did not reflect the mystification of the benevolence of the king, and we should avoid labeling it as "naïve monarchism."[65] As has been shown here, the slaves appealed to colonial political discourses of justice as a strategic, practical way to guarantee their freedom, which at the beginning of the war they defined in terms of being vassals of the king. The communities in Popayán, which were also part of a diasporic network of information, seem to have considered the possibility that emancipation could come from an African royal. In other words, at the same time that slaves produced arguments and actions based on legal reasoning, their lives and experience as slaves within the Hispanic context included broad connections with other Africans across the diaspora, with whom they seem to have shared a common imaginary. The slaves in Popayán conceived of freedom in terms of local economic, political, and military autonomy. They sought to take advantage of their liberty to provide either military or labor service to the king as a means of claiming rights and recognition as vassals. Yet once the absolutist government attempted to regain control over the slaves, the attacks of the royalists on their free communities in 1819 would have been a challenge to any illusion that slaves had about the intrinsic justice of the crown. Given that, during 1820 and 1821 the communities living in the mining region were still waging a war against any intrusions into their territory, be they from royalists or insurgents.[66]

An understanding of freedom as a situation in which enslaved people sought to gain recognition as vassals or citizens, and, as a corollary, would receive land, was not unique to Popayán. In the United States and across the Caribbean, slave participation in interimperial or independence wars was commonly rewarded with rights and land. In the British case hundreds of loyalist slaves ran away and embarked on a trans-Atlantic journey to receive their promised rewards. In Esmeraldas, south of Popayán, slaves negotiated with the royalists the payment of tribute in exchange for maintaining an autonomous right to exploiting the mines for themselves.[67]

---

[65] Childs, *The 1812 Aponte Rebellion*, 170–71.

[66] BLAA Archivo de Emiliano Díaz del Castillo, Caja 8, Carpeta 81, fols. 71–73.

[67] Studies of slave loyalists in the American Revolution are Pybus, *Epic Journeys of Freedom*; Jasanoff, *Liberty's Exiles*; Schama, *Rough Crossings*. Landers, *Atlantic Creoles in*

For the Popayán slaves, the promise of freedom was elusive because it was born out of the expediency of colonial officials, and the legality of such offers was put in question later by the crown in Madrid. But the slaves had a certain advantage in their numbers and, instead of waiting to receive freedom, they took control of the territory and defended it. Their communities did not limit their economies to subsistence agriculture, as most postemancipation studies assume was the goal of slaves after freedom. In the Pacific lowlands of Popayán, blacks worked in the mines and at other extractive labor and in that way continued to be at the center of global trade.[68]

the Age of Revolutions, documents cases of free-black militias that were rewarded with land in the circum-Caribbean. Rocío Rueda, "Territorio, movilización e identidad étnica: Participación de los esclavizados del norte de Esmeraldas en las guerras de independencia, 1809–1813," in *Indios, negros y mestizos*, ed. Bonilla, 125–27.

[68] A study of postemancipation peasant aspirations is Fick, *The Making of Haiti*. On the role of Afro-Colombians in the economic transformations across the Pacific lowlands during the nineteenth century, see Claudia Leal, "Disputas por tagua y minas: recursos naturales y propiedad territorial en el Pacífico colombiano, 1870–1930," *Revista Colombiana de Antropologia* 44, no. 2 (2008), 409–38.

6

"The yoke of the greatest of all tyrannical intruders, Bolívar"

The royalist rebels in Colombia's southwest (1820–1825)

By the third decade of the nineteenth century, what had begun as a crisis of sovereignty with immediate roots in the peninsula was already an irreversible struggle for independence in Spain's American territories. Leading the northern Andean process of independence was the Venezuelan Simón Bolívar, who was able to internationalize the anticolonial project and gain support from Britain, Haiti, and the United States. In mid-1819 Bolívar moved his campaign from Venezuela to New Granada, and this change in strategy paid off. The republican army had a break-through at the Battle of Boyacá, seventy-five miles (120 kilometers) from the viceregal capital. Viceroy Sámano had escaped and fled toward the Caribbean coast before Bolívar entered Santa Fe, triumphant, on August 9, 1819.[1] With this victory over the Spanish army, and the consequent destabilization of the royalist chain of command, republicans could ensure that the liberation of Caracas would be easier. But Bolívar's vision conceived of the independence struggle on a continental scale. His military ambitions included the liberation not only of Venezuela and New Granada but also of Peru. His goal was to connect the northern campaign with the southeastern struggle for independence, led by the Argentine general José de San Martín. Since 1810, when independence was first declared in Buenos Aires and Santa Fe, insurgent forces had strategically sought to take over Peruvian territory and make contact with each other to strengthen the independence cause. But between Peru, Quito, and Popayán, a royalist block with its heart in Lima kept the Pacific area free

[1] Earle, *Spain and the Independence of Colombia*, 135, 139.

of insurgents. By 1819 the situation was quite different. Independence forces made progress on both fronts, north and south of Peru. As Bolívar took over Santa Fe, San Martín was approaching Lima from the south, challenging the Spanish government there.

Then, in 1820, revolution returned to Spain. In January the troops that King Fernando had been planning to send to the Atlantic to fight the rebels in Buenos Aires revolted in Andalucía, demanding the restoration of the Cádiz Constitution. The king ceded to this pressure, and in March he swore allegiance to the 1812 charter and convoked the Cortes, thus reestablishing a constitutional monarchy. Any progress that had been achieved by Pablo Morillo in three years of reconquest in New Granada was suddenly brought to a halt and even reversed, because the news of the proconstitutional revolts in the peninsula signaled a serious crisis at the head of the monarchy. The inconsistency in the monarch's leadership gave way to deeper divisions among the American royalist authorities, as many – Viceroy Sámano in Cartagena, for example – chose to disregard the king's order to bring liberalism back to life.

One significant change brought about by the liberal turn of 1820 was that Fernando decided to temper the counterinsurgent offensive and attempt to negotiate with the rebels in Spanish America. The king hoped that in the new context the Creoles would find incentives to participate in the imperial representative government and give up their goal to separate from Spain. But, instead, the news reinvigorated the insurgents, from Rio de la Plata to Mexico, and they prepared to take advantage of those tensions to push their offensive and strike a final blow.[2] In South America, the Province of Guayaquil declared independence from the Kingdom of Quito in October 1820, fracturing the "Pacific royalist block" that had been solid throughout most of the decade.[3] Guayaquil's independence isolated the southwestern royalist bulwark in New Granada – Quito, Pasto, Barbacoas, and Patía – from Lima and cut off its support, which had financed the royalist resistance since 1809. Seeing that the last of New Granada's royalists were isolated and weakened, Bolívar began marching toward Popayán to attempt to penetrate the royalist bulwark in Pasto and Quito, which, in turn, had protected Peru from the insurrection in the north. In July 1821 San Martín finally reached Lima, and, in November of that year, Panama declared its independence. With the royalists out of

[2] Restrepo, *Historia de la Revolución*, Vol. III (1827), 23–24; Earle, *Spain and the Independence of Colombia*, 153–54.
[3] Rodríguez, *La revolución política*, 125.

the isthmus and Peru under direct attack, the Pacific Ocean became easier for the republicans to navigate, giving them an unprecedented advantage in the upcoming military struggles.

The royalist authorities in the southwestern region of New Granada faced this critical situation while they suffered internal divisions. The enmity between Popayán bishop Salvador Jiménez and Colonel Sebastián de la Calzada, who was in charge of the army, proved devastating. The Bishop had a strong ascendancy over the population and damaged Calzada's relations with the troops. Bishop Jiménez influenced Quito president Melchor Aymerich to replace Calzada with Basilio García, putting him in charge of the army in Popayán.[4] In part because of the divisions among the elite, Bolívar's offensive succeeded, defeating the Spanish army in April 1822 in the southwest at the battle of Bomboná.

Following the defeat of the Spanish army in Bomboná on April 7, 1822, the Spanish colonel Basilio García drafted a capitulation in which Pasto would concede the victory to Bolívar but expect fair treatment and protection of the civil and military population in the region. The terms of capitulation that Bolívar signed with the infamous Pastusos were indeed generous, because Bolívar understood that they were serious rivals, who had sustained a war against the anticolonial forces for a decade. Negotiating a settlement with them was a high priority for Colombia at that time. For the elites in Pasto the capitulation guaranteed the protection of their status, and, in the case of individuals who agreed to swear allegiance to the Republic, it also promised a transition from royalist government posts to positions within the republican state structure. The Catholic religion remained official, and no attempt would be made to change it. The local militias that were composed largely of town residents would not be forced to participate in the Colombian army's ongoing battles. In addition, the capitulation stated that all those conditions applied to the territory of Patía and the Patianos (including free blacks), who would also be protected from any retaliation for their long-lasting war against the republic. The document was signed by Bolívar's representatives on June 6, 1822, putting a formal end to the longest confrontation between royalists and republicans in New Granada.[5]

---

[4] Restrepo, *Historia de la Revolución*, Vol. III (1827), 18, 41; "Actas celebradas en Pasto por la Junta de Autoridades," in *Colección de documentos para la historia de Colombia*, ed. Ortiz, 226.

[5] See capitulation in Basilio García, "Manifiesto de lo acaecido en la última acción de Guerra que se dió en el territorio de Pasto en Costa Firme," 1822, in *Colección de documentos para la historia de Colombia*, ed. Ortiz, 282–96.

But this sort of diplomatic arrangement did not represent the spirit of people in Pasto. The Pastusos saw the capitulation as treason on the part of the Spanish army and the municipal council, and the popular royalist rebellion outlived the capitulation signed by the Spanish army and the local Creole elites in Pasto, represented by Popayán Bishop Salvador Jiménez. Five months later the Spanish lieutenant colonel Benito Boves and the captain Agustín Agualongo organized a rebellion in Pasto, becoming the leaders of a much deeper mobilization of the people, who were ready to act against the occupying forces of the republican government. Surely, one intention of this rebellion was to complicate Bolívar's plan to meet San Martín in Guayaquil.

The royalist rebellion that lasted between 1822 and 1825, its organization and territorial scope, suggest that royalism changed in this final phase of the struggle. This change was due in part to the unprecedented division between Pasto elites and the popular classes, after the elites chose to negotiate with Bolívar. That the royalist rebellion turned against Bolívar's republic was another innovation, making it explicitly antirepublican for the first time. This largely indigenous royalist movement was led by Spanish, Creole, and *mestizo* military figures who had survived the independence wars and were reluctant to surrender. Although Indians did not play a role within the leadership of the movement, they were, in fact, the majority and made up its core. My analysis widens the regional and ethnic scope of traditional accounts of the rebellion, which have considered it a movement exclusively involving Indians. As we will see, the movement was multiethnic; people from Patía (including free blacks) and enslaved people in the Pacific lowlands were also involved in and supported the royalist revolt. The royalist rebels evidently sought to establish an economic base in the coveted coastal mining region and had the expectation that they could overcome the republicans by rebuilding royalist power in the Pacific-Andean region.

THE END OF ROYALISM?

General Sucre won Quito for the republicans at the Battle of Pichincha, around the same time that Popayán fell to Bolívar's forces in Bomboná. Thus, in mid-1822 Bolívar thought that he had finally accomplished his goal of liberating New Granada. "Filled with joy," Bolívar wrote to Vice President Francisco de Paula Santander, "that we have finally put an end to the war with the Spaniards and secured for ever the Republic's fortune." But tension was in the air as Bolívar finally marched triumphant into the city of Pasto on June 8, watched by incredulous faces that could not accept the defeat or, even worse, the concession of victory to the republicans. Bolívar also mentioned to Santander that he knew very well that "the will of the people is against us," because during his speech people shouted that "they would rather die than concede surrender; that the Spanish were giving them away."[6] In these circumstances Bolívar's main practical goal was to collect all the weapons held by the population and hope that, with time, the Pastusos would accept the arrangement reached by the ruling classes, represented by Colonel García, the municipal council, and Bishop Jiménez. Returning to Quito, Bolívar left Bartolomé Salom stationed in Túquerres, charging him with this mission.

News of the victories at Bomboná and Pichincha circulated around Colombia, and praise was given for the end of war in the south and the incorporation of "a million Americans into the republican family."[7] Emboldened after his victories against Spain, and with most of New Granada and Venezuela under his command, Bolívar viewed the southwest as a strategic territorial obstacle and was determined to pacify the royalist remnants in the area by any means. Even if the republicans did not have complete legitimacy in Pasto, the tables had been turned, and Bolívar now had the authority to rule in the region. This was due to the fact that, at this turning point in 1822, once the independence movement attained superior military strength, the independence project and its republican ideals also gained territorial and ideological legitimacy. The standard for loyalty was no longer the king but the nation and the republic of Colombia. Along with losing its legitimacy, royalism was also stripped of its historical importance, because the prevailing nationalist metanarrative of liberation would not tolerate any alternative visions of the independence period, roundly condemning those who defended the Spanish colonial state. In practice, the royalist subversion allowed the republicans to transform them into agitators (*facciosos*), insurgents, and rebels. In the southwest – renamed the Cauca by the Bolivarian Republic – after the capitulation, any mobilization against other Colombians was susceptible to punishment for "treason."

Yet, in the royalists' memory, the independence movement that became dominant in South America after almost twenty years of bloody military conflicts had been the original "insurgency," battling against a legitimate,

---

[6] Cited in Ortiz, *Agustín Agualongo*, 445.
[7] "Gaceta Extraordinaria de Colombia," 1822, AGN Enrique Ortega Ricaurte, Proclamas y Decretos, Caja 341, fol. 7.

sovereign Spain. After the capitulation in Quito, a handful of officers from the Spanish army fled toward the north and made their way to Pasto. Among them were Benito Boves – a nephew of José Tomás Boves, the infamous royalist who had fought against Bolívar in the Venezuelan *llanos* a decade earlier – and Agustín Agualongo, a *mestizo* from Pasto who had been in the royalist army since 1811 and was captain of the royalist militias in 1822. In Pasto, Boves, Agualongo, and other Spanish colonels reorganized the royalist guerrillas to fight in the name of the king and against the usurpers of the rights of Fernando VII. According to the historian José Manuel Restrepo, "all of [Pasto's] population, with few exceptions," were in favor of the insurrection.[8] Although Restrepo was completely biased in favor of the republican cause, given the scarcity of sources pertaining to the movement, his account of the revolt has to be the starting point for any inquiry into the confrontation with Bolívar's regime in the Colombian southwest. This founding historian of Colombian independence strictly defined the rebels in negative terms, as anti-Colombian. In Restrepo's description, the royalists in Pasto who rose against Bolívar lacked depth of character as political actors, and, particularly when Indians or blacks were involved, they appeared as mere followers and dupes of religious figures among the elite. Yet it seems contradictory that Restrepo did not care to acknowledge the divisions at the heart of this royalist bulwark but instead affirmed that Pasto's population was decidedly promonarchical. Since he did not give details about the exceptions to that norm, Restrepo's generalized statement about Pasto's population being involved in the rebellion seems to reflect, more than anything, a racialized judgment about royalists and royalism. As we will see next, this matter of rejection of the rebellion among some sectors of Pasto's population is crucial to recognizing changes in the royalist faction after 1822. Additionally, it is necessary to make an effort to refute Restrepo's simplistic characterization of Pasto as royalist in order to clarify the royalist rebels' goals and practical possibilities for action after the capitulation.

PASTO DIVIDED

The rebel royalist forces succeeded in occupying the city of Pasto on October 28, 1822. They then removed from the government anyone

---

[8] Restrepo, *Historia de la Revolución*, Vol. IV (1969), 419.

who was not willing to cooperate, reinstituted the royalist militias, and named Estanislao Merchancano, a Creole from Pasto who had been committed to the royalist army, the Military and Political Governor. Leading the militias, Boves attacked Túquerres, in the province of Los Pastos, where Antonio Obando was in charge of the government. The rebels deposed Obando and rounded up large numbers of cattle, which they then sent to the north of the Juanambú River (close to the city of Pasto) as provisions for the militias.[9] Boves and Merchancano named Ramón Medina as *protector de naturales* and abolished Indian tribute.[10]

Let us not forget that Medina had been named *protector* by the Quito *Audiencia* in 1817 after a long confrontation that the caciques of Obonuco and Catambuco and some other towns had had with the earlier *protector*, Juan Díaz Gallardo. Gallardo was finally removed, and in his place the *audiencia* named Medina, who at the time was captain of the royalist militias in Pasto. The selection of Medina for the post of protector signals that during the war the holder of that position was deeply immersed in military dynamics. For Boves and Merchancano, having Medina as part of the government structure facilitated the mobilization of the communities through their caciques, leaders whom Medina himself appointed and who would have collaborated with the rebellion in favor of the king.

That Boves abolished tribute is possibly a sign that the Indian commoners had been able to negotiate their participation in the rebellion by pushing for that fundamental demand to be made one of the rebel government's top priorities. When Gallardo was the *protector*, he defended the interests of the commoners and advocated for tribute reduction. It seems likely that Medina also supported the tribute reduction – even its abolition – to gain the Indian masses' support for the 1822 rebellion. Ultimately, the caciques must also have accepted such a transformation, in spite of having rejected it a decade earlier when the independence wars began and negotiations over tribute were first incorporated into the royalist agenda. Such a change in the caciques' position suggests that the caciques' power now depended on their ability to mobilize the communities.[11]

---

[9] Ortiz, *Agustín Agualongo*, 451.
[10] J.C. Mejía Mejía, "El clero de Pasto y la insurrección del 28 de octubre de 1822," *Boletín de Estudios Históricos* 4, no. 46 (1932), 418–22.
[11] Cecilia Méndez found a similar situation in the Huanta rebellion of 1825–28. See Méndez, *The Plebeian Republic*, 23.

The Pasto elites rejected the revolt and denounced it as a mere tumult born of popular ignorance. They knew that disavowing the arrangement achieved with Bolívar that same year would be a dangerous step in the wrong direction. Many members of the clergy openly defied Boves and his rebel forces for claiming for themselves the right to govern in the name of the king; most notably, Aurelio Rosero, Pasto's priest and Ecclesiastic Judge, excommunicated them. In mid-November, in turn, Boves' government forcefully set out to collect high taxes from the "traitors" who had negotiated with Bolívar and accepted the republican government, including Rosero.[12]

These antagonisms made clear an outright division between elite and popular opinions in Pasto, and during this revolt the popular sectors acted largely autonomously from the elites, who had accepted republicanism after the 1822 capitulation. This was a significant change because previously the Pasto elites had considered the Indians to be crucial allies. When the Pasto municipal council requested recognition and rewards for its loyalty to the Spanish crown between 1809 and 1822, the letters they sent to the king always included explicit mention of the valued indigenous support for the royalist cause.[13] Now Bishop Jiménez openly supported Bolívar, becoming a key agent for the diffusion of the republican and nationalist doctrines. The political elites, who, as had been promised in the capitulation, had been incorporated into the republican government, were also interested in maintaining their positions and possessions intact. As this division deepened, the elites became central to Bolívar's strategy for pacifying the royalist rebels. For example, when Bolívar named Colonel Juan José Flores governor of Pasto, Flores was able to develop an alliance with the local elite and organize a counterinsurgent militia headed by Nicolás Chaves and Tomás Miguel Santacruz.[14]

The break between the elites and the popular classes changed the dynamic of the royalist struggle. For the first time in more than a decade of war in Pasto, the royalist alliance fractured along class lines, with most of the urban elites turning against the royalist rural population. Recent

---

[12] Ortiz, *Agustín Agualongo*, 451. See Charles Walker's analysis of the potent role that excommunication played in the repression of the Tupac Amaru rebellion. Walker, *The Tupac Amaru Rebellion.*

[13] A summary of the Pasto *cabildo*'s requests can be found in "Dictamen del Consejo de Indias sobre recompensas a la ciudad de Pasto, en vista de sus representaciones," in *Colección de documentos para la historia de Colombia*, ed. Ortiz, 110, 112.

[14] "Conducta y operaciones del coronel Juan José Flores, durante su permanencia en Pasto," in *Colección de documentos para la historia de Colombia*, ed. Ortiz, 297.

scholarship describes this turning point as the moment when the Indians began to act on their own, and not as clients of the elites. This shift has been interpreted as evidence that the previous (1809–22) royalist alliances in this region were the reflection of engrained patronage or clientelist relations between the Pasto elites and the Indians. Additionally, this interpretation states that the Indians finally began to act in their own interests once Bolívar had negotiated with the Spanish officers and certain sectors of the Creole elite.[15] But why would the indigenous communities have acted in a way that did not reflect or coincide with their interests and only pursue these interests after the elites turned republican? I believe a different argument is needed. It must take into account the fact that indigenous people in Pasto had been a crucial part of royalist alliances since 1809 and that their position in those alliances had been carefully negotiated in terms that benefited them. A clientelist conceptual framework, which depoliticizes the Indians and portrays them as dependent on the elites' interests, is insufficient for explaining the political relations that were visible when the caciques and the *protector de naturales* acted as intermediaries for the military mobilization of Indians in favor of royalism. In other words, since the outbreak of the war, indigenous people had not been manipulated or forced to enroll in the royalist faction but actually had been negotiating across class lines according to their interests. Precisely because royalism was not monolithic but had different meanings across class lines, even when the Creole elites participated in the alliances, the Indians' actions did not necessarily correspond to elite interests in a linear or direct way.

THE ROYALIST REBELS, AGUSTÍN AGUALONGO, AND COLOMBIAN HISTORY

Boves escaped and fled to the Amazon during a battle in 1822. After that point, Agustín Agualongo became the rebel government's longest lasting leader, fighting until his death at the hands of the republic in July 1824. From the nationalist perspective, in the historiography and popular accounts, Agualongo was an antihero who represented the stubbornness

---

[15] For Gutiérrez, *Los indios de Pasto contra la república*, 201, 206, this is the only moment when Indians acted independently and not under the influence of elites. That interpretation results from his framing of Indian royalism using a clientelist model that explains patronage and elite manipulations as the causes of Indian mobilization. See also Earle, *Spain and the Independence*, 164.

and backwardness of the people of Colombia's southwest region. As an officer of the Republic in 1823, José Hilario López, who later would be president of Colombia, wrote that "the Pastusos' innate barbarism and ignorance" was the only explanation for their ingratitude toward Colombia's national generosity.[16] In spite of the stigmatizing power of anti-Pastuso rhetoric, in Pasto regional history, Agualongo is evoked as a hero whose great virtue was loyalty. This is because the violence of the Bolivarian pacification of Pasto (this violent pacification will be considered in a moment) left a bad mark on the Pastuso memory of independence. Although sources for the caudillo's early life and military career are scarce, some historians have attempted to reconstruct his life and give meaning to his struggle. Perhaps the most significant controversy is linked to Agualongo's ethnicity. This is a matter that reveals the unstable foundation of the usual interpretations about his willingness to die fighting for the Spanish monarch and to lead a movement of plebeians that brought the wrath of the Colombian war to Pasto, resulting in devastating consequences for the region.

In the 1827 *History of the Colombian Revolution*, José Manuel Restrepo, the first historian of the Colombian Republic, established an authoritative narrative of the era, one that portrayed Agualongo and all people from Pasto (or Pastusos) as vile fanatics, "idolaters of Fernando VII."[17] Restrepo was a powerful political figure in his lifetime, having served as Bolívar's Minister of the Interior. Moreover, as an eyewitness of events of the independence era, his opinions had nearly unimpeachable credibility. Restrepo's account condemned Agualongo as an "ignorant Indian," and his negative portrayal influenced many later historical representations of this royalist caudillo. This depiction implied that Agualongo's ethnicity and ignorance led him to fight for the king for nearly fifteen years, repeatedly turning his back on the liberating, progressive promise of the new republic.[18] On the other hand, by describing and labeling him as an Indian, Restrepo highlighted Agualongo's lack of judgment by relying on the widespread, racist belief that all Indians were simple and incapable of making rational political judgments. In fact, indigenous people clearly understood Hispanic law, participated actively in the colonial economy, and positioned themselves strategically within the context of the political events that made up the independence process. But many

---

[16] López cited in Gutiérrez, *Los indios de Pasto contra la república*, 220.
[17] Restrepo, *Historia de la Revolución*, Vol. III (1827), 276.
[18] Restrepo, *Historia de la Revolución*, Vol. I (1969), 386; Vol. V (1969), 89.

Colombian elites clung to the belief that Indians were clearly inferior to people of Spanish descent, and Restrepo's representation of indigenous people from Pasto reveals the shaky concept of equality that existed in Creole visions of the Colombian Republic. By calling Agualongo – the symbol of southwestern royalism par excellence – an ignorant Indian, Restrepo explained away the caudillo's support for royalism as merely a reflection of the inherent poor judgment of the Indian people, in this way excusing Agualongo for his obviously delusional opposition to the independence cause. In presenting this negative, racist characterization, Restrepo set the tone for the complete dismissal of royalism as a legitimate political and ideological position during the period.

But was Agualongo really an Indian?[19] Based on documentation suggesting that Agualongo was not an Indian but rather a *mestizo*, historians in the twentieth century have challenged Restrepo's negative, racist portrayal of the royalist caudillo. Indeed, his birth certificate provides evidence that Agustín Agualongo Sisneros was born in the city of Pasto of *mestizo* parents.[20] But in spite of that "fact," the stories that echoed Restrepo's account prevailed and even multiplied in the twentieth century. For example, the first history book used for educating high school students in Colombia was published by Jesús María Henao and Gerardo Arrubla in 1910. In their influential work, Henao and Arrubla described Agualongo as an "astute and brave Indian," but they labeled royalists as "fanatics."[21] Other works used Agualongo's surname to brand him as a mere Indian who had worked as a servant for a wealthy family in Pasto. According to this account, the caudillo's name, "Agualongo," came from the many times that his masters asked Agustín to bring them water (*agua* in Spanish). The word *longo* was (and still is) used to refer to Indians, so his last name would have been the result of the

---

[19] Agualongo has become a mythical figure in the history of Pasto. Whether or not he was indigenous is relevant, but what the historiography has done with such a question is to racialize the memory of royalism in the region, adding essentialist overtones to its interpretation. In other words, no work to this date has accounted for the political project of the rebellion led by Agualongo, yet it has been characterized as religiously fanatic and as "idolatrous of Fernando VII." See Restrepo, *Historia de la Revolución*, Vol. IV (1969), 423; Restrepo, *Diario Político y Militar*, Vol. I, 256; Ortiz, *Agustín Agualongo*, 15–27; Bastidas, *Las guerras de Pasto*, 113; Guerrero, *Pasto en la guerra*, 141; Alberto Miramón, "Agualongo, el guerrillero indomable," *Boletín de Historia y Antigüedades* 27, nos. 313–314 (1940), 968–85.

[20] Ortiz, *Agustín Agualongo*, 14; Díaz del Castillo, *El Caudillo*, 5–6.

[21] Jesús María Henao and Gerardo Arrubla, *Historia de Colombia para la enseñanza secundaria*, Vol. II (1910; Bogota: Librería Colombiana, 1920), 410.

command "*¡agua, longo!*" or "Indian, bring the water!" This far-fetched explanation presents the stereotypical image of Indians as servile.[22] Indeed, that assumption underlies Restrepo's characterization of royalism; it was a movement of Indians who were ultimately manipulated into blindly following royalist leaders at the expense of their actual best interests.

Restrepo also called Agualongo an Indian probably because indigenous people were a significant segment of the population in southwest New Granada, and the royalist army in Pasto was largely composed of Indians. As a result, although historians have proven that Agualongo was a *mestizo* and not an Indian, his connection to the royalist cause in the area led people to associate him with the ethnic majority in that region. To be sure, the politics of the insurrection were entwined with the Pasto Indians' interest in reducing tribute and protecting their communal interests. Thus it is clear that Agualongo, although a *mestizo*, explicitly embraced the welfare of the indigenous people, who were fundamental to the royalist struggle. But the fact is that the Indian population was not the only group that comprised his army. Some people from the town of Patía, north of Pasto, still supported the Spanish cause during the years 1822 to 1824. Indeed, when Agualongo led the royalist resistance to Bolívar, some Patianos formed part of his army, making the royalist movement multiethnic. The Patianos had played a central role in the royalist defense of Popayán between 1809 and 1819. Yet their participation in the war varied over time. At first they mobilized in an autonomous fashion, as a guerrilla, but after 1815 they became part of the Spanish army. Then, once Bolívar arrived victorious in Popayán, some of the Patiano soldiers were willing to negotiate with his representatives and change sides.[23] What this suggests is that with Spain's defeat in New Granada, some royalists sought to secure their place in the new order and continue to benefit from their position in the military. Even if this may have generated fissures within Patiano society, the flexibility of their strategies is made clear by the fact that some Patianos continued to be royalists and fought with Agualongo after 1822.

Agualongo's last battle, which he lost to Tomás Cipriano de Mosquera, was in Barbacoas, in the Pacific lowlands gold-mining region, where enslaved blacks had mobilized in support of the king's cause

---

[22] Ortiz, *Agustín Agualongo*, 14; Alberto Miramón, *Hombres del tiempo heróico* (Bogotá: Empresa Nacional de Publicaciones, 1956), 92.

[23] Zuluaga, *Guerrilla y sociedad en el Patía*.

between 1810 and 1820. In Barbacoas, after the capitulation with Bolívar, some slaves seemed interested in the revolutionary project. In 1822 slaves from the mines revolted against their owners, with their leaders adopting the names of the main caudillos of independence of that time: Bolívar, Santander, and Sucre.[24] Bolívar, however, decided to send an officer to put down the revolt, an action that must have made it clear to the enslaved that their struggle for freedom was not supported by the republican government.

The three main leaders of the rebellion, Tomás Boves, Agustín Agualongo, and Estanislao Merchancano, had had ample experience in the war, which lent them prestige in the region. Their leadership was based on alliances with various lower-ranking individuals who were able to organize people at the community level. The caciques of Anganoy, Catambuco, and Cumbal mobilized Indians from Pasto and Los Pastos, the two jurisdictions where Indian communities lived. Two black men were also among the leaders of the rebellion. They strategically headed the royalist rebellion in the Pacific lowlands, in the region between Barbacoas and Buenaventura, including the Patía River Valley, where royalism had been a constant in the previous years. Additionally, Merchancano, a Creole from Pasto, who had been part of the royalist army, represented the rebel government in the city. By uniting Spanish, *mestizo*, Indian, and black leaders, the royalists represented the different population sectors living in and around Pasto and secured a wide following. The rebels' considerable strength was evident in their successive (at least three) occupations of the city of Pasto, where they instituted a royalist government that remained under siege by the republicans.

ANTIREPUBLICAN ROYALISM IN 1822–1824

The ideological confrontation between Colombians and Pasto royalists revolved around the opposition between anticolonial values and the defense of the Spanish monarch's sovereignty in the Americas. Even after

---

[24] This information has been reproduced in the historiography, but there is no clarity about its origin in the primary sources. Because of a lack of contextualization, it is hard to interpret the revolt further. See Idelfonso Díaz del Castillo, "El coronel Manuel Ortiz y Zamora. Breves apuntes sobre su vida," *Boletín de Estudios Históricos* 2, no. 21 (1929), 276; Fernando Jurado, *Esclavitud en la Costa Pacífica. Iscuandé, Tumaco, Barbacoas y Esmeraldas, Siglos XVI al XIX* (Quito: Ediciones Abya-Yala, 1990), 394–95; Arboleda "Entre la libertad y la sumisión," 28; Almario, *La invención del suroccidente colombiano*, 129.

the Spanish forces retreated from Pasto, the rebels expressed a commitment to the monarchical legal framework that guaranteed them certain rights. That the Colombian army and the government that Bolívar organized in the southwest were perceived as intruders suggests the nationalist discourse that was circulating had not convinced broad sectors of the Indian and *casta* populations in the southwest.[25] It is a fact that by right of "secuestro," the republicans confiscated significant amounts of property and land and gave the new landowners positions in the local government.[26] The royalist slaves and the free black and indigenous peasants were certainly defending their territory from being divided up among the victors of the conflict – the military and other government officials who represented Bolívar and Colombia on the ground.

That said, the people who mobilized as part of a royalist rebellion in 1822–25 shared ideas and values about governance and law that went beyond a merely instrumental search for material well-being. The proclamations of the royalist government signed by Agualongo and Merchancano denounced the illegitimacy of the Colombians, who were seen to be usurping the rights of Fernando VII. For example:

Inhabitants of the faithful City of Pasto:

You have seen and painfully experienced your people's devastation; you have suffered the strongest yoke of the greatest of all tyrannical intruders, Bolívar. ... It is time for us, faithful *pastusos*, to unite our courageous hearts in the defense of Religion, the King, and our Fatherland, because if we stop defending our most sacred rights, we will again fall into the hands of the enemies of the Church and Humanity.[27]

This and other proclamations express specific qualms about the dismantling of Spanish rule in the region, something with which the Indians and people of African descent mobilized in rebellion would have likely

---

[25] This does not mean that the royalist rebels were in any way backward or resentful toward any type of "outside" interference in their livelihood or communal space – as other scholars have suggested. This traditional interpretation assumes that Pasto was an isolated place and therefore out of touch with wider developments. It also conflates the late colonial context with the independence period without studying or acknowledging the transformations brought about during the years 1809–22 when people in Pasto were actively involved in royalist mobilization. See Earle, "Indian Rebellion and Bourbon Reform in New Granada," 123; Hamnett, "Popular Insurrection and Royalist Reaction," 311.

[26] José María Obando, *Apuntamientos para la historia* (1837; Medellín: Editorial Bedout, 1972), 59.

[27] This proclamation is probably from June 1823 (n.d.), in Cristóbal de Gangotena y Jijón, ed., *Documentos referentes a la campaña de Ibarra con la narración histórica de la campaña de Pasto* (Quito: Talleres Tipográficos Nacionales, 1823), 6.

identified. The rebels' denunciation of the Colombian Creole government's direct disavowal of the political pact with the Spanish monarch implies that such a pact was, in fact, valuable to the royalists rebels.

Yet the notion of a legal framework or political pact that Indians and slave royalists were upholding by rising in rebellion against Colombia's despotic attempt to conquer them was not a static one. Throughout the years of the independence wars, when Popayán was under royalist rule, Indians and slaves were able to expand their rights under the premise of their loyalty to the Crown. For them, after 1809 militia participation mediated their social standing. Based on that experience, the royalist rebellion in 1822–25 expressed the collective interest of the communities of indigenous and enslaved people in Popayán in restoring the conditions that had prevailed in the region when royalists governed the area.

At the start of the second decade of the nineteenth century, royalism among the Pasto Indian communities was once again influenced by the ethnic authorities, who were defending their prerogatives and wished to maintain a privileged status in the new political context. Among those interests was the continued right of Indians to their communal landholdings, an aspect of Hispanic legal and social organization that the Colombian Republic had explicitly attacked. This was manifest in the decree of May 20, 1820, in which Bolívar announced the republican plan to divide up communal lands to provide Indians with individual, private property; this provision was later included in Article 3 of the law of October 11, 1821. Both laws were consistent with the republican project to make Indians citizens equal to other Colombians.[28]

Additionally, *cacicazgos* were abolished after independence. As part of the republican policy of the integration of Indians into the nation on equal terms, the government no longer recognized the existence of hereditary rights to authority in indigenous communities. These measures had a liberal content in a sense that was different from the liberalism of Cádiz. However, the Bolivarian attack on caciques' privileges (including their right to administer communal lands, especially important in the southwestern region of Colombia) was also a response to the Indians' political opposition to the republic during the independence wars.

---

[28] See "Ley sobre la extinción de los tributos de los indígenas, distribución de sus resguardos y exenciones que se les conceden," in *Congreso de Cúcuta de 1821: Constitución y Leyes* (Bogotá: Biblioteca Banco Popular, 1971), 248–52; Friede, *El indio en lucha por la tierra*, 106. The law was also a continuation of the once aborted Bourbon project of division of Indian lands, which was carried out mostly in the region surrounding Santa Fe.

Precisely because this was a change introduced during the monarchical crisis, when Bolívar arrived in Pasto to institute a law to suppress ethnic authorities and abolish the Indian communities, the indigenous people there reacted against him. Similarly, the freedom struggles of enslaved blacks in the Pacific were entwined with the royalist rebellion during the time when royalists controlled the area, and since 1821 they had been defending themselves from the republican incursion meant to pacify them and restore slavery.[29]

A continuity with the royalist principles that underlaid the military mobilization of Indians and slaves in the southwestern region of Colombia was paralleled by a significant transformation visible after 1822 when, for the first time, their motives for going to war became explicitly anti-republican. That the advance of Colombian forces into the southwest was a violent imposition and encroachment explains that the rebels did not perceive a "revolutionary" or emancipatory potential in the Bolivarian Republic. The royalist rebellions after 1822 combined the creative and dynamic essence of the royalist rebellion with elements of a reaction to Bolivarian rule and the violence that it had unleashed during its pacification of the region. Hence, we can state that these rebellions were not reactionary.

The following two sections will explore the confrontation between the republicans and the Indian and black royalists in an armed struggle that led to the progressive escalation of violence and repression on the part of the republicans. As the royalist rebellion was expanding across the territory in an attempt to reestablish the royalist block in the Pacific region, it created major problems for Bolívar.

PASTO'S INVINCIBLE LIBERATORS

While he was in Quito, as soon as he heard the news of the October 1822 insurrection, alarmed but not surprised, Bolívar sent General Sucre with reinforcements to combat the rebellion. In December more men arrived

---

[29] The communities in Telembí (Barbacoas), Naya, Saija, and Iscuandé continued to be in a royalist revolt in 1821. BLAA Archivo de Emiliano Díaz del Castillo, Caja 8, Carpeta 81, fols. 89, 94. See also Almario, *La invención del suroccidente colombiano*, 125. A parallel case to this can be found in Florida when the Indians and free blacks who had organized their society around a relationship with the Spanish state were threatened by the encroachment of U.S. forces and a legal system that was antagonistic to their interests. Jane Landers, *Black Society in Spanish Florida* (Chicago: University of Illinois Press, 1999), ch. 10; and Landers, *Atlantic Creoles in the Age of Revolutions*, ch. 5.

from Bogotá, eventually outnumbering Boves and his local forces. The Pastusos were eager to defend their positions, and they knew that this time there would be no space or chance for mercy. Yet, unable to defend the city, Boves escaped from the city and fled toward the eastern Amazon lowlands, after which the guerrillas gave in. The wrath of the republican forces fell on the city for days, the soldiers punishing with death almost anyone they encountered and leaving the city devastated. When Bolívar entered Pasto again on January 2, 1823, he rescinded the gentle treatment offered in the previous capitulation, point by point. He imposed a tax levy to be collected from every family. Where the capitulation had promised to allow Pastusos to remain in their territory, Bolívar now demanded the recruitment of all males into the army. Instead of respecting the properties of prominent families, Bolívar ordered the confiscation of horses and other goods, which he distributed among his army. Any priest known to have defended the royalist rebellion was sent into exile, so Bolívar dispatched an order to Quito asking for priests loyal to the republic to be sent to Pasto as replacements. Bolívar reinstituted the tribute, a setback for indigenous people in the region since the abolition of tribute payment was perhaps the most important point of contention for them.[30]

The punishment for "treason" went even further once Bolívar returned to Quito in mid-January and Salom was left in charge. As military governor, Salom tricked the Pastusos by asking them to attend a meeting in the city to request citizenship papers, only to imprison all those who attended. Around a thousand men were later sent to Quito to join the army, including some two hundred Indians who were drafted by force from their towns. During their march south, many of these men died of hunger because, as a form of protest against their forced incorporation into the army, they did not accept the food provided. Others committed suicide. Preferring to die rather than collaborate with the republican cause, these Pastusos manifested the extent of their commitment to the war and resistance. In Pasto, other royalist prisoners were tied in pairs and thrown down an abyss into the Guáitara River, an execution method – called *matrimonio cívico* or "civic marriage" – that allowed the republicans to save ammunition.[31] As a result of those excesses, the

---

[30] Ortiz, *Agustín Agualongo*, 459–60.

[31] Ortiz, *Agustín Agualongo*, 460; Obando, *Apuntamientos para la historia*, 63. This information is central to the historiography of the period that was produced in Pasto, because it reveals the wickedness of a republican ruler such as Salom and the Pastusos' radical capacity for sacrifice.

people in Pasto had more reasons than ever to rise in rebellion. Added to their ideological rejection of the Bolivarian republic was the fact that the Pastusos now held Bolívar accountable for the widespread abuses and violence perpetrated against the local people.

After the first insurrection of October 1822 had been repressed, the survivors stayed hidden in the mountains for some time but did not give up their intention to fight back. Around the same time, after Salom returned to Quito, in April 1823 Bolívar named Colonel Juan José Flores governor of Pasto. A Venezuelan by birth, Flores represented the occupation of the region by forces perceived as – and that literally were – foreign. In spite of Flores' efforts to contain the rebellion, the guerrillas – composed mostly of indigenous men and peasants from the rural areas surrounding Pasto and the Patía Valley – seemed indomitable. The movement began to operate again in Funes and Sapuyes, soon to spread to the other Indian towns. In a report on the events, Flores summarized the situation saying that "the stupid rural people's opinion was against us."[32] In this vague statement, Flores used terms similar to those of the historian Restrepo to depict the rebels, combining racist assumptions with the intolerant rhetoric against royalists. Like Restrepo, Flores did not account specifically for his enemy's interests or for the composition of the movement in particular. However, his words suggest that most of the Indian towns in the Pasto district either were actively involved in the rebellion or supported it.

To pacify the rebels, Flores heightened his violent response to their actions, executing without trial anyone he was able to catch, aiming to "make the rebels and those who protected them afraid of punishment." In his reports of the military operations under his government, including some defeats at the hands of the "insurgents," Flores wrote that his opponents were "ferocious" and that such ferocity was enhanced "by their ignorance." Flores also noted that "in Colombia everyone knows that cold steel (*arma blanca*) is very powerful in the hands of a stubborn man."[33] These counterinsurgency reports obscured and belittled the perspective of the rebels and labeled them as inferior. Flores' reports even suggested that the royalist rebels lacked any strategy and that their military actions were merely savage reactions. Yet his written words also

---

[32] "Conducta y operaciones del coronel Juan José Flores, durante su permanencia en Pasto," in *Colección de documentos para la historia de Colombia*, ed. Ortiz, 298.

[33] "Conducta y operaciones del coronel Juan José Flores, durante su permanencia en Pasto," in *Colección de documentos para la historia de Colombia*, ed. Ortiz, 301.

expressed fear, fear of the incomprehensibleness of their actions and, moreover, fear of the decided passion with which the royalist guerillas waged war. In that sense, although Flores tried to portray the rebels in the rural areas of Pasto as irrational, we can see that their hit-and-run guerrilla strategies were successful precisely because they differed from the military tactics of the Colombian army.

Significantly, while most of the Colombian army was composed of people who had come from the north, including Bolívar's Haitian allies, the royalist rebels were local people who could count on support from their communities and families. It is also revealing that while Flores tried to diminish the image of these guerrillas by alluding to their simple weapons, in his report he also asserted that their capacity for victory was great, given their resolve. Ultimately Flores' words also tell us two things: one, that these royalist guerrillas possessed a special strength stemming from their "inversion" of their expected subordinate status and, two, their determination to disregard authority enabled them to intimidate Colombian soldiers.[34]

After Boves' escape, in 1823 new leadership emerged among the rebels: Agustín Agualongo and Estanislano Merchancano were both Pastusos with military backgrounds; the cacique of Catambuco, José Canchala, José Calzón from Cumbal, and Andrés Pianda from Anganoy traveled to the communities in Pasto and Los Pastos to mobilize the Indian communities; Jerónimo Toro, from Patía, returned to the valley to call the Patianos to fight; and Francisco "El negro" Angulo went to Barbacoas to make connections with free and enslaved blacks in the mines.[35] The documents that survive, most of them penned by the republicans, give us no hint as to what types of negotiations took place between the rebel leaders and the Indian and black communities in the area between Pasto and the Pacific lowlands. Yet the rebels' actions show an interest in two things: one, laying claim to the city of Pasto, and two, maintaining control of the area linking the province of Los Pastos to Barbacoas, since this was the corridor leading to the gold mines and the ocean. It also is likely that Indians were rebelling against the reinstitution of tribute attempted by Bolívar as punishment after the 1822 revolt.

---

[34] See Ranajit Guha, *Elementary Aspects of Peasant Insurgency in Colonial India* (Durham, NC: Duke University Press, 1999), ch. 2. Similar factors were in place in 1896 during the Cuban war of independence when U.S. soldiers stigmatized Cuban insurgents for their guerrilla tactics and race. See Louis Pérez, *Cuba Between Empires, 1878–1902* (Pittsburgh, PA: University of Pittsburgh Press, 1998), 199–205.

[35] Ortiz, *Agustín Agualongo*, 465.

In spite of Flores' attempts to defend the city, on June 12, 1823, the rebels occupied Pasto again. An army composed largely of Indians armed with a few rifles and bayonets, spears, sticks, and clubs entered the city yelling, "Long live the King!" (¡*Viva el Rey!*). Around 800 men (including 600 Indians) were responsible for defeating the 500 men in Flores' army. Colombians were shocked. How could these "poorly armed Indians" overcome their forces?[36] A few days after the occupation, Colombian authorities in Popayán interrogated Vicente Olave, a merchant who had been traveling from Pasto to Popayán. They asked him what he made of the rebel victory, to which he replied that they were strong because "they were fighting out of rage."[37] Olave's remarks corroborate that the movement was a violent reaction to the illegitimate government (*gobierno intruso*). The communities were defending themselves from the treatment they were receiving from republican officials stationed in the area. And as Flores' reports about the royalist insurgents indicated, their decisiveness and passion seemed to count in their favor. Other testimony provides evidence for the reasons the rebels had taken up arms. According to José A. Delgado, another merchant, the rebels in Pasto said that they were tired of hiding in the mountains from the Colombian forces. While their base would be in Pasto, they were planning to return to their homes and lands on the outskirts of the city to defend them. Delgado added that he had heard the rebels say that they were only acting in self-defense because their homes had been burnt and sacked, evidence that the authorities that governed in the name of the Colombian state had been abusive to an intolerable degree.

Agualongo and Merchancano took the leading positions in the new rebel government in Pasto, with Agualongo heading the military and Merchancano in charge of civil affairs. The organization of the royalist government into military and civil branches suggests an innovative change from the time of Spanish monarchical rule. While the Spanish government had always been dual, with the two pillars of government being the crown and the church, in 1823 the royalists in Pasto instead included the military as a fundamental component of government. They did not disregard religion – there were numerous priests who had

---

[36] BLAA Archivo de Emiliano Díaz del Castillo, Caja 8, Carpeta 85, fols. 91–94; "Informe del Coronel Juan José Flores al secretario de Guerra y Marina sobre la pérdida de Pasto el 12 de junio de 1823," in *Colección de documentos para la historia de Colombia*, ed. Ortiz, 233.

[37] BLAA Archivo de Emiliano Díaz del Castillo, Caja 8, Carpeta 85, fol. 95.

participated in the rebellion in Patía and the Indian towns, and Agualongo and Mechancano's official proclamations stressed that they were defending religion and the church. But the church did not have an administrative role in the government that the rebels formed in June of 1823. It is possible that given the alliance of Popayán Bishop Jiménez with Bolívar, and his active support for the new government, the rebels considered the official church leadership illegitimate.[38]

The significance of the military leadership is also made clear in a letter dated July 2, 1823, sent in the early days of the rebellion by the rebel "Government and General Headquarters" to the Colombian officer Murgueito, who was with his troops outside Barbacoas. The "commanders of Pasto's honorary liberators, the invincible troops of our lord the king" threatened Murgueito and gave him the chance to escape from "the undefeated Pasto soldiers" stationed in the mountain of Cumbal and "liberate himself from their ferocity." It is fascinating that the rebels had clearly appropriated the notion of "liberation" so central to Simón Bolívar's crusade and turned it on its head to signify that the Pastusos were the authentic liberators of the region in the face of the Bolivarian invasion. Likewise, just as Colonel Flores described the war tactics of the royalist rebels as "ferocious," the royalist army used the term to instigate fear in their enemies.[39] For the rebels in Pasto, the terms of the historical struggle they were waging against the republicans were not set in stone, as they might seem to be to us today. For the Pasto royalists, "liberation" could be defined differently from the way the revolutionaries saw it when they associated liberation with anticolonialism. This suggests that the rebels did not accept the absolute value of republicanism, did not equate republicanism with liberation, and, instead, maintained a direct campaign against the republican forces, one in which they proclaimed themselves the liberators of Pasto. Simultaneously, the rebels borrowed one of the terms prevalent in counterinsurgent discourse that portrayed them as "ferocious" to aggrandize the image of their power.

Although the royalists profited from the cruel image of themselves that circulated among Colombians, during their occupation of Pasto, they treated the people in the city and region selectively. Agualongo and Merchancano granted permission (*pasaporte*) to merchants such as Vicente Olave and Luciano Valdéz who needed to travel to Quito and Popayán. In the words of the latter, they "did not want to hurt anyone who

---

[38] Gangotena y Jijón, *Documentos referentes a la campaña de Ibarra*, 6.
[39] BLAA Archivo de Emiliano Díaz del Castillo, Caja 8, Carpeta 85, fol. 109.

was not a soldier or their enemy." But the rebels were not always lenient. A letter from Tomás Miguel de Santacruz to the Intendente in Popayán informed him that the *Juez Político* of Pasto, Joaquín Paz, had been murdered by indigenous people in the town of Aponte.[40] Following the 1822 occupation of Pasto by the royalists, the *Juez Político* had been appointed by Bolívar to directly oversee the collection of forced levies from people in Pasto as punishment for rebelling. As the local face of the republican government, Paz was an obvious target for taking retaliation.[41]

REGIONAL VISIONS AND RUMORS OF VICTORY

Having lost any direct contact with Spain, Lima, and Quito, the rebels lacked funds. To deal with that problem, they envisioned a plan to send 200 men to Barbacoas to bring money and salt back to Pasto. The rebels saw the Pacific mining region of Barbacoas as part of their territorial base, which implies that the mining economy was crucial to the rebels' material vision. According to Olave's declaration, "They also had high hopes of reuniting with Patía."[42] Projecting an alliance of Pasto with Barbacoas to the west and Patía to the north, the rebels sought to reunite the territories that until recently had been governed by the royalists. Moreover, they had the goal of expanding their revolt south into Ibarra and Quito. At the center of the revolt in Pasto, the Indians were in the majority, but they wanted to expand the social base of the rebellion to include free and enslaved blacks from the Patía Valley and the Pacific region. Throughout the years of fighting the independence war in conjunction with the Patianos and some slaves who were part of the royalist army, the Indians and *mestizos* in Pasto had established relations with blacks that were unmediated by the colonial state. In other words, the rebellion now included alliances between *mestizos*, Indians, and blacks that were evidently structured around the material importance of gold and trade that linked the province of Pasto to the Pacific lowlands (see Figure 6.1).

The rebels had a clear sense of their need for reinforcements to attempt any move into Popayán, where the Colombian government was located, and they saw cooperation with the forces in Patía and the Pacific lowlands as a viable possibility. But the rebels did not disregard Spanish support or

[40] BLAA Archivo de Emiliano Díaz del Castillo, Caja 8, Carpeta 85, fols. 90–91.
[41] Ortiz, *Agustín Agualongo*, 458.
[42] BLAA Archivo de Emiliano Díaz del Castillo, Caja 8, Carpeta 85, fol. 91.

FIGURE 6.1 Pasto and Pacific lowlands, 1822–25.
Map modified by Santiago Muñoz based on Marta Herrera "Provincia de Popayán, siglo XVIII. Relieve e hidrografía," in *Popayán*, 28.

consider it impossible or undesirable. At that time, rumors were circulating that 3,000 Spanish troops had arrived in Iscuandé and were marching toward Popayán through Micay. The arrival of Spanish reinforcements would have represented a reciprocal gesture from the monarch in support of the Pastuso royalist revolt against Bolívar. Moreover, the rumor also suggests that the rebellion seriously aimed to stand in for the Spanish monarch in Pasto and that it was not a parochial indigenous revolt launched to defend local interests and territories.[43] In the spring of 1823, the Holy Alliance in Europe contributed to the defeat of the Spanish liberals, and Fernando VII was able to reinstate absolutism. Although the Spanish monarch did not actually send reinforcements to fight the independence forces in South America, it is plausible that the rebels in Pasto and the Pacific lowlands interpreted the news to mean that such support would possibly be coming from the peninsula.

Along similar lines, the rebels circulated other information that – although not based on facts – reflected the hopes and military goals of the Pastusos and their allies. Olave said that they were spreading news about Bolívar leaving the mainland by sea to go to Panama because Guayaquil, Cuenca, and Quito had declared in favor of the king. This suggests that the rebels were clear about the geopolitical importance of Pasto's previous "Pacific" alliance with the southern Andean cities of Quito and Cuenca. The rumor also asserted the centrality and weight of Bolívar's defeat or departure as a goal of the rebellion.[44]

But, in fact, Bolívar remained in Quito preparing his march south. He publicly declared in a proclamation to Quito's inhabitants that if the "vile Pastusos do not surrender to Colombia, they will disappear from the list of towns."[45] Defiant, Agualongo went with the army to the village of Ibarra (located between Pasto and Quito) and successfully occupied it on July 12. At that time the royalist army had reached 1,500 in number, including men from the towns between Pasto and Ibarra who had joined Agualongo's anti-Bolivarian campaign. Ready to confront the Pastusos and prevent their reunion with the royalists in the south, Bolívar prepared his forces with reinforcements from Guayaquil, Ambato, and Otavalo. He set upon the Pastusos in Ibarra on the 17th of July, destroying them completely. At least half of Agualongo's men perished in Ibarra, about 800 in number, although Agualongo himself was able to escape and fled to Barbacoas. Victorious once more, Bolívar increased the level of his punishment of the Pastusos. Any man who did not present himself to be exiled to Guayaquil and was caught would be shot. All families of the

---

[43] Historians such as Eric Van Young have argued that indigenous people in Latin America were only defending their territorial interests and did not have a connection to the national "imagined communities" that allegedly emerged during the independence wars.

[44] BLAA Archivo de Emiliano Díaz del Castillo, Caja 8, Carpeta 85, fol. 91.

[45] In the original: "del catálogo de los pueblos." "A los habitantes de Quito," in *Simón Bolívar: Proclamas y Discursos*, ed. Gerardo Rivas Moreno (Cali: Fundación para la Investigación y la Cultura, 2001), 241.

insurgents would be exiled, and their land in Pasto was offered to any patriot who wished to move there to live. The possessions of those exiled were declared national patrimony.[46] Once more, Bolívar left General Salom in charge of the pacification of Pasto, allowing him to put into practice any measures that he deemed convenient.

The official proclamations that Bolívar and Santander circulated in the southwest in an effort to win the Pastusos and Patianos to the Colombian side oscillated between paternalist invitations and outright threats. Before entering Pasto in 1822 after the battle of Bomboná, Bolívar promised the "inhabitants of the south" that the liberating army would bring them calm and freedom (*reposo y libertad*). He directed a separate statement to the Pastusos and Patianos, promising to treat the first like brothers and the second like friends.[47] But after the rebellion, the Colombians saw no reason or logic in the reluctance of people in the region to accept their impending incorporation into the legal and territorial framework of Colombia, which had been brought into being by the war. This is evident in the following fragment of a private letter Bolívar wrote to Santander in 1823:

Pasto is the southern gate, and if we don't have it, we will always be cut off. Therefore we need that passage to be clear, without a single enemy in its way. . . . The worst of it is that . . . we have a force of more than 3,000 souls against us – souls made of unbending steel. Since the conquest, no other people has demonstrated more tenacity than they. . . . It has been proven we cannot win over [those wicked ones] and for that reason it is essential to destroy them to their very core.[48]

The unrest against Colombian rule in Pasto throughout 1822–25 certainly complicated Bolívar's plan to push south to Peru and establish a broad independent confederation. In those circumstances, Bolívar was not moved by the fraternal impulses of national solidarity but by a pragmatic need to incorporate a strategically located region into the republic he impatiently wanted to consolidate. As revealed by his own words, Bolívar equated the royalist rebels to objects of conquest who needed to be eliminated. And the royalist rebels confronted Bolívar precisely at that level.

Salom attempted to negotiate with the rebels but had to report to Bolívar that the Pastusos were convinced they were fighting a war to the

[46] Cited in Ortiz, *Agustín Agualongo*, 476.

[47] "A los habitantes del sur," and "A los patianos, pastusos y españoles," in *Simón Bolívar: Proclamas y Discursos*, 230–31.

[48] Bolívar to Santander, Quito, 21 July 1823, in *Cartas Santander-Bolívar 1823–1825*, Vol. 4 (Bogotá: Fundación Francisco de Paula Santander, 1988), 97.

death, especially considering the treatment they had received in Ibarra. According to Salom, "The furor with which they make war on us is indescribable."[49] To make matters worse, the guerrillas seemed to be multiplying. They appeared in the province of Los Pastos, where the Indian José Calzón and the priest Juan Benavides mobilized Indians to take over Túquerres and Sapuyes. Meanwhile Jerónimo Toro was in Patía with a small guerrilla group. Other groups were fighting as far as Buenaventura on the Pacific coast, trying to establish a contact in the port so they could purchase arms there.[50] On August 23, once more the royalists took over Pasto and stayed there until mid-September.

Seeing that neither the war nor the attempts of local officers to negotiate could bring the Pastusos under control, in November Vice President Santander sent a letter to Agualongo and Merchancano laying out the reasons they should accept defeat. Santander wrote they were extremely delirious and mad (*el colmo del delirio y de la locura*) to believe "that you [Pastuso royalists] could ever, in such an insignificant place, make us lose our liberty." He invited them to "enjoy the peace that all Colombians have," and to "rectify the erroneous perception that Spain could conquer Colombia again." Santander warned that the tragedy of a sustained war would be solely the responsibility of the Pastusos' obstinacy and blindness (*obstinación y ceguedad*). The vice president remarked that a people who had not feared Morillo and his Expeditionary Army would not be afraid of a few men cornered in Pasto without reinforcements or arms.[51] By the time that Agualongo and Merchancano received Santander's missive, in January 1824, Juan José Flores had returned to help Salom with the campaign against Agualongo's forces. In contrast to Santander's inviting words, Salom and Flores executed any combatant who fell into their hands. These men of war, who had to deal with the rebels on the ground, knew that Pastusos would never give in, and, with their actions, Salom and Flores demonstrated that they were aligned with Bolívar and with the message he had privately sent to Santander, that "it [wa]s essential to destroy [the royalists] to their very core."[52] Colombian military officers approached the Pastusos in an attitude of merciless "conquest," while the

---

[49] Salom cited in Ortiz, *Agustín Agualongo*, 479.
[50] Restrepo, *Historia de la Revolución*, Vol. III (1827), 383.
[51] Santander cited in Ortiz, *Agustín Agualongo*, 482–83.
[52] Bolívar to Santander, Quito, 21 July 1823, in *Cartas Santander-Bolívar 1823–1825*, Vol. 4, 97.

political discourse stemming from Santander and Bolívar's proclamations continued to invite them to join the Colombian nation.

Badly beaten but determined to continue fighting, Agualongo and another 100 men traveled to Barbacoas, seeking to enlarge their army with the free and enslaved blacks in the region. Agualongo's goal in 1824 seems to have been to expand his control over the Pacific littoral, where slaves from the gold mines continued to be potential allies of the royalist cause.[53] Despite the odds, they continued to harbor hopes for a royalist victory in Peru and were fighting to restore the Pasto-Quito-Lima corridor to royalist control. The royalist government in Pasto would be viable if the Andean-Pacific region were economically integrated. From the perspective of the Colombians, the connection between the Pasto rebellion and the ongoing insurrection among the slaves in the Pacific lowlands created serious territorial difficulties for the army. In an 1821 offensive, a battalion had tried to enter the mining region from Cali with the goal of pacifying the slaves and then penetrating Pasto from the northwest. But this ultimately proved to be impossible. On the one hand, the slaves and free blacks enjoyed complete control of the area and had already allowed the entrance of the Pastusos, giving the royalist army a tactical advantage. On the other hand, as the War and Maritime Secretary of Colombia concluded, "Any force that enters the Pacific lowlands will have to subsist with goods that arrive from the province of Los Pastos." One strategy of war used by the slaves on the Pacific coast was to block the flow of goods from the eastern plains, precisely as deterrent to a Colombian invasion.[54]

Surrounded, Agualongo's forces set fire to the city of Barbacoas and put up a fight with support from the locals, but the Colombians, headed by Tomás Cipriano de Mosquera, claimed victory on the third day. On June 24, José María Obando caught Agualongo and twelve of his men at El Castigo as they were retreating to Pasto. He shot Joaquín Enríquez, Francisco Terán, and Manuel Insuaste and then took Agualongo to Popayán, where the republican forces summarily shot him on July 13, 1824.[55] Although Obando wrote in his memoirs that Agualongo was interrogated and a document (*causa*) was produced laying out his defense, this affidavit has yet to be located in the archives.[56]

[53] AGN República, Secretaría de Guerra y Marina 43, fol. 681; Obando, *Apuntamientos para la historia*, 68.
[54] BLAA Archivo de Emiliano Díaz del Castillo, Caja 8, Carpeta 81, fols. 71–73.
[55] Ortiz, *Agustín Agualongo*, 492.   [56] Obando, *Apuntamientos para la historia*, 67.

REVERBERATIONS

With Agualongo's capture and death, the royalists were profoundly weakened, but a few small bands continued to roam across Pasto. Jerónimo Toro fell in Barbacoas, but Francisco "El negro" Angulo, whom Agualongo had named governor of Barbacoas, continued to move around the valley of Taminango close to Patía.[57] The fact that Angulo reportedly was granted a government post in the area of Barbacoas, where mostly black people lived, is significant. Men such as Angulo and Toro had privileged access to people in the mining region and the Patía River Valley and were able to rally them to the royalist cause. Their active participation and leadership in the royalist army indicates that horizontal links had formed within the militias, links that had the potential to mobilize more people in the Pacific lowlands to defend the cause. More striking was the decisive inclusion of a black man – also a captain in the royalist army – in the royalist government, an unprecedented gesture that was surely intended to signal to the free and enslaved blacks in the region that the rebellion would include them on equal terms in the leadership. It is not known whether Angulo fulfilled his role as "governor" of Barbacoas before Mosquera's victory, but his retreat to Patía after the defeat in June of 1824 suggests that he continued to seek and possibly attain support in a region where many free black people lived.

According to José Manuel Restrepo, the priest Benavides continued to lead an insurrection in the province of Los Pastos and the forests around the Juanambú River.[58] Restrepo's statement was based on a lampoon or *pasquín* signed with Benavides' name that appeared on a wall of the church in the town of San Pablo in the Patía River Valley in March 1825. A transcribed copy of this lampoon is today part of the Restrepo Collection, and the copy has a note (added by the transcriber) that denies that Benavides could have been the author of the *pasquín*.[59] It is impossible to know whether the note added to the transcription is correct, or, on the contrary, if Benavides was indeed the author of this text signed with his name. Even if he was not the author, it seems significant that his name would be used to issue a call to arms in the Patía Valley. In conjunction with Restrepo's affirmation that Benavides was mobilizing people in the province of Los Pastos, an area mostly inhabited by Indians,

---

[57] Restrepo, *Historia de la Revolución*, Vol. III (1969), 383.
[58] Restrepo, *Historia de la Revolución*, Vol. III (1969), 383.
[59] JCBL Archivo Restrepo, Fondo II, Vol. 47, fol. 89.

the lampoon suggests that, as a royalist rebel, Benavides also could have been a potential leader of free blacks. The text was allegedly written at the "general provincial headquarters." Again, although it is hard to certify that large numbers of rebels were mobilized at this point in time, the lampoon implied that, even in 1825, some rebels were organized in militias. There is not enough evidence of the persistence of the rebellion to back up that possibility, and it is also impossible to know whether or not Benavides had written the text. But it is significant that whoever transcribed it and added the note doubting that Benavides was the author explained with concern that any priest could have written it, given that the priests of the towns of San Pablo and La Cruz were royalists and were continuing to preach against the republic.

The lampoon begins with a "¡Viva el Rey!" ("Long live the King!"). Praising the "immortal and brave Patianos," it then calls on them to respond to their duty to mobilize against "the traitor" Bolívar. The lampoon says they surely were well aware of the abuses and desolation caused by the Colombians. As "intrepid defenders of a loving and benign king" they should, therefore, voluntarily join the fight against the "hungry wolves" that allegedly were traveling north from Quito. The assured triumph of the Patianos would make them "famous," the lampoon promised. Furthermore, Spanish troops would supposedly come to support that battle and recognize the Patianos' valor. As I mentioned earlier, the royalist rebels around Pasto had invoked promises of Spanish support at other times, even after the capitulation agreed to by Bolívar and the Spanish Colonel Basilio García. At the time this lampoon was publicized, the last military actions of the royalist resistance were taking place in Peru, in the region of Huanta, so the reference could have been to that specific royalist rebellion. Such a reference suggests continued hopes for a meeting taking place between royalists from southern Colombia and Peru.[60] Most importantly, the lampoon is a testament to the dependence of royalists on the Patianos and the extent to which the support from the Patianos had become linked to victory over and effective resistance to the republicans. By promising new rewards and recognition to men who mobilized in favor of the king, the lampoon also suggests that once the republicans acquired control over the region, the Patianos lost a lot of the power they had amassed throughout the course of the wars.[61]

---

[60] For a study of the monarchist rebellion in Huanta, see Méndez, *The Plebeian Republic*.
[61] JCBL Archivo Restrepo, Fondo II, Vol. 47, fol. 89.

The transcribed document also included two short poems (*coplas*), although it is unclear if these circulated along with the lampoon. The first one said, "Citizens, Bolívar is finished, forget all heresy, turn your eyes to God." The second read, "The mistake that has been committed is very grave, the devil and the so-called liberator fooled you." The first poem called citizens to repent for dealing with Bolívar's heretic regime. In this short text, there was a recognition of the people's new status under the law as citizens, but the verse presaged the destruction of Bolívar's government. Both poems emphasized the issue of religion, an aspect that had always been central to the royalists' confrontation with the republicans. The text in the lampoon also put religion at the forefront with two statements. The first was that the king should be defended "because we owe him our Christianity." This affirmation of the Christian legacy the Spanish had bequeathed to Spanish Americans cast the relationship of the Christian religion and the monarchical order in a positive light. Then, the lampoon turned to accusing the republicans of being masons, a negative use of religion to mark the difference between republicans and royalists in terms of their faith. If a priest had drafted the poems and the lampoon, as the note written by the transcriber of the lampoon suggests, this would not be surprising. Censuring the republicans for being "franc-masones" was a crucial aspect of the representation of Bolívar in official royalist propaganda as someone who was a danger to the religious foundations of society. Earlier proclamations authored by Agualongo and Merchancano in Pasto called Bolívar the "enemy of the Church and Humanity."[62] The reference to Bolívar in the poem as a heretic suggests that rejection of the republicans on account of their irreligiousness still resonated among the population in the towns of La Cruz and San Pablo well beyond Agualongo's death.

In the years of the independence wars, confrontations on religious grounds turned upon the royalist condemnation of republicans for being heretics and the republican claim that royalists (particularly Indians) were fanatics and prone to manipulation by priests. Both were subjects of propaganda that combined some degree of truth with outright exaggeration. For example, it is clear that in places such as Patía or Pasto, some priests were royalists, but others were central to the independence process in and around Cali. Thus, the antiroyalist propaganda that assumed that all priests were antiliberal was masking a complex aspect of reality. In a

---

[62] Ortiz, *Agustín Agualongo*, 468.

similar way, the antirepublican propaganda that claimed that Bolívar was a heretic ignored the appeal that republicanism had for members of the church who did not find the two discourses antagonistic. Additionally, the religious component of antirepublicanism had a long history in the anti-French rhetoric that had traveled across the Atlantic from the peninsula between the time of the French Revolution and 1808; it used images referring to profanation to describe (and warn against) revolutionary threats.[63]

In Pasto, the fear of republican impiety was borne out by a Colombian law decreed in Cúcuta on August 6, 1821; it targeted two religious institutions that were central to the lives of various social groups and classes, such as the Indians. According to this law, any convent or monastery that had fewer than eight members would be closed, and its property would pass to the state. Given the population's clear rejection of it, the law was not put into effect in Pasto, and, when it finally was enforced by the government of President José Ignacio Márquez eighteen years later, the Pastusos rose in rebellion. In what is locally called "La Guerra de los Conventos," Indians, free blacks, and slaves joined José María Obando to fight against Márquez and bring the royalist guerrillas back to life. A possible explanation for the problems this measure raised among the Indians and peasants in the region was the support these institutions gave to the communities for festivals and for the *cofradías* that had been established under Spanish rule and functioned as a kind of savings bank for the Indians.[64]

Judging from those aspects of Restrepo's writings that promoted the idea that royalists were just plain fanatics, it would seem that Bolívar and the republicans had a negative view of the church. But Bolívar's position vis-à-vis religion was more nuanced. For him the conflicts with the church were delicate, and over time he changed certain of his attitudes with the hope of reversing the alienation among the people that such an image had

---

[63] Santa Fe's "Papel Periódico" published an official critique of the French Revolution's anarchy in the late eighteenth century. See Silva, *Prensa y Revolución*, 130–46. A comparative analysis of the reaction to the French Revolution in Peru can be found in Rosas, "El miedo a la revolución." See also Chapter 4 where I analyzed an example of the circulation of anti-French propaganda during the 1809 crisis between Quito and Popayán.

[64] Rebecca Earle, "The War of the Supremes: Border Conflict, Religious Crusade or Simply Politics by Other Means?," in *Rumours of Wars: Civil Conflict in Nineteenth-Century Latin America*, ed. Earle (London: University of London, Institute of Latin American Studies, 2000), 131; Gutiérrez, *Los indios de Pasto contra la República*, 192–93.

caused him.[65] In Popayán and Pasto he sought an alliance with Bishop Jiménez, who until then had been a fundamental figure among the royalists. Although Jiménez later asked Bolívar for permission to leave for Rome, Bolívar in turn asked him to stay because he needed to rebuild the church with the help of supporters of the republic, such as the bishop. As we have seen, Jiménez's alliance with Bolívar did not prevent people in Pasto from defending the crown in the following years. That indigenous people, slaves, and people in Patía did not simply follow the lead of Bishop Jiménez and switch sides is perhaps the clearest contradiction of Restrepo's assessment of the royalist rebels as blind fanatics who were manipulated by priests.[66]

ROYALISM AND CHANGE

This chapter has studied the royalist, anti-Bolivarian revolt that took place in the region between Pasto and the Pacific lowlands during the years between 1822 and 1825. This revolt was the last episode in the long, deep history of Indian and black royalism in Popayán, a region that (as we have seen throughout this book) after 1809 was part of what I have called the "Pacific royalist block." Thus, the revolt was not simply a mechanical reaction to republican rule. At this turning point in the region's history, royalism evolved. From being principally the product of Indians' and slaves' negotiations with the representatives of the crown over their rights and duties throughout the ten years from 1809 to 1819, in the early 1820s, royalism expanded to include the rejection of Bolivarian rule. After Spain lost the war, in the perennially royalist areas south of Popayán, the Bolivarian project was perceived as illegitimate, and the Indians, slaves, and Patianos who had become invested in the king's cause during the previous decade took a stand against Bolívar's invading forces. Moreover, they all resented the extreme measures that Bolívar used to pacify the region, and they continued to fight for the expulsion of the Colombian government from their lands.

The royalist rebellion illustrated the war's political legacy in the southwest. Its multiethnic leadership brought together men who had acquired

[65] John Lynch, *Simón Bolívar: A Life* (New Haven, CT: Yale University Press, 2006), 244–45.

[66] In this I agree with Rebecca Earle and Jairo Gutiérrez. See Earle, "Indian Rebellion and Bourbon Reform in New Granada," 123; Gutiérrez, *Los indios de Pasto contra la República*, 215. Bolívar's letter to Jiménez can be found in Zawadzky, *Clero insurgente y clero realista*, 20–21.

power through their participation in the royalist army. Individuals such as Agualongo had been part of this force for more than a decade. At the time of Bolívar's arrival in the region, these men's individual interests in perpetuating their authority were intertwined with their continued goal of defending their homeland from being conquered by the illegitimate power that the republic represented. The impact of the politics of war was particularly visible among the indigenous people in Pasto and Los Pastos, whose caciques were now leaders of an armed rebellion. The Indian commoners, for their part, seem to have been able to influence the movement, motivated by their first priority, which was to have tribute abolished. At the juncture in time when the republic became a common enemy, caciques and commoners joined together in a struggle to defend their rights to self-government and land that the republic was attacking.

After 1821 the slave communities in the Pacific were under pressure from the republican forces' attempt to enter the lowlands territory in order to pacify their rebellion and to move east into Los Pastos. Agualongo and his allies sought the slaves' support and even recognized a representative in the region who would govern in their name. In spite of the paucity of records about the relations between the Pastusos and the rebel slaves living in the region between Barbacoas and Buenaventura, it seems that this was a crucial moment when their combined tactics guaranteed their control of a larger area. And their alliance was based on their successful control of the territory that linked the province of Pasto to the Pacific lowlands.

Conclusion

The law and social transformation in the early republic

In 1821 the Congress of Cúcuta elected Simón Bolívar president of the emerging Republic of Colombia. The Congress also began establishing a legal framework for the republic and assumed the right to govern the territory of Colombia, which encompassed the former *Audiencias* of Santa Fe, Panama, Caracas, and Quito. With antecedents in the many constitutional projects that were undertaken in New Granada during the 1810–15 period, the first Colombian constitution was centralist at its core, precisely as a reaction to the atomized, federalist model of the previous decade that Bolivarianists considered would be doomed to failure in the Colombian context.[1]

Influenced by numerous trends in contemporaneous revolutionary thought and by his allies, the "Liberator" equated colonialism with slavery and devised an anticolonial discourse of emancipation in which freedom and equality would be the pillars of political modernity. However, Creoles in the region espoused independence but not necessarily social change. Similarly to what happened in other places in the Atlantic world during the nineteenth century, economic pressures and fear of racial conflict narrowed down the possibilities of the integration of indigenous and Afro-descendant peoples into the newly founded nations.

As the cases analyzed throughout this book have revealed, until the 1820s the differences that separated Indians and slaves stemmed from their legal position within the Spanish monarchy. During the independence wars, in the royalist territory of Popayán Indians and slaves had new

---

[1] Sergio Mejía, *La revolución en letras: La Historia de la Revolución de Colombia de José Manuel Restrepo (1781–1863)* (Bogotá: Uniandes, 2007), 96, 97, 116.

opportunities to negotiate their duties and entitlements vis-à-vis the crown and local colonial officials. These groups acted within different legal frameworks but used similar strategies, both legal and military, during the unprecedented monarchical crisis and the war that had come to their homelands. In spite of the singular importance that equality as a legal goal enjoyed during this period, the differences between legal and political identities of the Indians and slaves continued to be produced and reproduced at the imperial level (in the Cádiz Constitution) and by the national state, once it was founded (the republic did not abolish slavery until 1852). Moreover, throughout those years Indians, in particular, also revitalized their corporate legal identities through their political activity and their search for protection of their distinct rights.

In the context of republican state formation, the 1822 royalist rebellion against the republic (analyzed in Chapter 6) reveals that indigenous people in Pasto did not welcome the project of transforming indigenous peoples into citizens, a principle that was at the core of the Colombian constitutional project. Furthermore, the republican intention to legally abolish indigenous rights and institutions, such as the *cacicazgo*, was not necessarily effective in transforming the way Indians perceived their authorities within the communities in Pasto. Throughout the nineteenth century, their political and military leaders continued to function as de facto caciques. Aside from being regarded as traditional sources of legitimacy, during the nineteenth century these caciques' participation in the civil wars was the main source of their political power.[2] In other words, the relevance of the military strategies that had begun to take shape during the war for independence only increased with the consolidation of the republican state.[3]

---

[2] Joanne Rappaport, *The Politics of Memory: Native Historical Interpretation in the Colombian Andes* (1990; Durham, NC: Duke University Press, 1998), 95–96, 98. See also Campo Chicangana, *Montoneras, deserciones e insubordinaciones*.

[3] The relevance of military strategies for political inclusion in the republican state has been studied in Cecilia Méndez, "Tradiciones liberales en los Andes o la ciudadanía por las armas: Campesinos y militares en la formación del estado peurano," in *La mirada esquiva*, ed. Irurozqui, 125–54; Marta Irurozqui, "*Los hombres chacales en armas*: Militarización y criminalización indígenas en la revolución federal boliviana de 1899," in *La mirada esquiva*, ed. Irurozqui, 285–320; Marta Irurozqui, "El bautismo de la violencia: Indígenas patriotas en la revolución de 1870 en Bolivia," in *Identidad, ciudadanía y participación popular desde la colonia al siglo XX*, ed. Josefa Salmón and Guillermo Delgado (La Paz: Editorial Plural, 2003), 115–52; Flavia Macías, "Ciudadanía armada, identidad nacional y estado provincial: Tucumán, 1854–1870," in *La vida política en Argentina del siglo XIX: Armas, votos y voces*, ed. Hilda Sábato and Alberto Lettieri (Buenos Aires: Siglo XXI, 2003), 137–52; Víctor Peralta, "El mito del ciudadano armado: La 'semana magna'

This raises important questions about the internal dynamics of Indian communities after independence was achieved and the transformation of their interests throughout the early years of the republic. The evidence presented in this book suggests that the abolition of tribute decreed by Spanish liberals and negotiated on the ground by military leaders during the war (1809–19) was appealing to Indian commoners if not to all the Indian authorities. Therefore, the economic measures promoted by Bolívar in the 1820s may have been attractive to some community members, especially those who had the means to position themselves advantageously in the new situation by buying lands and securing wealth. They could have been open to receiving the new "liberty" that derived from "smallholder republicanism." Nonetheless, developments in the late nineteenth century suggest that the Indian communities in the Colombian southwest, in fact, strongly defended their communal status as well as their *resguardos* against the new laws. Although thoroughly immersed in republican political dynamics and the new liberal legislation of the state, Indians in southwestern Colombia fought for and strongly supported a particular definition of citizenship that allowed them to preserve a certain degree of autonomy and protect their vested communal right to land.[4]

As the present study has demonstrated, the Indians' alliance with the royalist elites in southwestern New Granada was part of a long process of negotiation in which the Spanish elites, far from assuming Indian loyalty to the crown, transformed the terms of the relationship between the Indians and the monarchy to be able to guarantee Indian support for their political and military cause. From the mid- to the late nineteenth century, those same communities laid claim to a citizenship and republicanism that, in James Sanders' words, "did not deny their Indian identity but rather sought to protect it within the new nation."[5] The case of

---

y las elecciones de 1844 en Lima," in *Ciudadanía política y formación de las naciones. Perspectivas históricas en América Latina*, ed. Hilda Sábato (Mexico: Fondo de Cultura Económica, 1999), 231–52; Nicola Foote and René Harder Horst, eds., *Military Struggle and Identity Formation in Latin America: Race, Nation, and Community during the Liberal Period* (Gainesville: University Press of Florida, 2010).

[4] James Sanders, *Popular Politics, Race, and Class in Nineteenth-Century Colombia* (Durham, NC: Duke University Press, 2004), 41–42. Sanders did find a few cases in which leaders of the Indian *cabildos* attempted to take for themselves the largest portions of land during the process of *resguardo* division.

[5] James Sanders, "Belonging to the Great Granadan Family: Partisan Struggle and the Construction of Indigenous Identity and Politics in Southwestern Colombia, 1849–1890," in *Race and Nation in Modern Latin America*, ed. Nancy Appelbaum et al. (Chapel Hill: North Carolina University Press, 2003), 61.

southwestern New Granada, however, contrasts with what Steinar Saether describes as having happened in Santa Marta, the other royalist stronghold in New Granada, where some formerly royalist Indian communities opted for inclusion in the republic as non-Indian citizens.[6]

A comparison of the developments in Caribbean Santa Marta and the Andean city of Pasto shows the reactions of different royalist Indian communities to nineteenth-century republican politics. The path taken by the Indians in republican Popayán could be labeled "conservative," as Sanders argues, because of the similarity between their concept of law and the state and the views of the conservatives, as well as the eventual alliance of Indians with the Conservative Party. However, taking into account the different choices made by Indian communities in Santa Marta and Popayán reveals that there is no structural relationship between Indian royalism and conservatism. Given that Indians who lived in Indian towns had had juridical and political rights under the monarchy, the transition to citizenship according to the terms of the new government implied an opportunity for Indians to reinvent their place in society in political terms.[7] In other words, not even in the cases where community was strategically asserted after independence, such as in Popayán, does this continuity have to be explained as part of a parochial identity on the part of the Indians.[8] Rather, such developments were related to the regional demographic, economic, and political histories that made opportunities for Indian communities different in the republican context. When Indians participated in the royalist alliances, they did so for strategic reasons having to do with land and tribute. The Indians in Santa Marta welcomed citizenship in a liberal government at the cost of collective identity, communal resources, territory, and economy. In the southwest, the Pasto Indians did not accept that very costly bargain, a choice that cannot be reduced to an essentialist view of Indian "conservatism."

While insurgents in New Granada used the symbol of slavery to represent colonialism and defined their struggle as a means of breaking the chains of tyranny and achieving liberation, they did not intend to negotiate freedom with their slaves in order to be able to use them as soldiers. Insurgent slave owners who incorporated their slaves into their

---

[6] Saether, "Independence and the Redefinition of Indianness."   [7] Ibid., 60.

[8] Such as Heraclio Bonilla, "Rey o República: El dilemma de los indios frente a la independencia," in *Independencia y transición a los estados nacionales en los países andinos*, ed. Martínez, 357–69; Gutiérrez, *Los indios de Pasto contra la República*; and Van Young, *The Other Rebellion*, argue.

army did so by using them as they would have for any other form of labor. This was, in other words, a depoliticized incorporation of slaves into the insurgent struggle. In the 1814 battle of Calibío (near Popayán), for example, José Rafael Mosquera and Mariano Mosquera contributed more than one hundred of their slaves to the victorious insurgent forces. A gang captain controlled the slaves so they would not run away during the battle.[9] Even as the insurgent struggle became more widespread in the years to come, the Cali elites were particularly averse to recruiting people of color into their armies.[10]

Juan del Corral, a military officer who headed the independence government in Antioquia, led the first abolitionist experiment in New Granada. He drafted an important law, passed in April of 1814, which granted freedom to all newborn slaves once they reached the age of sixteen (called *libertad de vientres* or Free Womb Law). The Spanish revoked that law after they reconquered the region in 1816.[11] In Venezuela, a context where Creole insurgents were not linked to abolitionist interests, the measures taken by Simón Bolívar after 1815 and his alliance with Haitian President Alexandre Pétion had been extremely cautious. In June 1816, Bolívar decreed freedom for all slaves who would join him in the military fight for independence, but had little or no luck in

---

[9] Arboleda, "Entre la libertad y la sumisión," 33.

[10] From 1819 to 1820 an English man named Runnel led an insurgent guerrilla group of slaves and free blacks in the Cauca Valley. Runnel was disliked by all the members of the *cabildo* in Cali, who thought his alliance with the slaves made him dangerous, not to mention the fact that he was famous for promoting anarchism. See Arboleda, "Entre la libertad y la sumisión"; Matthew Brown, "Esclavitud, castas y extranjeros en las guerras de la independencia de Colombia," *Historia y Sociedad* 10 (2004), 109–125; Colmenares, "Castas, patrones de poblamiento y conflictos sociales," 147–49. Restrepo, *Historia de la Revolución*, Vol. III (1827), 16. In that sense, the mobilization of slaves in southwestern New Granada during the first years of the crisis of the monarchy followed a substantively different path than the one taken in Cuba in the 1860s, where insurgents were open to incorporating slaves into their ranks. Ada Ferrer has studied the relation between discursive and military mobilization of slaves during the Cuban war of independence (1868). She has argued that black politics during and after independence was defined by a dual process in which "rebel leaders and the enslaved struggled to define the boundaries, meanings, and implications of the arming of slaves." Ada Ferrer, "Armed Slaves and the Anticolonial Insurgency in Late Nineteenth-Century Cuba," in *Arming Slaves*, ed. Brown and Morgan, 305.

[11] Eduardo Posada, *La esclavitud en Colombia* (Bogotá: Imprenta Nacional, 1933), 41; Carlos Restrepo Canal, *Leyes de Manumisión* (Bogotá: Imprenta Nacional, 1933), 152; Restrepo, *Historia de la Revolución*, Vol. I (1969), 291; Fischer, "Bolívar in Haiti." This law had an impact in the long run, when, in the early 1830s, large numbers of blacks who had been born in the mid-1810s sought to secure their freedom.

recruiting slaves to the republican cause in this way. In a decree issued in Carúpano, Bolívar called on men between fourteen and seventy years of age to enlist in the army in their local parishes to fight for their freedom and that of their close kin. However, if they failed to enlist, these men and their families would lose the right to become citizens in the Venezuelan Republic. Bolívar was attempting to counter Tomás Boves' army of slaves that had fought against the independence project in 1813. Yet his authoritarian tone resulted in many slaves turning royalist instead of following the obligatory decree of enlistment to fight for their freedom and rights.

Once Bolívar crossed the Venezuelan plains into New Granada and was recognized as the leader of the Andean struggle for emancipation, he organized the first Colombian constituent congress in Angostura on 1819. It was there that Bolívar attempted to fulfill the promises of liberation and emancipation, which viewed slavery as a symptom of colonialism and the trafficking and exploitation of Africans as immoral practices. He made the abolition of slavery a central goal of the republic. The tensions between Bolívar's discourses of civic and political freedom and the interests of his social base (most of them wealthy Creoles who depended on the slave economy) were evident in the treatment that such a proposal received in Congress. The slave trade was outlawed, but abolition was not decreed. The outcome was the manumission law of July 21, 1821, drafted following the outline of preexisting laws, particularly those already in force in Antioquia and Venezuela.

Beyond the legislative assembly, Bolívar also took measures to integrate slaves into the liberationist force. The need for soldiers led him to call for the recruitment of 5,000 slaves, a decision that he carefully distinguished from general emancipation.[12] He said

We need robust, vigorous men who are accustomed to hardship and fatigue; men who will identify their interests with the public interest and men for whom death means little less than life itself.[13]

Additionally, Bolívar was concerned about the fact that "we have seen the free population die and the slave survive." As he told Vice President

---

[12] Harold Bierck, "The Struggle for Abolition in Gran Colombia," *Hispanic American Historical Review* 33, no. 3 (1953), 365–86.

[13] Letter of Bolívar to Santander, April 20, 1820. Cited in Bierck, "The Struggle for Abolition," 369, from Vicente Lecuna, ed., *Cartas del libertador*, II (Caracas: Lit. y Tip. del Comercio, 1929), 149.

Santander, his hope was that by recruiting slaves into the army the danger that "[black slaves] will outlive us" would be prevented.[14]

During the first half of the nineteenth century, the fear of Haiti was very present in the minds of the republican leaders, concerned as they were about social stability and the protection of property. Indeed, as John Lynch has demonstrated, Bolívar "had some misgivings" about having had incorporated *pardos* (or mulattos) and blacks into the army of liberation. In 1828, Bolívar called it "a necessary evil" during the war, "but now, in peacetime, [it] is an obstacle to peace and tranquility."[15] Thus, the racial politics of the revolutionaries was complicated, expressing the tensions between the language of liberty and equality and the material realities of the new Colombian nation.

Following the publication of the abolition laws, between 1814 and 1821 slaves used all the means available to them to press for the end of slavery. In other words, during this period the antislavery politics of the enslaved combined different strategies to achieve their goals. Self-purchase and other means of securing individual and collective manumission continued to be part of the repertoire, as well as a conscious appeal to the variety of laws that were transforming the political landscape during this period. Participation in the army, either on the royalist or patriot side, was also part of the calculations made by enslaved men who were seeking to benefit from the unprecedented openings that had emerged from the military needs of both sides. Peter Blanchard has documented numerous instances of slave inclusion in the royalist and republican ranks, noting how the incorporation of individual male slaves into the army tended to reduce the possibilities of a collective struggle against slavery. In Popayán, by becoming allies of the royalists, the enslaved who lived in the Pacific lowlands and had built communities there that included free blacks were able to claim the territory and live in de facto freedom for a decade. In other words, royalism represented an opportunity for Afro-descendants to defend their communities, and they did not understand freedom exclusively as freedom for the individual, as it was in the politically liberal sense of the word.[16]

---

[14] Ibid., 150–51.

[15] Lynch, *Simón Bolívar*, 108; Louis Peru de Lacroix, *Diario de Bucaramanga: Vida pública y privada del libertador* (1869; Caracas: Ediciones Centauro, 1976), 59.

[16] See Blanchard, *Under the Flags of Freedom*, for a complete account of slave mobilization during the independence wars in South America.

Although abolition was legislated in a way that guaranteed that it would take place only gradually and that it would protect the interests of slave owners, slaves pushed the institution to a level where it was close to becoming extinct. In Popayán in the early nineteenth century, manumission took place most commonly through self-purchase or purchase by a third party. Taking advantage of the lower prices of slaves during the years of the war, slave manumissions increased both through self-purchase and when freedom was granted as a prize for participating militarily on either of the contending sides.[17] A total of 226 manumissions were registered in Popayán's registry office (*notaría*) during the years from 1808 to 1830, when 248 slaves were freed.[18]

During the 1840s Colombia had its first civil war, called the War of the Supremes.[19] In this war the southwestern caudillo José María Obando mobilized slaves from the haciendas with promises of liberation. This was one of the last phases in the turbulent struggle for abolition; it was only in 1852, during the Liberal government of José Hilario López, that slavery was finally abolished.[20]

The recent historiography on republicanism and race in Colombia has focused on Cartagena and has tended to seek out the kind of patterns seen in Haiti's independence. While historians of Caribbean Colombia have proved that people of African descent played a crucial role in the independence struggle in that Caribbean city, some seem disappointed to find

---

[17] Rodríguez, "La manumisión en Popayán, 1800–1850," 81, 83.

[18] Arboleda, "Entre la libertad y la sumisión," 19. Arboleda says the average number of manumissions in Popayán during this period, around ten a year, shows an increase compared with the data analyzed by Colmenares for the 1720–1800 period, when the average was six per year. See Colmenares, *Historia económica y social*, II, 74. The fundamental role of slaves in the destruction of slavery that goes beyond their masters' reticent collaboration with the project of abolition was first proposed by Rebecca Scott, *Slave Emancipation in Cuba: The Transition to Free Labor, 1860–1899* (1985; Pittsburgh, PA: University of Pittsburgh Press, 2000), esp. part 2. For Peru, see Christine Hünefeldt, *Paying the Price of Freedom: Family and Labor among Lima's Slaves, 1800–1854* (Berkeley: University of California Press, 1994); Carlos Aguirre, *Agentes de su propia libertad* (Lima: Pontificia Universidad Católica del Perú, 1993); for Santa Fe, see Díaz Díaz, *Esclavitud, región y ciudad.*

[19] The War of the Supremes also was called *La guerra de los conventos* in Pasto. See Earle, "The War of the Supremes."

[20] The law of May 21, 1851, abolished slavery from January 1, 1852, onward. The mobilization of slaves so prevalent in Popayán in the 1830s and 1840s, either through legal or violent means, has been studied by Maria Camila Díaz, '*Salteadores y cuadrillas de malhechores': Una aproximación a la acción colectiva de la población negra en el suroccidente de la Nueva Granada, 1840–1851* (Popayán: Editorial Universidad del Cauca, 2015).

that blacks in the region failed to mobilize unanimously around the cause to overturn white racial domination.[21] Cartagena may seem like an anomaly if compared with Saint-Domingue, where a black republic was created. But racial solidarity among people of African descent is a controversial assumption that cannot be proven for all situations of this kind in Latin America.[22] Narrowly focused on republicanism, the studies about Cartagena moreover ignore that Indians and free blacks supported the royalist cause in other places in the Caribbean region of Colombia, such as Tolú and Sinú (in Cartagena Province) and Santa Marta.[23]

Marixa Lasso's study of Cartagena demonstrated that free blacks mobilized extensively around the liberal promises of equality espoused by insurgent Creoles and became a crucial social base for the independence struggle in the Caribbean.[24] But Cartagena's case cannot be generalized for the rest of Colombia. In Popayán we find evidence of the long-lasting alliance of slaves and free people of African descent (the Patianos) with royalist elites, forcing us to widen the scope of analysis when it comes to establishing links between republicanism and groups of Indians and free or enslaved blacks. Although Popayán, like Cartagena, also had a growing population of free blacks, the alignment of free blacks from Patía with royalism, and their centrality to the royalist military campaigns during the 1809–19 period in the southwest, evokes the situation of many free blacks across Spanish America who believed that a monarchical government offered a better life for people of all social classes and ethnicities.[25]

---

[21] See Helg, *Liberty and Equality*.

[22] Barbara Weinstein has highlighted the fact that "the militancy of free people of color [to gain access to citizenship] did not necessarily have implications for the institution of slavery itself" in nineteenth-century Brazil. Weinstein, "Erecting and Erasing Boundaries: Can We Combine the 'Indo' and the 'Afro' in Latin American Studies?" *Estudios Interdisciplinarios de América Latina y el Caribe* 19, no. 1 (2008), 3. See also, Hebe Maria Mattos, *Escravidão e cidadania no Brasil monárquico* (Rio de Janeiro: Jorge Zahar, 2000); Hendrik Kraay, *Race, State, and Armed Forces in Independence-Era Brazil: Bahia, 1790s–1840s* (Stanford, CA: Stanford University Press, 2001).

[23] An exception is Steinar Saether, *Identidades e Independencia*. See also Saether, "Estudios recientes sobre raza e independencia en el caribe colombiano (1750–1835)," in *Historias de Raza y Nación en América Latina*, ed. Claudia Leal and Carl H. Langebaek (Bogotá: Uniandes, 2010), 399.

[24] Lasso, *Myths of Harmony*. See also Múnera, *El fracaso de la nación*.

[25] Landers, *Atlantic Creoles in the Age of Revolutions*, 233. Marixa Lasso, "Los grupos afro-descendientes y la independencia: ¿un nuevo paradigma historiográfico?" in *L'atlantique Revolutionnaire: Une Perspective Ibéro-Américain*, ed. Clément Thibaud, Gabriel Entin, Alejandro Gómez, and Federica Morelli (Bécherel: Éditions Les Perséides, 2013), 359–378.

In Popayán, those strategic alliances of enslaved and free blacks with the royalists did not, on the other hand, imply that the previously royalist groups were more prone to being mobilized by conservatives. As Sanders has shown, in Popayán it was the Liberal Party that ultimately incorporated people of African descent into republican party politics and promoted a politically inclusive racial discourse.[26] This suggests that royalism did not lead exclusively to modern conservatism and that the divide between conservatives and liberals traditionally ascribed to elite antagonism can be looked at more broadly and fluidly by including popular struggles going back to the time of the independence process.

This study of royalism is thus not (and should not be understood as) a genealogy of conservatism in Colombia or, more broadly speaking, in Latin America as a whole. Highlighting contingency and complexity as essential traits of politics in the revolutionary period, I have avoided dichotomist classifications such as liberal/conservative or progressive/backward, and thus countered the tendency to view royalism as a conservative (or backward) choice for Indians and slaves. I have shown how a proper understanding of the context and process whereby indigenous and enslaved people defended Spanish rule can revise our traditional view of popular political agency and consciousness as resistance or anticolonialism and, indeed, turn it on its head. Royalism allowed Indians and slaves to align their diverse and particular struggles for inclusion within the evolving imperial political landscape during the first decades of the nineteenth century.

The multiethnic royalist alliances in Popayán during the wars of independence illustrate the complexity of Indian and slave politics in the revolutionary Atlantic world. The cross-class and multiethnic composition of the alliances that developed in Popayán has allowed us to observe a diverse range of social actors (Europeans, Creoles, Indians, slaves, *mestizos*, and free blacks) within a single regional frame and to study together subjects who are usually treated in isolation from one another. Royalist elites perceived Indians and slaves as valuable allies, and for that reason these elites were willing to negotiate with them and offer them concessions to secure their loyalty. Far from being a story about backwardness or naïveté, the royalist politics of Indians and slaves in Popayán expands our understanding of their historical political strategies, offering evidence of the importance of vertical alliances between elites and Indians and slaves.

---

[26] Sanders, *Contentious Republicans.*

As a consequence, the cases analyzed here invite us to reconsider historiographic expectations about anticolonialism among Indians and enslaved people, and to rethink our approach to the study of independence processes. Most studies of Indians' and slaves' political consciousness in the nineteenth century assume that rebelliousness and anticolonialism are corollaries of domination. Thus, historians look for the centrality of indigenous or enslaved people in cases of rebellions and revolutions, which are equated with radical politics, while Indians or slaves who were loyal to the imperial power are ignored or marked as ignorant or parochial. In the cases presented in this book, the political goals of Indians and slaves were not necessarily antagonistic to the imperial legal framework. These cases are evidence that the radical politics of Indians and slaves encompassed a wide scope that includes royalism. To understand the Indian and slave royalists' goals in Popayán, we have needed to look at them from the perspective of their own experience and not in the light of later political parameters.

The Bolivarian narrative of republicanism and national unity produced and disseminated a negative discourse of these royalists. To avoid mirroring this antagonism constitutive of Colombian historiography, this book did not explain royalism exclusively as a reaction against the Bolivarian project. Instead, the book has contributed to an understanding of royalist politics within a wider temporal frame. Placing royalism away from the republican narrative has allowed me to reconstruct the antecedents and continuity of Indians' and slaves' engagement with a monarchical ideology that continued to serve them in changing circumstances. This does not mean that the dynamic relation of Indians and slaves to the crown in the eighteenth century predetermined their royalist stance during the nineteenth-century conflicts. Rather, the emergence of a "Pacific royalist block" provides the context for understanding the contingencies of royalist alliances across Popayán during the independence process.

The story presented here challenges modernizing teleologies, without recreating an alternative teleology about the necessity of royalism for the region of my study. To explain Indian and slave royalism in Popayán during the Spanish monarchical crisis (that took place from 1808 onward), I began this book with a study of the relationships that Indians and slaves had with the monarchy. I outlined the concepts of law and monarchy held by each of these groups and described patterns of legal action and violent action that were available to each group in the three decades before the nineteenth-century crisis broke out. Illustrating the centrality of legal politics to antebellum political culture, I argued that Indians' and slaves' appeals to the king's justice were not naïve or mystical, as has been suggested by earlier historiography. Monarchist political culture was continually reinterpreted by different social sectors, including Indians and slaves, and its continuous state of flux reflected the constant on-the-ground negotiation characteristic of colonial politics. During the years of this study, imperial policies moved with dizzying speed from the mandates of Bourbon rule to the liberal precepts of the Cádiz Constitution and then back to absolutism. In the wake of the 1808 monarchical crisis, Spanish vassals confronted novel opportunities to take advantage of the changing political landscape, lending new, specific meanings to royalism.

In seeing royalism as linked – not opposed – to liberalism, my analysis in this book has revealed that the marked divide between the colonial period (presumed prepolitical) and the republican era (i.e., modern) is insufficient in allowing one to understand the independence *process*. My processual approach instead has captured the sophisticated ways in which absolutism and liberalism coexisted.[27] This was clear, for example, in the growing antagonism among the members of the indigenous communities in Pasto. While in the aftermath of the 1800 Túquerres rebellion, Indian elites and commoners drew on the rhetoric of Indian rusticity to defend their community, during the independence wars, between 1809 and 1819, the Indian caciques and commoners had different motives for defending the king, and each sector used seemingly opposing discourses to guard their interests within the changing political and legal context.

To understand the complex case of Popayán, in this book we have moved away from Colombian history's preconceived ideas about political geography. Preconceptions about the shape of independent Colombia have led historians to look for its roots in the colonial past. Clearly what happened in the southwestern Andean and Pacific regions of Popayán differed greatly from the larger autonomist trend in New Granada (excepting, notably, Santa Marta and Riohacha), yet we would find that divergence surprising only if we hark back to the nationalist history that condemns their royalism. The rise of a royalist block in the Pacific was a crucial condition that made possible the continuation of royal power across Peru and Popayán between 1809 and 1822. In fact, Popayán's

---

[27] According to Brian McConville's study of American prerevolutionary political culture, "royalism was a primary force of change *before* 1776" (emphasis added). This temporal demarcation ignores royalism's centrality to the revolutionary process itself. See *The King's Three Faces The Rise & Fall of Royal America, 1688–1776* (Chapel Hill: Omohundro Institute of Early American History and Culture/University of North Carolina Press, 2006), 10.

southward orientation during the monarchical crisis was consistent with the colonial jurisdictional organization that had tied places such as Barbacoas and Pasto to Quito's *Audiencia* (as noted in Chapter 1 of the book). This ambiguity, furthermore, continued into the 1830s when Gran Colombia fragmented, and the oscillating Ecuadorian frontier at times included Pasto.

The monarchical crisis also offers an opportunity to explore the on-the-ground rivalries and alliances that characterized the period, which led to the rapid political fragmentation of the territory. The Pacific region gives us a window into the process and consequences of the Spanish monarchical crisis and allows us to explore it in a new light. The resulting story, one that emphasizes the contingent nature of politics over time and the differences in regional reactions to the crisis, can serve as a counterpoint to the revolutionary narratives that have come to dominate the history of the Atlantic world.

Finally, this book is one of still relatively few works that combine the stories of Indians and people of African descent in Spanish America, thus helping scholars of Latin America to understand how the study of these two groups within a single conceptual framework can expand the political history of Latin America.[28] Through the study of these two groups within the same geographic space, the book has shown the specific ways in which communal interests shaped fluid colonial identities at the institutional and subjective levels. During the early years of state formation, the Bolivarian Republic attempted to homogenize the citizenry, but this project failed because the differences the state wanted to eliminate were ultimately restored by the state as well as through Indian and slave political action. Thus, a scrutiny of legal and ethnic politics from the late-eighteenth century into the early-nineteenth century, paying close attention to transformations in the rights and the legal definition of both social groups, yields new insight into the possibilities, interests, and diversity in the agency of Indians and enslaved Afro-descendant people in the making of early Colombian politics.

This historical perspective is of particular importance today given that contemporary Colombia recognizes the ethnic rights of Afro-Colombians,

---

[28] Lewis, *Hall of Mirrors*; Matthew Restall, ed., *Beyond Black and Red: African-Native Relations in Colonial Latin America* (Albuquerque: University of New Mexico Press, 2005); Matthew Restall, *The Black Middle: Africans, Mayas, and Spaniards in Colonial Yucatan* (Stanford, CA: Stanford University Press, 2009); O'Toole, *Bound Lives*; Yuko Miki, "Insurgent Geographies: Blacks, Indians, and the Colonization of Nineteenth-Century Brazil" (PhD. diss., New York University, 2010).

which were incorporated into the 1991 multicultural constitution and modeled after indigenous people's long-standing ethnic rights in the country. Since the late twentieth century, scholars and activists have studied how the advent of multiculturalism in an increasingly globalized framework of cultural politics has impacted the politics of Indians and blacks in Colombia.[29] However, there is much less understanding of the depth and background of the entwined political history of both groups in the region and their engagement with legal politics. Particularly in the case of Afro-Colombians, anthropologists and political scientists risk equating political visibility and recognition by the state in the late twentieth century with the initial appearance of their political consciousness and strategies. Although not a study of the transformations of the politics of Indians and blacks in Colombia from the colonial context to the present, this book contributes to our understanding of the crucial historical relationship between state structures, indigenous rights, and the emergence of black ethnic rights, which were sanctioned by the 1991 constitution but which have also had a long history in the activism of Indians and Afro-descendants in New Granada and Colombia.

---

[29] Peter Wade, *Race and Ethnicity in Latin America* (London: Pluto Press, 1997) is one of the first works to deal with the relationship between Indians and blacks from the colonial period to the present. See also Bettina Ng'wengo, *Turf Wars: Territory and Citizenship in the Contemporary State* (Stanford, CA: Stanford University Press, 2007); Kiran Asher, *Black and Green: Afro-Colombians, Development, and Nature in the Pacific Lowlands* (Durham, NC: Duke University Press, 2009); Diana Bocarejo, "Reconfiguring the Political Landscape after the Multicultural Turn: Law, Politics, and the Spacialization of Difference in Colombia" (PhD. diss., University of Chicago, 2008).

Bibliography

ARCHIVES AND ABBREVIATIONS

Archivo Central del Cauca, Popayán (ACC)
Archivo del Congreso de los Diputados, Madrid (ACD)
Archivo General de Indias, Seville (AGI)
Archivo General de la Nación, Bogotá (AGN)
Archivo Histórico Nacional, Madrid (AHN)
Archivo Municipal de Pasto, Pasto (AMP)
Archivo Nacional del Ecuador, Quito (ANE)
Archivo Nacional Militar, Madrid (ANM)
Biblioteca Luis Angel Arango, Bogotá (BLAA)
John Carter Brown Library, Providence R.I. (JCBL)
Real Academia de la Historia, Madrid (RAH)

PRIMARY SOURCES

Abascal y Sousa, José Fernando de. *Memoria de Gobierno,* Vol. 2. Sevilla: Escuela de Estudios Hispano-Americanos de Sevilla, 1944.

Arroyo y Valencia, Santiago. "Memoria para la historia de la revolución de Popayán." *Revista Popayán* 5 (1910): 29–34.

Burns, Robert, ed. *Las Siete Partidas,* trans. Samuel Parsons Scott, Vol. 4. Philadelphia: University of Pennsylvania Press, 2001.

Cartas Santander-Bolívar 1823–1825, Vol. 4. Bogotá: Fundación Francisco de Paula Santander, 1988.

Congreso de Cúcuta de 1821. Constitución y Leyes. Bogotá: Biblioteca Banco Popular, 1971.

De Gangotena y Jijón, Cristóbal, ed. *Documentos Referentes a la batalla de Ibarra con la narración histórica de la campaña de Pasto.* Quito: Talleres Tipográficos Nacionales, 1823.

De Santa Gertrudis, Fray Juan. *Maravillas de la Naturaleza*, Vol. 2. 1799; Bogotá: Empresa Nacional de Publicaciones, 1956.

"Diario de las noticias y hechos ocurridos que nos dieron los senores limeños, desde el 1 de octubre de 1813 hasta el 15 de enero de 1814." *Boletín Histórico del Valle* 23–24 (1934): 450.

Fernández García, Antonio, ed. *La Constitución de Cádiz (1812) y Discurso Preliminar a la Constitución*. Madrid: Editorial Castalia, 2002.

Guerrero, Gustavo. *Documentos históricos de los hechos ocurridos en Pasto en la Guerra de Independencia*. Pasto: Imprenta del Departamento, 1912.

Juan, Jorge, and Antonio de Ulloa. *Noticias Secretas*. 1826; Bogotá: Banco Popular, 1983.

Konetzke, Richard. *Colección de documentos para la formación social de Hispanoamérica 1493–1810*, 3:2. Madrid: Consejo Superior de Investigaciones Científicas, 1962.

Lecuna, Vicente, ed. *Cartas del libertador*, Vol. 2. Caracas: Lit. y Tip. del Comercio, 1929.

Obando, José María. *Apuntamientos para la historia*. 1837; Medellín: Editorial Bedout, 1972.

Ortiz, Sergio Elías, ed. *Colección de documentos para la historia de Colombia. Época de la independencia*. Bogotá: Academia Colombiana de Historia, 1964.

Peru de Lacroix, Louis. *Diario de Bucaramanga: Vida pública y privada del libertador*. 1869; Caracas: Ediciones Centauro, 1976.

Real Academia Española. *Diccionario de Autoridades*. 3 Vols. Madrid: Gredos, 1990.

Recopilación de las leyes de los reynos de las Indias. [1681; Madrid: Viuda de Joaquín de Ibarra, 1791] Madrid: Facsimile reprint, 1941.

Report from a Select Committee of the House of Assembly Appointed to Inquire into the Origins, Causes, and Progress of the Late Rebellion. Barbados: House of Assembly, 1818.

"Representación del Cabildo de Santa Fe, capital del Nuevo Reino de Granada, a la Suprema Junta Central de España" (1809). In *Constituciones de Colombia: recopiladas y precedidas de una breve reseña histórica*, Vol. 1, edited by Manuel Antonio Pombo and José Joaquín Guerra, 57–86. Bogotá: Ministerio de Educación Nacional, 1951.

Restrepo, José Manuel. *Historia de la Revolución de la República de Colombia en la América Meridional*. 10 Vols. Paris: Librería Americana, 1827.

Diario Político y Militar: Memorias sobre los sucesos importantes de la época para servir a la historia de la revolución de Colombia y de la Nueva Granada, desde 1819 para adelante. 4 Vols. Bogotá: Imprenta Nacional, 1854.

ed. *Documentos importantes de Nueva Granada, Colombia y Venezuela (Apéndice de la Historia de Colombia, Tomo V)*. 1861; Bogotá: Imprenta Nacional, 1969.

Historia de la Revolución de Colombia. 5 Vols. 1827; Medellín: Editorial Bedout, 1969.

Rivas Moreno, Gerardo, ed. *Simón Bolívar: Proclamas y Discursos*. Cali: Fundación para la Investigación y la Cultura, 2001.

SECONDARY SOURCES

Adelman, Jeremy. *Sovereignty and Revolution in the Iberian Atlantic*. Princeton, NJ, and Oxford: Princeton University Press, 2006.

"Iberian Passages: Continuity and Change in the South Atlantic." In *The Age of Revolutions in Global Context, c. 1760–1840*, edited by David Armitage and Sanjay Subrahmanyam, 59–82. New York: Palgrave Macmillan, 2010.

Aguirre, Carlos. *Agentes de su propia libertad*. Lima: Pontificia Universidad Católica del Perú, 1993.

Alda, Sonia. *La participación indígena en la construcción de la república de Guatemala, S XIX*. Madrid: Universidad Autónoma de México, 2002.

Aljovín, Cristóbal. "Monarquía o república: 'ciudadano' y 'vecino' en Iberoamérica, 1750–1850." *Jahrbuch für Geschichte Lateinamerikas* 45 (2008): 31–55.

Almario, Oscar. *La invención del suroccidente colombiano: Independencia, etnicidad y estado nacional entre 1780 y 1930*. Medellín: Universidad Pontificia Bolivariana, 2006.

Andrés-Gallego, José. *La esclavitud en la América Española*. Madrid: Ediciones Encuentro y Fundación Ignacio Larramendi, 2005.

Andrews, George Reid. *Afro-Latin America, 1800–2000*. Oxford: Oxford University Press, 2004.

Andrews, Norah. "Taxing Blackness: Tribute and Free Colored Community in Colonial Mexico." PhD diss., Johns Hopkins University, 2014.

Andrien, Kenneth. "Soberanía y Revolución en el Reino de Quito, 1809–1810." In *En el umbral de las revoluciones hispánicas, 1808–1810*, edited by Roberto Breña, 313–34. Mexico and Madrid: El Colegio de México-Centro de Estudios Políticos y Constitucionales, 2010.

Annino, Antonio. "Cádiz y la revolución territorial de los pueblos mexicanos." In *Historia de las elecciones en Iberoamérica, siglo XIX*, 177–226. Buenos Aires: Fondo de Cultura Económica, 1995.

Arboleda, Gustavo. *Historia de Cali desde los orígenes de la ciudad hasta la expiración del periodo colonial*. Cali: Imprenta Arboleda, 1928.

Arboleda, Juan Ignacio. *Entre la libertad y la sumisión: Estrategias de libertad de los esclavos en la gobernación de Popayán durante la independencia, 1808–1830*. Bogotá: Universidad de Los Andes, 2006.

Arocha, Jaime. "La inclusion de los afrocolombianos, ¿meta inalcanzable?" In *Geografía Humana de Colombia, Tomo VI, Los Afrocolombianos*, edited by Luz Adriana Maya, 339–96. Bogotá: Instituto Colombiano de Antropología e Historia, 1998.

Arze, René Danilo. *Participación popular en la independencia de Bolivia*. La Paz: Fundación Cultural Quipus, 1987.

Asher, Kiran. *Black and Green: Afro-Colombians, Development, and Nature in the Pacific Lowlands*. Durham, NC: Duke University Press, 2009.

Baber, R. Jovita. "The Construction of Empire: Politics, Law and Community in Tlaxcala, New Spain, 1521–1640." PhD diss., University of Chicago, 2005.

Barcia, Manuel. "Fighting with the Enemy's Weapons: The Usage of the Colonial Legal Framework by Nineteenth-Century Cuban Slaves." *Atlantic Studies* 3, no. 2 (2006): 159–81.

Basadre, Jorge. "El régimen de la mita." In *El virreinato del Perú*, edited by José Manuel Valega, 187–203. Lima: Editorial Cultura Ecléctica, 1939.

Bassi, Ernesto. "Between Imperial Projects and National Dreams: Communication Networks, Geopolitical Imagination, and the Role of New Granada in the Configuration of a Greater Caribbean Space, 1780s–1810s." PhD diss., UC Irvine, 2012.

Bastidas Urresty, Edgar. *Las guerras de Pasto*. Pasto: Ediciones Testimonio, 1979.

Basto Girón, Luis J. *Las mitas de Huamanga y Huancavelica*. Lima: Editora Médica Peruana, 1954.

Beatty-Medina, Charles. "Between the Cross and the Sword: Religious Conquest and Maroon Legitimacy in Colonial Esmeraldas." In *Africans to Spanish America: Expanding the Diaspora*, edited by Sherwin Bryant, Rachel O'Toole, and Ben Vinson III, 95–113. Chicago: Illinois University Press, 2012.

Bellingeri, Marco. "Sistemas jurídicos y codificación en el primer liberalismo mexicano, 1824–1834." In *Dinámicas de Antiguo Régimen y orden constitucional: Representación, justicia y administración en Iberoamérica, Siglos XVIII–XIX*, edited by Marco Bellingeri, 367–95. Turin: Otto Editore, 2000.

Bennett, Herman L. *Africans in Colonial Mexico: Absolutism, Christianity, and Afro-Creole Consciousness, 1570–1640*. Bloomington and Indianapolis: Indiana University Press, 2003.

 Colonial Blackness: A History of Afro-Mexico. Bloomington and Indianapolis: Indiana University Press, 2010.

Benton, Lauren. *Law and Colonial Cultures: Legal Regimes in World History, 1400–1900*. New York: Cambridge University Press, 2002.

Bergad, Laird. *Slavery and the Demographic and Economic History of Minas Gerais, Brazil, 1720–1888*. New York: Cambridge University Press, 1999.

Bernal, Alejandro. "La circulación de productos entre los pastos en el siglo XVI." *Revista Arqueológica del Area Intermedia* 2 (2000): 125–51.

Bierck, Harold. "The Struggle for Abolition in Gran Colombia." *Hispanic American Historical Review* 33, no. 3 (1953): 365–86.

Blackburn, Robin. *The Making of New World Slavery: From the Baroque to the Modern, 1942–1800*. New York: Verso, 1997.

 The Overthrow of Colonial Slavery, 1776–1848. 1988; London and New York: Verso, 2000.

Blanchard, Peter. "Slave Soldiers of Spanish South America: From Independence to Abolition." In *Arming Slaves: From Classical Times to the Modern Age*, edited by Christopher Leslie Brown and Philip Morgan, 255–73. New Haven, CT: Yale University Press, 2006.

 Under the Flags of Freedom: Slave Soldiers and the Wars of Independence in Spanish South America. Pittsburgh, PA: University of Pittsburgh Press, 2008.

Bocarejo, Diana. "Reconfiguring the Political Landscape After the Multicultural Turn: Law, Politics, and the Spacialization of Difference in Colombia." PhD. diss., University of Chicago, 2008.

Bonilla, Heraclio. "Clases populares y estado en el contexto de la crisis colonial." In *La independencia en el Perú*, edited by Heraclio Bonilla and Karen Spalding, 13–69. Lima: Instituto de Estudios Peruanos, 1981.

"La economía política de la conducción de los indios a Mariquita: La experiencia de Bosa y Ubaque en el Nuevo Reino de Granada." *Anuario Colombiano de Historia Social y de la Cultura* 32 (2005): 11–30.

"Rey o República: El dilemma de los indios frente a la independencia." In *Independencia y transición a los estados nacionales en los países andinos: Nuevas perspectivas*, edited by Armando Martínez, 357–69. Bucaramanga: Universidad Industrial de Santander/Bogotá: Organización de Estados Iberoamericanos, 2005.

ed. *Indios, negros y mestizos en la independencia*. Bogotá: Editorial Planeta-Universidad Nacional de Colombia, 2010.

Bonnett, Diana. *El protector de naturales en la Audiencia de Quito, siglos XVII y XVIII*. Quito: FLACSO, 1992.

Tierra y comunidad un problema irresuelto: El caso del altiplano cundiboyacense (Virreinato de la Nueva Granada) 1750–1800. Bogotá: ICANH, Universidad de Los Andes, 2002.

Borah, Woodrow. *Justice by Insurance: The General Indian Court of Colonial Mexico and the Legal Aides of the Half Real*. Berkeley: University of California Press, 1983.

Borrero, Manuel María. *La revolución quiteña, 1809–1812*. Quito: Editorial Espejo, 1962.

Borucki, Alex, David Eltis, and David Wheat. "Atlantic History and the Slave Trade to Spanish America." *The American Historical Review* 120, no. 2 (2015): 433–61.

Brading, David. *The First America: The Spanish Monarchy, Creole Patriots, and the Liberal State, 1492–1867*. New York: Cambridge University Press, 1993.

Bragoni, Beatriz. "Esclavos, libertos y soldados: La cultura política plebeya en tiempo de revolución." In *¿Y el pueblo dónde está? Contribuciones a la historia popular de la revolución de independencia rioplatense*, ed. Raúl Fradkin, 107–50. Buenos Aires, Prometeo ediciones, 2008.

Brandes, Stanley. *Power and Persuasion: Fiestas and Social Control in Rural Mexico*. Philadelphia: University of Pennsylvania Press, 1988.

Breña, Roberto. *El primer liberalismo español y los procesos de emancipación de América, 1808–1824*. México: Colegio de México, 2006.

Brown, Christopher. "The Arming of Slaves in Comparative Perspective." In *Arming Slaves: From Classical Times to the Modern Age*, edited by Christopher Leslie Brown and Philip Morgan, 330–53. New Haven, CT: Yale University Press, 2006.

Brown, Matthew. "Esclavitud, castas y extranjeros en las guerras de la independencia de Colombia." *Historia y Sociedad* 10 (2004): 109–125.

Bryant, Sherwin. "Enslaved Rebels, Fugitives, and Litigants: The Resistance Continuum in Colonial Quito." *Colonial Latin American Review* 13, no. 1 (2004): 7–46.

"Finding Gold, Forming Slavery: The Creation of a Classic Slave Society, Popayán, 1600–1700." *The Americas* 63, no. 1 (2006): 81–112.

Rivers of Gold, Lives of Bondage: Governing through Slavery in Colonial Quito. Chapel Hill: University of North Carolina Press, 2014.

Bryant, Sherwin, Rachel O'Toole, and Ben Vinson III, eds. *Africans to Spanish America: Expanding the Diaspora.* Chicago: Illinois University Press, 2012.

Burbank, Jane. *Russian Peasants Go To Court: Legal Culture in the Countryside, 1905–1917.* Bloomington and Indianapolis: Indiana University Press, 2004.

Burgos, Roberto, ed. *Rutas de Libertad: 500 años de travesía.* Bogotá: Ministerio de Cultura y Universidad Javeriana, 2011.

Burns, Kathryn. *Into the Archive: Writing and Power in Colonial Peru.* Durham, NC: Duke University Press, 2010.

"Making Indigenous Archives: The Quilcaycamayoc of Colonial Cuzco." *Hispanic American Historical Review* 91, no. 4 (2011): 665–89.

Buve, Raymond. "La influencia del liberalismo doceañista en una provincia novohispana mayormente indígena: Tlaxcala, 1809–1824." In *La trascendencia del liberalismo doceañista en España y en América,* edited by Manuel Chust and Ivana Frasquet, 115–35. Valencia: Generalitat Valenciana, 2004.

Calderón, María Teresa, and Clément Thibaud. *La magestad de los pueblos en la Nueva Granada y Venezuela, 1780–1832.* Bogotá: Taurus, Instituto Francés de Estudios Andinos, Universidad Externado de Colombia, 2010.

Calero, Luis Fernando. *Chiefdoms under Siege: Spain's Rule and Native Adaptation in the Southern Colombian Andes, 1535–1700.* Albuquerque: University of New Mexico Press, 1997.

Calloway, Colin. *The American Revolution in Indian Country: Crisis and Diversity in Native American Communities.* New York: Cambridge University Press, 1995.

Campo Chicangana, Ary R. *Montoneras, deserciones e insubordinaciones: Yanaconas y Paeces en la guerra de los Míl Días.* Cali: Secretaría de Cultura, Archivo Histórico, 2003.

Campos García, Melchor. *Castas, feligresía y ciudadanía en Yucatán.* Mérida: Universidad Autónoma de Yucatán, 2005.

Cañeque, Alejandro. *The King's Living Image: The Culture and Politics of Viceregal Power in Colonial Mexico.* New York and London: Routledge, 2005.

Cantor, Eric Werner. *Ni aniquilados, ni vencidos: Los Emberá y la gente negra del Atrato bajo el dominio español. Siglo XVIII.* Bogotá: Instituto Colombiano de Antropología e Historia, 2000.

Carrera Damas, Germán. *Boves: Aspectos socioeconómicos de la guerra de independencia.* Caracas: Ediciones de la Biblioteca de la Universidad Central de Venezuela, 1972.

Carroll, Patrick J. "Mandinga: The Evolution of a Mexican Runaway Slave Community, 1735–1827." *Comparative Studies in Society and History* 19, no. 4 (1977): 488–505.

Cerón, Benhúr, and Rosa Isabel Zarama. *Historia socio espacial de Túquerres, siglos XVI–XX: De Barbacoas hacia el horizonte nacional.* San Juan de Pasto: Universidad de Nariño, 2003.

Chandler, David. "Health and Slavery in Colonial Colombia." Dissertations in European Economic History. New York: Arno Press, 1981.

Charles, John. "More *Ladino* than Necessary: Indigenous Litigants and the Language Policy Debate in Mid-Colonial Peru." *Colonial Latin American Review* 16, no. 1 (2007): 23–47.

Chaves, María Eugenia. *Honor y Libertad: Discursos y recursos en la estrategia de libertad de una mujer esclava (Guayaquil a fines del periodo colonial).* Gothenburg: University of Gothenburg, 2001.

"Esclavos, libertades y república: Tesis sobre la polisemia de la libertad en la primera república antioqueña." *Estudios Interdisciplinarios de América Latina y el Caribe* 22, no. 1 (2011): 81–104.

Childs, Matt. *The 1812 Aponte Rebellion in Cuba and the Struggle against Atlantic Slavery.* Chapel Hill: University of North Carolina Press, 2006.

Chopra, Ruma. *Unnatural Rebellion: Loyalists in New York City during the Revolution.* Charlottesville: University of Virginia Press, 2011.

Chust, Manuel. "De esclavos, encomenderos y mitayos: El anticolonialismo en las Cortes de Cádiz." *Mexican Studies/Estudios Mexicanos* 11, no. 2 (1995): 179–202.

La cuestión nacional americana en las Cortes de Cádiz (1810–1814). Valencia: Instituto de Historia Social, 1999.

ed. *1808, la eclosión juntera en el mundo hispano.* México, D.F.: Fondo de Cultura Económica, 2007.

Clavero, Bartolomé. *Derecho indígena y cultura constitucional en América.* México: Siglo XXI, 1994.

Colmenares, Germán. "Castas, patrones de poblamiento y conflictos sociales en las provincias del Cauca, 1810–1830." In *La Independencia: Ensayos de Historia Social*, edited by Germán Colmenares, Zamira Díaz de Zuluaga, José Escorcia, and Francisco Zuluaga, 137–73. Bogotá: Instituto Colombiano de Cultura, 1986.

"La Historia de la Revolución por José Manuel Restrepo: Una prisión historiográfica." In *La Independencia: Ensayos de Historia Social*, edited by Germán Colmenares, Zamira Díaz de Zuluaga, José Escorcia, and Francisco Zuluaga, 9–23. Bogotá: Instituto Colombiano de Cultura, 1986.

Historia Económica y Social de Colombia, 1537–1719. 1973; Bogotá: Tercer Mundo Editores, 1997.

Historia económica y social de Colombia, vol. 2: Popayán: Una sociedad esclavista, 1680–1800. 1979; Bogotá: Tercer Mundo Editores, 1999.

Cooper, Frederick, Thomas Holt, and Rebecca J. Scott. *Beyond Slavery: Explorations of Race, Labor, and Citizenship in Postemancipation Societies.* Chapel Hill: University of North Carolina Press, 2000.

Craton, Michael. *Testing the Chains: Resistance to Slavery in the British West Indies.* Ithaca, NY, and London: Cornell University Press, 1982.

Cummins, Tom, and Joanne Rappaport. *Beyond the Lettered City: Indigenous Literacies in the Andes.* Durham, NC: Duke University Press, 2012.

Cunill, Caroline. "Tomás López Medel y sus instrucciones para defensores de indios: Una propuesta innovadora." *Anuario de Estudios Americanos* 69, no. 1 (2012): 539–63.

Curcio-Nagy, Linda. *The Great Festivals of Colonial Mexico City: Performing Power and Identity.* Albuquerque: University of New Mexico Press, 2004.

Cutter, Charles. *The Protector de Indios in Colonial New Mexico, 1659–1821.* Albuquerque: University of New Mexico Press, 1986.
"The Legal Culture of Spanish America on the Eve of Independence." In *Judicial Institutions in Nineteenth-Century Latin America*, edited by Eduardo Zimmerman, 8–24. London: Institute of Latin American Studies, University of London, 1999.
Dantas, Mariana. *Black Townsmen: Urban Slavery and Freedom in the Eighteenth-Century Americas.* New York: Palgrave MacMillan, 2008.
De Armellada, Cesáreo. *La Causa Indígena Americana en las Cortes de Cádiz.* Caracas: Universidad Católica Andrés Bello, 1979.
De Granda, Germán. "Onomástica y procedencia africana de esclavos negros en las minas del sur de la gobernación de Popayán, siglo XVIII." *Revista Española de Antropología Americana* VI (1971): 388–90.
De la Fuente, Alejandro. "'Su único derecho': los esclavos y la ley." *Revista Debate y Perspectivas* 4 (2004): 7–21.
"Slave Law and Claims-Making in Cuba: The Tannenbaum Debate Revisited," *Law and History Review* 22, no. 2 (2004): 339–69.
"Slavery and the Law: A Reply," *Law and History Review* 22, no. 2 (2004): 383–87.
"Slaves and the Creation of Legal Rights in Cuba: *Coartación* and *Papel*." *Hispanic American Historical Review* 87, no. 4 (2007): 659–92.
De la Puente Brunke, José. "Notas sobre la Audiencia de Lima y la 'protección de los naturales' (siglo XVII)." In *Passeurs, mediadores culturales y agentes de la primera globalización en el Mundo Ibérico, siglos XVI–XIX*, edited by Scarlett O'Phelan Godoy and Carmen Salazar-Soler, 221–48. Lima: PUCP-Instituto Riva-Agüero-Instituto Francés de Estudios Andinos, 2005.
De la Puente Luna, José Carlos. "Into the Heart of the Empire: Indian Journeys to the Habsburg Royal Court." PhD diss., Texas Christian University, 2010.
"The Many Tongues of the King: Indigenous Language Interpreters and the Making of the Spanish Empire." *Colonial Latin American Review* 23, no. 2 (2014): 143–70.
De la Torre Curiel, José Refugio. "Un mecenazgo fronterizo: El protector de indios Juan De Gándara y los ópatas de Opodepe (Sonora) a principios del siglo XIX." *Revista de Indias* 70, no. 248 (2010): 185–212.
Del Castillo, Nicolas. *La llave de las Indias.* Bogotá: Ediciones El Tiempo, 1981.
Di Meglio, Gabriel. *¡Viva el bajo pueblo!: La plebe urbana de Buenos Aires y la política entre la Revolución de Mayo y el Rosismo.* Buenos Aires: Prometeo Libros, 2007.
Díaz, Maria Camila. *"Salteadores y cuadrillas de malhechores": Una aproximación a la acción colectiva de la población negra en el suroccidente de la Nueva Granada, 1840–1851.* Popayán: Editorial Universidad del Cauca, 2015.
Díaz, Maria Elena. *The Virgin, the King, and the Royal Slaves of El Cobre: Negotiating Freedom in Colonial Cuba, 670–1780.* Stanford, CA: Stanford niversity Press, 2000.
"Beyond Tannenbaum." *Law and History Review* 22, no. 2 (2004): 371–76.

Díaz, Zamira. *Oro, sociedad y economía: El sistema colonial en la Gobernación de Popayán, 1533–1733.* Bogotá: Banco de la República, 1994.

Díaz del Castillo, Emiliano. *El Caudillo: Semblanza de Agualongo.* Pasto: Tipografía y Fotograbado Javier, 1983.

Díaz del Castillo, Idelfonso. "El coronel Manuel Ortiz y Zamora: Breves apuntes sobre su vida." *Boletín de Estudios Históricos* 2, no. 21 (1929): 271–95.

Díaz Díaz, Rafael. *Esclavitud, region y ciudad: El sistema esclavista urbano-regional en Santafé de Bogotá, 1700–1750.* Bogotá: Centro Editorial Javeriano, 2001.

Dubois, Laurent. *Avengers of the New World: The Story of the Haitian Revolution.* Cambridge, MA: Belknap Press, 2004.

A Colony of Citizens: Revolution and Slave Emancipation in the French Caribbean, 1787–1804. Chapel Hill: Omohundro Institute of Early American History and Culture/University of North Carolina Press, 2004.

"Citizen Soldiers: Emancipation and Military Service in the Revolutionary French Caribbean." In *Arming Slaves: From Classical Times to the Modern Age,* edited by Christopher Leslie Brown and Philip Morgan, 233–54. New Haven, CT: Yale University Press, 2006.

"An Enslaved Enlightenment: Rethinking the Intellectual History of the French Atlantic." *Social History* 31, no. 1 (2006): 1–14.

"Calling Down the Law: Prophetic Rumor and the Coming of Emancipation in the Caribbean, 1789–1848." Unpublished manuscript.

Dueñas, Alcira. "Ethnic Power and Identity Formation in Mid-Colonial Andean Writing." *Colonial Latin American Review* 18, no. 3 (2009): 407–33.

Indians and Mestizos in the "Lettered City": Reshaping Justice, Social Hierarchy, and Political Culture in Colonial Peru. Boulder: University Press of Colorado, 2010.

Dym, Jordana. "La soberanía de los pueblos: Ciudad e independencia en Centroamérica, 1808–1823." In *Revolución, independencia y las nuevas naciones de América,* edited by Jaime Rodríguez, 309–38. Madrid: Fundación Mapfre-Tavera, 2005.

From Sovereign Villages to National States: City, State and Federation in Central America, 1759–1839. Albuquerque: University of New Mexico Press, 2006.

"Napoleon and the Americas." Unpublished manuscript.

Earle, Rebecca. "Indian Rebellion and Bourbon Reform in New Granada: Riots in Pasto, 1780–1800." *Hispanic American Historical Review* 73, no. 1 (1993): 99–124.

Spain and the Independence of Colombia, 1810–1825. Exeter: University of Exeter Press, 2000.

"The War of the Supremes: Border Conflict, Religious Crusade or Simply Politics by Other Means?" In *Rumours of Wars: Civil Conflict in Nineteenth-Century Latin America,* edited by Rebecca Earle, 119–34. London: University of London, Institute of Latin American Studies, 2000.

"Creole Patriotism and the Myth of the 'Loyal Indian.'" *Past and Present* 172 (2001): 125–45.

The Return of the Native: Indians and Mythmaking in Spanish America, 1810–1930. Durham, NC: Duke University Press, 2007.

Eastman, Scott. *Preaching Spanish Nationalism across the Hispanic Atlantic, 1759–1823*. Baton Rouge: Louisiana University Press, 2012.

Echeverri, Marcela. "'Enraged to the Limit of Despair': Infanticide and Slave Judicial Strategies in Barbacoas, 1789–1798." *Slavery & Abolition* 30, no. 3 (2009): 403–26.

"Popular Royalists, Empire, and Politics in Southwestern New Granada, 1809–1819." *Hispanic American Historical Review* 91, no. 2 (2011): 237–69.

"Race, Citizenship, and the Cádiz Constitution in Popayán (New Granada)." In *The Rise of Constitutional Government in the Iberian Atlantic World: The Impact of the Cádiz Constitution of 1812*. Edited by Scott Eastman and Natalia Sobrevilla Perea, 91–110. Tuscaloosa: University of Alabama Press, 2015.

Edwards, Laura F. "Enslaved Women and the Law: Paradoxes of Subordination in the Post-Revolutionary Carolinas." *Slavery & Abolition* 26, no. 2 (2005): 305–23.

Elkins, Stanley. *Slavery: A Problem in American Institutional and Intellectual Life*. Chicago, IL: University of Chicago Press, 1968.

Elliott, J.H. *Empires of the Atlantic World: Britain and Spain in America, 1492–1830*. New Haven, CT, and London: Yale University Press, 2006.

Eltis, David. *The Rise of African Slavery in the Americas*. New York: Cambridge University Press, 2000.

Fernández Albaladejo, Pablo. *Fragmentos de Monarquía: Trabajos de historia política*. Madrid: Alianza Universidad, 1992.

Ferrer, Ada. *Insurgent Cuba: Race, Nation, and Revolution, 1868–1898*. Chapel Hill: University of North Carolina Press, 1999.

"Armed Slaves and the Anticolonial Insurgency in Late Nineteenth-Century Cuba." In *Arming Slaves: From Classical Times to the Modern Age*, edited by Christopher L. Brown and Philip D. Morgan, 304–29. New Haven, CT, and London: Yale University Press, 2006.

"Speaking of Haiti: Slavery, Revolution, and Freedom in Cuban Slave Testimony." In *The World of the Haitian Revolution*, edited by David Geggus and Norman Fiering, 223–47. Bloomington and Indianapolis: Indiana University Press, 2009.

"Haiti, Free Soil, and Antislavery in the Revolutionary Atlantic." *American Historical Review* 117, no. 1 (2012): 40–66.

Freedom's Mirror: Cuba and Haiti in the Age of Revolution. New York: Cambridge University Press, 2014.

Fick, Carolyn. *The Making of Haiti: The Saint Domingue Revolution from Below*. Knoxville: University of Tennessee, 1990.

Fischer, Sibylle. "Bolívar in Haiti: Republicanism in the Revolutionary Atlantic." In *Haiti and the Americas*, edited by Carla Calarge, Raphael Dalleo, Luis Duno-Gottberg, and Clevis Headley, 25–53. Jackson: University Press of Mississippi, 2013.

Fisher, Andrew, and Matthew O'Hara. "Introduction: Racial Identity and Their Interpreters in Colonial Latin America." In *Imperial Subjects: Race and*

Identity in Colonial Latin America, edited by Andrew Fisher and Matthew O'Hara, 1–38. Durham, NC: Duke University Press, 2009.

Fisher, John, Allan Kuethe, and Anthony McFarlane, eds. *Reform and Insurrection in Bourbon New Granada and Peru*. Baton Rouge: Louisiana University Press, 1990.

Foote, Nicola, and René Harder Horst, eds. *Military Struggle and Identity Formation in Latin America: Race, Nation, and Community during the Liberal Period*. Gainesville: University Press of Florida, 2010.

Fradera, Josep Maria. *Gobernar Colonias*. Barcelona: Ediciones Península, 1999.

Friede, Juan. *El Indio en la lucha por la tierra: Historia de los resguardos del macizo central colombiano*. 1944; Bogotá: Editorial La Chispa, 1972.

García, Gloria. *La esclavitud desde la esclavitud*. La Habana: Editorial de Ciencias Sociales, 2003.

Garofalo, Leo. "The Shape of a Diaspora: The Movement of Afro-Iberians to Colonial Spanish America." In *Africans to Spanish America: Expanding the Diaspora*, edited by Sherwin Bryant, Rachel O'Toole, and Ben Vinson III, 27–49. Chicago: Illinois University Press, 2012.

Garrett, David T. *Shadows of Empire: The Indian Nobility of Cusco, 1750–1825*. New York: Cambridge University Press, 2005.

Garrido, Margarita. *Reclamos y representaciones: Variaciones sobre la política en el Nuevo Reino de Granada, 1770–1815*. Bogotá: Colección Bibliográfica del Banco de la República, 1993.

"'Free Men of All Colors' in New Granada: Identity and Obedience before Independence." In *Political Cultures in the Andes, 1750–1950*, edited by Nils Jacobsen and Cristóbal Aljovín de Losada, 165–83. Durham, NC: Duke University Press, 2005.

Geggus, David P. "Slavery, War, and Revolution in the Greater Caribbean." In *A Turbulent Time: The French Revolution and the Greater Caribbean*, edited by David B. Gaspar and David P. Geggus, 1–50. Bloomington and Indianapolis: Indiana University Press, 1997.

"The Caribbean in the Age of Revolution." In *The Age of Revolutions in Global Context, c. 1760–1840*, edited by David Armitage and Sanjay Subrahmanyam, 83–100. New York: Palgrave Macmillan, 2010.

Genovese, Eugene. "Materialism and Idealism in the History of Negro Slavery in the Americas." In *Slavery in the New World: A Reader in Comparative Perspectives*, edited by Laura Fones and Eugene Genovese, 238–55. Englewood Cliffs, NJ: Prentice-Hall, 1969.

From Rebellion to Revolution: Afro-American Slave Revolts in the Making of the Modern World. Baton Rouge: Louisiana State University Press, 1979.

Ghachem, Malick W. *The Old Regime and the Haitian Revolution*. New York: Cambridge University Press, 2012.

Giménez, Manuel. "Las doctrinas populistas en la Independencia de Hispanoamérica." *Anuario de Estudios Americanos* 3 (1946): 534–54.

Gomez, Michael. *Exchanging our Country Marks: The Transformation of African Identities in the Colonial and Antebellum South*. Chapel Hill: University of North Carolina Press, 1998.

González Sevillano, Pedro H. *Marginalidad y exclusion en el Pacífico colombiano: Una visión histórica.* Cali: Editorial Universidad Santiago de Cali, 1999.

Grandin, Greg. *The Blood of Guatemala: A History of Race and Nation.* Durham, NC: Duke University Press, 2000.

Graubart, Karen. "Learning from the *Qadi*: The Jurisdiction of Local Rule in the Early Colonial Andes." *Hispanic American Historical Review* 95, no. 2 (2015): 195–228.

Guardino, Peter F. *Peasants, Politics, and the Formation of Mexico's National State: Guerrero, 1800–1857.* Stanford, CA: Stanford University Press, 1996.

The Time of Liberty: Popular Political Culture in Oaxaca, 1750–1850. Durham, NC: Duke University Press, 2005.

Guarisco, Claudia. *Los indios del valle de México y la construcción de una nueva sociabilidad política, 1770–1835.* Zinacantepec: El Colegio Mexiquense, 2003.

Gudmundson, Lowell, and Justin Wolfe. *Blacks and Blackness in Central America: Between Race and Place.* Durham, NC: Duke University Press, 2010.

Guerra, François-Xavier. *Modernidad e independencias: Ensayos sobre las revoluciones hispánicas.* México, D.F.: Editorial MAPFRE-Fondo de Cultura Económica, 1992.

Guerrero, Gerardo León. *Pasto en la guerra de independencia, 1809–1824.* Bogotá: Tecnoimpresores, 1994.

Guha, Ranajit. *Elementary Aspects of Peasant Insurgency in Colonial India.* Durham, NC: Duke University Press, 1999.

Gutiérrez, Daniel. *Un Nuevo Reino: Geografía política, pactismo y diplomacia durante el interregno en Nueva Granada (1808–1816).* Bogotá: Universidad Externado de Colombia, 2010.

"Las políticas abolicionistas en el Estado de Antioquia (1812–1816)." Unpublished manuscript.

Gutiérrez, Jairo. "'El infame tumulto y criminal bochinche': Las rebeliones de los indios de Pasto contra la República (1822–1824)." In *Independencia y transición a los estados nacionales en los países andinos: Nuevas perspectivas*, edited by Armando Martínez, 371–99. Bucaramanga: Universidad Industrial de Santander, 2005.

Los indios de Pasto contra la República (1809–1824). Bogotá: Instituto Colombiano de Antropología e Historia, 2007.

"La Constitución de Cádiz en la Provincia de Pasto, Nueva Granada, 1812–1822." *Revista de Indias* 68, no. 242 (2008): 207–24.

Hall, Gwendolyn Midlo. *Slavery and African Ethnicities in the Americas: Restoring the Links.* Chapel Hill: University of North Carolina Press, 2005.

Hamnett, Brian. "The Counter Revolution of Morillo and the Insurgent Clerics of New Granada, 1815–1820." *The Americas* 32, no. 4 (1976): 597–617.

Revolución y contrarrevolución en México y el Perú: Liberalismo, realeza y separatismo. México, D.F.: Fondo de Cultura Económica, 1978.

"Popular Insurrection and Royalist Reaction: Colombian Regions, 1810–1823." In *Reform and Insurrection in Bourbon New Granada and Peru*, edited by John Fisher, Allan Kuethe, and Anthony McFarlane, 292–326. Baton Rouge: Louisiana University Press, 1990.

"El momento de decisión y de acción: El virreinato del Perú en el año de 1810." *Historia y Política* 24 (2010): 143–68.

Harris, Marvin. *Patterns of Race in the Americas.* New York: Walker and Co., 1964.

Helg, Aline. *Liberty and Equality in Caribbean Colombia, 1770–1835.* Chapel Hill: University of North Carolina Press, 2004.

Henao, Jesús María, and Gerardo Arrubla. *Historia de Colombia para la enseñanza secundaria*, Vol. 2. 1910; Bogota: Librería Colombiana, 1920.

Herrera, Marta. "En un rincón de ese imperio en que no se ocultaba el sol: Colonialismo, oro y terror en Las Barbacoas. Siglo XVIII." *Anuario Colombiano de Historia Social y de la Cultura* 32 (2005): 31–50.

Popayán: La unidad de lo diverso: Territorio, población y poblamiento en la provincia de Popayán, siglo XVIII. Bogotá: Ediciones Uniandes-CESO, 2009.

Herzog, Tamar. "De la historia y el mito: Las rebeliones de Quito (1592–1765)." *Reflejos* 7 (1998): 72–80.

Hespanha, Antonio. *La gracia del derecho: Economía de la cultura en la Edad Moderna.* Madrid: Centro de Estudios Políticos y Constitucionales, 1993.

Higgins, Kathleen. *"Licentious Liberty" in a Brazilian Gold-Mining Region: Slavery, Gender, and Social Control in Eighteenth-Century Sabará, Minas Gerais.* University Park: Pennsylvania State University Press, 1999.

Holt, Thomas. *The Problem of Freedom: Race, Labor, and Politics in Jamaica and Britain, 1832–1938.* Baltimore, MD, and London: Johns Hopkins University Press, 1992.

Honores, Renzo. "La asistencia jurídical privada a los señores indígenas ante la Real Audiencia de Lima, 1552–1570." Paper Presented at the 2003 Latin American Studies Association meeting.

"Colonial Legal Polyphony: Caciques and the Construction of Legal Arguments in the Andes, 1550–1640." Paper Presented to the 2010 Seminar on the History of the Atlantic World, *Justice: Europe in America, 1500–1830.*

Hünefeldt, Christine. "Los indios y la Constitución de 1812." *Allpanchis* 11–12 (1978): 33–57.

Lucha por la tierra y protesta indígena: Las comunidades indígenas del Perú entre Colonia y República, 1800–1830. Bonn: Estudios Americanistas de Bonn, 1982.

Paying the Price of Freedom: Family and Labor among Lima's Slaves, 1800–1854. Berkeley: University of California Press, 1994.

Hurtado, Alberto Montezuma. "Los Clavijos y la casa de los muertos." *Boletín Cultural y Bibliográfico* 9, no. 8 (1968): 7–105.

Irurozqui, Marta. "El bautismo de la violencia: Indígenas patriotas en la revolución de 1870 en Bolivia." In *Identidad, ciudadanía y participación popular desde la colonia al siglo XX*, edited by Josefa Salmón and Guillermo Delgado, 115–52. La Paz: Editorial Plural, 2003.

"De cómo el vecino hizo al ciudadano y de cómo el ciudadano conservó al vecino: Charcas, 1808–1830." In *Revolución, independencia y las nuevas naciones de América*, edited by Jaime Rodríguez, 451–84. Madrid: Fundación Mapfre-Tavera, 2005.

"*Los hombres chacales en armas*: Militarización y criminalización indígenas en la revolución federal boliviana de 1899." In *La Mirada Esquiva: Reflexiones históricas sobre la interacción del estado y la ciudadanía en los Andes (Bolivia, Ecuador y Perú), siglo XIX*, edited by Marta Irurozqui, 285–320. Madrid: Consejo Superior de Investigaciones Científicas, 2005.

Jackson, Robert, ed. *Liberals, the Church, and Indian Peasants: Corporate Lands and the Challenge of Reform in Nineteenth-Century Latin America*. Albuquerque: University of New Mexico Press, 1997.

Jaramillo Uribe, Jaime. *Ensayos de Historia Social*. 1989; Bogotá: Ediciones Uniandes, 2001.

Jasanoff, Maya. "The Other Side of Revolution: Loyalists in the British Empire," *The William and Mary Quarterly* 65, no. 2 (2008): 205–32.

"Revolutionary Exiles: The American Loyalist and French Émigré Diasporas." In *The Age of Revolutions in Global Context, c. 1760–1840*, edited by David Armitage and Sanjay Subrahamanyam, 37–58. New York: Palgrave Macmillan, 2010.

Liberty's Exiles: American Loyalists in the Revolutionary World. Knopf/Harper Press, 2011.

Jiménez, Orián. "La conquista del estómago: Viandas, vituallas y ración negra. Siglos XVII–XVIII." In *Geografía Humana de Colombia, Tomo VI, Los Afrocolombianos*, edited by Luz Adriana Maya, 219–40. Bogotá: Instituto Colombiano de Antropología e Historia, 1998.

El Chocó: Un paraíso del demonio: Nóvita, Citará y El Baudó, siglo XVIII. Medellín: Editorial Universidad de Antioquia, 2004.

Johnson, Lyman, *Workshop of Revolution: Plebeian Buenos Aires and the Atlantic World, 1776–1810*. Durham, NC: Duke University Press, 2011.

Johnson, Walter. *Soul by Soul: Life Inside the Antebellum Slave Market*. Cambridge, MA, and London: Harvard University Press, 1999.

"On Agency," *Journal of Social History* 37, no. 1 (2003): 113–24.

Jouve Martín, José Ramón. *Esclavos de la ciudad letrada: Esclavitud, escritura y colonialismo en Lima (1650–1700)*. Lima: Instituto de Estudios Peruanos, 2005.

Jurado, Fernando. *Esclavitud en la Costa Pacífica: Iscuandé, Tumaco, Barbacoas y Esmeraldas, Siglos XVI al XIX*. Quito: Ediciones Abya-Yala, 1990.

Kahle, Louis G. "The Spanish Colonial Judiciary." *The Southwestern Social Science Quarterly* 32 (1951): 26–37.

Kellogg, Susan. *Law and the Transformation of Aztec Culture, 1500–1700*. Norman: University of Oklahoma Press, 1995.

Kiddy, Elizabeth. "Who Is the King of Congo? A New Look at African and Afro-Brazilian Kings in Brazil." In *Central Africans and Cultural Transformations in the American Diaspora*, edited by Linda M. Heywood, 153–82. New York: Cambridge University Press, 2002.

King, James. "A Royalist View of the Colored Castes in the Venezuelan War of Independence." *Hispanic American Historical Review* 33, no. 4 (1953): 526-37.

Klein, Herbert. *Slavery in the Americas: A Comparative Study of Virginia and Cuba*. Chicago, IL: The University of Chicago Press, 1967.

The Atlantic Slave Trade. 1999; New York: Cambridge University Press, 2010.

"The African American Experience in Comparative Perspective: The Current Question of the Debate." In *Africans to Spanish America: Expanding the Diaspora*, edited by Sherwin Bryant, Rachel O'Toole, and Ben Vinson III, 206–222. Chicago: Illinois University Press, 2012.

Klein, Herbert, and Francisco Vidal Luna. *Slavery in Brazil*. New York: Cambridge University Press, 2010.

Klein, Herbert, and Ben Vinson III. *African Slavery in Latin America and the Caribbean*. 2nd ed. Oxford: Oxford University Press, 2007.

Klooster, Wim. "Le décret d'émancipation imaginaire: Monarchisme et esclavage en Amérique du Nord et dans la Caraïbe au temps des révolutions." *Annales Historiques de la Révolution Française* 1 (2011): 111–28.

König, Hans-Joachim. *En el camino hacia la nación: Nacionalismo en el proceso de formación del estado y de la nación en la Nueva Granada, 1750–1856*. Bogotá: Banco de la República, 1994.

Kraay, Hendrik. *Race, State, and Armed Forces in Independence-Era Brazil: Bahia, 1790s–1840s*. Stanford, CA: Stanford University Press, 2001.

Krug, Jessica. "Social Dismemberment, Social Remembering: Contested Kromanti Identities, Nationalism, and Obeah, 1675–Present." MA Thesis, University of Wisconsin, 2007.

Kuethe, Allan. "The Status of the Free Pardo in the Disciplined Militia of New Granada." *The Journal of Negro History* 56, no. 2 (1971): 105–117.

Military Reform and Society in New Granada, 1773–1808. Gainesville: University Presses of Florida, 1978.

"More on 'The Culmination of the Bourbon Reforms': A Perspective from New Granada." *Hispanic American Historical Review* 58, no. 3 (1978): 477–80.

"The Early Reforms of Charles III in the Viceroyalty of New Granada, 1759–1776." In *Reform and Insurrection in Bourbon New Granada and Peru*, edited by John Fisher, Allan Kuethe, and Anthony McFarlane, 19–40. Baton Rouge: Louisiana University Press, 1990.

Kuethe, Allan, and Kenneth Andrien. *The Spanish Atlantic World in the Eighteenth Century: War and the Bourbon Reforms, 1713–1796*. New York: Cambridge University Press, 2014.

Landavazo, Marco A. *La máscara de Fernando VII: Discurso e imaginario monárquico en una época de crisis. Nueva España 1808–1822*. México, D.F.: Colegio de México, 2001.

Landázuri Camacho, Carlos. "La independencia del Ecuador (1808–1822)." In *Nueva Historia del Ecuador*, 6, edited by Enrique Ayala Mora, 79–126. Quito: Grijalbo, 1994.

Landers, Jane. "'In Consideration of Her Enormous Crime': Rape and Infanticide in Spanish St Augustine." In *Sex and Race in the Early South*, edited by Catherine Clinton and Michele Gillespie, 205–17. Oxford: Oxford University Press, 1997.

Black Society in Spanish Florida. Chicago: University of Illinois Press, 1999.

"*Cimarrón* and Citizen: African Ethnicity, Corporate Identity, and the Evolution of Free Black Towns in the Spanish Circum-Caribbean." In *Slaves, Subjects and Subversives: Blacks in Colonial Latin America*, edited by Jane

Landers and Barry Robinson, 111–46. Albuquerque: University of New Mexico Press, 2006.

"Transforming Bondsmen into Vassals: Arming Slaves in Colonial Spanish America." In *Arming Slaves: From Classical Times to the Modern Age*, edited by Christopher Leslie Brown and Philip Morgan, 120–45. New Haven, CT: Yale University Press, 2006.

Atlantic Creoles in the Age of Revolutions. Cambridge, MA: Harvard University Press, 2010.

Langley, Lester. *The Americas in the Age of Revolution, 1750–1850.* New Haven, CT: Yale University Press, 1996.

Lane, Kris. "The Transition from *Encomienda* to Slavery in Seventeenth-Century Barbacoas (Colombia)." *Slavery & Abolition* 21, no. 1 (2000): 73–95.

"Gone Platinum: Contraband and Chemistry in Eighteenth-Century Colombia." *Colonial Latin American Review* 20, no. 1 (2011): 61–79.

Larson, Brooke. "Explotación y economía moral en los Andes del sur: Hacia una reconsideración crítica." *Historia Crítica* 6 (1992): 75–92.

Cochabamba, 1550–1900: Colonialism and Agrarian Transformation in Bolivia. 1988; Durham, NC: Duke University Press, 1998.

Trials of Nation Making: Liberalism, Race, and Ethnicity in the Andes, 1810–1910. New York: Cambridge University Press, 2004.

Lasso, Marixa. *Myths of Harmony: Race and Republicanism during the Age of Revolution, Colombia 1795–1831.* Pittsburgh, PA: University of Pittsburgh Press, 2007.

"Población y Sociedad." In *Colombia: Crisis Imperial e Independencia* (Tomo I, 1808–1830), edited by Eduardo Posada Carbó, 199–247. Madrid: Taurus, Fundación MAPFRE, 2010.

"Los grupos afro-descendientes y la independencia: ¿un nuevo paradigma historiográfico?" In *L'atlantique revolutionnaire: Une perspective Ibéro-Américain*, edited by Clément Thibaud, Gabriel Entin, Alejandro Gómez, and Federica Morelli, 359–378. Bécherel: Éditions Les Perséides, 2013.

Lavallé, Bernard. "Presión colonial y reivindicación indígena en Cajamarca (1785–1820) según el Archivo del Protector de Naturales." *Allpanchis* 35–36 (1990): 105–37.

"Aquella ignomiosa herida que se hizo a la humanidad': El cuestionamiento de la esclavitud en Quito a finales de la época colonial." *Procesos* 6 (1994): 23–48.

Laviña, Javier. "La sublevación de Túquerres de 1800: Una revuelta antifiscal." *Boletín Americanista* 28 (1978): 189–96.

Leal, Bernardo. "Pido se me ampare en mi libertad: Esclavizados, manumisos y rebeldes en el Chocó (1710–1810) bajo la lente colonial y contemporánea." MA Thesis, Universidad Nacional de Colombia, 2006.

Leal, Claudia. "Disputas por tagua y minas: recursos naturales y propiedad territorial en el Pacífico colombiano, 1870–1930." *Revista Colombiana de Antropologia* 44, no. 2 (2008): 409–38.

Levaggi, Abelardo. "La condición juridical del esclavo en la época hispánica." *Revista de Historia del Derecho* 1 (1973): 83–175.

Lewis, Laura. *Hall of Mirrors: Power, Witchcraft, and Caste in Colonial Mexico.* Durham, NC: Duke University Press, 2003.

Lohmann, Guillermo. *Las minas de Huancavelica en los siglos XVI y XVII.* Seville: Escuela de Estudios Hispano-Americanos, 1949.

Lucena Giraldo, Manuel. "La constitución atlántica de España y sus Indias." *Revista de Occidente* 281 (2004): 29–44.

Lucena Salmoral, Manuel. *Sangre sobre piel negra: La esclavitud quiteña en el contexto del reformismo borbónico.* Quito: Centro Cultural Afroecuatoriano, Ediciones Abya-Yala, Colección Mundo Afro 1, 1994.

Los códigos negros de la América española. Ediciones Unesco/Universidad de Alcalá, 1996.

Lynch, John. *The Spanish American Revolutions, 1808–1826.* 1973; New York: W. W. Norton, 1986.

Simón Bolívar: A Life. New Haven, CT: Yale University Press, 2006.

Macías, Flavia. "Ciudadanía armada, identidad nacional y estado provincial: Tucumán, 1854–1870." In *La vida política en Argentina del siglo XIX: Armas, votos y voces,* edited by Hilda Sábato and Alberto Lettieri, 137–52. Buenos Aires: Siglo XXI, 2003.

Martínez, Armando, and Daniel Gutiérrez. *La contrarrevolución de los pueblos de las Sabanas de Tolú y el Sinú (1812).* Bucaramanga: Universidad Industrial de Santander, 2010.

Martínez, María Elena. "The Black Blood of New Spain: *Limpieza de Sangre,* Racial Violence, and Gendered Power in Early Colonial Mexico." *William and Mary Quarterly* 61, no. 3 (2004): 479–520.

Marzahl, Peter. *Town in the Empire: Government, Politics, and Society in Seventeenth-Century Popayán.* Austin: University of Texas, 1978.

Mattos, Hebe Maria. *Escravidão e cidadania no Brasil monárquico.* Rio de Janeiro: Jorge Zahar, 2000.

Maya, Luz Adriana. *Brujería y reconstrucción de identidades entre los africanos y sus descendientes en la Nueva Granada, siglo XVII.* Bogotá: Ministerio de Cultura, 2005.

McConville, Brian. *The King's Three Faces The Rise and Fall of Royal America, 1688–1776.* Chapel Hill: Omohundro Institute of Early American History and Culture/University of North Carolina Press, 2006.

McFarlane, Anthony. "*Cimarrones* and *Palenques*: Runaways and Resistance in Colonial Colombia." *Slavery & Abolition* 6, no. 3 (1985): 131–51.

"The Rebellion of the *Barrios.*" In *Reform and Insurrection in Bourbon New Granada and Peru,* edited by John Fisher, Allan Kuethe, and Anthony McFarlane, 197–254. Baton Rouge: Louisiana University Press, 1990.

Colombia antes de la independencia: Economía, sociedad y política bajo el dominio borbón. Bogotá: Banco de la República, 1997.

War and Independence in Spanish America. New York and London: Routledge, 2014.

Mckinley, Michelle. "Fractional Freedoms: Slavery, Legal Activism, and Ecclesiastical Courts in Colonial Lima, 1593–1689." *Law and History Review* 28, no. 3 (2010): 749–90.

Meiklejohn, Norman. "The Observance of Negro Slave Legislation in Colonial Nueva Granada." PhD diss., Columbia University, 1968.

"The Implementation of Slave Legislation in Eighteenth-Century New Granada." In *Slavery and Race Relations in Latin America*, edited by Robert Brent Toplin, 176–203. Westport, CT: Greenwood Press, 1974.

Meisel Roca, Adolfo. "¿Situado o contrabando?: La base económica de Cartagena de Indias a fines del Siglo de las Luces." In *Cuadernos de Historia Económica y Empresarial* 11 (2003).

Mejía, Sergio. *La revolución en letras: La Historia de la Revolución de Colombia de José Manuel Restrepo (1781–1863)*. Bogotá: Uniandes, 2007.

Mejía Mejía, J.C. "El clero de Pasto y la insurrección del 28 de octubre de 1822." *Boletín de Estudios Históricos* 4, no. 46 (1932): 418–22.

Méndez, Cecilia. *The Plebeian Republic: The Huanta Rebellion and the Making of the Peruvian State, 1820–1850*. Durham, NC: Duke University Press, 2005.

"Tradiciones liberales en los Andes o la ciudadanía por las armas: Campesinos y militares en la formación del estado peurano." In *La Mirada Esquiva: Reflexiones históricas sobre la interacción del estado y la ciudadanía en los Andes (Bolivia, Ecuador y Perú), siglo XIX*, edited by Marta Irurozqui, 125–54. Madrid: Consejo Superior de Investigaciones Científicas, 2005.

Miki, Yuko. "Insurgent Geographies: Blacks, Indians, and the Colonization of Nineteenth-Century Brazil." PhD. diss., New York University, 2010.

"Fleeing into Slavery: The Insurgent Geographies of Brazilian Quilombolas (Maroons), 1880–1881." *The Americas* 64, no. 4 (2012): 495–528.

Miramón, Alberto. "Agualongo, el guerrillero indomable." *Boletín de Historia y Antigüedades* 27, nos. 313–14 (1940): 968–85.

Hombres del tiempo heróico. Bogotá: Empresa Nacional de Publicaciones, 1956.

Minaudier, Jean Pierre. "Pequeñas patrias en la tormenta: Pasto y Barbacoas a finales de la colonia y en la independencia." *Historia y Espacio* 3, nos. 11–12 (1987): 130–65.

Mora de Tovar, Gilma Lucía. *Aguardiente y conflictos sociales en el Nuevo Reino de Granada durante el siglo XVIII*. Bogotá: Universidad Nacional de Colombia, 1988.

Morelli, Federica. "La publicación y el juramento de la constitución de Cádiz en Hispaoamérica: Imágenes y valores (1812–1813)." In *Observation and Communication: The Construction of Realities in the Hispanic World*, edited by Johannes-Michael Scholz and Tamar Herzog, 135–49. Frankfurt am Main: Vittorio Klostermann, 1997.

Territorio o Nación: Reforma y disolución del espacio imperial en Ecuador, 1765–1830. Madrid: Centro de Estudios Políticos y Constitucionales, 2005.

"Quito en 1810: La búsqueda de un nuevo proyecto político." *Historia y Política* 24 (2010): 119–41.

Moreno Yáñez, Segundo. *Sublevaciones indígenas en la Audiencia de Quito: Desde comienzos del siglo XVIII hasta finales de la Colonia*. Quito: Centro de Publicaciones Pontificia Universidad Católica del Ecuador, 1977.

Morgan, Philip. "The Cultural Implications of the Atlantic Slave Trade: African Regional Origins, American Destinations and New World Developments." *Slavery & Abolition* 18, no. 1 (1997): 122–45.

Múnera, Alfonso. *El fracaso de la nación*. Bogotá: Banco de la República, El Ancora Editores, 1998.

Muñoz, Lidia Inés. *La última insurrección indígena anticolonial*. Pasto: Imprenta Departamental, 1982.

Murra, John V. *The Economic Organization of the Inca State*. Greenwich, CT: JAI Press, 1980.

Nelson, Eric. *The Royalist Revolution: Monarchy and the American Founding*. Cambridge, MA: Belknap Press, 2014.

Ng'wengo, Bettina. *Turf Wars: Territory and Citizenship in the Contemporary State*. Stanford, CA: Stanford University Press, 2007.

Ogle, Gene E. "The Trans-Atlantic King and Imperial Public Spheres: Everyday Politics in Pre-Revolutionary Saint-Domingue." In *The World of the Haitian Revolution*, edited by David Geggus and Norman Fiering, 79–96. Bloomington and Indianapolis: Indiana University Press, 2009.

O'Phelan Godoy, Scarlett. "Abascal y la reformulación del espacio del virreinato del Perú, 1806–1816." *Revista Política Internacional* 95–96 (2009): 30–46.

Ortiz, Sergio Elías. *Agustín Agualongo y su tiempo*. Bogotá: Editorial A.B.C., 1958.

O'Shaughnessy, Andrew Jackson. *The Men Who Lost America: British Leadership, the American Revolution, and the Fate of Empire*. New Haven, CT: Yale University Press, 2013.

Ossa, Juan Luis. *Armies, Politics and Revolution: Chile, 1808–1826*. Liverpool: Liverpool University Press, 2014.

O'Toole, Rachel. "'In a War against the Spanish': Andean Protection and African Resistance on the Northern Peruvian Coast." *The Americas* 63, no. 1 (2006): 19–52.

Bound Lives: Africans, Indians, and the Making of Race in Colonial Peru. Pittsburgh, PA: University of Pittsburgh Press, 2012.

Ots y Capdequí, José María. *Manual de Historia del Derecho Español en las Indias y del Derecho Propiamente Indiano*. Buenos Aires: Instituto de Historia del Derecho Argentino, 1943.

Oviedo, Ricardo. *Los Comuneros del Sur: Levantamientos Populares del Siglo XVIII*. San Juan de Pasto: Editorial de Nariño, 2001.

Owensby, Brian P. "How Juan and Leonor Won Their Freedom: Litigation and Liberty in Seventeenth-Century Mexico." *Hispanic American Historical Review* 85, no. 1 (2005): 39–80.

Empire of Law and Indian Justice in Colonial Mexico. Stanford, CA: Stanford University Press, 2008.

Pagden, Anthony. *The Fall of Natural Man: The American Indian and the Origins of Comparative Ethnology*. New York: Cambridge University Press, 1987.

Palomeque, Silvia. "El sistema de autoridades de 'pueblos de indios' y sus transformaciones a fines del período colonial: El partido de Cuenca." *Memoria Americana* 6 (1997): 10–47.

Paquette, Gabriel. *Imperial Portugal in the Age of Atlantic Revolutions: The Luso-Brazilian World, c. 1770–1850*. New York: Cambridge University Press, 2013.

Patterson, Tiffany Ruby, and Robin Kelley. "Unfinished Migrations: Reflections on the African Diaspora and the Making of the Modern World." *African Studies Review* 43, no. 1 (2000): 11–45.

Patzi, Felix. "Rebelión indígena contra la colonialidad y la transnacionalización de la economía: Triunfos y vicisitudes del movimiento indígena desde 2000 a 2003." In *Ya es otro tiempo el presente: Cuatro momentos de insurgencia indígena*, edited by Forrest Hylton, Felix Patzi, Sergio Serulnikov and Sinclair Thomson, 199–279. Bolivia: Muela del Diablo Editores, 2003.

Peralta, Víctor. *En pos del tributo: Burocracia estatal, elite regional y comunidades indígenas en el Cuzco rural (1826–1854)*. Cuzco: Centro de Estudios Andinos Regionales, 1991.

"El mito del ciudadano armado: La 'semana magna' y las elecciones de 1844 en Lima." In *Ciudadanía política y formación de las naciones: Perspectivas históricas en América Latina*, edited by Hilda Sábato, 231–52. México, D.F.: Fondo de Cultura Económica, 1999.

"Los inicios del sistema representativo en Perú: Ayuntamientos constitucionales y diputaciones provinciales (1812–1815)." In *La mirada esquiva: Reflexiones sobre la interacción del estado y la ciudadanía en los Andes (Bolivia, Ecuador y Perú), siglo XIX*, edited by Marta Irurozqui, 65–92. Madrid: Consejo Superior de Investigaciones Científicas, 2005.

Pérez, Louis. *Cuba between Empires, 1878–1902*. Pittsburgh, PA: University of Pittsburgh Press, 1998.

Pérez de la Riva, Juán. "Introduction." In *Correspondencia reservada del Capitán General Don Miguel Tacón con el gobierno de Madrid, 1834–1836*. La Habana: Consejo Nacional de Cultura, 1963.

Phelan, John L. "Authority and Flexibility in the Spanish Imperial Bureaucracy." *Administrative Science Quarterly* 5, no. 1 (1960): 47–65.

The People and the King: The Comunero Revolution in Colombia. Madison: University of Wisconsin Press, 1978.

Pita Pico, Roger. *El reclutamiento de negros durante las guerras de independencia de Colombia, 1810–1825*. Bogotá: Academia Colombiana de Historia, 2012.

Platt, Tristan. *Estado Boliviano y ayllu andino: Tierra y tributo en el Norte de Potosí*. Lima: Instituto de Estudios Peruanos, 1982.

"Liberalism and Ethnocide." *History Workshop Journal* 17 (1984): 3–18.

Platt, Tristan, Thérèse Bouysse-Cassagne, and Olivia Harris, eds. *Qaraqara-Charka. Mallku, Inka y Rey en la provincia de Charcas (siglos XV–XVII): Historia antropológica de una confederación aymara*. La Paz: Instituto Francés de Estudios Andinos, Plural Editores, University of St Andrews, University of London, IAF, Banco Central de Bolivia, 2007.

Portillo, José María. *Revolución de Nación: Orígenes de la cultura constitucional en España, 1780–1812*. Madrid: Centro de Estudios Políticos y Constitucionales, 2001.

Crisis atlántica: Autonomía e independencia en la crisis de la monarquía hispana. Madrid: Marcial Pons, 2006.

Posada, Eduardo. *La esclavitud en Colombia*. Bogotá: Imprenta Nacional, 1933.

Powers, Karen. *Andean Journeys: Migration, Ethnogenesis, and the State in Colonial Quito*. Albuquerque: University of New Mexico, 1995.

Premo, Bianca. *Children of the Father King: Youth, Authority, and Legal Minority in Colonial Lima*. Chapel Hill: University of North Carolina Press, 2005.

"An Equity against the Law: Slave Rights and Creole Jurisprudence in Spanish America." *Slavery & Abolition* 32, no. 4 (2011): 495–517.

Price, Richard. *Maroon Societies: Rebel Slave Communities in the Americas*. 1973; Baltimore: Johns Hopkins University Press, 1996.

Proctor, Frank T. III. *Damned Notions of Liberty: Slavery, Culture, and Power in Colonial Mexico, 1640–1769*. Albuquerque: University of New Mexico, 2010.

Pybus, Cassandra. *Epic Journeys of Freedom: Runaway Slaves of the American Revolution and Their Global Quest for Liberty*. Boston: Beacon Press, 2006.

Quijada, Mónica. "Las 'dos tradiciones': Soberanía popular e imaginarios compartidos en el mundo hispánico en la época de las grandes revoluciones atlánticas." In *Revolución, Independencia y las nuevas naciones de América*, edited by Jaime Rodríguez, 61–86. Madrid: Fundación MAPFRE Tavera, 2005.

Quintero, Inés, and Ángel Rafael Almarza. "Autoridad militar vs. legalidad constitucional: El debate en torno a la Constitución de Cádiz (Venezuela 1812–1814)." *Revista de Indias* 68, no. 242 (2008): 181–206.

Ramos, Gabriela, and Yanna Yannakakis, eds. *Indigenous Intellectuals: Knowledge, Power, and Colonial Culture in Mexico and the Andes*. Durham, NC: Duke University Press, 2014.

Rappaport, Joanne. *Cumbe Reborn: An Andean Ethnography of History*. Chicago, IL: University of Chicago Press, 1994.

The Politics of Memory: Native Historical Interpretation in the Colombian Andes. 1990; Durham, NC: Duke University Press, 1998.

Restall, Matthew. *Seven Myths of the Spanish Conquest*. Oxford: Oxford University Press, 2004.

ed. *Beyond Black and Red: African-Native Relations in Colonial Latin America*. Albuquerque: University of New Mexico Press, 2005.

The Black Middle: Africans Mayas, and Spaniards in Colonial Yucatan. Stanford, CA: Stanford University Press, 2009.

Restrepo Canal, Carlos. *Leyes de Manumisión*. Bogotá: Imprenta Nacional, 1933.

Rieu-Millan, Marie Laure. *Los diputados americanos en las Cortes de Cádiz*. Madrid: Consejo Superior de Investigaciones Científicas, 1990.

Roca, José Luis. "Las expediciones porteñas y las masas altoperuanas (1811–1814)." *Historia y Cultura* 13 (1988): 111–38.

Rodríguez, Jaime. "Las primeras elecciones constitucionales en el Reino de Quito, 1809–1814 y 1821–1822." *Revista Procesos* 14 (1999): 13–52.

La revolución política durante la época de la independencia: El reino de Quito, 1808–1822. Quito: Universidad Andina Simón Bolívar, Corporación Editora Nacional, 2006.

La independencia de la América española. 1996; México, D.F.: Fondo de Cultura Económica, 2008.

Rodríguez, Pablo. "La manumisión en Popayán, 1800–1850." *Revista de Extensión Cultural* 7/10 (1981): 77–85.

"Aspectos del comercio y la vida de los esclavos: Popayán, 1780–1850." *Boletín de Antropología* 23 (1990): 11–26.

Romero, Mario Diego. *Poblamiento y sociedad en el Pacífico colombiano, siglos XVI al XVIII*. Cali: Universidad del Valle, Editorial Facultad de Humanidades, 1995.

Rosas, Claudia. "El miedo a la revolución: Rumores y temores desatados por la Revolución Francesa en el Perú 1790–1800." In *El miedo en el Perú: Siglos XVI al XX*, edited by Claudia Rosas, 139–68. Lima: Universidad Católica, 2005.

Rueda, Rigoberto. "El 20 de Julio de 1810: Una lectura en clave social." In *El Nuevo Reino de Granada y sus Provincias: Crisis de la Independencia y experiencias republicanas*, edited by Aristides Ramos, Oscar Saldarriaga, and Radamiro Gaviria, 165–87. Bogotá: Editorial Universidad del Rosario, 2009.

Rueda, Rocío. *Zambaje y autonomía: Historia de la gente negra de la provincia de Esmeraldas, siglos XVI–XVIII*. Quito: Ediciones Abya-Yala, 2001.

"Territorio, movilización e identidad étnica: Participación de los esclavizados del norte de Esmeraldas en las guerras de independencia, 1809–1813." In *Indios, negros y mestizos en la independencia*, edited by Heraclio Bonilla, 125–27. Bogotá: Editorial Planeta-Universidad Nacional de Colombia, 2010.

"Rutas, caminos y la apertura de la frontera minera en la costa pacífica esmeraldeña (Ecuador, siglo XVIII)." Unpublished manuscript.

Ruggiero, Kristin. "Not Guilty: Abortion and Infanticide in Nineteenth-Century Argentina." In *Reconstructing Criminality in Latin America*, edited by Carlos A. Aguirre and Robert Buffington, 149–66. Wilmington, DE: Jaguar Books, 2000.

Ruigómez, Carmen. *Una política indigenista de los Habsburgo: El protector de Indios en el Perú*. Madrid: Ediciones de Cultura Hispánica, 1988.

Saether, Steinar. *Identidades e independencia en Santa Marta y Riohacha, 1750–1850*. Bogotá: Instituto Colombiano de Antropología e Historia, 2005.

"Independence and the Redefinition of Indianness around Santa Marta, Colombia, 1750–1850." *Journal of Latin American Studies* 37 (2005): 55–80.

"Estudios recientes sobre raza e independencia en el caribe colombiano (1750–1835)." In *Historias de Raza y Nación en América Latina*, edited by Claudia Leal and Carl H. Langebaek, 381–406. Bogotá: Uniandes, 2010.

Sala i Vila, Nuria. "El levantamiento de los pueblos de Aymaraes en 1818." *Boletín Americanista* 39–40 (1990): 203–26.

Salomon, Frank. *Native Lords of Quito in the Age of the Incas: The Political Economy of North Andean Chiefdoms*. New York: Cambridge University Press, 1986.

Sanders, James. "Belonging to the Great Granadan Family: Partisan Struggle and the Construction of Indigenous Identity and Politics in Southwestern Colombia, 1849–1890." In *Race and Nation in Modern Latin America*, edited by Nancy Appelbaum, Anne McPherson, and Karin Alejandra Rosemblatt, 56–86. Chapel Hill: North Carolina University Press, 2003.

Contentious Republicans: Popular Politics, Race, and Class in Nineteenth-Century Colombia. Durham, NC: Duke University Press, 2004.

Sartorius, David. *Ever Faithful: Race, Loyalty, and the Ends of Empire in Spanish Cuba.* Durham, NC: Duke University Press, 2013.

Schama, Simon. *Rough Crossings: Britain, the Slaves, and the American Revolution.* New York: Harper, 2006.

Schmidt-Nowara, Christopher. "Still Continents (and an Island) with Two Histories?" *Law and History Review* 22, no. 2 (2004): 377–82.

Slavery, Freedom, and Abolition in Latin America and the Atlantic World. Albuquerque: University of New Mexico Press, 2011.

Schultz, Kirsten. *Tropical Versailles: Empire, Monarchy, and the Portuguese Royal Court in Rio de Janeiro, 1808–1821.* New York and London: Routledge, 2001.

Schwartz, Stuart. *Slaves, Peasants, and Rebels: Reconsidering Brazilian Slavery.* Chicago: University of Illinois Press, 1992.

Scott, David. *Conscripts of Modernity: The Tragedy of the Colonial Enlightenment.* Durham, NC: Duke University Press, 2004.

Scott, Julius. "The Common Wind: Currents of Afro-American Communication in the Era of the Haitian Revolution." PhD diss., Duke University, 1986.

Scott, Rebecca. *Slave Emancipation in Cuba: The Transition to Free Labor, 1860–1899.* 1985; Pittsburgh, PA: University of Pittsburgh Press, 2000.

Seijas, Tatiana. *Asian Slaves in Colonial Mexico: From Chinos to Indians.* New York: Cambridge University Press, 2014.

Semprún, José, and Alonso Bullón de Mendoza. *El ejército realista en la independencia Americana.* Madrid: Editorial MAPFRE, 1992.

Serulnikov, Sergio. "Disputed Images of Colonialism: Spanish Rule and Indian Subversion in Northern Potosí, 1777–1780." *Hispanic American Historical Review* 76, no. 2 (1996): 189–226.

Subverting Colonial Authority: Challenges to Spanish Rule in Eighteenth-Century Southern Andes. Durham, NC: Duke University Press, 2003.

"Andean Political Imagination in the Late Eighteenth Century." In *Political Cultures in the Andes, 1750–1950,* edited by Nils Jacobsen and Cristóbal Aljovín de Losada, 257–77. Durham, NC: Duke University Press, 2005.

Revolution in the Andes: The Age of Túpac Amaru. Durham, NC: Duke University Press, 2013.

Sharp, William F. *Slavery on the Spanish Frontier: The Colombian Chocó, 1680–1820.* Norman: University of Oklahoma Press, 1976.

Sheller, Mimi. *Democracy after Slavery: Black Publics and Peasant Radicalism in Haiti and Jamaica.* Gainesville: University of Florida Press, 2001.

Sidbury, James. *Becoming African in America: Race and Nation in the Early Black Atlantic.* New York: Oxford University Press, 2007.

Silva, Renán. *Prensa y Revolución a finales del Siglo XVIII.* Bogotá: Banco de la República, 1988.

Soriano, Cristina. *Tides of Revolution: Information and Politics in Late Colonial Venezuela.* Albuquerque: University of New Mexico Press, forthcoming.

Sosa, Guillermo. *Representación e Independencia, 1810–1816.* Bogotá: Instituto Colombiano de Antropología e Historia, 2006.

Soto, Ángel and León Gómez Rivas. "Los orígenes escolásticos de la independencia Iberoamericana (en el bicentenario de la emancipación 1810–2010)." *Bicentenario. Revista de Chile y América* 4, no. 2 (2005): 115–45.

Soulodre-La France, Renée. "Por el amor!: Child Killing in Colonial Nueva Granada." *Slavery and Abolition* 23, no. 1 (2002): 87–100.

Región e Imperio: El Tolima Grande y las Reformas Borbónicas en el siglo XVIII. Bogotá: Instituto Colombiano de Antropología e Historia, 2004.

"'Los esclavos de su Magestad': Slave Protest and Politics in Late Colonial New Granada." In *Slaves, Subjects, and Subversives: Blacks in Colonial Latin America*, edited by Jane G. Landers and Barry M. Robinson, 175–208. Albuquerque: University of New Mexico Press, 2006.

Soux, Maria Luisa. *El complejo proceso hacia la independencia de Charcas (1808–1826): Guerra, ciudadanía, conflictos locales y participación indígena en Oruro*. La Paz: Instituto Francés de Estudios Andinos, 2010.

Spalding, Karen. *Huarochirí: An Andean Society under Inca and Spanish Rule*. Stanford, CA: Stanford University Press, 1988.

Stern, Steve, ed. *Resistance, Rebellion, and Consciousness in the Andean Peasant World*. Madison: University of Wisconsin Press, 1987.

Peru's Indian Peoples and the Challenge of the Spanish Conquest: Huamanga to 1640. 2nd ed. Madison: University of Wisconsin Press, 1993.

Stoetzer, Carlos. *El pensamiento político en la América española durante el período de la emancipación (1789–1825)*. Madrid: Instituto de Estudios Políticos, 1966.

Las raíces escolásticas de la emancipación en la América española. Madrid: Centro de Estudios Constitucionales, 1982.

Straka, Tomás. *La voz de los vencidos: Ideas del partido realista de Caracas, 1810–1821*. Caracas: Facultad de Humanidades y Educación-Universidad Central de Venezuela, 2000.

Tandeter, Enrique. *Coacción y mercado: La minería de la plata en Perú colonial, 1692–1826*. Buenos Aires: Editorial Sudamericana, 1996.

Tannenbaum, Frank. *Slave and Citizen: The Negro in the Americas*. 1946; New York: Vintage Books, 1963.

Tau Anzoategui, Victor. *Casuismo y Sistema*. Buenos Aires: Instituto de Investigaciones de Historia del Derecho, 1992.

Taylor, William B. *Drinking, Homicide, and Rebellion in Colonial Mexican Villages*. Stanford, CA: Stanford University Press, 1979.

Thibaud, Clément. *Repúblicas en Armas: Los ejércitos Bolivarianos en la guerra de independencia en Colombia y Venezuela*. Bogotá: Planeta, Instituto Francés de Estudios Andinos, 2003.

"De la ficción al mito: Los llaneros de la independencia de Venezuela." In *Mitos politicos en las sociedades andinas: Orígenes, invenciones y ficciones*, edited by Germán Carrera Damas, Carole Leal, Georges Lomné, and Frédéric Martínez, 327–42. Caracas: Instituto Francés de Estudios Andinos, 2006.

Thomson, Sinclair. *We Alone Will Rule: Native Andean Politics in the Age of Insurgency*. Madison: University of Wisconsin Press, 2002.

Thornton, John. "I Am the Subject of the King of Kongo." *Journal of World History* 4, no. 2 (1993): 181–214.

Africa and Africans in the Making of the Atlantic World, 1400–1800. 1992; New York: Cambridge University Press, 1998.

Thurner, Mark. *From Two Republics to One Divided: Contradictions of Post-colonial Nationmaking in Andean Peru*. Durham, NC: Duke University Press, 1997.

Tierney, Brian. *The Idea of Natural Rights: Studies on Natural Rights, Natural Law, and Church Law, 1150–1625*. Atlanta, GA: Emory University Press, 1997.

Tovar, Hermes. *De una chispa se forma una hoguera: Esclavitud, insubordinación y liberación*. Tunja: Nuevas Lecturas en Historia, 1992.

Convocatoria al poder del número: Censos y estadísticas de la Nueva Granada, 1750–1850. Bogotá: Archivo General de la Nación, 1994.

Townsend, Camilla. "'Half My Body Free, the Other Half Enslaved': The Politics of the Slaves of Guayaquil at the End of the Colonial Era." *Colonial Latin American Review* 7, no. 1 (1998): 105–28.

Van Deusen, Nancy. *Global Indios: The Indigenous Struggle for Justice in Sixteenth Century Spain*. Durham, NC: Duke University Press, 2015.

Van Young, Eric. *The Other Rebellion: Popular Violence, Ideology, and Struggle for Independence*. Stanford, CA: Stanford University Press, 2001.

Verdo, Geneviève. *L'indépendance argentine entre cités et nation (1808–1821)*. Paris: Sorbonne, 2006.

Villa-Flores, Javier. *Dangerous Speech: A Social History of Blasphemy in Colonial Mexico*. Tucson: University of Arizona Press, 2006.

Vinson, Ben III. *Bearing Arms for His Majesty: The Free-Colored Militia in Colonial Mexico*. Stanford, CA: Stanford University Press, 2001.

Vinson, Ben III, and Matthew Restall. "Black Soldiers, Native Soldiers: Meanings of Military Service in the Spanish American Colonies." In *Beyond Black and Red: African-Native Relations in Colonial Latin America*, edited by Matthew Restall, 15–52. Albuquerque: University of New Mexico Press, 2005.

Wade, Peter. *Race and Ethnicity in Latin America*. London: Pluto Press, 1997.

Walker, Charles. *Smoldering Ashes: Cuzco and the Creation of Republican Peru, 1780–1840*. Durham, NC: Duke University Press, 1999.

The Tupac Amaru Rebellion. Cambridge, MA: Harvard University Press, 2014.

Weinstein, Barbara. "Erecting and Erasing Boundaries: Can We Combine the 'Indo' and the 'Afro' in Latin American Studies?" *Estudios Interdisciplinarios de América Latina y el Caribe* 19, no. 1 (2008), www1.tau.ac.il/eial/index .php?option=com_content&task=view&id=240&Itemid=162.

West, Robert. *Colonial Placer Mining in Colombia*. Baton Rouge: Louisiana State University Press, 1952.

Wheat, David. "The Afro-Portuguese Maritime World and the Foundations of Spanish-Caribbean Society, 1570–1640." PhD diss., Vanderbilt University, 2009.

Williams, Caroline. *Between Resistance and Adaptation: Indigenous Peoples and the Colonisation of the Chocó, 1510–1753*. Liverpool: Liverpool University Press, 2004.

Williams, Derek. "Acomodación, negociación y el actuar político: Resistencia y revuelta indígena en el altiplano de los Pastos." MA thesis, Universidad del Valle, 1994.

"'Who Induced the Indian Communities?': The Los Pastos Uprising and the Politic of Ethnicity and Gender in Late-Colonial New Granada." *Colonial Latin American Historical Review* 10, no. 3 (2001): 277–309.

Wilson, Fiona. "Reconfiguring the Indian: Land–Labour Relations in the Post-colonial Andes." *Journal of Latin American Studies* 35 (2003): 221–47.

Yannakakis, Yanna. *The Art of Being In-between: Native Intermediaries, Indian Identity, and Local Rule in Colonial Oaxaca*. Durham, NC: Duke University Press, 2008.

"*Costumbre*: A Language of Negotiation in Eighteenth-Century Oaxaca." In *Negotiation within Domination: Colonial New Spain's Indian Pueblos Confront the Spanish State*, edited by Ethelia Ruiz Medrano and Susan Kellogg, 137–72. Boulder: University Press of Colorado, 2011.

Zahler, Reuben. *Ambitious Rebels: Remaking Honor, Law, and Liberalism in Venezuela, 1780–1850*. Tucson: The University of Arizona Press, 2013.

Zarama, Rosa Isabel. "Consolidación de Túquerres al final del periodo colonial, 1750–1810." In *Historia socio espacial de Túquerres, siglos XVI–XX: De Barbacoas hacia el horizonte nacional*, edited by Behur Cerón and Rosa Isabel Zarama, 141–56. Pasto: Universidad de Nariño, 2003.

Zawadzky, Alfonso. *Las ciudades confederadas del Valle del Cauca en 1811: Historia, actas, documentos*. Cali: Imprenta Bolivariana, 1943.

Clero insurgente y clero realista: Estudio de los Informes Secretos del Obispo de Popayán doctor Salvador Jiménez al Rey de España sobre la actuación de Saterdotes de su Diócesis durante la Guerra de Independencia. Cali: Imprenta Bolivariana, 1948.

Zuluaga, Francisco. *Guerrilla y sociedad en el Patía: Una relación entre el clientelismo político y la insurgencia social*. Cali: Universidad del Valle, 1993.

"La independencia en la gobernación de Popayán." In *Historia del Gran Cauca: Historia Regional del Suroccidente Colombiano*, 91–98. Cali: Universidad del Valle, 1996.

Index

Abad chiefdom, 24
Abascal y Sousa, José Fernando de, 43–44,
  136
  Tacón alliance with, 46–48
African slaves
  communities of, 120–22
  ethnic origins of, 28–29
  legal definition of, 21
  mining and, 29, 102–4
  Popayán Province, 27
Afro-descendants
  in Colombian wars of independence, 188
  communities of, 120–22
  in contemporary Colombia, 236–37
  indigenous people and, 20–21
  in Mexico, 20–21
  military duty for, 151
  in New Granada, 20–21
  in Popayán Province, 20–21, 32, 101
  in Spanish Caribbean, 231–32
  in Viceroyalty of Peru, 20–21
Age of Revolution, 6
  freedom for slaves during, 186–90
  Latin America during, literature on, 5–7
  rights for slaves during, 186–90
  royalism during, 9
  slaves as loyal to monarchy during,
    186–90
Agualongo, Agustín, 194, 196, 199–203
  liberation of Pasto and, 201, 209–11, 217
  mestizo background of, 201–2
aguardiente (cane liquor), reform policies
  for, 66–70

Alfonso X, 97–98
Andean chiefdoms. See cacicazgo
Andes region, indigenous intellectuals in, 87
Angulo, Francisco "El negro," 209, 218
Angulo, Gregorio, 124, 128–30, 135
Anticolonialism
  in Kingdom of Quito, 11–12
  in New Granada, 11–12
  in Viceroyalty of Peru, 11–12
Antioquia Province, slave conspiracy in,
  19–20
anti-Republican royalism, in Colombia,
  203–6
Aponte Rebellion, 173
Arrubla, Gerardo, 201
Asian (chino) slaves, freedom modeled by,
  20
Asmasa, Salvador, 70
audiencias (royal judicial courts), 33–34
  creation in Santa Fe and Quito, 23
  in Quito, 92–93, 145–46
  response to Túquerres Indian revolt,
    86–87
Aymerich, Melchor, 193

Balboa, Vasco Nuñez de, 27
Barbacoas
  cabildo, 165
  infanticides in, 119–20
  justice for slaves in, 106–13
  loyalty to Tacón in, 165
  Quito's expansionism and, 41–42
Baron de Carondelet, 41

Battle of Boyacá, 191–92
Battle of Pichincha, 194
the beloved. *See el deseado*
Benavides, Juan, 216, 218–19
Blanchard, Peter, 174, 230
Boasé mine, 92–93
Bolívar, Simón, 8, 156
    abolition of slavery under, 229
    Battle of Boyacá and, 191–92
    Bolivarian Army, 8–9
    end of royalism in New Granada and,
        194–96
    independence movements and, 58–59
    integration of slaves into liberation forces,
        229–31
    liberation of Pasto and, 206–17
    negotiations with Creole royalists, 199
    in New Granada, 59, 191–94
    in Popayán Province, 2
    as president of Colombia, 224
    Quito and, 196–99, 206–17
    royalist rebellions and, 194, 199–203
    slavery and, 54, 229
Bolivarian Army, 8–9
    including large numbers of blacks, 59
Bomboná, battle of, 215
Botina, Francisco, 149
Botina, Jesús, 149
Bourbon monarchy
    centralization of government under,
        15–16
    Comunero Rebellion against, 19–20, 37
    in Pasto, 72–73
    Pastusos and, 61
    Quito under, 41–43
    reforms, 34–38
    royalism and, 3, 15–16
    royalists and, 3, 15–16
Boves, Benito, 194, 196
Boves, José Tomás, 58–59, 164, 196–99,
        203

cabildo (municipal council), 26–27
    in Pasto, 137–38
    in Popayán Province, 159
cacicazgo (Andean chiefdoms), 138, 205
caciques (native authorities), 71–75, 77–78
    hierarchy vis-à-vis commoners and
        community structures, 72
    in Pasto, 130–32
    tribute collection by, 130–33

during Túquerres Indian revolt, 77–78
Cádiz region, 8–9. *See also* Constitution of
    Cádiz
Calama, Pérez, 41
Caldas, Francisco José de, 57
Caldas, José Ilario, 166
Caldas, Rafael, 167
Caldas, Salvador, 167
Cali, city of, 23–54
    alliance with Quito junta, 47
    enslaved workers in haciendas, 27
    exclusion of blacks from insurgent forces,
        60, 175–76
    independence partisans in, 46
    mine- and slave-owning families from, 30
    opposition to royalists in, 158–62
    Pacific lowlands colonization and, 27,
        30–31
    Popayán and, 30–31
    priests and independence project in, 222
    rejection of Tacón, 46, 48, 159
    royalist slaves in mines and, 176–77
    slaves against insurgents in, 161
Calzada, Sebastián de la, 193
Calzón, José, 209, 216
Canchala, José, 209
Cañeque, Alejandro, 33
Captain (enslaved)
    claiming right to freedom, 187
    conflicts with, 120–21
    controlling slaves during battle, 228
    knowledge of Spanish, 103
    leadership roles, 15–16, 103
    as legal representative of the *cuadrilla*,
        120–21, 161
    mastery of law, 15–16
    as recipient of news and legislation, 162
Carlosama, Julián, 62–63, 76, 85
Carrasco, Miguel, 125–26
Carrera Damas, Germán, 164
Cartagena
    Bourbon military reform in, 35–36
    confederations sought with, 46
    first independence project and ideals of
        racial equality, 52–53
    free blacks in, 52–53, 232
    links with Quito and Popayán, 29
    Pablo Morillo's pacification of, 56–57
    Pétion's support to proindependence
        families from, 58
    port of, 23

Quito's junta ambitions to expand into,
41–43
relocation of Audiencia to, 56–57
republicanism and race in, 231–32
slave imports through, 28
Cauca River, 23
Cauca Valley, 161–64, 228
Charcas, Kingdom of, 41–43
Charles III (King), 10
Charles IV (King), 98
Chaves, Nicolás, 198
Chocó
frontier expansion, 30–31
merchants in the region bringing news, 170
native resistance, 24
Cieza de León, Pedro, 25
citizenship
under Constitution of Cádiz, 51–52
exclusion of people of African descent
from, 52
for free blacks who could prove merit, 59
for Indians, under Constitution of Cádiz,
51–52
Indians' particular definition of, 226
for indigenous people, under Constitution
of Cádiz, 51–52
in New Granada, 49–55
royalists Indians and slaves and ideas of, 8
vecindad and, 51
welcomed by Indians in Santa Marta, 227
Clavijo, Atanacio R., 62–64, 85
changes in tithe collection, 63
Clavijo, Francisco R., 62–64, 85
appointment of *caciques*, 74
conflicts with, 73–74
as *corregidor*, 73–75, 78–80
dispossession of Indian lands and, 74–75
Indian complaints against, 80
Colombia. *See also* Popayán Province
abolition of slavery in, 229
Afro-descendants in, 236–37
Antirepublican royalism in, 203–6
Bolívar presidency in, 224
Cartagena, 231–32
development as republican state, 224–37
Guayaquil Province in, 192–93
nationalist myths in, 2
1991 multicultural constitution, 236–37
pardo politics in, 188
preconceived national territorial frame,
11–12, 235

royalism in, 3–6
royalist rebellion in, 194, 199–203
royalists in, 3–6, 191–94
social transformation in, after end of
Spanish rule, 224–37
War of the Supremes in, 231
wars for independence in, 188
colonialism
justifications for, 78
as slavery, 227–29
communal gathering. *See minga*
communities
of Africans, as result of slavery, 120–22
cuadrillas as, 102–3, 115–16, 120–21
of Indians, in Popayán province, 31–32,
37
palenque, 104–5
community lands. *See resguardos*
Comunero Rebellion, 19–20, 37, 65
Consejo de Guerra Permanente (Permanent
Court-Martial), 57
Constitution of Bayonne, 49
Constitution of Cádiz, 48, 50–53
citizenship under, 51–52
constitutional debates, American
representation in, 40
Indians under, 51–52
indigenous people under, 51–52
in Pasto, 155–56
in Quito, 155–56
restoration of, 192
slavery under, 52–53
constitutions
in New Granada, 49–55
treatment of slaves under, 52–54
Corral, Juan del, 54, 228–29
corregidor (Spanish magistrate), 70–75
Clavijo, Francisco R., as, 73–75
during Túquerres Indian revolt, 78–80,
82–83
corregimientos (political units administered
by a *corregidor*), 26–27
Cortés, Casimiro, 93–97, 114
Cortés, Marcos, 92, 107–9, 114–16
Cortes authority, 39–40, 158
Costa Firme Expeditionary Army, 56
Creole juntas, 169–70
ambitions, 40
in Quito and Charcas, 41
Quito's second junta, 47
Creole nationalism, 2–3

Creole royalists, 43–44
  Bolívar's negotiations with, 199
  Indians and, 199
  in Popayán Province, 158
Creoles, in Popayán Province, 31, 35–36
  nationalism of, 2–3
Cruz, Gerónimo, 76
cuadrillas (slave gangs), 102–3
  captains of, 15–16, 103
  as community, 120–21
  excessive cruelty toward, 115–16
  legal defense in Barbacoas, 116–17
  political structure and dynamics, 116
Cuba, Aponte Rebellion in, 173
Cundinamarca, Kingdom of, 49

de la Cruz, Mónica, 107
"el deseado" (the beloved), 9
Dias, Pablo, 63, 66, 74–75, 84–85, 87–88
Diaz, Leandro, 75
Domínguez, Pedro, 180
Dubois, Laurent, 93–94, 159
Dueñas, Alcira, 87

Earle, Rebecca, 66, 151
Ecuador, royalists and royalism in, 4–5
1800 rebellion. *See* Túquerres, Indian revolt in
encomenderos (Spaniards who were
    assigned native settlements and who
    had rights to their labor and tribute),
    26–27
Enríquez, Joaquín, 217
Erazo, Bernardo, 63–64
Espinoza Ibarra, Antonio, 125

Fernando VI (King), 10
Fernando VII (King), 8–9, 21–22, 38,
    56–57, 125, 139
  Costa Firme Expeditionary Army and, 56
  Junta Central and, 41–43
  reinstatement of tribute collection by, 153
  restoration of royal absolutism, 147
Ferrer, Ada, 228
Ferrín, Manuel, 93
Fisher, Andrew, 31
Flores, Juan José, 198, 208–9, 216
forasteros, 138
France, 38–43. *See also* Napoleonic
    invasion
free blacks, 20
  in Cartagena, 232
  militancy of, 232

in Popayán Province, 233
  royalism among, 233
freedom, for slaves
  during Age of Revolution, 186–90
  for Asian slaves, 20
  black queen and, rumors of, 170–73
  legalization of, by slaves, 175–83
  manumission as reward for loyalty, 183
  for slave mineworkers, 183–86
  in Spanish Empire, 13–14
French Revolution, 124

Gallardo, Juan Díaz, 135, 139–43
  removal as *protector partidario*, 147–49
García, Basilio, 193, 219
García, Juan, 27
Getial, Manuel, 73–75
gold production, in Popayán Province,
    29–31
Gómez, Domingo, 109
González del Palacio, Miguel, 68–69
Guadeloupe, slave revolt on, 160
Guáitara River, 128
  execution of prisoners in, 207–8
  military confrontations along, 128
Guayaquil Province, in Colombia, 192–93
"La Guerra de los Conventos," 221
Guinulté mine, 92–93
Gutiérrez, Daniel, 43
Gutiérrez de Piñeres, Francisco, 35

Haitian Revolution, 172–73
Henao, Jesús María, 201
Herrera, Marta, 93
Historia de la Revolución de Colombia
    (Restrepo), 2–3, 164, 200–1
Hurtado, Damasco, 166
Hurtado, Dionicio, 167
Hurtado, Francisco, 167
Hurtado, Marcelino, 166
Hurtado, Maria Josefa, 166–67
Hurtado, Mauricio, 167–68
Hurtado, Roque María, 167

identity, for Indians, 87–91
independence wars. *See also* War of
    Independence
  Bolívar and, 58–59
  Indians during, 59–61
  indigenous people during, 59–61
  in Latin America, 10
  slaves mobilized during, 59–61, 157–58

Indian revolts. *See also* Túquerres, Indian
   revolt in
  in New Granada, 64–66
  in Quito, 64–66
Indianness
  in New Granada, 89
  in Pasto, 87–91
  royalism and, 152
Indians. *See also* indigenous people; tribute
   collection; Túquerres, Indian revolt in
  abusive conduct toward, 79
  aguardiente reform and, 66–70
  attack on Los Pastos, 125–27
  caciques and, 71–75
  citizenship for, under Constitution of
   Cádiz, 51–52
  in Colombian wars of independence,
   188
  under colonialism, justifications for, 78
  commoners in the royalist army seeking
   tribute reduction, 60–61
  complaints against Clavijo brothers, 80
  Creole elites and, 199
  elites among, 87
  during formation of republican states,
   after independence, 226–27
  as homogeneous group, 66
  identity for, 87–91
  during independence wars, 59–61
  labor service for, 139–43
  legal definition of, 21
  legal rights of, 65–66, 86–87
  local politics and, 66–70
  loyalty toward Spanish monarchy,
   82–85
  military duty for, 139–43, 150–56
  in New Granada, revolts by, 64–66
  in Pasto, as royalists, 151–54
  politicization of, in Pasto, 132–33
  in Popayán Province, 31–32, 37
  population by region, 25–26
  protector partidario de naturales for,
   134–39
  in Quito, revolts by, 64–66
  under *Recopilación de las leyes de Indias*,
   63–64
  recruited as soldiers, 126–27
  revolts by, 64–66
  royalism among, 131, 150
  self-government by, 70–75
  tithing requirements for, 62–64
  tribute collection, 72–73

indigenous people
  Afro-descendants and, 20–21
  in Andes region, 87
  citizenship for, under Constitution of
   Cádiz, 51–52
  defense of territorial interests by, 214
  forasteros and, 138
  during independence wars, 59–61
  intellectuals among, 87
  in Pasto, 2, 7–8, 24
  Pastusos, 61
  in Popayán Province, 7
  royalism for, 16
  Spanish liberalism and, impact of,
   155–56
infanticides
  in Barbacoas, 119–20
  defined, 92
  economic impact of, 93
  in Popayán Province, 92–93
  as religious practice, 111
  by slaves, 107–13, 119–20
  by women, 112
Instrucción sobre la educación, trato y
   ocupaciones de los esclavos, 93–94,
   98–99, 117–20
Insuaste, Manuel, 217
Iscuandé community, 206
  battle of, 168

Jasanoff, Maya, 6–7
Jiménez, Salvador, 193–94
Johnson, Walter, 95–96
Juan, Jorge, 73
Juanambú River
  during Agualongo rebellion, 196–97
  royalist Indian towns around, 133
Junta Central authority, 39–43
  in Popayán Province, 158
  in Quito, 42–43

Kingdom of Charcas. *See* Charcas, Kingdom
  of
Kingdom of Cundinamarca. *See*
  Cundinamarca, Kingdom of
Kingdom of Quito. *See* Quito, Kingdom
  of

La Paz, 41–43
Landázuri, Mariano, 108–9
Landázuri y Eraso, Josef, 76
Landers, Jane, 6–7

Lasso, Marixa, 188, 232
Latin America
  during Age of Revolution, literature on,
    5–7
  independence wars in, 10
  liberalism in, 9–10
law. *See* legal regimes
Laws of the Indies, 97–98
legal regimes
  slaves' knowledge of, 13
  in Spanish Empire, 12
legal rights
  of Indians, 65–66, 86–87
  for slaves, 34, 113–14
liberalism, Spanish
  indigenous people and, impact on,
    155–56
  in Latin America, 9–10
  royalism and, 155–56, 235
López, José Hilario, 200, 231
López, Tomas, 72–73
Lozano, Jorge Tadeo, 57
Lynch, John, 230

manumission, royalist slaves' request for,
  183
maroon community. *See palenque*
Márquez, José Ignacio, 221
Martínez, Maria Elena, 21
Martínez de Segovia, Francisco, 77, 83–84,
  135
Mazo, María, 107
Medina, Ramón, 143–50, 197
Meiklejohn, Norman, 94–95
Mendinueta, Pedro de, 76
Mera, Gerardo, 83
Merced, María, 107
Merchancano, Estanislao, 196–97, 203
  liberation of Pasto and, 209–11
Messía de la Cerda, Pedro, 67
Mexico
  Afro-descendants in, 20–21
  protector partidario de naturales in,
    144–50
military duty
  for Afro-descendants, 151
  for Indians, 139–43, 150–56
  protector partidario de naturales and,
    139–43
military reform, for Spanish army, 35–36
mines, slaves in, 93–94

in Barbacoas, 106–13
Boasé mine, 92–93
cuadrillas, 102–3, 115–16, 120–21
freedom for, 183–86
Guinulté mine, 92–93
in Popayán Province, 92–94, 102–3,
  106–13, 169–75
San Juan mine, 169–75, 186–90
Teranguará mine, 92–93
minga (communal gathering), 142
  War of a Thousand Days and, 142
Molina, Joaquín, 47
monarchical crisis, 21–22, 53–54
  changes in community representation by
    caciques, 145
  Napoleonic Invasion and, 1
  opportunity for the enslaved during, 157
Montalvo, Francisco de, 56–57
Montes, Toribio, 47–48, 137, 155–56
Montúfar, Carlos, 47, 133–34
Montúfar, Juan Pio, 123
Morillo, Pablo, 56–58, 60–61, 139, 148,
  192
Mosquera, Felipe, 166–67
Mosquera, José Rafael, 228
Mosquera, Mariano, 228
Mosquera, Tomás Cipriano de, 202–3, 217
Múnera, Alfonso, 188
municipal council. *See cabildo*

naïve monarchism, 189
Nanny (slave), as black queen, 170–73
Napoleon, Joseph, 38
Napoleonic invasion
  news about and fear of, 124
  Quito during, 41–43, 123–27
  of Spain, 39–43
  Spanish monarchical crisis and, 1
Nariño, Antonio, 54
nationalist myths, in Colombia, 2
  royalists and royalism as part of, 3–6
native authority. *See caciques*
Naya community, revolt, 206
New Granada, Viceroyalty of. *See also*
    Colombia; Popayán Province
  abolishment of, 50–51
  Afro-descendants in, 20–21
  aguardiente reform in, 66–70
  anticolonial movements in, 11–12
  Bolívar in, 59, 191–94
  citizenship in, after 1810, 49–55

Comunero Rebellion in, 19–20, 37, 65
Consejo de Guerra Permanente in, 57
constitutional debates in, 40
constitutions in, after 1810, 49–55
Indian revolts in, 64–66
Indianness in, 89
justice for Indians in, 86–87
population in, 25–26
reform movements in, 34–38
response to French Revolution, 124
restoration of Spanish monarchy in,
    56–61
royalism in, 46–47, 194–96
slavery in, 94–95
sovereignty of Spanish monarchy in,
    39–43
Nieto, Diego Antonio, 63, 100
cacique appointments in Yascual and
    Túquerres and, 73–74
investigation of Túquerres revolt and,
    75–76, 85
Northern Andes region. *See* New Granada;
    Popayán Province

Obando, Antonio, 196–97
Obando, José María, 217, 221, 231
O'Hara, Matthew, 31
Olano, Nuflo de, 27–29
Olave, Vicente, 211–12
Olaya, Manuel, 163–64
Ordóñez de Lara, Ramón, 62
originarios, 138
O'Toole, Rachel, 21

Pacific Lowlands region, population of,
    25–26
Pacific royalist block, 11–12, 137, 222–23,
    234
attempts to reestablish, 206
as condition for continuation of royal
    power across Peru and Popayán,
    235–36
as context for royalist alliances in
    Popayán, 234
fractured in 1820, 192–93
in Peru, Quito, and Popayán, 191–92
rivals, Quito and Santa Fe, 46
pacts. *See* political pacts
Padilla, José, 54–55
palenque (maroon community), 104–5
pardo politics, 188

Pasto, City of
Agualongo and, 201, 209–11, 217
aguardiente reform in, 68
antirepublican royalism in, 203–6
Bolívar and, 196–99, 206–17
Bourbon reforms in, 72–73
cabildo in, 137–38
caciques in, 71–75
chiefdom societies in, 25
Constitution of Cádiz in, 155–56
district governed by the city, 25
"La Guerra de los Conventos" and, 221
Indian royalists in, 151–54
indigenous people in, 2, 7–8, 24
liberation of, 201, 206–22
Merchancano in, 209–11
politicization of Indians in, 132–33
politics of Indianness in, 87–91
population in, 25–26
protector partidario de naturales in,
    134–39, 144–50, 154
rebel royalists in, 196–99
Spanish liberalism in, 155–56
Spanish rule in, 1–2, 25–26
tribute collection in, 72–73
Los Pastos, 72–73
Angulo and, 124, 128–30
estanquillos destruction in, 75–76
Indian attack on, 125–27
Indian mobilization during Aqualongo
    rebellion, 203, 209
Indian royalists in, 133–34
Indian tribute collection in, 127–34
links with Barbacoas, 209
mobilized by priest Benavides, 218
royalist guerillas in, 215–16
search for autonomy from the city of
    Pasto, 134
tribute collection in, 72–73
Pastusos, 61
Bolívar's proclamations to, 215
faithful, 204
as ignorant and fanatics, 200–1
as liberators, 211
military goals of, 214
punishment for treason and
    rebelliousness, 207, 214–15
reaction to terms of capitulation with
    Bolívar, 193–94
Patía River Valley, 101
during Agualongo rebellion, 203, 218

Patía River Valley (cont.)
  runaways in "El Castigo," 104–5,
    115–16
Patianos, 202
  as allies of Pasto elites, 198
  Bolívar's proclamations to, 215
  in capitulation, 193
  lampoon to mobilize, 219
  relations with Indians, 212–18
Paz, Joaquín, 211–12
Paz, Melchor, 84
Peredo, Josef Ignacio, 68, 86
Pérez, Benito, 168
Permanent Court-Martial. *See Consejo de
  Guerra Permanente*
Peru, Viceroyalty of
  Afro-descendants in, 20–21
  Creole royalists in, 43–44
  Pacific Royalist Block and, 11–12
  protector partidario de naturales in,
    144–50
  royalism in, 4–5
  royalists in, 4–5, 43–48
  Túpac Amaru rebellion in, 64–65
Pétion, Alexandre, 58–59, 228–29
Philip V (King), 10
Pianda, Andrés, 149, 209
Piar, Manuel, 54–55
Pirio, Marcelino, 107–8
Piscal, Lorenzo, 63, 85
political pacts, within Spanish Empire,
  14–15
Popayán Province. *See also* Pasto, City of;
  Los Pastos
  Abad chiefdom in, 24
  African slaves in, 27
  Afro-descendants in, 20–21, 32, 101
  alliance with French, 123–27
  audiencias in, 33–34
  Bolívar in, 2
  Bolivarian Army in, 8–9
  cabildo in, 26–27, 159, 165
  Cauca Valley, 161–64
  Cortes authority in, 158
  Creole royalists in, 158
  Creoles in, 31, 35–36
  elites in, 26–27
  free blacks in, 233
  freedom for slaves in, 100–6, 161–63
  gold production in, 29
  historical development of, 22–34

imperial subjecthood in, 31
Indian communities in, 31–32, 37
Indians as royalists in, 222–23
indigenous peoples in, 7
infanticides in, 92–93
judicial authority in, 33–34
Junta Central in, 158
political authority in, 33–34
population in, 25–26
Quillacinga chiefdom in, 24
reformist movements in, 10–11
Regency authority in, 158
rejection of Spanish monarchy in, 1, 23–26
revolutionary movements in, 10–11
royalism in, 3–6
royalist alliances in, 3–6, 46–48
slave economy in, 27–29, 53–54, 101–2
slaves as mineworkers in, 92–94, 102–3,
  106–13, 169–75
slaves as royalists in, 60–61, 157–69,
  222–23
slaves in, 27–29, 53–54, 60–61, 93–97,
  100–6, 157–58
Spanish arrival in, 23–26
spatial methodological strategy for, 11–12
sub-regions in, 30
populations, 25–26
Proctor, Frank, 96
protector partidario de naturales, 134–39
  conflict between, 153
  Gallardo as, 135, 139–43, 147–49
  historical development of, 144–50
  Medina as, 143–50
  military duty for Indians and, 139–43
  in Pasto, 134–39, 144–50, 154
  politicization of position, 143–50
protests. *See* rebellions

Quillacinga chiefdom, 24
Quito, Kingdom of
  aguardiente reform in, 66–70
  alliance with French invaders, 123–27
  anticolonialism in, 11–12
  audiencias in, 92–93, 145–46
  Bolívar and, 196–99, 206–17
  under Bourbon monarchy, 41–43
  Constitution of Cádiz in, 155–56
  forasteros and, 138
  independence proclamation from Spain,
    133–34
  Indian revolts in, 64–66

Junta Central authority in, 42–43
during Napoleonic invasion, 41–43, 123–27
protector partidario de naturales in, 144–50
Regency authority in, 47
response to French Revolution, 124

Ramírez, Marcelo, 63
Real Cédula, 98
Rebellion of *Los Barrios*, 67
rebellions. *See also* Indian revolts; slave
    resistance; slave revolts; Túquerres,
    Indian revolt in
    aguardiente reform as cause of, 66–70
    in Antioquia Province, 19–20, 37
    Aponte Rebellion, 173
    in Colombia, 194, 199–203
    Comunero Rebellion, 19–20, 37, 65
    Haitian Revolution, 172–73
    by Indians, 62–66
    in Pasto, by slaves, 2
    slave-led, 95, 160
    Túpac Amaru rebellion, 64–65, 132–33
Recopilación de las leyes de Indias, 63–64,
    97–98
reforms
    historiographic interpretations of, 36
    in Popayán province, 10–11
    within Spanish Empire, 34–38
    in Spanish military, 35–36
Regency authority, 39–40
    in Quito, 47
Remo, Ramón Cucas, 63, 85
republican states, formation of
    antirepublican royalism and, 203–6
    Cartagena and, race as factor in, 231–32
    Colombia as, 224–37
    Indians during, 226–27
    smallholder republicanism, 226
resguardos (community lands), 37
Restall, Matthew, 151
Restrepo, José Manuel, 2–3, 164, 196,
    200–1, 218–19
revolutions
    Haitian Revolution, 172–73
    in Popayán Province, 10–11
Reyes, Pablo, 83
rights
    for slaves, during Age of Revolution,
        186–90
    in Spanish Empire, 13–14
Río de la Plata, Viceroyalty of, 41–43

Riofrio, José, 125
Rodríguez, Pablo, 101–2
Rosero, Aurelio, 198
Roxas, Juan de, 86
royal judicial courts. *See audiencias*
royalism
    during Age of Revolution, 9
    Bourbon context for, 3, 15–16
    in Colombia, 3–6, 203–6
    defined, 5–6
    in Ecuador, 4–5
    among free blacks, 233
    Indian tributes and, 127–34
    Indianness and, 152
    among Indians, 131, 150
    for indigenous people, 16
    in nationalist myths, 3–6
    in New Granada, 46–47, 194–96
    among Pasto Indians, 205
    in Peru, 4–5
    political context of, during nineteenth
        century, 9
    for slaves, 16
    as socially embedded, 12
    Spanish liberalism and, 155–56,
        235
    in Venezuela, 4–5
royalists
    Bourbon context for, 3, 15–16
    in Cali, opposition movements against,
        158–62
    in Colombia, 3–6, 191–94
    Creole, 43–44, 158, 164–65, 199
    Creole juntas, 169–70
    defined, 5–6
    in Ecuador, 4–5
    Indians as, in Popayán Province, 222–23
    in nationalist myths, 3–6
    in Pasto, Indians as, 151–54
    in Los Pastos, 133–34
    in Peru, 4–5, 43–48
    political context of, during nineteenth
        century, 9
    in Popayán province, 3–6, 46–48
    slaves as, in Popayán province, 60–61,
        157–69, 222–23
    slaves as, under Tacón, 53–54,
        157–58
    in Venezuela, 4–5
Ruggiero, Kristin, 112
Ruiz, Miguel, 27

Saether, Steinar, 226–27
Saija community, 206
Saint-Domingue, slaves in, 172–73
Salom, Bartolomé, 195
Salvador, Bernardo, 93, 120
Salvador, Manuel, 93, 115–16, 120
Sámano, Juan, 48
San Juan mine, 169–75
  freedom for slaves in, 186–90
San Martín, José de, 8, 191–92
Sánchez, José Joaquín, 178–79
Sanclemente, José Joaquín, 183
Sanders, James, 226–27
Santa Cruz, Tomás Miguel, 135–36,
  211–12
Santa Fe, Manuel, 114–15
Santa Marta, 131, 139
Santacruz, Tomás Miguel, 198
Sarasti, Cayetano, 166–67
Sarasti, Francisco, 133–34
Sarasti, Victorino, 166
Sartorius, David, 6–7
Seijas, Tatiana, 20
Selva Alegre, Marqués de, 123
Séptimo, Fernando, 139
Serulnikov, Sergio, 65, 81
Las Siete Partidas, 97–98
slave gangs. *See cuadrillas*
slave owners
  *Instrucción sobre la educación, trato y
    ocupaciones de los esclavos*, 117–20
  slaves mobilized against, by Spanish
    monarchy, 1–2
slave patrol. *See zambos*
slave resistance, 95–96
slave revolts
  Aponte Rebellion, 173
  in Cauca Valley, 228
  on Guadeloupe, 160
  Haitian Revolution, 172–73
  justification by slaves for, 174
  in the Pacific Lowlands, 2
  royalist revolts compared to, 173
  in San Juan mine, 169–75, 186–90
  in Spanish Caribbean, 160
slave trade
  abolition of, 52–55
  under Constitution of Cádiz, 52–53
  European domination of, 28
slavery
  abolition of, under Bolívar, 229

in Antioquia Province, 19–20
colonialism as, 227–29
communities of Africans as result of,
  120–22
under Constitution of Cádiz, 52–53
humane legislation of, 94–95
during independence wars, 59–61,
  157–58
*Instrucción sobre la educación, trato y
  ocupaciones de los esclavos*, 93–94,
  98–99
laws of, 97–100
mediated by authority of king, 120–22
in New Granada, 94–95
in Pasto, 2
in Popayán Province, 27–29, 53–54,
  60–61, 101–2
under *Real Cédula*, 98
in Spanish Caribbean, 97–100
under Tacón, 53–54, 157–58
throughout Spanish Empire, 27–29
slavery laws
  Code Noir, 99
  in favor of servitude, 113–20
  *Instrucción sobre la educación, trato y
    ocupaciones de los esclavos*, 93–94,
    98–99
  Real Cédula, 98
  in Spanish Caribbean, 97–100
slaves. *See also* African slaves
  in Antioquia Province, 19–20
  Asian, 20
  in Barbacoas, 106–13
  black queen and, rumors among,
    170–73
  in Boasé mine, 92–93
  Bolívar and, 54
  in Bolívar army, 54
  Creole royalists and, 164–65
  cuadrillas, 102–3, 115–16, 120–21
  excessive cruelty towards, by Cortés, M.,
    115–16
  excessive cruelty towards, in Popayán
    Province, 93–97
  freedom for, in Popayán province, 100–6,
    161–63
  freedom for, under Tacón, 161–63
  freedom through self-purchase, 96,
    103–4
  in Guinulté mine, 92–93
  infanticides by, 107–13, 119–20

Instrucción sobre la educación, trato y ocupaciones de los esclavos, 93–94, 98–99
integration into liberation forces, by Bolívar, 229–31
intellectual history of, 93–94
knowledge of law, 13
law in favor of servitude and, 113–20
legal identity for, 93–94
legal rights for, 34, 113–14
legalization of freedom for, 175–83
manumission of, 183
meetings in juntas, 169
as mineworkers, 92–94, 102–3, 106–13, 115–16, 120–21, 169–75
mobilization against slave owners, by Spanish monarchy, 1–2
mobilization of, during independence wars, 59–61, 157–58
mobilization of, under Tacón, 157
in Pasto, 2
political culture for, 93–94
political identity for, 93–94
political radicalization of, 55
in Popayán Province, 27–29, 53–54, 60–61, 93–97, 100–6, 157–58
under *Real Cédula*, 98
rebellions by, 95
as royalists, 60–61, 157–69, 222–23
in Saint-Domingue, 172–73
in San Juan mine, 169–75, 186–90
in Spanish Caribbean, 97–100
in Spanish Empire, 27–29
strategy of war used by, on Pacific coast, 217
in Teranguará mine, 92–93
smallholder republicanism, 226
Spain. *See also* Spanish Empire; Spanish monarchy
Napoleonic invasion of, 39–43
War of Independence for, 38–43
Spanish Caribbean
Afro-descendants in, 231–32
Real Cédula, 98
response to French Revolution in, 124
rumors of black queen in, 170–73
Saint-Domingue, 172–73
slave revolts in, 160
slavery laws in, 97–100
Spanish Empire. *See also* New Granada
Cortes authority in, 39–40

gold production for, 29–31
Junta Central authority in, 39–43
legal regimes in, 12
military reform in, 35–36
mobilization of slaves against slave owners, 1–2
in Pasto, 1–2, 25–26
political pacts within, 14–15
in Popayán Province, 23–26
Recopilación de las leyes de Indias in, 63–64
reform movements within, 34–38
Regency authority in, 39–40, 47
rights and freedoms in, 13–14
slave economy as part of, 27–29
sovereignty of Spanish monarchy throughout, 39–43
War of Independence and, 38–43
Spanish magistrate. *See corregidor*
Spanish monarchy. *See also* Bourbon monarchy
during Age of Revolution, loyalty of slaves to, 186–90
crisis of sovereignty for, 1–18
destabilization of, 21–22
Indians' loyalty toward, 82–85
in Popayán Province, rejection of, 1
restoration of, in New Granada, 56–61
War of Independence and, 21–22, 38–43

Tacón, Miguel, 123–25, 177–78
Abascal alliance with, 46–48
Angulo and, 124, 128–30
Barbacoas and, loyalty to, 165
after battle of Iscuandé, 168
mobilization of slaves under, 53–54, 157–58
negotiations with Indians over tribute, 130–32
promises of freedom for slaves, 161–63
recruitment of slaves as loyalists, 158–69
slavery under, 53–54, 157–58
Telembí community, 206
Terán, Francisco, 217
Teranguará mine, 92–93
tithing requirements, 62–64
Toro, Jerónimo, 209, 216, 218
Torres, Camilo, 57, 175–83, 187
Torres, Gerónimo, 169, 176, 180, 183–86

tribute collection, 72–73
  conflicts under Clavijo's government and,
    71–72
  under Fernando VII, 153
  under Gallardo, 139–43
  Indians' control of, 72
  offers made by *caciques* in favor of the
    king, 130–33
  reduction in exchange for loyalty, 130
  royalism and, 127–34
Túpac Amaru rebellion, 64–65, 132–33
Túquerres, Indian revolt in, 62–64, 75–83
  audiencias' response to, 86–87
  caciques in, 77–78
  Clavijo brothers and, 78–80
  denunciations of the *corregidor* in, 78–80,
    82–83
  legal status of Indians, 88–89
  punishment of Indians after, 85–87

Ulloa, Antonio de, 73
Uribe, Jaime Jaramillo, 101–2

vagamundos, 138
Valdéz, Luciano, 211–12
Valiente, Juan, 27
Valverde, García de, 72–73
Valverde, Manuel Silvestre, 163–64,
  176–78
Van Young, Eric, 214
Velasco, Manuel Alonso de, 177–80

Venezuela
  First Republic of, 58–59
  Morillo army in, 148
  royalists and royalism in, 4–5
  Second Republic of, 58–59
Viceroyalty of New Granada. *See* New
  Granada, Viceroyalty of
Viceroyalty of Peru. *See* Peru, Viceroyalty of
Viceroyalty of Río de la Plata. *See* Río de la
  Plata, Viceroyalty of
Villa-Flores, Javier, 111–12
Villalonga, Jorge de, 35
Vinson, Ben, 151

Walker, Charles, 79
war, jurisdiction and sovereignty, 39–41
War of a Thousand Days, 142
War of Independence, 21–22, 38–43
War of the Supremes, 231
wars of independence, in Colombia,
  188
Weinstein, Barbara, 232

yanaconas, 138
Yupanqui, Dionisio Inca, 147
Yurumanguí, mine of, 159

zambos (slave patrol), 164
Zambrano, Manuel, 125
Zumpango, 141
Zúñiga, José María, 177

Printed in the USA
CPSIA information can be obtained
at www.ICGtesting.com
LVHW040505310723
753816LV00001B/55